HOW WE WORK

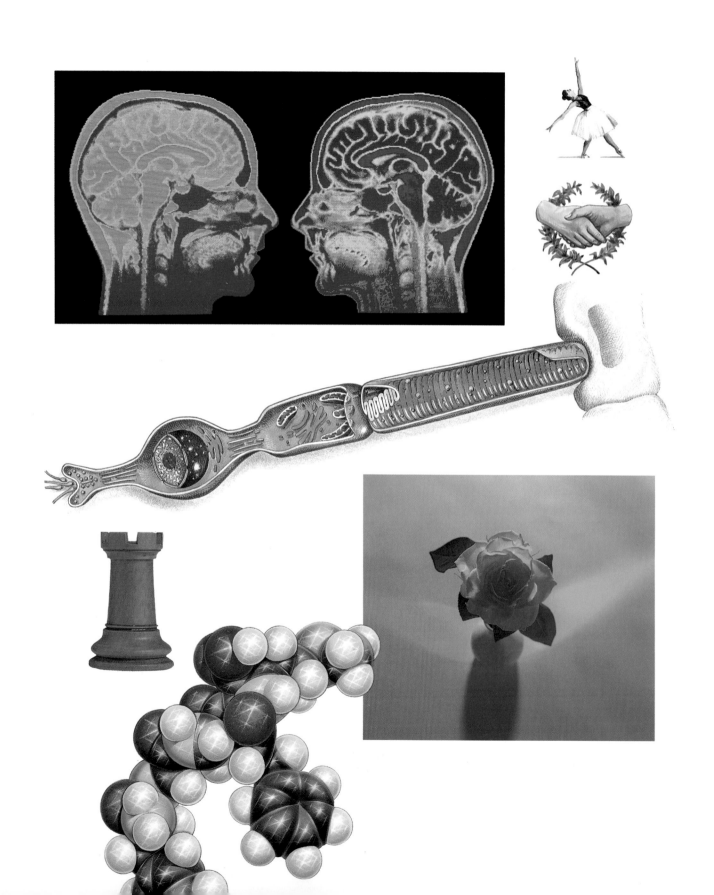

HOW WE WORK

UNDERSTANDING THE HUMAN BODY AND MIND

Dr. Philip Whitfield
and Dr. Susan Greenfield

MARSHALL EDITIONS
LONDON

Contents

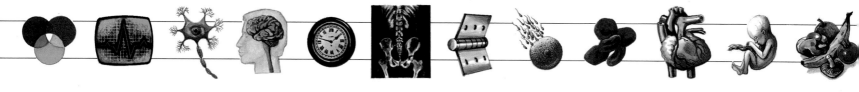

A Marshall Edition
170 Piccadilly, London, W1V 9DD

Copyright © 1997 by Marshall Editions
Developments Limited

First published in the UK in 1997

ISBN 0 9507901 4 1

PROJECT EDITOR   Jon Kirkwood
ART EDITOR   Simon Adamczewski
PICTURE EDITOR   Zilda Tandy

CONTRIBUTORS   Jerome Burne
                   John Farndon
                   Steve Parker
                   Dr. Philip Whitfield

Printed and bound in Italy by
New Interlitho SpA, Milan

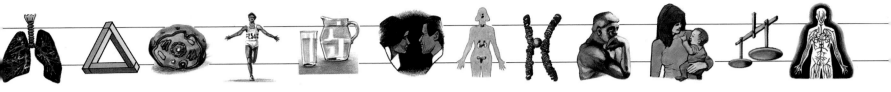

Introduction

This book's nine interlinked sections, each looking at different aspects of the body's and brain's functions, reveal their workings and structure, how we interact with the world around us and how we survive both individually and as a species.

SUPPORT AND MOVEMENT
A bony framework, along with other less rigid tissues, holds the body in shape while muscles make it move. **Support and Movement** delves into muscle action – from the mechanics of getting around to the beating of the heart.

ENERGY
Among the countless billions of chemical reactions taking place inside us every second are those that provide power for the body. **Energy** keeps track of how we acquire, produce and use energy both in cells and on a larger scale.

CIRCULATION, MAINTENANCE AND DEFENCE
Blood – a complex fluid driven by a tireless pump – is in constant motion. **Circulation, Maintenance and Defence** examines all the body's moving fluids and the phenomenal systems it uses to defend and repair itself.

REPRODUCTION AND GROWTH
The development of a person from the fertilization of an egg by a sperm to full adult maturity is a part of the amazing story of how humans populate the Earth. **Reproduction and Growth** explores human reproduction in the light of new facts about our genetic make-up.

SURVEYING THE MIND
Starting with an enquiry into the nature and workings of the mind, **Surveying the Mind** moves on to the most powerful and up to date techniques for investigating the brain and then provides vital anatomical and functional maps.

BUILDING THE BRAIN
The myriad microscopic components of the brain – its cells – are the key to understanding how it all works. **Building the Brain** explores their structure and function and sees how they change from conception to old age.

INPUTS AND OUTPUTS
Sensory signals stream into the brain, keeping it in touch with what is going on outside and inside the body. **Inputs and Outputs** shows how these signals are made and interpreted and how the brain sends out its messages of control.

FAR HORIZONS
Learning, memory and the growth from infancy to adulthood of a new human mind are extraordinary enough, but **Far Horizons** goes a step farther and probes the world of the intellect and the higher functions of the brain.

STATES OF MIND
We know that we are self-aware and that life can have its emotional ups and downs, yet it is hard to grasp just what makes up each unique human mind. **States of Mind** looks at how we experience the positive and negative aspects of being alive and explores the boundaries, if any, to thought and behaviour.

Getting the picture
Photographic images, backed up with informative captions, reveal the living details of the brain and body.

Section tag
Colour-coded arrows help you key into the nine sections that explain the workings of the body and mind.

Introducing the subject
A two-line "read first" introduces each topic and highlights its outstanding elements.

Now read on...
A clear, concise text enables readers to grasp the exciting complexities of the human body and mind. Using everyday analogies, as well as examples of the body and mind in action, it provides understanding with ease.

Feature box
To expand understanding, box features focus on the details of the body's systems and functions, giving contrasting or complementary examples. Here, the discovery that nerve cells communicate using special chemicals is explained in detail.

HOW TO USE THIS BOOK
Photographs and illustrations are the starting points that lead to knowledge and an understanding of the nature and workings of the body and the mind. Each of the book's double-page spreads is a self-contained story. But since topics do not always fit under the headings on them, connections lead from the edge of each right-hand page to other topics, both within the same section and in different sections.

In order to promote flexibility of thought and depth of interest, the connections made are often deliberately wide ranging. This helps to forge links of understanding between different, yet complementary, aspects of human body functions.

Support and Movement, Circulation, Maintenance and Defence, Reproduction and Growth are devoted to specific areas of the body's function and performance. **Energy** deals with the overall process whereby the human body machine powers its many activities. **Surveying the Mind, Building the Brain** and **Inputs and Outputs** are devoted to exploring and explaining specific areas of the brain's function and performance. **Far Horizons** and **States of Mind** deal more widely with the processes of thought and the way we experience our mind in action.

Connections
Follow the routes to suggested topics that contain back-up facts to boost your grasp of each subject. The connections also track down related ideas and explore parallel pathways of knowledge so that the diverse themes are bound together into a coherent body of knowledge.

Linked topics in the same section are listed first, followed by topics in other sections. Each topic title is followed by its page number for easy access.

Connection icon
Graphic icons help you to make the link between a specific topic and connecting topics in the same or different sections.

Close-up on the body and brain
Dramatic large-scale illustrations unravel complex multistranded stories by projecting the topic to a fuller, more complete level. Where necessary, these meticulous artworks explain in step-by-step sequence or break the topic down into manageable pieces by homing in on the essential details.

Case histories and animal comparisons
Sometimes box features contain case histories to give insights into the workings of the body and mind; these are indicated by the medical symbol of a staff twined with snakes. Other box features compare and contrast animal and human brains or behaviour; these are indicated by a paw print.

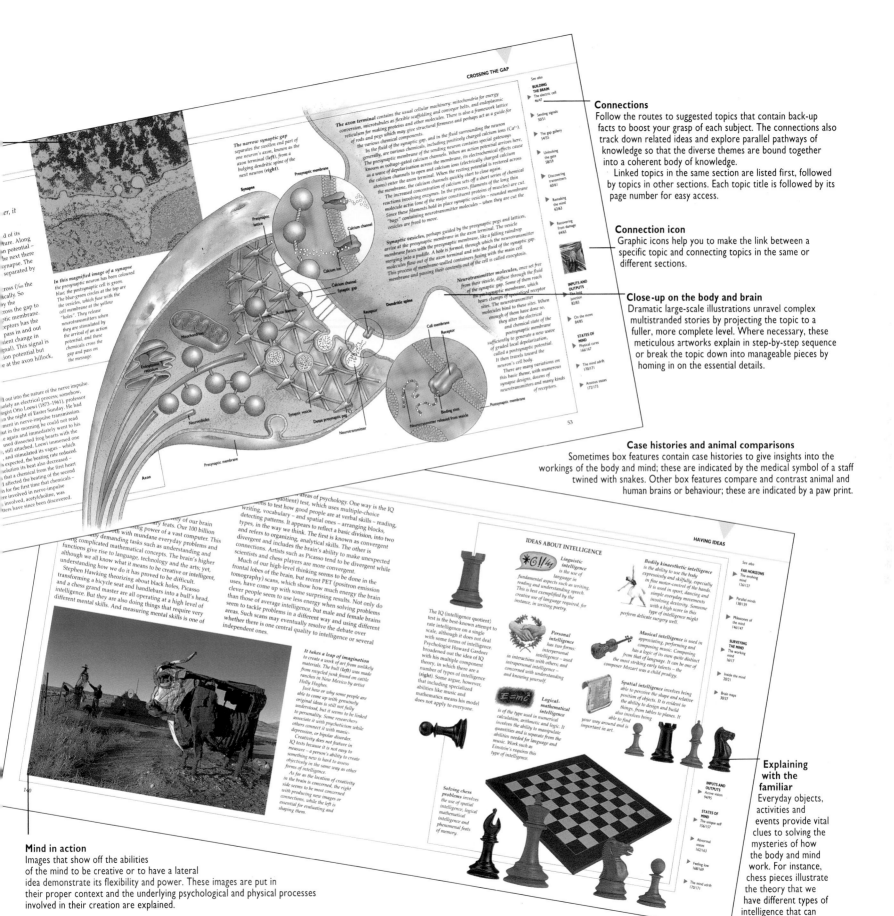

See also
BUILDING THE BRAIN
- The electric cell 46/47
- Sending signals 50/51
- The gap gallery 54/55
- Unlocking the gate 58/59
- Discovering transmitters 60/61
- Remaking the mind 62/63
- Recovering from damage 64/65

INPUTS AND OUTPUTS
- The limb junction 82/83
- On the move 84/85

STATES OF MIND
- Physical cures 170/171
- The mind adrift 170/171
- Anxious states 172/173

The axon terminal contains the usual cellular machinery: mitochondria for energy conversion, microtubules as flexible scaffolding and conveyor belts, and endoplasmic reticulum for making proteins and other molecules. There is also a framework lattice of rods and pegs which may give structural firmness and perhaps act as a staging-for the various chemical components.

In the fluid of the synaptic gap, and in the fluid surrounding the neuron generally, are various chemicals, including positively charged calcium ions (Ca^{2+}). The presynaptic membrane of the sending neuron contains special gateways known as voltage-gated calcium channels. When an action potential arrives here, as a wave of depolarization across the membrane, its electrochemical effects cause the calcium channels to open and calcium ions (electrically charged calcium atoms) enter the axon terminal. When the resting potential is restored across the membrane, the calcium channels quickly start to close again.

The increased concentration of calcium sets off a short series of chemical reactions involving enzymes. In the process, filaments of the long thin molecule actin (one of the major constituent proteins of muscles) are cut. Since these filaments hold in place synaptic vesicles – rounded membrane "bags" containing neurotransmitter molecules – when they are cut the vesicles are freed to move.

Synaptic vesicles, perhaps guided by the presynaptic pegs and lattices, arrive at the presynaptic membrane in the axon terminal. The vesicle membrane fuses with the presynaptic membrane, like a falling raindrop merging into a puddle. A hole is formed, through which the neurotransmitter molecules flow out of the axon terminal and into the fluid of the synaptic gap. This process of membrane-walled containers fusing with the main cell membrane and passing their contents out of the cell is called exocytosis.

Neurotransmitter molecules, once set free from their vesicle, diffuse through the fluid of the synaptic gap. Some of them reach the postsynaptic membrane, which bears clumps of specialized receptor sites. The neurotransmitter molecules bind to these sites. When enough of them have done so, they alter the electrical and chemical state of the postsynaptic membrane sufficiently to generate a new wave of graded local depolarization, called a postsynaptic potential. It then travels toward the neuron's cell body.

There are many variations on this basic theme, with numerous synapse designs, dozens of neurotransmitters and many kinds of receptors.

The narrow synaptic gap separates the swollen end part of one neuron's axon, known as the axon terminal (left), from a bulging dendritic spine of the next neuron (right).

In this magnified image of a synapse the presynaptic neuron has been coloured blue; the postsynaptic cell is green. The blue-green circles at the top are the vesicles, which fuse with the cell membrane at the yellow "holes". They release neurotransmitters when they are stimulated by the arrival of an action potential, and these chemicals cross the gap and pass on the message.

Labels: Synapse · Presynaptic membrane · Presynaptic lattice · Calcium channel · Calcium ion · Synaptic gap · Dendritic spine · Receptor · Axon filament · Mitochondrion · Cell membrane · Binding sites · Neurotransmitter released from vesicle · Postsynaptic membrane · Endoplasmic reticulum · Synaptic vesicle · Dense presynaptic peg · Neurotransmitter · Presynaptic membrane · Axon

...out into the nature of the nerve impulse. ...olely an electrical process, somehow, ...ogist Otto Loewi (1873-1961), professor ...n the night of Easter Sunday. He had ...ment in nerve-impulse transmission. ...ut in the morning he could not read ...e again and immediately went to his ...used dissected frog hearts with the ..., still attached. Loewi immersed one ..., and stimulated its vagus – which ...s expected, the beating rate reduced. ...olution its beat also decreased – ...that a chemical from the first heart ...affected the beating of the second ...n for the first time that chemicals – ...re involved in nerve-impulse ...involved, acetylcholine, was ...tters have since been discovered.

53

...areas of psychology. One way is the IQ ...ions to test how good people are at verbal skills – reading, writing, vocabulary – and spatial ones – arranging blocks, detecting patterns. It appears to reflect a basic division, into two types, in the way we think. The first is known as convergent and refers to organizing, analytical skills. The other is divergent and includes the brain's ability to make unexpected connections. Artists such as Picasso tend to be divergent while scientists and chess players are more convergent.

Much of our high-level thinking seems to be done in the frontal lobes of the brain, but recent PET (positron emission tomography) scans, which show how much energy the brain uses, have come up with some surprising results. Not only do clever people seem to use less energy when solving problems than those of average intelligence, but male and female brains seem to tackle problems in a different way and using different areas. Such scans may eventually resolve the debate over whether there is one central quality to intelligence or several independent ones.

It takes a leap of imagination to create a work of art from unlikely materials. The bull (left) was made from recycled junk found on cattle ranches in New Mexico by artist Holly Hughes.

Just how or why some people are able to come up with genuinely original ideas is still not fully understood, but it seems to be linked to personality. Some researchers associate it with psychoticism while others connect it with manic-depression, or bipolar disorder.

Creativity does not feature in IQ tests because it is not easy to measure – a person's ability to create something new is hard to assess objectively in the same way as other forms of intelligence.

As far as the location of creativity in the brain is concerned, the right side seems to be most concerned with producing new images or connections, while the left is essential for evaluating and shaping them.

Mind in action
Images that show off the abilities of the mind to be creative or to have a lateral idea demonstrate its flexibility and power. These images are put in their proper context and the underlying psychological and physical processes involved in their creation are explained.

140

IDEAS ABOUT INTELLIGENCE

Linguistic intelligence is the use of language in fundamental aspects such as writing, reading and understanding speech. This is best exemplified by the creative use of language required, for instance, in writing poetry.

Bodily kinaesthetic intelligence is the ability to use the body expressively and skilfully, especially in fine motor-control of the hands. It is used in sport, dancing and simple everyday movements involving dexterity. Someone with a high score in this type of intelligence might perform delicate surgery well.

The IQ (intelligence quotient) test is the best-known attempt to rate intelligence on a single scale, although it does not deal with some forms of intelligence. Psychologist Howard Gardner broadened out the idea of IQ with his multiple component theory, in which there are a number of types of intelligence (right). Some argue, however, that including specialized abilities like music and mathematics means his model does not apply to everyone.

Personal intelligence has two forms: interpersonal intelligence – used in interactions with others; and intrapersonal intelligence – concerned with understanding and knowing yourself.

Musical intelligence is used in appreciating, performing and composing music. Composing has a logic of its own quite distinct from that of language. It can be one of the most striking early talents – the composer Mozart was a child prodigy.

$E=mc^2$

Logical-mathematical intelligence is of the type used in numerical calculation, arithmetic and logic. It involves the ability to manipulate quantities and is separate from that needed for language and music. Work such as Einstein's requires this type of intelligence.

Spatial intelligence involves being able to perceive the shape and relative position of objects. It is evident in the ability to design and build things, from tables to planes. It also involves being able to find your way around and is important in art.

Solving chess problems involves the use of spatial intelligence, logical mathematical intelligence and phenomenal feats of memory.

See also
FAR HORIZONS
- The evolving mind 126/127
- Parallel minds 138/139
- Milestones of the mind 146/147

SURVEYING THE MIND
- The working mind 16/17
- Inside the mind 20/21
- Brain maps 30/37

INPUTS AND OUTPUTS
- Active vision 94/95

STATES OF MIND
- The unique self 156/157
- Abnormal states 162/163
- Feeling low 168/169
- The mind adrift 170/171

Explaining with the familiar
Everyday objects, activities and events provide vital clues to solving the mysteries of how the body and mind work. For instance, chess pieces illustrate the theory that we have different types of intelligence that can be measured.

How Your Body Works

Humans are inquisitive creatures. We investigate and explore. We are continually searching for new experiences, objects and surroundings. When confronted with some new phenomenon or with something inexplicable, we want to understand how it works, what makes it tick. All the knowledge and understanding achieved in the many different branches of science and technology are the result of people down the ages asking the question "how does it work?"

Over many thousands of years people have asked that question about the most complex living machine of all – the human body. Using the most up-to-date sources available, this section explains the ways in which the human body machine works. The information in it has been gained by different types of specialists – anatomists, physiologists, neurologists, psychologists, pharmacologists, biochemists and molecular biologists. Each area of specialism has provided knowledge of the way in which parts of the body function, from the way in which the heart beats and the digestive tract processes food to the way the brain thinks and babies grow.

In these and in all other facets of its working, the body can be fully understood only by knowing what happens at the three levels of organs, cells and molecules. For instance, the movements of your eyes as they scan this line of text can be understood as the coordinated contractions of the set of six muscles (organs) that move each eye, as the actions of the specialized muscle cells from which those muscles are built, or as the interactions of the proteins actin and myosin (molecules) in the muscle cells which enable them to contract. This illustrated manual describes the workings of all parts of your body at these three levels.

Support and Movement

A self-repairing internal framework stronger weight-for-weight than steel and a tireless pump controlled by electric signals from a powerful computer sound like some of the specifications for a superman. But they are just attributes of each and every human body – the skeleton and the bones that make it, and a muscle pump, the heart, whose rate of beating is timed by the brain.

Muscles and bones, together with the connective tissues, share the job of supporting the body and making it move. But muscles also play vital roles in other types of movements. Blood vessels with muscular walls act as circulatory control valves, while some muscles in the eyes focus the lens and others constrict the iris. Then there are the muscles in the digestive tract that force food through the gut and others that keep body wastes contained.

Left (clockwise from top): homing in on the living skeleton; a tough nut to crack, like the skull; a joint's stressful life; the watery way to stay in shape. This page (top): moving is easy with good connections; (left) resilient fibres.

Staying in shape

The shape we are is determined by evolution, but how is the familiar outline of the body supported?

All vertebrates, or backboned creatures (humans included), have endoskeletons – strong internal frames made of bone or cartilage. In fact, the shape of human beings reflects millions of years of evolutionary changes acting on the basic body plan of a land-living, four-limbed vertebrate. Fossil evidence shows how, some 350 million years ago, the fleshy-based fins of ancient fish developed into four limbs, each with five digits. The result was the earliest amphibians, which lumbered onto the land. Through the stages of early reptiles, mammal-like reptiles and then the first shrewlike mammals over 200 million years ago, the basic skull-and-backbone-and-four-limbs design persisted.

When the dinosaurs disappeared some 65 million years ago, mammal evolution took off. We can trace our origins within the mammal group, through the first primates, to the early apes, and then via "ape-humans" *Australopithecus* to our own group, *Homo*, and the human species today, *Homo sapiens*.

The general plan of the human body is typically mammalian. The breathing and eating inlets, as well as the main senses of sight, hearing, smell and taste, are sited at the head end. The respiratory and pumping sections of the circulatory system are packed into the chest. Most of the digestive, excretory (waste disposal) and reproductive parts are in the abdomen. The four limbs have five digits each.

The lobster
is kept in shape by its hard shell. Other crustaceans, as well as insects and molluscs, also have rigid outer frameworks, known as exoskeletons, which give their soft internal tissues shape and support and provide solid anchorage points for their muscles.

More mammalian characteristics feature both outside and within. Externally, the body has elastic, wear-resistant skin that protects it from knocks, germs and rays from the Sun and prevents leakage of body fluids. The skin's strong fibres (similar to any mammal leather) give shape and support to the contours of muscles and softer organs below. Our strong endoskeleton, "the skeleton", supports and protects the softer fleshy parts and provides points for muscle anchorage. The only major anatomical features that make us unique among

The jellyfish *has neither solid endoskeleton nor exoskeleton, since it is a creature whose muscle groups do not need a rigid frame inside or out. Its form is maintained by the tension in its outer layers which take their shape when stretched by the soft internal tissues with their high water content. A shape maintained in this way is said to be supported hydrostatically.*

mammals are an unusually large and complex brain and our status as the only species that habitually stands and moves in an upright posture.

By contrast, most of the invertebrates – creatures without backbones, which make up the vast majority of animals and include crustaceans, molluscs and insects – have rigid external shells, or exoskeletons, which support and protect the internal organs. Exoskeletons become impossibly heavy with increasing size, and the largest exoskeleton-clad animals live in the sea, their weight partly supported by water. They are virtually helpless on land.

Some invertebrates, such as jellyfish and worms, seem to have no body support at all and plainly do not have the sophisticated endoskeletons of the vertebrates. These creatures do, however, have a support in the form of a hydrostatic "skeleton", which relies on fluid under pressure. Their essentially fluidlike internal organs press against a flexible "skin", or outer layer, to keep them in shape, rather like a plastic bag full of water. This system works well for simple creatures, especially those that live in water where the surrounding fluid helps them stay in shape.

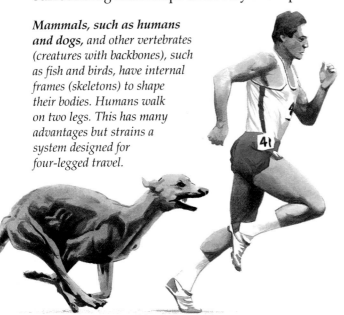

Mammals, such as humans and dogs, and other vertebrates (creatures with backbones), such as fish and birds, have internal frames (skeletons) to shape their bodies. Humans walk on two legs. This has many advantages but strains a system designed for four-legged travel.

THE SHAPE YOU ARE IN

Most of us have similar body shapes, and variation between individuals is not great. Most obvious differences are in height and bulk. Laurel, on the left, is slim while Hardy is taller and stocky.

The body's size and shape depends on three main factors: skeletal size and proportions; muscular development; and stored fat. The relation of skeletal height and the lengths of limbs to the widths of skull and hipbone remains remarkably constant from the tall to the short. The skeleton determines our height and is the factor we can least influence.

But it is possible to add or lose muscle and fat. Almost anyone who exercises can build up muscle mass, thereby bulking up the shoulders, arms, torso and legs. People who do not exercise, and who eat too much, round out in the face, neck and abdomen, where the excess food is converted to stores of body fat.

Bearing the load

The body's internal framework, the skeleton, is an extraordinary study in engineering design.

Without a skeleton the body would collapse in a floppy heap, like a jellyfish on dry land. But more than 200 bones, linked at over 100 movable joints, provide rigid strength and support coupled with flexibility and agility.

Evolution has produced bones whose size and shape are perfectly matched to their roles. The primary roles are support for the softer parts, anchor points for muscles and protection for delicate parts within. The long bones in the arms and legs function both as load-bearing beams and columns and as mechanical levers; the broad, flat bones in the shoulders and hips provide large areas for the attachment of many powerful muscles; and the rounded bones of the skull, ribcage and pelvis shield the more delicate parts within, such as the brain, heart, lungs and intestines, from knocks and damage. Certain bones are formed from several bones which have fused together during development. For example, each pelvic, or hip, bone has three fused elements; and the sacrum at the base of the spine has five elements.

Bones have anatomical names and most have everyday names as well (shown in brackets). Bones also lend their names to other body parts near them, such as blood vessels and nerves. Thus, the subclavian artery runs under the clavicle (collarbone).

The body's backbone, or spinal column, is like a spiral staircase. All the treads and central rings of the staircase are fixed firmly together so the whole structure does not sway about like beads on a string. The weight of the staircase is carried by the central supporting column.

The spine has a similar segmented, load-bearing structure – taking the entire weight of the upper body – but in addition, it is flexible. Each bone, known as a vertebra, is separated from its fellows by a tough "washer", the disc, which allows a limited amount of movement. The spinal column is supported and held in place by muscles and ligaments which allow movement but prevent motions that might damage the vertebrae or, crucially, the spinal cord that runs down its centre. This contains nerves that control muscles and carry sensory messages.

Like a walnut shell, the skull protects its contents within a hard covering. Both shell and skull are rigid containers that enclose and protect a rounded, wrinkled-looking object. In the skull's case, the object is the brain. The curved upper brain-box part is the cranium and consists of eight rounded bones which are fused strongly at wavy-line joints called sutures. Another 14 fused bones form the facial skeleton. Some of these create two bowl-shaped depressions – the orbits, or sockets, which house and shield the eyes.

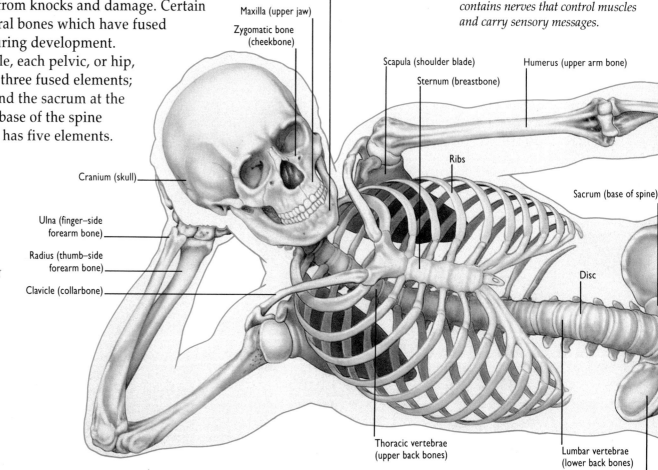

Mandible (lower jaw)

Maxilla (upper jaw)

Zygomatic bone (cheekbone)

Scapula (shoulder blade)

Humerus (upper arm bone)

Sternum (breastbone)

Ribs

Sacrum (base of spine)

Cranium (skull)

Ulna (finger–side forearm bone)

Radius (thumb–side forearm bone)

Clavicle (collarbone)

Disc

Thoracic vertebrae (upper back bones)

Lumbar vertebrae (lower back bones)

Ilium

SKELETON FACT FILE

Some individuals have extra or fewer bones: one person in 20 has an extra pair of ribs, making 13 pairs instead of 12.

Total no. of bones	adult	206
	child	300*
No. of bones in	skull and neck	23
	each ear	3
	spinal column	26
	chest	25
	arm and hand	32
	hip, leg and foot	31
Weight of skeleton in 50-kg adult	7 kg
	(110-pound)	(15½ pounds)
Longest bone	femur	27% of height of an adult
Widest bone	pelvis	body width at hip
Smallest bone	stapes	0.5 cm (⅕ inch) long

*Some bones fuse together as a child grows.

Semicircular canals

Malleus (hammer)

Incus (anvil)

Stapes (stirrup)

Cochlea

Tympanic membrane (eardrum)

Three tiny bones, known as the auditory ossicles (**left**), deep in the inner ear, are little larger than rice grains. They have no load-bearing or supporting function at all.

Despite their minute size, they have all the usual bone features: a nerve and blood supply, lubricated joints with their neighbours and muscle attachments.

The word "ossicle" comes from the Latin for "small bone". The bones' individual Latin names, and the translations, reflect their resemblance in shape to a blacksmith's hammer (mallet) and anvil, and to a stirrup used in horseriding. The function of the bones in hearing is to transmit and amplify the vibrations that represent sound waves from the tympanic membrane (eardrum) to the cochlea.

The leg and hip bones work like the tower and jib of a tall crane. The tower is built to withstand both downward compression forces and sideways forces as the crane lifts a weight.

In a similar manner, the thigh and shin bones not only support the body's downward weight but also resist sideways forces, since they are cantilevered out from the midline of the body by the width of the hips. Generally, though, the body's long bones are designed to bear compression forces along their long axes.

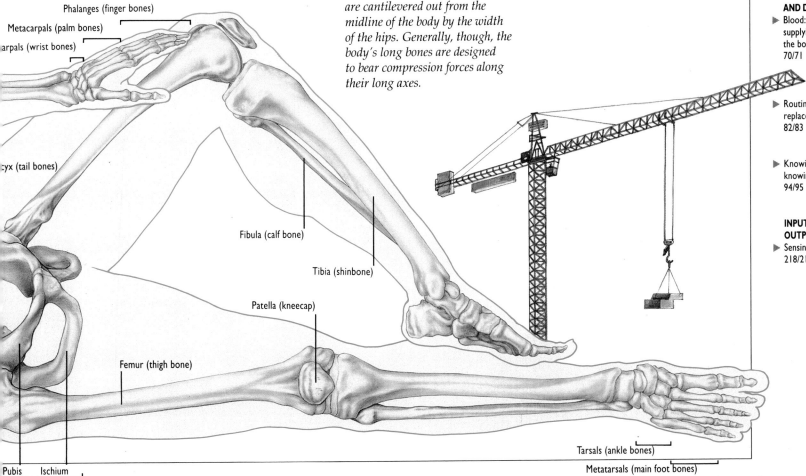

Phalanges (finger bones)

Metacarpals (palm bones)

arpals (wrist bones)

cyx (tail bones)

Femur (thigh bone)

Patella (kneecap)

Fibula (calf bone)

Tibia (shinbone)

Tarsals (ankle bones)

Metatarsals (main foot bones)

Phalanges (toe bones)

Pubis   Ischium

vis

See also

SUPPORT AND MOVEMENT
▶ Staying in shape 12/13

▶ The living framework 16/17

▶ Bone junction 18/19

▶ Holding it together 20/21

▶ Making a move 22/23

CIRCULATION, MAINTENANCE AND DEFENCE
▶ Blood: supplying the body 70/71

▶ Routine replacement 82/83

▶ Knowing me, knowing you 94/95

INPUTS AND OUTPUTS
▶ Sensing sound 218/219

The living framework

Skeletons are made from incredibly strong material that is constantly changing, adapting and rebuilding.

Bone is tough. It can withstand compression forces almost twice as well as granite, and stretching forces four times better than concrete. Yet despite this strength, bone is astonishingly light. If the skeleton were built of steel to an equivalent strength, it would weigh about five times as much. In the correct environment – the human body – bone can last for many years, even repairing itself when broken. For living bone is far from dry, brittle and static. It is physiologically busy and is constantly exchanging minerals and other substances with other body parts via the bloodstream.

Like many other tissues, bone consists of cells surrounded by a substance called a matrix. Some 30 to 40 percent of this matrix is protein, chiefly fibres of the protein known as collagen. The rest is made up of minerals, mostly calcium and phosphate. These two components – collagen and minerals – are complementary, each performing a vital role. Without collagen, bone would be as brittle as glass. Without minerals, it would be as bendy as a rubber toy.

Embedded in the matrix are three main types of bone cells. In mature bone they are mostly spidery osteocytes. These maintain the matrix, removing or adding proteins and minerals as required. A typical osteocyte lives for decades deep in a prison of its own making. It was once

Cartilage is softer and more bendy than bone, but still strong and resilient. Eight curved cartilage plates form the squashable framework of the nose, with a ninth dividing the two nostrils.

an osteoblast, or bone-making cell, near the bone's surface. As the bone grew during body development, more bone tissue was added around it, and the osteoblast matured into an osteocyte. Osteoclasts, the third type of cell, can erode the matrix if the body requires minerals and other ingredients elsewhere. The architecture of bone is far from fixed. While the osteoclasts dismantle bone, osteoblasts rebuild it elsewhere, for example at regions where strain increases with age or injury.

Bone has an intricate microstructure of rods, each of which has a channel, or Haversian canal, at its centre. Packed densely together these rods form compact bone, which provides a strong outer layer or "shell" for the whole bone where stresses are greatest. Other rods are arranged in the open honeycomb structure of spongy bone, which can be trellislike or made up of plates and sheets. This type of bone forms where stress is lower. In the spaces inside spongy bone are various types of marrow, which produce blood cells or store fatty nutrient reserves.

Lacking the rigid mineral crystals found in bone, cartilage – the other main supportive tissue in the body – is a more flexible alternative. It is found in many organs, giving shape to the ears, nose and trachea, helping you to sneeze, breathe, speak and hear effectively.

AS GOOD AS NEW

Most parts of the body can mend themselves, like skin, which heals over with scar tissue. A fractured bone can also self-repair, provided its stresses are relieved by other bones and muscles, and the broken ends are still close to each other. This is why a broken limb needs a splint or a plaster cast in order to heal. First blood from the vessels inside the bone clots to stop its continued leakage (**1**). Then a callus of fibrous tissue forms around the fracture (**2**). The callus is manufactured by cells known as fibroblasts. These cells also make cartilage,

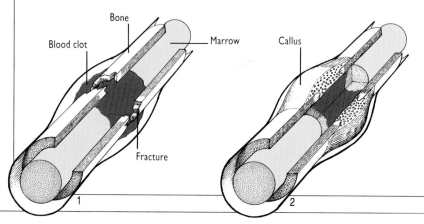

Bone

Blood clot — Marrow — Callus

Fracture

1

2

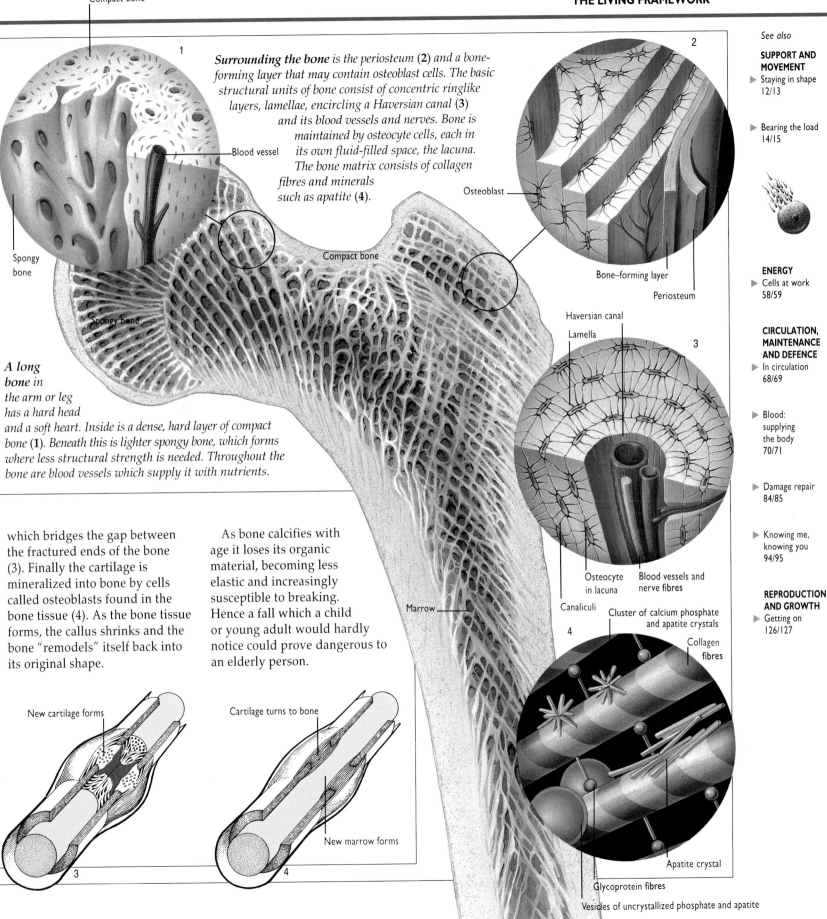

Compact bone

1

Surrounding the bone is the periosteum (**2**) and a bone-forming layer that may contain osteoblast cells. The basic structural units of bone consist of concentric ringlike layers, lamellae, encircling a Haversian canal (**3**) and its blood vessels and nerves. Bone is maintained by osteocyte cells, each in its own fluid-filled space, the lacuna. The bone matrix consists of collagen fibres and minerals such as apatite (**4**).

2

Blood vessel

Spongy bone

Osteoblast

Compact bone

Bone–forming layer

Periosteum

Spongy bone

A long bone in the arm or leg has a hard head and a soft heart. Inside is a dense, hard layer of compact bone (**1**). Beneath this is lighter spongy bone, which forms where less structural strength is needed. Throughout the bone are blood vessels which supply it with nutrients.

Haversian canal

Lamella

3

Osteocyte in lacuna

Blood vessels and nerve fibres

Canaliculi

4

which bridges the gap between the fractured ends of the bone (3). Finally the cartilage is mineralized into bone by cells called osteoblasts found in the bone tissue (4). As the bone tissue forms, the callus shrinks and the bone "remodels" itself back into its original shape.

As bone calcifies with age it loses its organic material, becoming less elastic and increasingly susceptible to breaking. Hence a fall which a child or young adult would hardly notice could prove dangerous to an elderly person.

Marrow

Cluster of calcium phosphate and apatite crystals

Collagen fibres

New cartilage forms

Cartilage turns to bone

New marrow forms

3

4

Apatite crystal

Glycoprotein fibres

Vesicles of uncrystallized phosphate and apatite

See also

SUPPORT AND MOVEMENT
▶ Staying in shape 12/13

▶ Bearing the load 14/15

ENERGY
▶ Cells at work 58/59

CIRCULATION, MAINTENANCE AND DEFENCE
▶ In circulation 68/69

▶ Blood: supplying the body 70/71

▶ Damage repair 84/85

▶ Knowing me, knowing you 94/95

REPRODUCTION AND GROWTH
▶ Getting on 126/127

Bone junction

Virtually every move you make depends on one of the body's engineering marvels – the joints between bones.

Nature has solved the problem of how to protect the ends of adjoining bones in a remarkably effective way. Movable bones do not actually touch, but instead have a long-lasting, wear-resistant bearing between them – a joint. The main type, which usually allows great freedom of movement, is the synovial joint. Its basic design is similar in all mammals, including humans. Bone is rough and hard, so its surfaces need a hardy, smooth coating. Inside a synovial joint, bone is covered by a pearly-smooth elastic substance – the articular cartilage. This is similar in structure to bone, being collagen (protein fibres) in a stiff matrix, but it does not have bone's hardening minerals. The cartilage-covered parts of bone can thus pivot or rotate on each other with little friction and wear. The cartilage also acts as a shock-absorber, so if the joint is jarred, the bones do not shatter.

Synovial joints have lubrication, too. The cartilage-covered bone ends are encased in a flexible bag – the articular capsule – which links the two bones together. This bag encloses a space, the synovial cavity. It is lined by a thin, shiny membrane, the synovial membrane, which produces synovial fluid. This thick, slippery substance fills the synovial capsule and is the "oil" that lubricates the joint. The articular capsule is thickened and strengthened by collagen at various sites, to form ligaments. These elastic strips link the two bones, to stop them pulling apart or moving too far and dislocating the joint.

In the body, there is great variety in the numbers of bones in a joint, the shapes of their cartilage-covered ends, and the type and amount of movement they allow. The similarities to mechanical joints give them various names, such as pivots and hinges. There are also several other types of joints in the body, including fixed joints that allow no movement at all.

Ball-and-socket joints, such as those at the shoulder and hip, have a spherical head (ball) that fits into a bowl-shaped cavity (socket). They allow movement in two planes plus some twisting. The socket in the shoulder blade (scapula) is shallower than that in the hip (pelvis), allowing more freedom of movement, but reducing stability.

Hinge joints, as at the elbow and knee, move in only one plane, but they trade limited movement for great stability. Other hinge-type joints are found in the smaller knuckles of the fingers and toes and between some bones in the ankle.

When you throw a ball, the shallow ball-and-socket shoulder joint lets the upper arm swing from behind the body, right round to the front. The hinged elbow joint snaps the arm straight, to flick the hand. It is aided by more than 20 hinge, gliding and other joints between the 8 wrist bones and their neighbours. The fingers push and straighten at their shallow hinge joints, giving the final impetus to send the ball on its way.

Washered joints are a special feature of the spinal column. Between each pair of vertebrae is a pad of squashy fibrous cartilage, the inter-vertebral disc, which lets them both rock slightly. These movements, over all its bones, enable the whole spine to bend double.

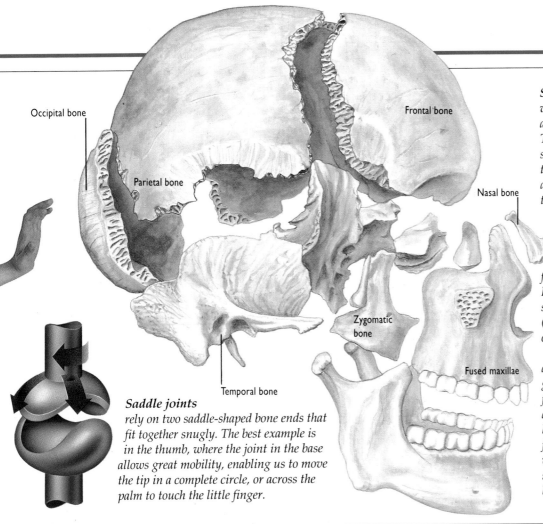

Occipital bone

Frontal bone

Parietal bone

Nasal bone

Zygomatic bone

Fused maxillae

Temporal bone

Saddle joints
rely on two saddle-shaped bone ends that fit together snugly. The best example is in the thumb, where the joint in the base allows great mobility, enabling us to move the tip in a complete circle, or across the palm to touch the little finger.

Some bones are joined in a secure way so that they move little, if at all, and are unlikely to come apart. The most solid joints are fibrous sutures, found between the bones of the adult skull. The various bones are butted and united by fibrous tissue and function as a solid unit.

In fibrous syndesmoses the bones are linked firmly by fibres but are not touching and can move slightly, as with the two forearm bones, the radius and ulna. In cartilaginous joints, the bones, such as the ribs and the breastbone (sternum), are cemented to a bridge of flexible cartilage between them.

Perhaps the simplest joint that allows significant movement is the gliding joint, where two almost flat surfaces slide across or twist against each other, but only by a limited amount. Gliding joints are found between various bones in the wrist and ankle, and between the shoulder blade (scapula) and collar bone (clavicle).

See also

SUPPORT AND MOVEMENT
▶ Staying in shape 12/13

▶ Bearing the load 14/15

▶ The living framework 16/17

▶ Holding it together 20/21

▶ Making a move 22/23

INPUTS AND OUTPUTS
▶ On the move 206/207

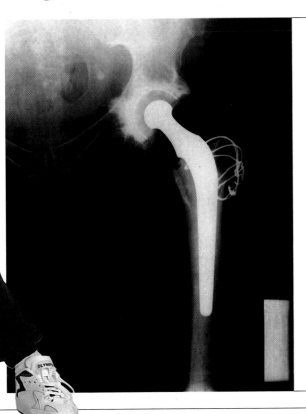

REPLACING THE NATURAL JOINT

Since Roman times, physicians have tried to treat joint problems, such as osteoarthritis where the cartilage flakes and degenerates, with prostheses (artificial parts). Arthritic hips, in particular, can severely limit mobility. In medieval times the prosthesis was external, strapped onto the skin over the joint to help take the weight. In the 1960s British surgeon John Charnley devised a successful internal prosthesis, the artificial hip joint. Its ball-and-socket design mimicked the natural version. The ball is of highly polished stainless steel, mounted on a long spike cemented into the marrow cavity of the thigh bone (femur). The socket, made of high-density polythene, is cemented onto the hip bone. Artificial elbows, knuckles and even knees are now available. The hunt continues for tougher, longer-lasting joint materials that can withstand the tremendous stresses imposed by body movements – stresses that can be observed in photographs of plastic models taken in polarized light (**right**).

Holding it together

Connective tissues, the body's "living glues and fillers", hold our tissues and organs together.

The body is made up of cells, grouped into tissues, grouped into organs. Connective tissues are found between organs, between various types of tissues and even in the spaces between cells. They fill, pack, support, protect, wrap, restrict, cushion, contain, restrain, insulate and, of course, connect.

Connective tissue has three major components. The first is cells – mainly fibroblasts, which make all-important fibres. Other connective tissue cells include adipose cells, swollen with globs of fat; macrophages, which eat germs and debris to keep the tissue clean; and reticular cells, plasma cells and others involved in body defence and immunity.

The second and distinctive component is fibres such as collagen, elastin and reticulin. The main type is the whitish protein collagen – resembling a microscopic length of rope – found in almost all connective tissues. Collagen is tough and can bend but hardly stretch; its fibres can be packed densely or scattered loosely, and can be neatly woven and well aligned or irregular and random. The highly flexible and elastic yellowish elastin gives young skin its rubbery stretchiness. Thinner, branching reticulin fibres are embedded in connective tissue's third component, known as the matrix or ground substance. This ranges from a runny syrup to a thick, stiff gel and is made mainly of large molecules such as glycoproteins.

Almost every body part has some type of connective tissue. In loose, or areolar, irregular connective tissue, the fibres are arranged at random and far apart in their jellylike matrix, to form spongy, flexible wrappings for body organs, blood vessels and nerves. In dense irregular connective tissue, the fibres are close together; in regular connective tissue they are aligned. Adipose, or fatty, connective tissue has many adipose cells and is soft and squidgy, for insulation and cushioning. More specialized types of connective tissue are bone and cartilage – and blood. Of course, blood does not connect anything. But it has the same embryonic origins as other connective tissues, as well as the three components: cells, fibres (for blood clotting) and a liquid matrix – the plasma.

This model giraffe collapses in a heap (below right) when a button on its base is pressed. The button releases the tension in a set of cords that run through its separate parts; without the tension the parts flop.

The human body would do the same if its connective tissue was magicked away. Bone, the stiffening structural core of the body, is a type of connective tissue, and so is cartilage, which forms the framework of parts such as the nose, ears and larynx (voice box). Cartilage also plays an important role in another body part, the trachea, or windpipe. Bands of cartilage hold it in shape and prevent it being squashed flat so that air can pass in and out of the lungs.

Dense irregular connective tissue is flexible and tough, able to stretch in almost any direction. It is widespread inside and around organs, forming sheaths and capsules and linking parts together. It forms the middle layer of skin, encases nerves, muscles and blood vessels, forms the outer capsules of glands and the eyeball and makes up the outer "skin" of bones and cartilages.

Dense irregular connective tissue

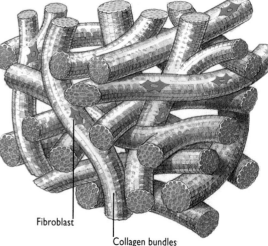

Ligament

Fibroblast

Collagen bundles

Ligaments, the stretchy straps that hold bones together in and around joints, are made of ligamentous regular connective tissue. The bundles of collagen, sometimes interwoven with elastin, curve gently and are packed in layers or sheets. Their curves can be straightened under tension, but spring back when released.

Extensor retinaculum

Tendons connect to forearm muscles

Beneath the outer layer of the skin, and just above the underlying muscles and tendons, is the adipose connective tissue, or fat. This type of connective tissue is unusual in that it does not have a supportive role; it does, however, provide insulation against heat loss and both cushions and protects.

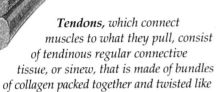

Tendon

Tendons, which connect muscles to what they pull, consist of tendinous regular connective tissue, or sinew, that is made of bundles of collagen packed together and twisted like rope fibres. Sheets of tendinous connective tissue on and within muscles are known as fascia and help to bind and align the tissues in the muscle. Sheets of tendinous and ligamentous tissue combined form aponeuroses, which act as anchor points for tendons and muscles.

Connections between tendons

Tendons attach to finger bones

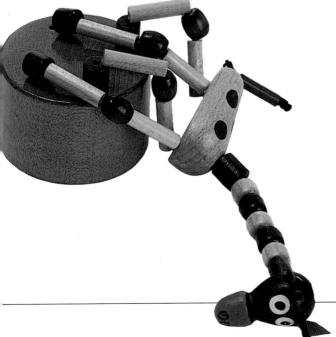

Connecting the fingers to the muscles in the upper forearm that make them move are tendons. In fact, 21 long, cordlike tendons run through the wrist. They are "glued" to the finger bones at one end and to the forearm bones near the elbow at the other end.

Wrapped around the tendons at the wrist, like a watchstrap under the skin, are two bands of fibrous tissue called retinacula. They keep the tendons aligned and following the correct line of pull as they slide beneath it. For instance, the extensor retinaculum on the back of the wrist restrains the extensor muscle tendons which straighten the fingers.

At sites where the tendons might rub and chafe adjacent tissues, they are encased in slippery bags known as synovial sheaths. These have the same membranes, smooth surfaces and lubricating fluid as bone-to-bone synovial joints.

Making a move

Every body movement is powered by muscles.
But muscles can only pull, so how do you push?

Our muscles – what we call the "red meat" on other
animals – make up almost half the body's weight and
produce all the body's movements and postures. The muscles
that move you around are called skeletal, or voluntary,
muscles and are under direct control of your will.

A muscle is a biological puller. It works by getting shorter,
or contracting, and moving the bones that are attached to it.
The body has opposing, or antagonistic, pairs of muscles – one
to lift the leg, for example, the other to lower it. The "lifting"
muscle pulls its bone one way and its opposing partner, or
antagonist – the "lowering" muscle – pulls the same bone in
the opposite direction. In each case, as one muscle contracts
and exerts a force, its opposite number automatically relaxes
and is passively stretched.

However, this two-way partnership is a considerable
simplification. In reality, muscles work in teams of 20, 30 or
even more. They move, lift and rotate bones so that you can
pull, push, squeeze, stretch, walk, jump and run. As muscle
teams in one region of the body make the primary movements,
others elsewhere adjust and compensate so that you are
always poised and balanced.

MUSCLES FACT FILE

*The most variable muscle is probably the platysma
in the side of the neck: it covers the whole region in
some people, is straplike in others, and completely
missing in a few.*

No. of skeletal, or voluntary, muscles		640 approx.
Bulkiest	gluteus maximus	1 kg (2¼ pounds) or more
Smallest	stapedius	0.5 cm (⅕ inch)
Longest	sartorius	50 cm (19½ inches)
Longest group	erector spinae	90 cm (35½ inches)
Widest	external oblique	45 cm (17¾ inches)
Percentage of body weight as muscle	male	40–50
	female	30–40
Muscle fibre length	av.	3 cm (1⅕ inches)
	max.	30 cm (12 inches)
	min.	0.1 cm (¹⁄₂₅ inch)

*The typical skeletal muscle has a
bulging body, or belly, that tapers at
either end into a cordlike tendon,
which is firmly anchored into a bone
of the skeleton. Some muscles are
triangular, others are sheetlike,
according to the job they do and
how they are attached. For instance,
the upper back is dominated by the
trapezius, a large triangular muscle
that extends up into the neck
and from the spine to the*

*shoulder blade (scapula). By pulling
or lifting this bone, it can alter
the position of the whole arm. The
deltoid, one of six main muscles that
stabilize the shoulder joint, lifts and
twists the arm. The shoulder joint
requires support since it is inherently
unstable – the upper-arm bone is set
in the shallowest of sockets.*

*The brain automatically
controls muscles for everyday
activities such as walking and
sitting. Only when learning new
physical skills, such as harp playing
or windsurfing, do you become
aware of the complexity and
coordination involved in controlling
more than 600 individual pulling
devices simultaneously. The major
muscles involved in moving the
body about are shown on the right.
Such is the complexity of the body's
musculature that the muscles
depicted here are only the superficial
ones; beneath is another layer, and
in some places in the body there is a
third, deep muscle set.*

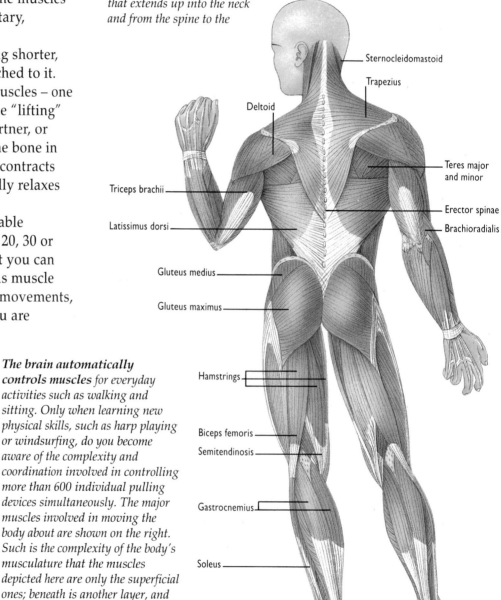

Sternocleidomastoid

Trapezius

Deltoid

Teres major
and minor

Triceps brachii

Erector spinae

Latissimus dorsi

Brachioradialis

Gluteus medius

Gluteus maximus

Hamstrings

Biceps femoris

Semitendinosis

Gastrocnemius

Soleus

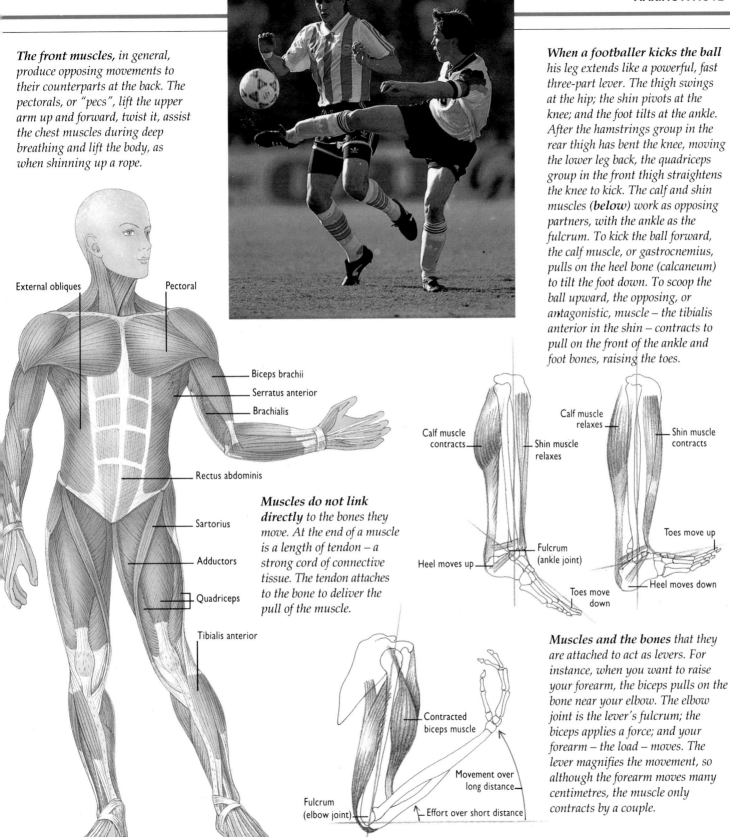

The front muscles, in general, produce opposing movements to their counterparts at the back. The pectorals, or "pecs", lift the upper arm up and forward, twist it, assist the chest muscles during deep breathing and lift the body, as when shinning up a rope.

External obliques

Pectoral

Biceps brachii

Serratus anterior

Brachialis

Rectus abdominis

Sartorius

Adductors

Quadriceps

Tibialis anterior

Muscles do not link directly to the bones they move. At the end of a muscle is a length of tendon – a strong cord of connective tissue. The tendon attaches to the bone to deliver the pull of the muscle.

When a footballer kicks the ball his leg extends like a powerful, fast three-part lever. The thigh swings at the hip; the shin pivots at the knee; and the foot tilts at the ankle. After the hamstrings group in the rear thigh has bent the knee, moving the lower leg back, the quadriceps group in the front thigh straightens the knee to kick. The calf and shin muscles (below) work as opposing partners, with the ankle as the fulcrum. To kick the ball forward, the calf muscle, or gastrocnemius, pulls on the heel bone (calcaneum) to tilt the foot down. To scoop the ball upward, the opposing, or antagonistic, muscle – the tibialis anterior in the shin – contracts to pull on the front of the ankle and foot bones, raising the toes.

Calf muscle contracts

Shin muscle relaxes

Heel moves up

Fulcrum (ankle joint)

Calf muscle relaxes

Shin muscle contracts

Toes move up

Heel moves down

Toes move down

Muscles and the bones that they are attached to act as levers. For instance, when you want to raise your forearm, the biceps pulls on the bone near your elbow. The elbow joint is the lever's fulcrum; the biceps applies a force; and your forearm – the load – moves. The lever magnifies the movement, so although the forearm moves many centimetres, the muscle only contracts by a couple.

Contracted biceps muscle

Movement over long distance

Fulcrum (elbow joint)

Effort over short distance

See also

SUPPORT AND MOVEMENT
▶ Staying in shape 12/13

▶ Bearing the load 14/15

▶ The living framework 16/17

▶ Bone junction 18/19

▶ Holding it together 20/21

▶ Fine movement 24/25

▶ Muscles at work 26/27

ENERGY
▶ Fuelling the body 38/39

REPRODUCTION AND GROWTH
▶ Building bodies 104/105

BUILDING THE BRAIN
▶ Sending signals 172/173

▶ On the move 206/207

Fine movement

Some carefully controlled muscles create extremely delicate movements.

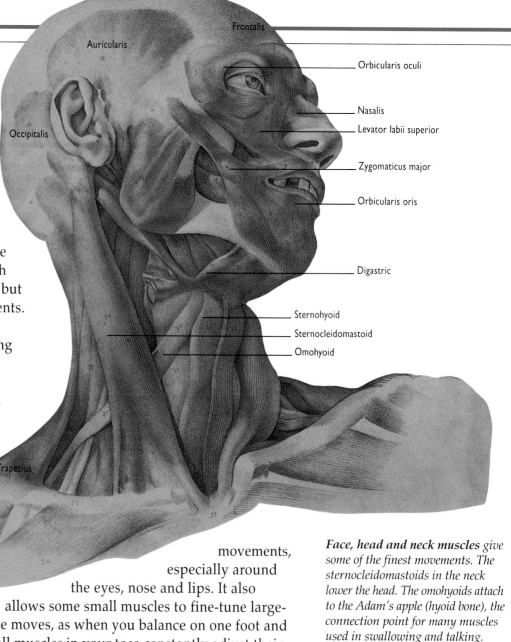

Auricularis

Frontalis

Occipitalis

Trapezius

Orbicularis oculi

Nasalis

Levator labii superior

Zygomaticus major

Orbicularis oris

Digastric

Sternohyoid

Sternocleidomastoid

Omohyoid

Look in the mirror, and raise your eyebrows slowly. As they lift, your expression changes from slight surprise to total astonishment. Along with body movements, facial expressions are a major part of our everyday life, as we flash a smile or frown in anger. Like the bigger movements, such as running and kicking, they depend on muscles – but thinner, shorter muscles for tiny, delicate movements. For instance, a complex network of neck muscles adjusts the larynx, or voice box, to control speaking volume and pitch. If the combined effect of these muscles stretches your vocal cords by just 2 mm (1/10 inch), the pitch of your voice will rise sharply, making it into a shrill shriek.

Dozens of the body's muscles, especially those around the face and in the hands and feet, are as thin as string. They cannot pull with any great strength, but they can make delicate, well-controlled movements. This is due to their small size and to the way in which the nerves are wired up to the hair-thin muscle fibres that are the basic units of a muscle. The biggest muscles have hundreds of thousands of muscle fibres; the smallest ones possess only a few hundred. In a large muscle, such as the gluteus in the hip, one nerve fibre (motor neuron) stimulates the contraction of thousands of muscle fibres. In a small muscle, like the straplike muscles that swivel an eye, each nerve fibre stimulates as few as 12 muscle fibres. This gives amazing precision of control, allowing some small muscles to make their own delicate movements, especially around the eyes, nose and lips. It also allows some small muscles to fine-tune large-scale moves, as when you balance on one foot and small muscles in your toes constantly adjust their pressure to keep you upright.

Face, head and neck muscles give some of the finest movements. The sternocleidomastoids in the neck lower the head. The omohyoids attach to the Adam's apple (hyoid bone), the connection point for many muscles used in swallowing and talking.

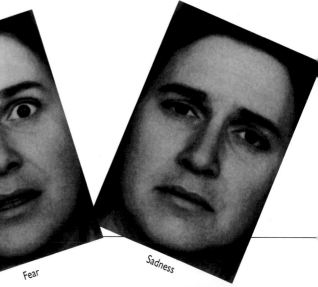

Neutral

Fear

Sadness

LOOKING AROUND

When you shift your gaze from a tree in the distance to another tree next to it, your eyeball swivels in an arc of less than one degree. This calls for extremely small and accurate movements by the muscles that move the eye. In fact they work to tolerances of tenths of a millimetre, and their stretch sensors tell the brain about the eye's angle of view for distance and depth perception.

Each eyeball has six muscles, fixed by their front ends to different areas around its sides. Most of the muscles extend backward to anchor in a ring of fibrous tissue at the rear of the eye socket (orbit). The muscles partially contract or relax with great precision to swivel the eye from side to side, up and down, twist it clockwise and anticlockwise, and any combination thereof. The angle of pull of one eye muscle – the superior oblique – is altered where its tendon passes around a trochlea, or bony "pulley". So this muscle rotates or twists one eye clockwise, the other anticlockwise.

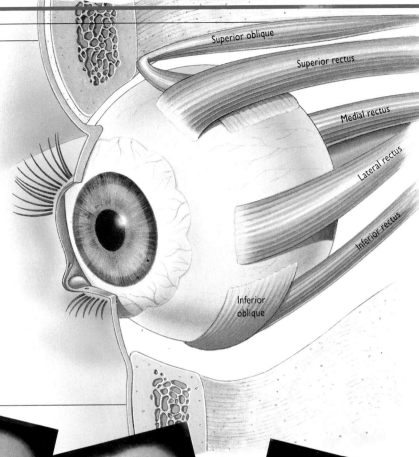

Superior oblique
Superior rectus
Medial rectus
Lateral rectus
Inferior rectus
Inferior oblique

See also

SUPPORT AND MOVEMENT
▶ Bearing the load 14/15

▶ Making a move 22/23

▶ Muscles at work 26/27

ENERGY
▶ Chewing it over 42/43

BUILDING THE BRAIN
▶ Sending signals 172/173

INPUTS AND OUTPUTS
▶ On the move 206/207

▶ Levels of seeing 214/215

▶ Seeing the light 210/211

▶ Staying upright 234/235

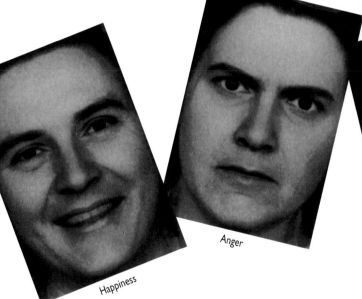

Happiness

Anger

Surprise

Disgust

More than 50 small muscles crisscross the face and head, just under the skin. Some are attached to the skull bones at both ends. Others have a bone anchorage at only one end and are fixed either to each other or to a common anchor point by fibrous straps or sheets. In closely coordinated action, they produce a galaxy of facial expressions. Each zygomaticus major runs from the cheekbone down to the corner of the mouth, and less than 5 mm (⅕ inch) contraction in them produces the flicker of a smile. The orbicularis oris purses lips and has an important role in speech; each nasalis flares a nostril; each frontalis raises an eyebrow; the occipitalis draws the scalp back; the levator labii superior raises the top lip; and in a few people the auricularis wiggles an ear.

After intensive research psychologists have found that there are seven universally recognized facial expressions. Computer-created composites can be made using photographs of actors whose features are accurately measured while assuming each of these expressions. Such images are now being used in research into areas such as autism and Parkinson's disease, whose sufferers may have problems controlling facial expressions.

Muscles at work

Powered molecular hinges are the basis of all muscle movement.

With your palms down and fingertips facing each other, slide the straight fingers of one hand between those of the other, so that the fingers interlock. On a scale millions of times smaller, at the level of molecules, this is a simple model of how your arm and hand muscles are producing the very movements you are now making.

Your fingers correspond to two body proteins, actin and myosin, the essential ingredients of muscle tissue. They are extremely small – about 80,000 myosins laid side by side would form a flat multistrand ribbon 1 mm ($\frac{1}{25}$ inch) wide, and actins are half as thick. Actin is a long ropelike molecule; myosin consists of a main backbone, with armlike cross bridges protruding at regular intervals. Each cross bridge supports a myosin head, which is instrumental in muscular contraction.

The myosin heads attach to a neighbouring actin and bend, pulling the actin along. The heads then detach from the actin, straighten and repeat the process again. It is like pulling on a rope with your hands. Billions of these incredibly small movements happen in a fraction of a second throughout the muscle, to make it contract. The process is driven by high-energy molecules of ATP (adenosine triphosphate), which the body uses to power many of its chemical processes. Muscle contraction is controlled by nerve signals from the brain, arriving along motor nerves.

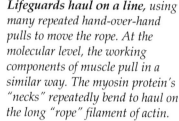

Lifeguards haul on a line, using many repeated hand-over-hand pulls to move the rope. At the molecular level, the working components of muscle pull in a similar way. The myosin protein's "necks" repeatedly bend to haul on the long "rope" filament of actin.

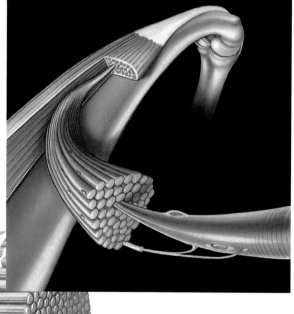

The muscles that move us are made of bundled fibres. These fibres in turn consist of hair-fine "threads" known as muscle cells, or myofibres. These rod-shaped cells have many nuclei and can be up to 30 cm (1 foot) long. Each myofibre contains a bundle of hundreds of yet smaller fibres, the myofibrils, which are made of two types of muscle filaments (myofilaments) – actin and myosin. Seen through a microscope, the myofibrils give the myofibres a regular pattern of stripes and bands.

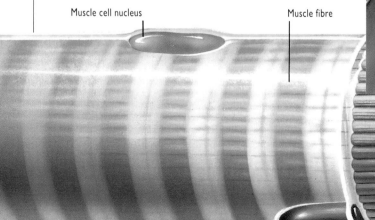

Muscle cell nucleus

Muscle fibre

Motor nerve endings

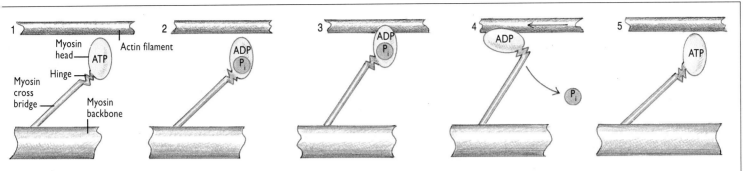

The chemical mechanism that pulls individual muscle filaments past each other (*above*), making muscles contract, is known as the cross-bridge cycle. Energy-rich ATP (adenosine triphosphate) attaches to the myosin head (**1**). It then breaks down into ADP (adenosine diphosphate) and P_i, an inorganic phosphate group (**2**). This split changes the shape of the myosin head and it attaches, or binds, to the actin myofilament (**3**). As the P_i leaves the myosin head, the "neck", or hinge, kinks and drags the actin along slightly (**4**). Finally the ADP separates, to be replaced by another high-energy ATP molecule, and the myosin neck straightens (**5**). The whole cycle repeats hundreds of times a second, on thousands of actin–myosin myofibrils in each myofibre, to produce the powerful pull of the whole muscle.

Actin is made of sub-units twisted together. Troponin proteins switch myosin head binding on and off under the influence of calcium.

Troponin protein **Actin filament**

Myosin cross bridge

Myosin head

Myosin filament Myosin backbone

Myosin, the thick myofilament, has a long backbone with many armlike cross bridges. These end in heads, which tilt to and fro producing muscular contraction.

In a fully relaxed, or stretched out, muscle, the ends of the actin filaments project only slightly into the bundles of myosins (**1**) and the I-band is at its widest. During contraction, thousands of myosin heads pull the actin myofilaments past, "hand over hand". The result is that the adjacent contractile units (sarcomeres) of the myofibre shorten (**2**). The I-bands become shorter while the A-bands stay the same width. Fully contracted, the I-bands narrow to nearly nothing and the H-zone (within the A-band) can disappear (**3**). At full contraction the whole muscle is almost half of its relaxed length.

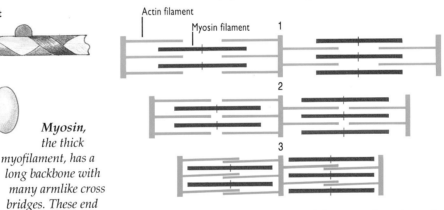

Actin filament

Myosin filament

1

2

3

Skeletal muscle is striped because of the way actin and myosin interlock and overlap. The A-band is a stack of myosins. The I-band is actins where they do not overlap myosins. The actins are joined at their ends to their neighbours, forming the Z-lines.

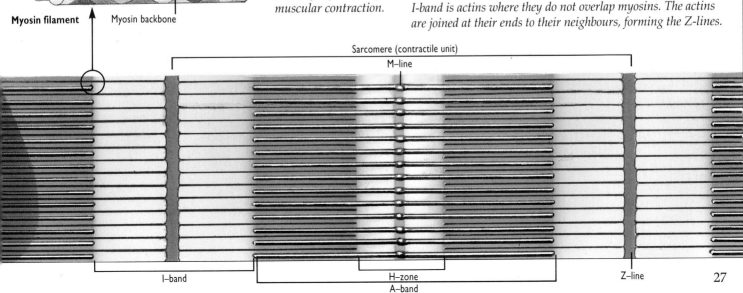

Sarcomere (contractile unit)

M–line

I–band

H–zone

A–band

Z–line

The heart's special muscle

Human life depends on the heart muscle's untiring and automatic contractions, continuously pumping blood around the body.

Unlike the muscles in, say, your arm, heart, or cardiac, muscle never tires. One reason for this is that the blood supply to heart muscle is copious. It has to be to supply the cardiac muscle with the oxygen and high-energy glucose it needs, and to flush away wastes, such as lactic acid, that might otherwise cause fatigue and cramps.

Heart muscle is like a combination of skeletal and visceral, or smooth, muscle. Looked at through a microscope, it has the regularly patterned bundles of fibres of skeletal muscle, but they branch, recalling the random arrangement of smooth fibres. Cardiac muscle also has its own built-in rhythm of about 100 beats each minute. Nerve signals from the brain usually slow this to about 60–80 in resting adults.

The inherent beating rhythm starts in a small patch of cells – the sinoatrial node – in the wall of the upper right atrium. This is the heart's pacemaker. It generates electrical signals that pass along nervelike tracts to a relay station at the base of the right atrium – the atrioventricular node. The signals continue along a thick conducting tract known as the bundle of His, then through its left and right branches, which subdivide further into a network of modified muscle fibres – the Purkinje fibres – in the walls of the ventricles. As each burst of electricity from the sinoatrial node reaches the muscle fibres, they contract, and so the heart pumps. The design of the wiring system means that the wave of contraction starts at the pointed base of the heart and works its way upward. Blood is thus ejected up into the main vessels, rather than being trapped in the bottom of the heart.

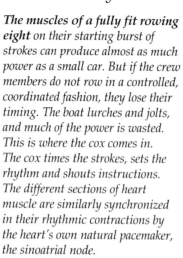

The muscles of a fully fit rowing eight on their starting burst of strokes can produce almost as much power as a small car. But if the crew members do not row in a controlled, coordinated fashion, they lose their timing. The boat lurches and jolts, and much of the power is wasted. This is where the cox comes in. The cox times the strokes, sets the rhythm and shouts instructions. The different sections of heart muscle are similarly synchronized in their rhythmic contractions by the heart's own natural pacemaker, the sinoatrial node.

SHOCKED BACK TO LIFE

Cardiac arrhythmias are medical conditions in which the heart loses its coordinated, rhythmic beating. Its various sets of muscles "do their own thing" and contract incompletely or out of sequence, upsetting the regular pumping of blood. Cardiac arrhythmias can be due to problems with the electrical coordinating system of the heart, with heart muscle itself or with its blood supply.

In ventricular fibrillation, for example, the lower main pumping chambers – the ventricles – contract very quickly, almost in a trembling fashion, yet pump hardly any blood. This can be a life-threatening emergency. One treatment is defibrillation: giving the heart a brief electric shock to jerk it out of its arrhythmia. The electric current, produced by a machine termed a defibrillator, is dispensed via two large metal plates (electrodes) held against the chest. The heart stops beating momentarily, in many cases allowing the sinoatrial node to regain control.

Defibrillator electrodes, pressed onto the chest skin on either side of the heart, deliver a burst of electricity that overwhelms the heart's own electrical conducting system. Several bursts may be needed, and the electricity makes other muscles contract too, so the patient may convulse and jerk about. Other people must stand well clear.

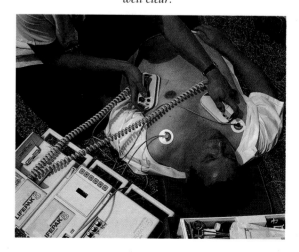

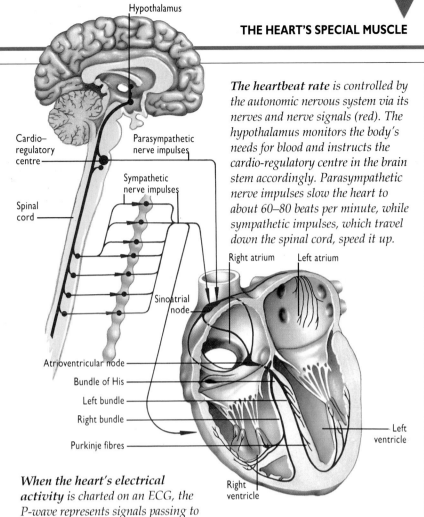

Hypothalamus

Cardio-regulatory centre

Parasympathetic nerve impulses

Spinal cord

Sympathetic nerve impulses

Sinoatrial node

Right atrium

Left atrium

Atrioventricular node

Bundle of His

Left bundle

Right bundle

Purkinje fibres

Right ventricle

Left ventricle

The heartbeat rate is controlled by the autonomic nervous system via its nerves and nerve signals (red). The hypothalamus monitors the body's needs for blood and instructs the cardio-regulatory centre in the brain stem accordingly. Parasympathetic nerve impulses slow the heart to about 60–80 beats per minute, while sympathetic impulses, which travel down the spinal cord, speed it up.

When the heart's electrical activity is charted on an ECG, the P-wave represents signals passing to the atrioventricular from the sinoatrial node. This is followed by atrial systole, when the atria pump blood into the ventricles. The dip at Q records signals passing along the bundle of His, and R and S mark their passage along the bundle branches and Purkinje fibres. These signals trigger ventricular systole, the contraction of the main chambers. At T the ventricles are relaxing during diastole.

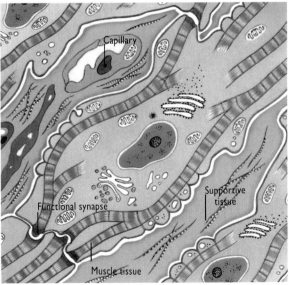

Capillary

Functional synapse

Supportive tissue

Muscle tissue

Purkinje fibres (above) are the heart's "nerve cells". They are cardiac muscle cells that also have impulse-transmitting membranes typical of true nerve cells. The impulses, which they conduct at 1.6 m/sec (5¼ feet/sec), reach every minute nook and cranny of the ventricle walls to stimulate heart muscle to contract. Signals cross from fibre to fibre at gaps that are similar to nerve-cell synapses.

The first heart sound – heard using a stethoscope – is the two valves between the ventricles and atria closing. The second is the two exit valves from the ventricles slamming shut.

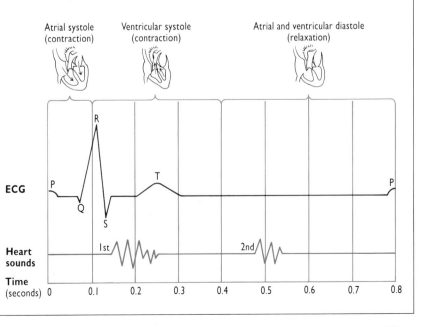

Atrial systole (contraction)

Ventricular systole (contraction)

Atrial and ventricular diastole (relaxation)

ECG

P   Q   R   S   T   P

Heart sounds

1st   2nd

Time (seconds)   0   0.1   0.2   0.3   0.4   0.5   0.6   0.7   0.8

Smooth operators

The next time you hear your stomach gurgle, the chances are that you are listening to muscles in action.

When a person is asleep, most of the skeletal (voluntary, or striped) muscles show little activity. But the breathing and heart muscles continue their rhythmic contractions, under autopilot control from the brain. There is also activity of muscles in the walls of internal body organs, such as the oesophagus (gullet), stomach, intestines and bladder, and in the small airways in the lungs and small arteries all over the body. These never-resting muscles are made of a type of tissue which – to contrast it with skeletal muscle – is known as visceral, involuntary or smooth muscle. This is because it makes up much of the bulk of the visceral (abdominal) organs, is largely under involuntary, or unconscious, control from the brain, and has a smooth, unstriped appearance under a microscope.

Smooth muscle is not connected to bones. Generally, it forms tubes or sacs and contracts to lessen the space it encloses. The fibres of smooth muscle are also usually arranged in layers, each contracting in a different direction. In a tube such as the gullet, fibres arranged in a longitudinal layer (lengthways) contract to shorten and widen the tube, while the circular layer (fibres arranged around the circumference) contracts to narrow and lengthen it. This so-called peristalsis pushes its contents along.

ASTHMA AND SMOOTH MUSCLE

The lungs' airways, the bronchi and bronchioles, have smooth muscle in their walls. In susceptible people, this muscle may go into spasm (contract) due to an allergic or hypersensitive reaction. The spasm is associated with inflammation of the bronchial lining and excess production of mucus.

Each of these three factors – muscle spasm, swollen lining and excess mucus – makes the airway narrower, leading to shortness of breath and also to breathing problems known as asthma. This condition tends to occur in episodes and can be triggered by a number of things, from exposure to house dust, pollen, animal fur or feathers to emotional upset or sudden inhalation of cold air.

Many asthma sufferers gain relief from symptoms – which in a bad attack can cause the sufferer literally to gasp for breath – using a bronchodilator drug. Because the smooth muscles in the airways have contracted, air is held in the lungs, and the sufferer cannot breathe out properly. The drug is squirted from an aerosol and is inhaled as a fine mist, deep into the lungs, to act directly on the narrowed airways and dilate (widen) them.

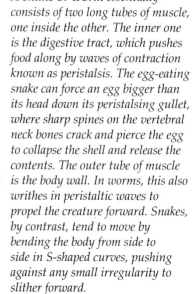

A snake or worm essentially consists of two long tubes of muscle, one inside the other. The inner one is the digestive tract, which pushes food along by waves of contraction known as peristalsis. The egg-eating snake can force an egg bigger than its head down its peristalsing gullet, where sharp spines on the vertebral neck bones crack and pierce the egg to collapse the shell and release the contents. The outer tube of muscle is the body wall. In worms, this also writhes in peristaltic waves to propel the creature forward. Snakes, by contrast, tend to move by bending the body from side to side in S-shaped curves, pushing against any small irregularity to slither forward.

Circular muscle

Longitudinal muscle

Resting muscle

Contracted circular muscle

Bolus

Relaxed muscle

Contracted longitudinal muscle

One of the clearest examples of peristalsis is found in the oesophagus (gullet), which propels swallowed lumps (boluses) of food down to the stomach. The gullet's circular muscle layer contracts behind the bolus in a travelling wave, massaging it on its way. Meanwhile, the longitudinal layer ahead of the bolus also contracts, making space for it by widening the tube. Gullet peristalsis is so strong that you can swallow even while upside down. It can also go into reverse and throw the stomach contents up and out of the mouth. In the intestines, where the semi-digested food has a more souplike consistency, peristalsis does not deal with individual boluses. It has a general massaging effect on the liquid contents.

In car tyres the strengthening materials – cords or plies – are arranged in bands of fibres lying in different orientations, rather like layers of smooth muscle in body organs. Each layer gives strength and stability in a certain direction, so that the whole design is firm yet supple.

Smooth muscles in certain arterial walls can contract or relax to vary the diameter of the vessel, controlling blood pressure and distribution.

Sphincters – ring-shaped structures with a central hole – are also made of smooth muscle. They stay contracted involuntarily, keeping the hole shut; the muscles are relaxed voluntarily to open the hole and let out the contents. One such sphincter is in the anus at the end of the digestive tract.

At the molecular level, the fibres (myofibres) of smooth muscle contract in much the same way as skeletal myofibres, although they are shorter and more spindle shaped. They also work a "rota system": while some contract, others relax and recover so that overall contraction in smooth muscle is maintained without fatigue.

See also

SUPPORT AND MOVEMENT
▶ Muscles at work 26/27

▶ The heart's special muscle 28/29

ENERGY
▶ Chewing it over 42/43

▶ The food processor 44/45

▶ Absorbing stuff 48/49

▶ A deep breath 52/53

CIRCULATION, MAINTENANCE AND DEFENCE
▶ In circulation 68/69

▶ The water balance 76/77

INPUTS AND OUTPUTS
▶ Body links 202/203

▶ Keeping control 238/239

▶ Dealing with drives 240/241

AVON CR5?B

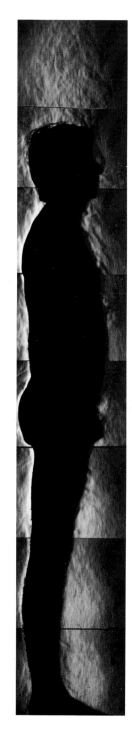

Energy

O*n the scale with which we are familiar –
that of the everyday world – humans are
great users of energy, driving about in cars,
illuminating the night with electric lights, flying in
aircraft and manufacturing products as diverse
as bread to eat and rockets to send satellites into
space. But we also use energy on a less familiar scale – a
molecular one – to power the chemical processes that occur within
the body's cells.*

*Our rate of internal energy use depends on the level of activity of the
community of cells that makes up the body. To match the demand for
energy, we take in fuel in the form of food. This is broken down into
smaller chemical components and absorbed, some to be stored and
used later, and some to provide the building blocks for
assembly into living tissue. Our lungs take in
oxygen, which is necessary for the series of
complex chemical reactions that take place
in the heart of each cell to release energy
from the fuel derived from food.*

Left (clockwise from top): *inside the
intestine; fibre; lung volume; heat energy.*
This page (top): *liver, duodenum
and pancreas;* **(right)**
energetic sperm.

The energy cycle

Humans are voracious consumers of energy, using it in two quite different ways.

Every living thing is a user of energy, and as energy is used it is transformed from one form to another. Thus plants which use light energy for photosynthesis turn electromagnetic radiation from the Sun into stored energy. When humans eat plants and digest them, molecules containing the stored energy are broken down and the energy is released and turned into, for example, movement via chemical reactions in the muscles. Thus energy which started as light became chemical energy and eventually kinetic, or movement, energy, which in time becomes heat energy.

Human bodies are complex metabolic machines that need energy to work – whether that work is the pull of a muscle, secretion by a gland or the transmission of a nerve impulse in the brain or spinal cord. Ultimately, that energy supply comes from food – fuel for the body machine. Parts of it are broken down in body cells in ways that release the chemical energy that drives all the other activities of the body. This energy-releasing metabolism, which normally requires oxygen for its completion, is termed internal respiration.

We also use external sources of energy to cook our food, heat our homes, power our computers, fuel transport systems, drive mechanical machinery, and manufacture materials and finished goods. These external sources include fossil fuels such as coal, oil and natural gas; nuclear power; and other sources such as solar, wind, geothermal, wave and tidal power, all of which maintain our energy-hungry existence. In industrialized societies most of these sources are used to produce electricity.

Flying high in a jet aircraft, passengers are served food by the cabin crew. The passengers' internal energy needs are being taken care of and, at the same time, they are flying in a plane which consumes external energy at a high rate. Not only is aviation fuel needed to keep a plane running, but a great deal is also used in its manufacture. The aluminium for its body is extracted from ore using vast amounts of electricity, for instance. Even the plastic insulating its wiring and the fabric covering the seats are made using energy, usually electricity generated from fossil fuel.

Different energy-generating techniques have varying indirect impacts. Burning fossil fuels, for instance, produces vast volumes of carbon dioxide, and this has contributed to the slow but steady increase in atmospheric levels of carbon dioxide in the 20th century. Carbon dioxide is one of the "greenhouse gases" that may induce global warming if its concentration in the atmosphere increases.

When *Homo sapiens* emerged, more than a million years ago, primitive human energy usage was almost entirely metabolic, driven by the food that was consumed. With the discovery of fire, however, the first rung on the ladder of external technological energy use was attained. Since then, the amount of external energy use has increased exponentially – the average energy consumption in the United States today is the equivalent of burning 8 tonnes of oil per person per year.

Almost every energy source that humans consume is, in the final analysis, derived from solar energy, which comes in turn from nuclear fusion reactions deep in the heart of the Sun, the star at the centre of our solar system.

All our foodstuffs depend on that energy because, apart from some bizarre deep-sea food webs centred on bacteria that

LIVING ALL OVER THE WORLD

Humans have made permanent homes in all regions of the Earth except for the polar areas.

☐	☐	☐	•
0–3	3–50	More than 50	Cities with population above one million

Population density per km²

Wherever humans go we use energy. We use some to stoke the internal "fires" of metabolism, and some to make changes to the world around us. In fact, if we have access to energy we can live in virtually any environment. The key extra ingredients are our intelligence, the ability to pass on information from generation to generation and the aptitude to make and use tools. In the colder regions of the Earth we can learn how to catch animals such as seals, thus providing food for internal use, skins that can be made into garments to keep out the cold and fat for fuel. Now other fuels can also be used to heat buildings. In hot regions buildings can be designed to keep cool in the fiercest sun, using air-conditioning units run on electricity.

metabolize hydrogen sulphide in complete darkness, all other land- or sea-based ecosystems are constructed around the ability of green plants and other photosynthesizing organisms to trap light energy.

Plants use light energy from the Sun to make organic substances such as sugars, fats and amino acids from inorganic ones like water, carbon dioxide and mineral salts. Human foods include light-trapping plants themselves or products made from them, such as bread from grain; animals that eat plants (herbivores such as sheep or chickens); animals that eat other animals (carnivores such as salmon); or decomposer organisms such as fungi that can break down the bodies of dead plants and animals. Humans are thus omnivores (we eat almost anything), and all our foods ultimately owe their existence to solar power. Even fossil fuels, which supply us with external energy, can be thought of as stores of ancient solar power. Coal, oil and natural gas are derived from the transformed remains of terrestrial or marine photosynthesizers that lived millions of years ago. The chemical energy locked up in their organic molecules came originally from light energy trapped by ancient living things. The energy from fossil fuels, and from nuclear and other sources, is used in countless ways in modern technological life.

The speed of life

A range of factors determines the rate at which you use energy. So how fast does your body run?

Put simply, the human body is a chemical machine in which countless billions of chemical reactions take place every split second. The sum total of all these reactions is known as metabolism, which is usually divided up into the reactions that build up complex molecules from simpler ones (known as anabolism) and those that break down large molecules into smaller ones (catabolism). In general, building processes use up energy when they take place, while many types of breakdown reactions release energy. In fact, one of the key roles of the food we eat is to provide us with nutrients that can be broken down in chemical reactions to supply us with energy; this energy then powers the body's metabolic machinery.

The amount of energy that the body uses over a given time is the metabolic rate. The rate of energy use depends on many factors, including body size, age and a person's typical level of activity. To find a metabolic rate that can be compared between different people, their rate of energy use when at rest is measured, thus eliminating such variable factors. The rate obtained under these conditions is known as the basal metabolic rate (BMR) and is usually expressed as the number of kilocalories (kcals or Calories) – units of energy – used per square metre of the person's body surface per hour. A BMR for a typical 20-year-old man would be about 26 kilocalories per square metre per hour. The BMR is often calculated by measuring a person's rate of oxygen use, since almost all the energy produced in a body is obtained from chemical reactions that use up oxygen.

ENERGY FOR THE BODY

The simple six-carbon sugar glucose has a central role because it can be broken down to produce carbon dioxide and water, along with useful energy for the body. This energy comes from the breaking of chemical bonds in glucose and the transfer of some of this chemical energy into the production of the molecule adenosine triphosphate (ATP). ATP is the direct chemical source of energy for most of the body's energy-demanding processes.

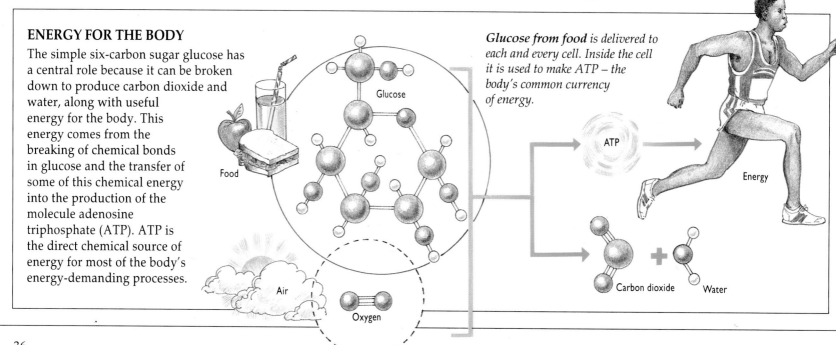

Glucose from food is delivered to each and every cell. Inside the cell it is used to make ATP – the body's common currency of energy.

Food

Glucose

Air

Oxygen

ATP

Energy

Carbon dioxide

Water

748

700 — **Kilocalories/30 minutes**

The amount of energy a person uses depends on a number of factors, including activity level. For instance, sprinting requires much more energy than, say, sleeping.

600

For an average-sized person who takes little or no exercise the rate of energy use is about 2,000 kcals (Calories) a day for a woman and 2,500 kcals a day for a man (men typically use more energy for any given activity than women). This is the amount of energy the body needs to keep the heart beating, to digest the food it eats, to perform many other functions – from thinking to breathing – and to account for minimal physical activity such as sitting, some standing, and a little walking in the course of 24 hours.

Sprinting 516

500

400

For short periods the body can power its activity with energy-providing ATP stored in its cells. This means that a 100-m (110-yard) sprint can be finished on a single deep breath. But longer periods of intense activity require high-efficiency aerobic (oxygen using) phases of cell energy production. So during a marathon, runners will be breathing hard to get as much oxygen to their muscle cells as possible so that glucose can react with oxygen to make more ATP.

321

300

Mountain climbing 241

.221

200

173

Playing tennis 166

Golfing 130

112

Walking 84

100

Eating 33

44

Sleeping 28

38

Women 0 — **Men**

As well as age, body size and general levels of activity, there are a number of other factors that can have an effect on BMR and the metabolic rate generally. For instance, for each degree Celsius that the body temperature rises, there is a 10 percent rise in metabolic rate, so people with fevers burn up energy at a higher rate than normal. The metabolic rate is also increased and largely controlled by the production of thyroxine in the thyroid gland. And increased food intake, especially of proteins, can raise the metabolic rate as the body works hard to digest it. But if increased food intake exceeds the body's metabolic needs, a person will put on weight; conversely, not eating enough can result in weight loss. Ideally, metabolic rate and energy intake from food should balance.

Fuelling the body

All parts of the body have a constant need for fuel to power their metabolic processes.

A space shuttle sits on its launch pad at Cape Kennedy. It is full of potential chemical energy, some in the form of liquid hydrogen and liquid oxygen in its main engine fuel tanks. When ignition begins, the potential chemical energy of this fuel (hydrogen) and oxidant (oxygen) is converted, in a controlled explosion, into superheated water vapour. The energy released from this reaction helps lift the craft into Earth orbit.

Energy production in the human body performs the same basic chemical trick but in a less violent, more everyday, fashion. The potential chemical energy locked up inside nutrients derived from food – especially the sugar glucose, the body's most-used primary fuel source – is liberated to power the functions of the body. This process, which requires the presence of oxygen, happens inside cells in a process known as cellular respiration. Examples of work done using released energy are the muscle contractions that move the body, metabolic activities such as the construction of proteins from amino acids, the transmission of nerve impulses and the generation of body heat.

In fact, heat production is perhaps the most obvious sign of energy-releasing activity – and hence the use of fuel – in the body. We are hot-blooded mammals able, like birds and a few specialized fish such as tuna, to maintain our bodies at a higher temperature than that of the surroundings and to hold that raised temperature within narrow limits. It is the stability of the internal body temperature that allows precise nervous and hormonal control of activity and metabolism.

In addition, the high, constant body temperature (around 37°C/98.6°F) means that body physiology – essentially the chemical reactions in cells – can be carried out at a fast rate, since a higher temperature increases the rate at which chemical reactions take place. This has evolutionary benefits. Generally speaking, the speed of chemical reactions in the cells allows mammals, including humans, to respond rapidly to the outside world, whether the need is to pursue prey quickly or to run from a threat. Maintaining a constant temperature is a fuel- (and thus food-) demanding process. But while a cold-blooded creature may need less fuel to keep itself going, if it gets too cold it dies.

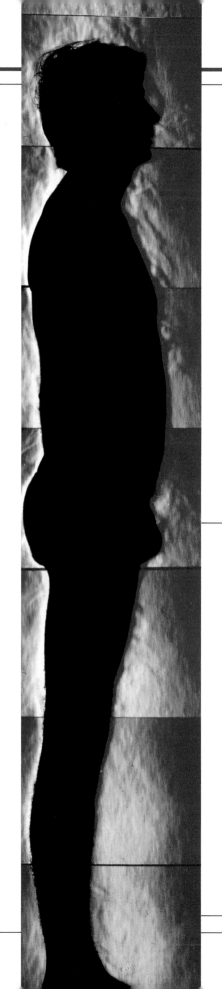

As warm-blooded mammals, humans generate heat through metabolic activities in order to hold body temperature at a constant 37°C (98.6°F).

The heat is generated in myriad chemical reactions that take place constantly in all the body's cells. The fuel for this heat production is ultimately the food we eat.

Images made using the so-called Schlieren method graphically illustrate the body's production of heat. The technique takes advantage of the fact that air of different temperatures has different refractive indices (it bends light to different extents). The specialized optics of the cameras used in the Schlieren method can capture the heated air around a person as it rises in smokelike plumes, warmed by body heat. In this image, red is coldest and light yellow warmest.

THE SMALL LIVE FAST

Metabolic rate in warm-blooded mammals is closely linked to the size of the animal. The larger the animal the lower the rate; conversely, the smaller the animal the higher its metabolic rate. This is mainly because warm-blooded animals have to maintain a constant, relatively high temperature, and the ratio of surface area to volume is much bigger in a small object than in a large one of the same general shape.

The amount of heat an animal generates as a by-product of energy-using actions such as muscle movement is related to its bulk, or volume. Its rate of heat loss is proportional to its skin size, or surface area. An

The brain accounts for about one-fifth of the total energy use of the body at rest. This is a remarkable statistic for a medium-sized organ that has no muscles and thus does not perform an energy-hungry process such as moving about. Much of the energy-requiring activity in the brain, which has a continual need for glucose (a sugar) as fuel, is linked with powering the electrochemical nerve impulses in its many billions of nerve cells.

So important is the brain that the first place a lack of fuel is noticed is in the effects it has on the brain: concentration goes and tiredness and listlessness set in. The brain's need for fuel is more or less constant. It uses just as much when you are concentrating hard as it does when you are "thinking of nothing" or even asleep.

The body's main muscles, such as those that move the arms and legs, do much physical work. The energy to power them comes from respiration in the cells of the muscles. Muscle activity, like brain activity, accounts for about one-fifth of the body's total energy use. However, the rate rises dramatically when the muscles work hard – when the body is at extremes of physical effort, muscles generate several times as much energy as all the other body systems put together. The muscles do not immediately require oxygen when they start to work, since they carry a small store of fuel. When this is exhausted, though, oxygen is needed for energy releasing reactions.

The heart's cardiac muscles have a self-evident energy demand: they pump continuously from "cradle to grave". This energy powers the ceaseless rhythmic contractions of the muscular walls of the two atria and two ventricles that push blood under pressure into the lungs and the rest of the body. Even without the extra work done when the body undertakes arduous physical activity, the action of the pumping heart at rest uses about one-tenth of the body's total energy requirement. The heart's need for fuel and oxygen, like the brain's, is soon noticed by its absence. If an artery carrying supplies of glucose and oxygen to the heart is blocked, the intense pain of a heart attack is experienced as the heart muscle supplied by that artery effectively dies for want of nutrients.

Oxygen consumption is a good measure of the total energy use – and thus fuel use – in a tissue, since oxygen is used in all energy-producing reactions in cells. In the human body, muscle and the liver use most energy, followed by the brain.

Adipose	9%
Brain	19%
Heart	11%
Kidney	8%
Liver	20%
Muscle	20%
Other	13%

Percentage of total oxygen consumption

See also

ENERGY
▶ The energy cycle 34/35

▶ The speed of life 36/37

▶ You are what you eat 40/41

▶ The energy storehouse 50/51

▶ The cell and energy 56/57

▶ Cells at work 58/59

SUPPORT AND MOVEMENT
▶ Muscles at work 26/27

▶ The heart's special muscle 28/29

CIRCULATION, MAINTENANCE AND DEFENCE
▶ The living pump 64/65

INPUTS AND OUTPUTS
▶ The big picture 236/237

▶ Dealing with drives 240/241

animal one-ninth the bulk of another has a skin surface area only one-third that of the other. It needs to generate roughly three times more heat kilogram for kilogram than the larger animal to maintain the same temperature. A harvest mouse, for instance, produces energy at a rate some 35 times higher than an elephant. If it used energy at the same rate as the elephant it would be unable to stay warm because its skin surface area, through which it loses heat, is proportionately much greater.

When metabolic rate – the sum total of all the chemical activity of an organism's cells – is estimated by the typical rate of oxygen consumed per unit of body weight per hour, the remarkable relationship between metabolic rate and body size shows up clearly.

What this means is that the smaller the creature, the faster on average all its cells are using energy as they perform their chemical functions. The champion mammal in terms of how fast its cells operate is the shrew, which has a rate 35 times faster than a human's.

Elephant	70
Horse	110
Human	210
Sheep	220
Dog	330
Cat	680
Rat	870
Ground squirrel	1,030
Mouse	1,650
Kangaroo mouse	1,800
Harvest mouse	2,500
Shrew	7,400

Oxygen consumption (ml/kg per hour)

You are what you eat

Food gives us both energy and the materials to build and maintain our bodies.

There are two basic ways for organisms to obtain the nutrition they need. They can, like plants and some bacteria, use light energy or the energy of chemical reactions to build the nutrients they require from scratch. Alternatively, like animals (including humans), fungi and some other bacteria, they can grab their nutrients ready formed from other organisms which they eat and digest.

A plant constructs each component of its nutrition from the simplest beginnings – photosynthesis in a leaf builds a component like glucose (a simple sugar). Using energy from sunlight, carbon dioxide from the air and water from the soil, a plant can construct a molecule of glucose atom by atom. Humans, and other animals, cannot do this. Our glucose nutrients arrive pre-synthesized in food. For instance, the glucose in honey is made by a plant and put into its nectar; bees collect the nectar; we collect the honey from the bees' hive.

Glucose is one of the most basic nutrients, but our food nutrients come mostly in the form of giant, complex organic molecules – macro-molecules – themselves made out of large numbers of organic sub-unit

The food we eat should contain all the fuel and raw materials the body needs. In this meal, the fish has protein and fat, and the rice has carbohydrate for energy as do the vegetables and fruit, which also contain fibre and vitamins.

molecules, like glucose, linked together in complex ways. Thus carbohydrates such as starch are polysaccharides – made of many (poly) sugar molecules (saccharides) joined together. Proteins are made of similarly large numbers of sub-units – amino acids. Fats are combinations of glycerol and fatty acids.

When macromolecular foods pass through the gut, they are disassembled into their sub-units by digestive processes and absorbed in that form. Within the body the sub-units are used as building blocks to construct human macromolecules in cells under the instruction of human genes.

Complex carbohydrates like those found in cereals are the best basis for the main supply of energy (Calories) in the diet. Vegetables and fruits, which provide minerals, vitamins and fibre, should also be eaten in large quantities, whereas smaller amounts of animal protein and fats are needed. Indeed, simple sugars, oils and fats should form only a small part of the diet.

This can be summed up in the food pyramid, the width of the pyramid representing the proportion of the type of food that should be eaten in a healthy diet.

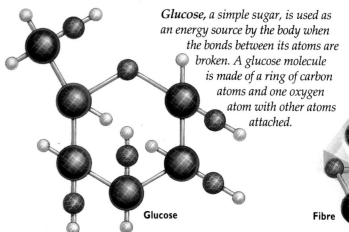

Glucose, a simple sugar, is used as an energy source by the body when the bonds between its atoms are broken. A glucose molecule is made of a ring of carbon atoms and one oxygen atom with other atoms attached.

Glucose

Fibre

Proteins in food are built of long folded chains of sub-units known as amino acids. Eating a varied range of protein-rich foods, such as fish, meat, nuts, eggs, pulses, and dairy products, ensures that all types of the 20 different amino acids are released by protein digestion in the gut and then absorbed in the intestines for use by the body. The average adult needs something like 60 g (2 ounces) of protein per day.

Amino acids are the building blocks used in the manufacture of all body tissues since they are the components strung together under the instruction of DNA in cells. There are, in fact, thousands of different proteins made by cells.

Sugar molecules, like glucose, link together to form large carbohydrate molecules, or polysaccharides. In the diet the most important ones are the starches, which are digested into their simple sugar sub-units and absorbed, and the cellulose fibre (roughage) – found in parts of vegetables, fruits, grains and pulses – which is made of polysaccharides that the gut cannot digest. This indigestible material provides the bulk in the gut contents and faeces, enabling gut peristalsis – the movement of matter through the intestines – to operate efficiently. The indigestible matter gives the contracting muscles that make up a peristaltic movement something to push against. A lack of fibre in the diet can lead to constipation and in the long run make a person more prone to bowel disease.

Minerals are found in foods in the form of ions (charged particles) and are directly absorbed from the gut. There are two classes, the macrominerals and the microminerals, or trace elements. Macrominerals are those that have to be taken in at a rate of more than 100 mg a day. They include ions of sodium, calcium, magnesium, potassium, chlorine, sulphur and phosphorus. Microminerals include copper, chromium, iron, cobalt, fluorine, iodine, manganese and zinc.

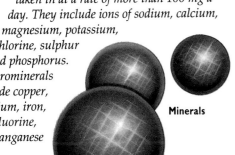

Hydrogen
Oxygen
Carbon
Minerals

Protein
Vitamin C

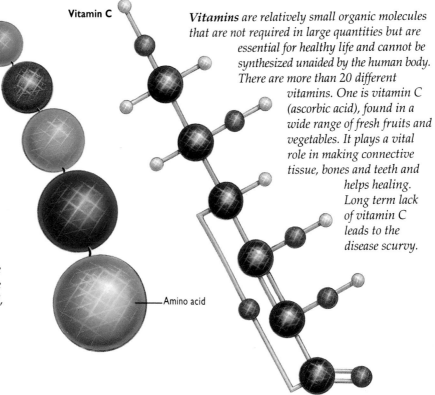

Amino acid

Vitamins are relatively small organic molecules that are not required in large quantities but are essential for healthy life and cannot be synthesized unaided by the human body. There are more than 20 different vitamins. One is vitamin C (ascorbic acid), found in a wide range of fresh fruits and vegetables. It plays a vital role in making connective tissue, bones and teeth and helps healing. Long term lack of vitamin C leads to the disease scurvy.

A CLOSE-UP ON GOOD FATS AND BAD FATS

In saturated fatty acids all the carbon atoms are linked by single bonds. Unsaturated fatty acids have some double bonds between the carbon atoms.

The body needs fats, just as it needs carbohydrates, proteins, minerals and vitamins. The fatty acid portion of the fats and oils from animal and plant foods in our diet is used after digestion and absorption to make our own fats. The fat cholesterol, for instance, is a key part of cell membranes.

Research indicates that diets containing a high proportion of saturated fatty acids, found typically in many animal fats, may be relatively harmful in relation to cardiovascular disease. But the unsaturated fatty acids, found typically in plant oils, are relatively protective, reducing the chance of illness.

Unsaturated fat   **Saturated fat**

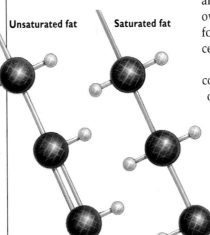

Chewing it over

Open your mouth and look in a mirror to see the first part of the body's food processing system.

Most of the digestive tract is hidden from us and works automatically and involuntarily (without being consciously controlled). The input sections of the tract, however, can be seen and are controlled in a largely voluntary way. The initial processing of foodstuffs starts with the lips, which are mobile for grasping food. The lips close to form a seal and the teeth chop and grind the food into small fragments. Meanwhile, the tongue manipulates the chewed food, compacting it into a rounded lump, or bolus. This is then pushed to the back of the throat for swallowing – it passes down the oesophagus (gullet) on the way to the stomach.

This breaking up of food is known as mechanical digestion. It changes food into fine particles which are further mechanically digested in the stomach and then chemically digested in the stomach and small intestine. The smaller the chewed particles, the faster chemical digestion occurs.

Saliva, the watery secretion of the salivary glands, is made in vast quantities when food is in the mouth. It aids chewing, lubricates the movement of food boluses and contains the digestive enzyme amylase that begins the chemical digestion of starch even before food is swallowed.

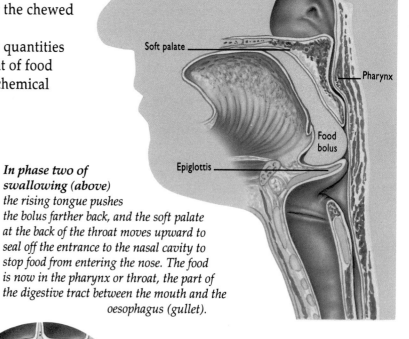

Three pairs of salivary glands, with ducts on each side of the face that empty into the mouth, produce saliva. This not only moistens the mouth but also helps chewing and swallowing by wetting food so it does not stick.

In phase two of swallowing (above) the rising tongue pushes the bolus farther back, and the soft palate at the back of the throat moves upward to seal off the entrance to the nasal cavity to stop food from entering the nose. The food is now in the pharynx or throat, the part of the digestive tract between the mouth and the oesophagus (gullet).

In phase one of swallowing (above) food (yellow) that has been chewed into small fragments and processed into a rounded soft ball, called a bolus, is propelled by complex movements of the tongue to the back of the mouth cavity. During the biting, chewing and grinding stage, the food is mixed with saliva from the salivary glands until the bolus is a uniform fine slurry of food particles suitable for swallowing.

A cross-sectional view of the mouth (left) shows how the tongue can act as a muscular piston that pushes a food bolus. The bolus, positioned between the tongue and the roof of the mouth, or the hard palate, starts to be squeezed toward the throat when the tip of the tongue rises to the front of the palate.
The section also reveals how the upper and lower sets of molar teeth at the rear of the mouth can meet one another for grinding food.

In phase three of swallowing (below) the combined action of the tongue moving backward and the muscles in the pharynx squeezing the bolus move it farther on. The trachea, or windpipe, rises up and the epiglottis swings down to close off its upper end like a spring-loaded trapdoor so that no food or liquid can enter. Swallowing is a reflex action and the coordination of the complex tongue and throat muscle contractions is automatic.

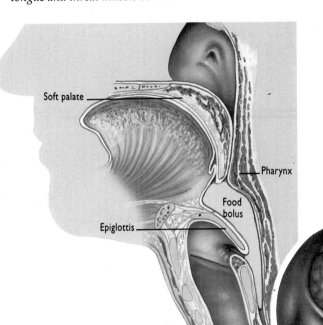

Soft palate

Pharynx

Food bolus

Epiglottis

In phase four of swallowing (right) more backward pressure by the tongue and constriction of the muscles of the pharynx push the food bolus past the epiglottis and down into the oesophagus, or gullet. Muscle contractions (peristalsis) in the oesophagus carry the food down into the stomach for the next stage of food processing.

Soft palate

Pharynx

Food bolus

Oesophagus

Uvula

Food bolus

Epiglottis

In this view down the throat (left) the food bolus has passed the uvula, the last part of the soft palate at the back of the roof of the mouth, and is moving down the throat. The epiglottis – a flap of cartilage – is shown here in its horizontal position, sealing off the trachea, or windpipe, during swallowing.

TEETH

Permanent teeth (blue), already formed in cavities within the jaw bones, eventually replace a child's 20 first, or milk, teeth.

Extra-hard white enamel forms the tough outer layer of a tooth; within that is a layer of softer dentine which itself encloses the pulp cavity containing blood vessels and nerves. Canines and incisors tear and cut bite-sized chunks of food; molars and premolars then grind them to a pulp. Adults have 4 canines, 8 incisors and 16 premolars and molars; many have 4 extra molars: wisdom teeth.

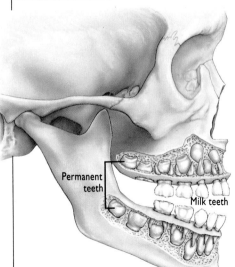

Permanent teeth

Milk teeth

Enamel

Gum

Jaw

Dentine

Pulp

Root

Molar   Premolar   Canine   Incisor

Molars are flat, with grooved tops. Canines are pointed. Incisors are flat topped and look like shears.

The food processor

More than just a store for food, the stomach is an active organ of digestion.

Swallowed food is broken up into ever smaller bits by the churning action of the stomach, which also blends the food with a mixture of chemicals, known as gastric juice, secreted by the stomach's thick wall. The main component is strong hydrochloric acid, which kills most of the bacteria and other dangerous microorganisms that might be swallowed and helps dissolve food. The stomach secretes pepsinogen as well, and this is converted into the protein-splitting enzyme pepsin by the acid. It also gives out small quantities of a fat-digesting lipase and a protein called intrinsic factor which enables the body to absorb and use vitamin B_{12}.

After several hours of churning, acid treatment and chemical digestion, the partly digested food, now called chyme, passes in controlled spurts into the upper part of the small intestine – the duodenum. Here secretions from the pancreas and gall bladder continue the digestion process. Since enzymes below the stomach work only in non-acid conditions, pancreatic secretions contain alkalis which neutralize the acid chyme. Pancreatic juice also contains the enzymes amylase, chymotrypsin, trypsin and lipase, as well as nucleases which break down or digest various components of food.

Since fats do not dissolve in water, it would be difficult for the water-soluble digestive enzymes of the intestines to deal with them without help. But bile enters the duodenum via the bile duct and acts as a biological detergent that emulsifies fats into minute droplets. These become suspended in the watery contents of the intestines so that the enzymes can work on them to split them up.

It is possible to swallow food even while hanging upside down. This is because powerful muscle layers in the oesophagus, which joins the throat to the stomach, generate strong contractions, or peristaltic waves, that push the food along. Mucus from glands in the oesophagus wall acts as a lubricant.

On its way down, food spends only minutes or less in the mouth and oesophagus (dark blue). It can spend a total of eight hours in the stomach and duodenum (red): four in the stomach before passing through the pyloric sphincter into the duodenum, where it spends a further four hours before going farther into the small intestine.

Cross section of oesophagus

Muscle layer

Mucous gland

Submucous layer

Salivary glands

Oesophagus

Liver

Stomach

Pyloric sphincter

Gall bladder

Duodenum

Pancreas

Small intestine

Colon

Appendix

Rectum

0   12

Hours spent in digestive system

In the stomach wall (below) surface cells make mucus which protects the lining from acid. Cells in pits in the wall secrete hydrochloric acid, other digestive chemicals and the hormone gastrin which helps control gastric juice production.

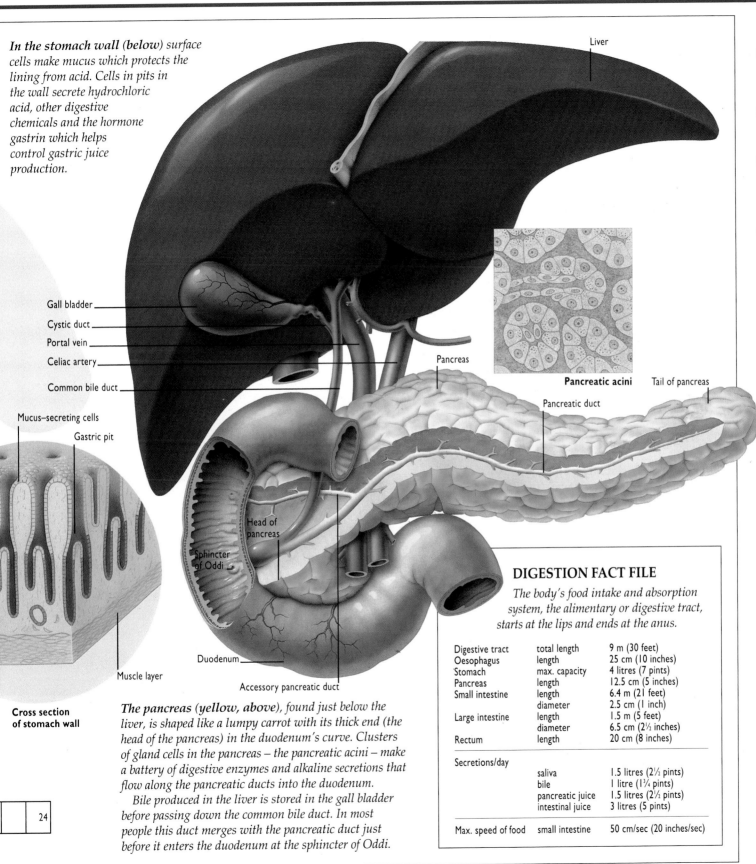

Liver

Gall bladder

Cystic duct

Portal vein

Celiac artery

Common bile duct

Mucus–secreting cells

Gastric pit

Head of pancreas

Sphincter of Oddi

Pancreas

Pancreatic acini

Tail of pancreas

Pancreatic duct

Duodenum

Muscle layer

Cross section of stomach wall

Accessory pancreatic duct

The pancreas (yellow, above), found just below the liver, is shaped like a lumpy carrot with its thick end (the head of the pancreas) in the duodenum's curve. Clusters of gland cells in the pancreas – the pancreatic acini – make a battery of digestive enzymes and alkaline secretions that flow along the pancreatic ducts into the duodenum.

Bile produced in the liver is stored in the gall bladder before passing down the common bile duct. In most people this duct merges with the pancreatic duct just before it enters the duodenum at the sphincter of Oddi.

24

DIGESTION FACT FILE

The body's food intake and absorption system, the alimentary or digestive tract, starts at the lips and ends at the anus.

Digestive tract	total length	9 m (30 feet)
Oesophagus	length	25 cm (10 inches)
Stomach	max. capacity	4 litres (7 pints)
Pancreas	length	12.5 cm (5 inches)
Small intestine	length	6.4 m (21 feet)
	diameter	2.5 cm (1 inch)
Large intestine	length	1.5 m (5 feet)
	diameter	6.5 cm (2½ inches)
Rectum	length	20 cm (8 inches)
Secretions/day		
	saliva	1.5 litres (2½ pints)
	bile	1 litre (1¾ pints)
	pancreatic juice	1.5 litres (2½ pints)
	intestinal juice	3 litres (5 pints)
Max. speed of food	small intestine	50 cm/sec (20 inches/sec)

See also
ENERGY
▶ You are what you eat 40/41

▶ Chewing it over 42/43

▶ Enzymes: chemical cutters 46/47

▶ Absorbing stuff 48/49

SUPPORT AND MOVEMENT
▶ Holding it together 20/21

▶ Smooth operators 30/31

CIRCULATION, MAINTENANCE AND DEFENCE
▶ Repelling invaders 88/89

BUILDING THE BRAIN
▶ Food for thought 188/189

INPUTS AND OUTPUTS
▶ Keeping control 238/239

▶ Dealing with drives 240/241

Enzymes: chemical cutters

Many body processes use highly specialized chemical tools to cut up or assemble molecules to order.

The human body depends on innumerable precisely controlled chemical reactions, many of which need catalysts to speed them up and facilitate them. Evolution has produced thousands of biological catalysts in the form of enzymes, each of which is normally capable of stimulating only one specific chemical reaction. Some enzymes join small molecules together to form larger ones, as when amino acids join to form the proteins that make up the body. Others break down large molecules into smaller ones, as in the digestion of food into small, absorbable sub-units, or in the severing of the bonds holding a sugar together to release energy.

Most enzymes are large globe-shaped protein molecules with a complex surface shape. This surface usually has a precisely patterned groove or cavity – the enzyme's "active centre". It is shaped so that the substance on which the enzyme acts to stimulate a reaction – the substrate – fits precisely into it. Fitting like a chemical key in the lock of the active centre, the substrate is activated, bringing about the desired reaction. It then leaves the enzyme, freeing up the active centre to receive a new substrate – and the process begins again. Enzymes are dependent on conditions being constant; the enzymes in the body generally work best at about 37°C (98.6°F) – the normal body temperature maintained by homeostasis.

Digestive enzymes break down large food molecules into small nutrient molecules that can be absorbed by the wall of the small intestine. There are three major types of large food molecules – the polysaccharides (starches), lipids (fats and oils) and proteins.

Polysaccharides, the starch in rice for instance, are made up of long chains of individual (monosaccharide) sugars, such as glucose, fructose and galactose. Starch-splitting enzymes digest them by breaking the links between the sugars. The process starts in the mouth with the enzyme salivary amylase. But most is done in the small intestine, where polysaccharide fragments are attacked by pancreatic amylase. This converts them into two-sugar disaccharides, such as sucrose, lactose and maltose. Specific disaccharidases (disaccharide-splitting enzymes), such as sucrase, lactase and maltase, on the surface of the small intestine split disaccharides into monosaccharide sugars. These are then absorbed by the gut wall.

Stomach

Disaccharide

Amino acid unit

Proteoses

Dextrin

Protein

Salivary amylase

Starch (polysaccharide chain)

Monosaccharide unit

Mouth

Stomach

Proteins are made of chains of amino acids joined together by links known as peptide bonds. The digestive enzymes that work on proteins such as those in fish do so by breaking the bonds. Such digestion takes place in the stomach and small intestine. The main enzyme in the stomach is pepsin, which can operate in the high acid levels found there. Pepsin breaks down proteins into smaller chains of amino acids known as proteoses and peptones and also some individual amino acids. In the small intestine the potent enzyme trypsin, along with enzymes called aminopeptidases, completes the breakdown of proteins, peptones and proteoses into single amino acids which can be absorbed by the body.

Pepsin

Trypsin, chymotrypsin, or carboxypeptide

Erepsin

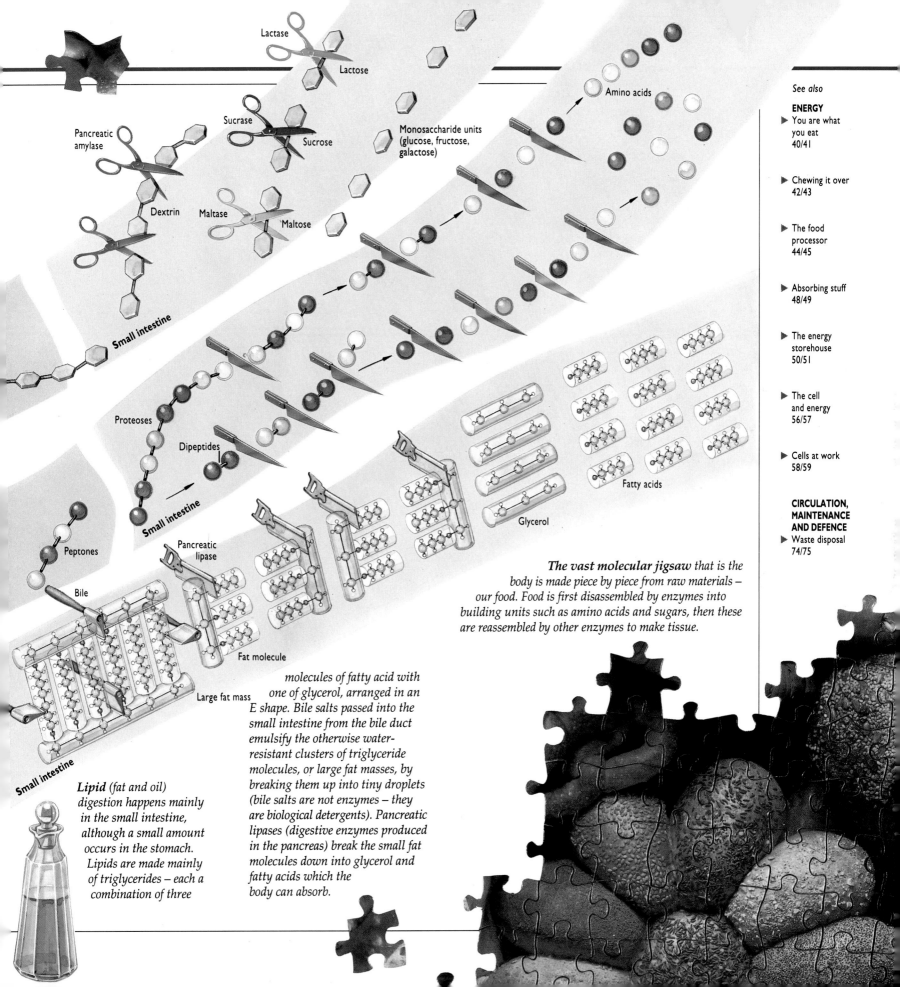

Lactase

Lactose

Sucrase

Sucrose

Pancreatic amylase

Dextrin

Maltase

Maltose

Amino acids

Monosaccharide units (glucose, fructose, galactose)

Small intestine

Proteoses

Dipeptides

Small intestine

Peptones

Bile

Pancreatic lipase

Fatty acids

Glycerol

Fat molecule

Large fat mass

Small intestine

Lipid (fat and oil) digestion happens mainly in the small intestine, although a small amount occurs in the stomach. Lipids are made mainly of triglycerides – each a combination of three

molecules of fatty acid with one of glycerol, arranged in an E shape. Bile salts passed into the small intestine from the bile duct emulsify the otherwise water-resistant clusters of triglyceride molecules, or large fat masses, by breaking them up into tiny droplets (bile salts are not enzymes – they are biological detergents). Pancreatic lipases (digestive enzymes produced in the pancreas) break the small fat molecules down into glycerol and fatty acids which the body can absorb.

The vast molecular jigsaw that is the body is made piece by piece from raw materials – our food. Food is first disassembled by enzymes into building units such as amino acids and sugars, then these are reassembled by other enzymes to make tissue.

Absorbing stuff

The primary function of the alimentary tract is to absorb nutrient molecules from digested foods.

Once food has been chewed and churned and broken down into tiny bits of organic nutrients by enzymes, it can be absorbed into the body. This is done extraordinarily efficiently – up to 95 percent of fats and 90 percent of amino acids (protein building blocks) produced by digestion are absorbed in the small intestine, which lies between the stomach and large intestine.

The small intestine has three parts: the duodenum, where most digestion occurs, and the jejunum and the ileum, where most absorption takes place. During the one to six hours (the average time is two hours) that it takes for digested food to pass through the small intestine, it is pushed along by the peristaltic action of muscles in the intestinal walls.

Uptake of nutrients into the blood vessels and lymph vessels of the gut wall is aided by an amplification of the surface area of the intestinal lining. This expands the simple inner surface of the small intestine by about 600 times – if the small intestine had a smooth inner surface it would need to be not 6 m (20 feet) but 3.6 km (2¼ miles) long.

The folded surface of the intestinal walls is expanded by millions of finger-shaped projections, or villi (right), and by intuckings, called crypts, between the villi. The villi wave about helping to stir the gut contents. Each villus is covered by absorptive epithelial cells (below) and contains a tiny arteriole and venule, linked by capillaries, and a lymph vessel known as a lacteal.

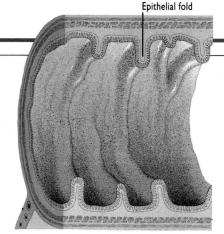

Epithelial fold

Section of small intestine

The inner wall of the small intestine (left) has folds, or plicae circulares, which extend around the inner lining like circular shelves. These shelves are the first step in increasing the area available for the uptake of nutrients. Muscles in the intestinal wall contract rhythmically to drive the contents along. The contractions help to swirl matter around so that it comes into contact with the absorbing cells.

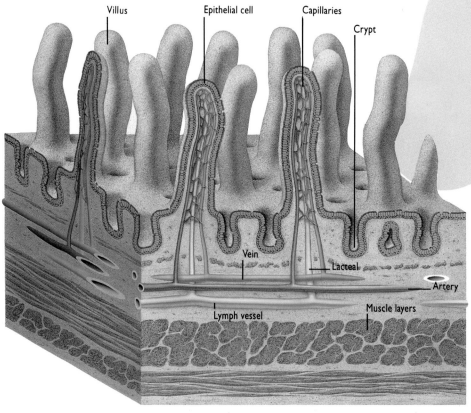

Villus   Epithelial cell   Capillaries

Crypt

Vein

Lacteal

Artery

Lymph vessel   Muscle layers

Detail of epithelial fold

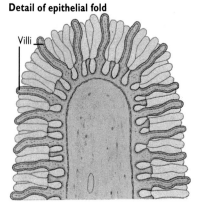

Villi

Nutrients such as sugars and amino acids pass across the epithelial cells into the blood in the capillaries to be transferred to the rest of the body. Products of fat digestion merge with the cell membrane, eventually drifting into the lacteals, which in due course empty into the blood system in a vein near the heart.

Detail of villus   Microvilli

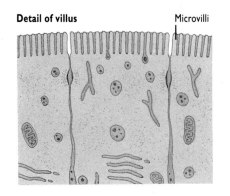

A fuzzy coat – the so-called brush border – covers the outer surface of each villus. The border is made up of thousands of microvilli (left), which are thin, membrane-bounded extensions of the cell. Nutrient absorption at an ultimate, molecular, level occurs across the outer membranes of the microvilli.

0

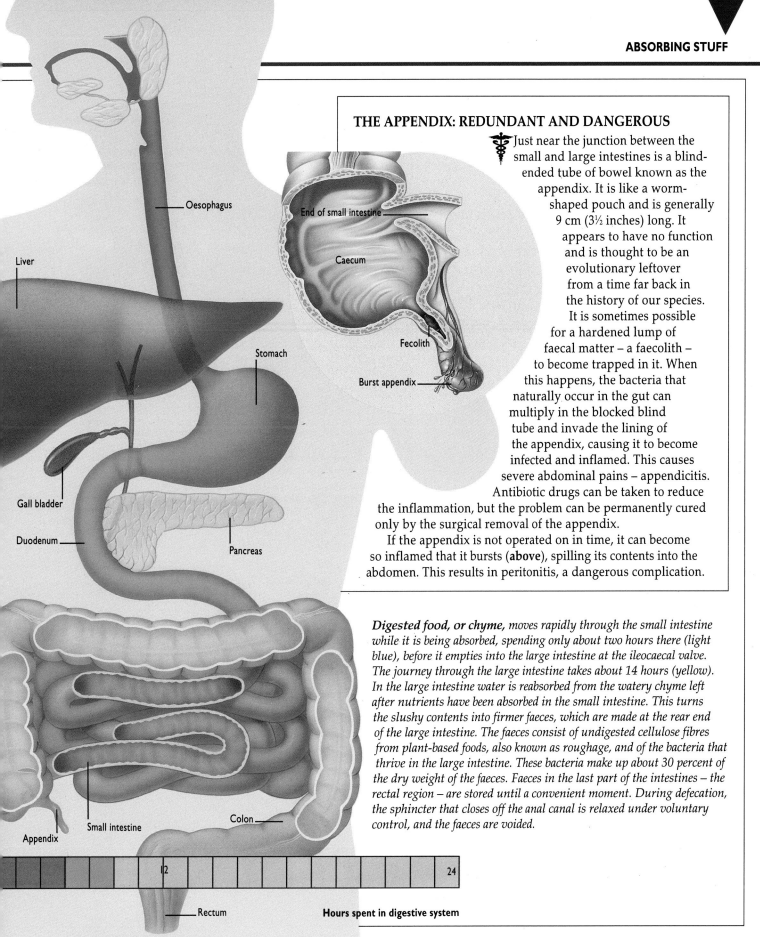

Oesophagus

Liver

Stomach

Gall bladder

Duodenum

Pancreas

End of small intestine

Caecum

Fecolith

Burst appendix

Appendix

Small intestine

Colon

Rectum

Hours spent in digestive system

12

24

THE APPENDIX: REDUNDANT AND DANGEROUS

Just near the junction between the small and large intestines is a blind-ended tube of bowel known as the appendix. It is like a worm-shaped pouch and is generally 9 cm (3½ inches) long. It appears to have no function and is thought to be an evolutionary leftover from a time far back in the history of our species. It is sometimes possible for a hardened lump of faecal matter – a faecolith – to become trapped in it. When this happens, the bacteria that naturally occur in the gut can multiply in the blocked blind tube and invade the lining of the appendix, causing it to become infected and inflamed. This causes severe abdominal pains – appendicitis. Antibiotic drugs can be taken to reduce the inflammation, but the problem can be permanently cured only by the surgical removal of the appendix.

If the appendix is not operated on in time, it can become so inflamed that it bursts (**above**), spilling its contents into the abdomen. This results in peritonitis, a dangerous complication.

Digested food, or chyme, moves rapidly through the small intestine while it is being absorbed, spending only about two hours there (light blue), before it empties into the large intestine at the ileocaecal valve. The journey through the large intestine takes about 14 hours (yellow). In the large intestine water is reabsorbed from the watery chyme left after nutrients have been absorbed in the small intestine. This turns the slushy contents into firmer faeces, which are made at the rear end of the large intestine. The faeces consist of undigested cellulose fibres from plant-based foods, also known as roughage, and of the bacteria that thrive in the large intestine. These bacteria make up about 30 percent of the dry weight of the faeces. Faeces in the last part of the intestines – the rectal region – are stored until a convenient moment. During defecation, the sphincter that closes off the anal canal is relaxed under voluntary control, and the faeces are voided.

The energy storehouse

It is difficult to find any aspect of bodily functions not influenced by the many activities of the liver.

Lying at the top of the abdominal cavity, nestling under the diaphragm and over the stomach, the liver – the body's largest gland – plays a truly central role in the body's nutrient transportation and metabolic processes. For instance, it takes the key energy-supplying molecule glucose (a sugar) from blood arriving from the intestine and converts it into the starchlike carbohydrate glycogen for storage. When glucose levels in the blood fall, it then converts the glycogen back into glucose for transport around the body. The liver can also store fats and amino acids and convert them into glucose. It forms the waste product urea from waste proteins and amino acids and manufactures the key molecules – lipoproteins, cholesterol and phospholipids – that make cell membranes.

In addition to these storage and conversion functions, the liver is also responsible for keeping the body at the correct temperature by warming blood as it passes through its inner spaces. It even defends the body by changing harmful chemicals like poisons, drugs, pesticides and environmental pollutants into harmless products which can then be removed from the body in bile or urine.

In a container port materials are stored ready for access and transport to other regions. Similarly, the liver stores nutrients from the digestive system ready for distribution and use in the body.

Inferior vena cava

Hepatic vein

Aorta

Liver

Hepatic artery

Portal vein

Capillaries of spleen, pancreas, stomach, intestines

The liver is supplied (via the hepatic artery) with blood which brings the oxygen and nutrients that enable it to do its work.
It also receives blood for processing that comes, via the portal vein, direct from capillaries that drain those parts of the digestive system that absorb nutrients from the gut contents. All blood leaves the liver via the hepatic vein.

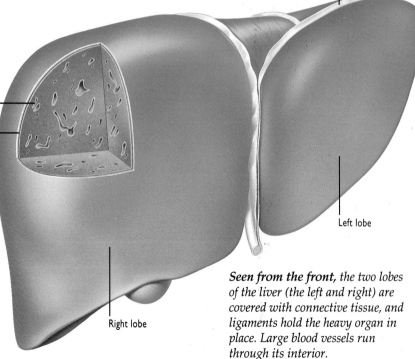

Supporting ligament

Section through blood vessels

Peritoneum

Left lobe

Right lobe

Seen from the front, the two lobes of the liver (the left and right) are covered with connective tissue, and ligaments hold the heavy organ in place. Large blood vessels run through its interior.

Left lobe

Portal vein

Inferior vena cava

Right lobe

Supporting ligament

Hepatic artery

Cross section of lobule

Branch of bile duct

Hepatic artery

Bile canaliculi

Liver cells

Sinusoids

Gall bladder

Branch of portal vein

Branch of bile duct

Branch of hepatic artery

Branch of portal vein

Branch of hepatic artery

Central vein (leads to hepatic vein)

Lobule

Sinusoid

Branch of hepatic artery

Branch of bile duct

Branch of portal vein

Hepatic vein

Central vein

The gall bladder temporarily stores bile, which contains water, sodium bicarbonate, bile salts, bile pigments and cholesterol. It concentrates the bile, extracting 90 percent of its water, making it mucusy. About 30 minutes after a meal, when the duodenum first contains partly digested food, the gall bladder contracts to push bile into the duodenum, where it turns fat droplets into an emulsion so that they can be digested.

Each lobe of the liver is made up of thousands of small lobes, or lobules. A lobule is made of liver cells, or hepatocytes, which are supplied with blood by tiny branches of the hepatic artery and portal vein. Blood flows in channels known as sinusoids.

A liver lobule's hepatocytes are piled up in irregularly shaped rows, radiating outward from a central vein. They are surrounded by blood which is carried in channels, or sinusoids, from the outside of the lobule toward the central vein. The blood comes from a branch of the portal vein and, after traversing the lobule, it drains into a branch of the hepatic vein.

As the blood passes through the lobule, hepatocytes get to work on it. One of their many roles in dealing with nutrients arriving from the intestines is to convert the sugars galactose and fructose into glucose, the body's essential fuel.

They also make bile – essential for the digestion of fats – which is collected by tiny bile ducts, or canaliculi, and taken to the gall bladder via the bile duct.

LIVER FACT FILE

The liver acts as a store for glucose, in the form of glycogen, the vitamins A, D, E, K and B₁₂, minerals such as iron as well as fats and amino acids.

Dimensions	width	20–22 cm (8–9 inches)
	height	15–18 cm (6–7 inches)
	thickness	10–13 cm (4–5 inches)
Weight of liver		1.5 kg (3 pounds)
Percentage of adult body weight		2.5
Percentage of infant body weight		4
No. of lobes		2
Diameter of lobules		0.1 cm (¹⁄₂₅ inch)
Blood supplied to liver		1.5 litres/min (2½ pints/min)
Blood supply from hepatic artery		20%
Blood supply from portal vein		80%
Rate of bile secretion		1 litre/day (1¾ pints/day)

A deep breath

Life depends on a continuous supply of oxygen, which we get from the air around us when we breathe.

The air we need is pumped in and out of two lungs which sit protected inside the ribcage of the chest. In the lungs oxygen is removed from the air and passed into the blood; the waste gas carbon dioxide leaves the blood to be eliminated in exhaled air. Breathing can be consciously controlled, but more usually this vital function is taken care of and coordinated automatically by the nervous system.

During breathing air enters through the nose or mouth. It then passes down the trachea, or windpipe, which is supported by tough cartilage hoops that keep it open at all times. On the way it is warmed and humidified.

From the windpipe air goes down the left or right bronchus (airway) into one or other of the lungs. The airways divide into finer and finer branches, or bronchioles; the narrowest bronchioles end in alveoli – tiny blind-ended air sacs where most of the gas exchange between air and blood takes place.

The whole inner lining of the breathing, or pulmonary, system is kept moist by secretions of mucus from the epithelial (lining) cells of the air spaces. And specialized cells in the airway wall have many cilia (short, hairlike projections) which beat and move the mucus along so it flows upward from the bronchioles. The system works like a watery conveyor belt, removing inhaled particles such as dust from the lungs to the top of the trachea from where the mucus can be coughed up or swallowed.

The total volume of air in a pair of lungs filled right to the top is the same as that of eight large mineral-water bottles – 6 litres (10½ pints).

The outside of the right lung, seen from the left, has indentations for central chest organs, including the trachea and oesophagus. Pulmonary veins take blood to the heart, and the pulmonary artery brings blood from the heart. The fissures mark the divisions of the lung into separate lobes.

In cross section, the spongy alveolar tissue and the bronchi (main airways) and bronchioles (smaller airways) are obvious.

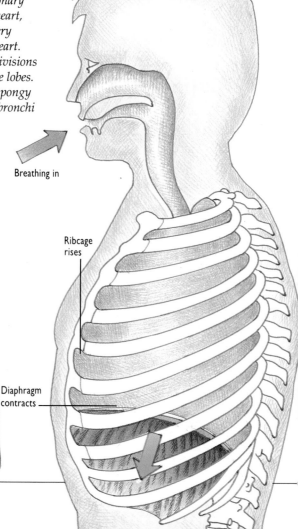

Breathing in

Ribcage rises

Diaphragm contracts

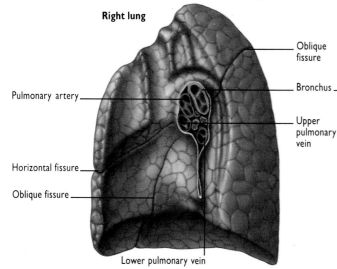

Right lung

Pulmonary artery

Horizontal fissure

Oblique fissure

Lower pulmonary vein

Oblique fissure

Bronchus

Upper pulmonary vein

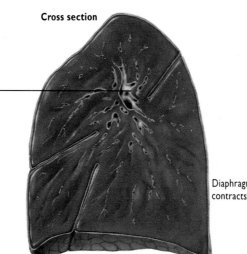

Cross section

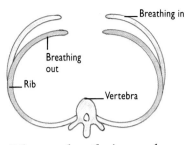

When you breathe in, labels: Breathing in, Breathing out, Rib, Vertebra

When you breathe in, *muscles raise and expand the ribcage while the diaphragm, a domed muscular sheet under the lungs, flattens. These movements increase the volume of the pleural cavity, the space in which the lungs sit, and air rushes in to equalize pressure. With the reverse movements, the volume decreases and air is pushed out.*

Breathing out

Ribcage falls

Diaphragm relaxes

BREATHING FACT FILE

The lungs are not identical – the right has three lobes; the left, which is smaller than the right, has two.

Av. weight of left lung	565 g (20 ounces)
Av. weight of right lung	625 g (22 ounces)
Total surface area of lungs	60–70 m² (645–755 sq. feet)
Av. no. of breaths a minute	16
Breathing rate (adult man) max.	300 litres/min (530 pints/min)
resting	8 litres/min (14 pints/min)
No. of alveoli per lung	More than 350 million
Diameter of alveoli	25 micrometres (¹/₁,₀₀₀ inch)
Thickness of alveoli walls	4 micrometres (¹/₆,₀₀₀ inch)
Oxygen	inhaled air 21% by volume
	exhaled air 16% by volume
Carbon dioxide	inhaled air 0.04% by volume
	exhaled air 4% by volume

Lung capacity chart: 6,000 / 5,000 / 4,000 / 3,000 / 2,000 / 1,000 axis. 4,800 ml, 3,100 ml, 500 ml, 1,200 ml, 6,000 ml, 1,200 ml

Lung capacity (millilitres)

1 — Total lung capacity
Vital lung capacity
Inspiratory reserve volume
2 — Resting tidal volume
3 — Expiratory reserve volume
4 — Residual volume

Resting tidal volume *is the amount of air breathed in and out during light breathing (**2**). The extra volume that can be filled with the deepest breath is the inspiratory reserve volume; together they add up to the inspiratory capacity (**1**). The extra volume breathed out by the strongest possible exhalation is the expiratory reserve volume (**3**). Air left in the airways after the strongest exhalation is the residual volume (**4**). The vital lung capacity is the amount of air that can be taken in by the strongest inhalation after the strongest exhalation. Vital lung capacity added to residual volume gives the total lung capacity.*

Lung air passages

Labels: Lower trachea, Bronchus, Bronchioles, Alveoli

Inside a lung *the airway divides and redivides like the branches of a tree or the tributaries of a river system. Each lung has 10 segments, each served by individual bronchi and bronchioles. Segments are further divided into lobules, each of which is served by a single tiny bronchiole – the final division in the system.*

*In each individual lobule are hundreds of alveoli (**inset**). It is in the alveoli that inhaled air comes into contact with tiny blood vessels containing deoxygenated blood. Gases are exchanged between the air and the blood, which picks up oxygen and gives out carbon dioxide.*

See also

ENERGY
▶ Fuelling the body 38/39

▶ The gas exchange 54/55

▶ Cells at work 58/59

SUPPORT AND MOVEMENT
▶ Holding it together 20/21

▶ Smooth operators 30/31

CIRCULATION, MAINTENANCE AND DEFENCE
▶ Transport systems 62/63

▶ Repelling invaders 88/89

REPRODUCTION AND GROWTH
▶ The newborn baby 120/121

INPUTS AND OUTPUTS
▶ Keeping control 238/239

▶ Dealing with drives 240/241

The gas exchange

Deep in the lungs tiny molecules move to and fro between air from outside and blood from within.

Each lung is an absorbent sponge, and breathing pulls air into the spaces of that sponge with every inhalation. The tiniest air-filled spaces are known as alveoli and in them oxygen passes into the bloodstream for circulation around the body and waste carbon dioxide leaves the blood to be discharged in exhaled air.

There are about 700 million alveoli in both lungs, and their combined surface area is some 70 m² (84 sq. yards) – not far short of the surface area of a tennis court. Gases such as oxygen and carbon dioxide move across this huge area by diffusion, which takes place because substances tend to move from a region where they are highly concentrated to one where they are relatively less concentrated. Since the oxygen concentration in the air of the alveoli is higher than that in the deoxygenated blood in the capillaries around the alveoli, oxygen moves into the capillaries from the air. Similarly, capillary blood contains more carbon dioxide than inhaled air, so this waste gas from the respiration (energy production) of body tissues passes from the blood into the alveolar air spaces to be breathed out.

The alveoli themselves are clustered around the blind inner endings of the thinnest branches of the airways (the terminal bronchioles) like minute bunches of grapes. Each individual alveolus "grape" is only 25 micrometres (¹⁄₁,₀₀₀ inch) in diameter, so 40 would have to be placed side by side to make a bunch 1 mm (¹⁄₂₅ inch) across.

The lungs have a spongy texture and are shot through with branching airways – bronchi and bronchioles – and blood vessels.

Deoxygenated blood on the right side of the heart is pushed by the right ventricle through the two pulmonary arteries and along a series of fine arterioles until it reaches the capillaries around an alveolus. There it picks up oxygen and returns to the left side of the heart via a network of veins that become increasingly wide and ultimately form the pulmonary vein. The oxygen is then pumped around the body from the left ventricle.

Alveoli occur in bunches (*inset*). Each bunch is fed by its own tiny airway, or bronchiolus, and the cluster of air sacs is surrounded by a mesh of branching capillaries. As you breathe, air moves in and out of the central spaces and gas exchanges take place across the alveolar wall: blood takes oxygen from the air and returns carbon dioxide to the air for exhalation.

Flour in a sieve stays there until the sieve is shaken. Then the fine flour particles fall through the much wider holes in the sieve. This movement is rather like the diffusion of oxygen across the wall of an alveolus in the lungs.

Oxygen molecules are so small that they can move easily through the alveolar wall. The energy source that moves them is the vibration energy that all molecules have; this is like the shaking of the sieve which sends the flour through the holes under the influence of gravity. Gravitational force can be likened to the concentration difference that allows oxygen to diffuse from air to blood.

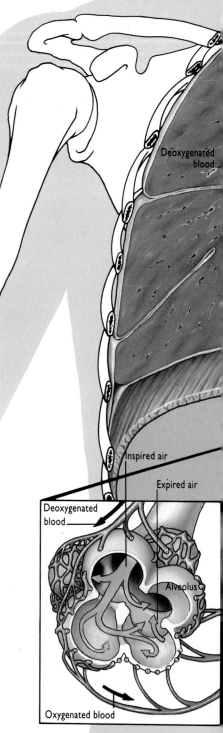

Deoxygenated blood

Inspired air

Expired air

Deoxygenated blood

Alveolus

Oxygenated blood

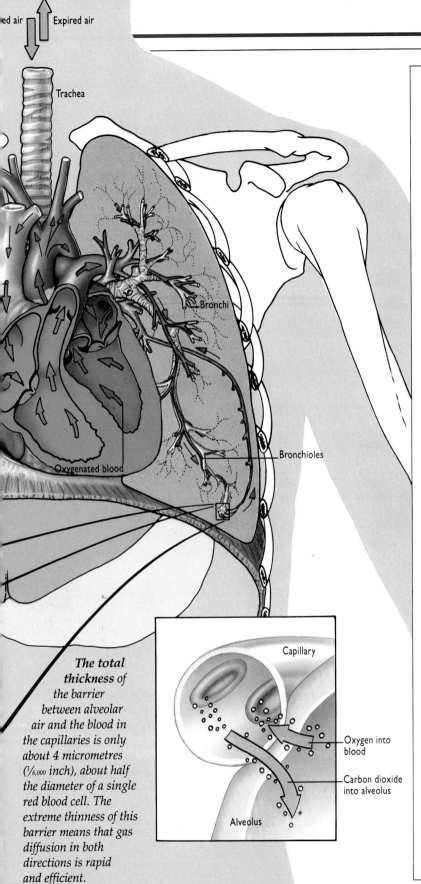

Expired air

Trachea

Bronchi

Bronchioles

Oxygenated blood

The total thickness of the barrier between alveolar air and the blood in the capillaries is only about 4 micrometres ($\frac{1}{6,000}$ inch), about half the diameter of a single red blood cell. The extreme thinness of this barrier means that gas diffusion in both directions is rapid and efficient.

Capillary

Oxygen into blood

Carbon dioxide into alveolus

Alveolus

CROSSING THE BARRIER

Although the barrier that oxygen and carbon dioxide have to cross during gas exchange in the lungs is extremely thin, it is nevertheless a complex, multilayered sandwich of tissue. The "bread" consists of two flattened layers of thin cells: one slice of alveolar cells, the other slice of cells that make up the capillary wall. A thin filling of basement membrane fibres separates the two cell layers. To an oxygen molecule, however, these layers seem insubstantial and the gas molecules, dissolved in a watery liquid, move across them by diffusion.

Oxygen diffusing into the blood from an alveolus first meets a biodetergent known as lung surfactant that is secreted by cells on the inner wall of the alveolus. This reduces the surface tension inside each alveolus so that it can easily be inflated by inhaled air.

The oxygen passes through a membrane into the alveolar cell and out through the other side. It then crosses the basement membrane before traversing a cell in the wall of the capillary. There it meets up with a red blood cell and oxygenates it.

Carbon dioxide moving from the blood into the air in the alveolus passes across the same barriers by diffusion but in the opposite direction.

Blood cells

Cell membrane

Capillary cell

Cytoplasm

Basement membrane fibres

Alveolar cell

Surfactant layer

Path of oxygen molecule

Air in lung

See also

ENERGY
▶ Fuelling the body 38/39

▶ A deep breath 52/53

▶ The cell and energy 56/57

SUPPORT AND MOVEMENT
▶ Holding it together 20/21

CIRCULATION, MAINTENANCE AND DEFENCE
▶ The living pump 64/65

▶ Growing heart 66/67

▶ In circulation 68/69

▶ Blood: supplying the body 70/71

REPRODUCTION AND GROWTH
▶ Being born 118/119

INPUTS AND OUTPUTS
▶ Dealing with drives 240/241

The cell and energy

Inside a typical cell are various sub-units, each with its own vital function. All of them need energy.

Every part of a person's body is made of microscopic cells or their products. There are trillions of cells in total and they vary enormously in shape, dimensions and function. But all of them, except for a few specialized types, have essentially the same organization. The basic plan is a volume of semifluid matter, or cytoplasm, held in shape by a cell membrane. Within the cytoplasm is the controlling nucleus. It contains the set of 46 chromosomes that carry the DNA molecules that hold the genes responsible for passing inherited characteristics from one generation to the next.

The cytoplasm and the nucleus house the specialized "tools" of the cell's living machinery. Some hold the cell in shape, others are manufacturing sites that make the products the cell needs. Others are power plants that provide energy: in mitochondria – the main energy generators – the energy-rich molecule ATP is formed.

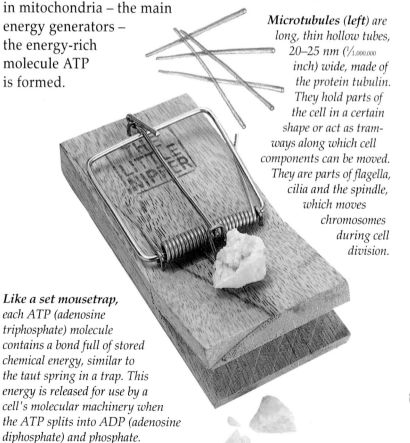

Microtubules (left) *are long, thin hollow tubes, 20–25 nm ($\frac{1}{1,000,000}$ inch) wide, made of the protein tubulin. They hold parts of the cell in a certain shape or act as tramways along which cell components can be moved. They are parts of flagella, cilia and the spindle, which moves chromosomes during cell division.*

Like a set mousetrap, *each ATP (adenosine triphosphate) molecule contains a bond full of stored chemical energy, similar to the taut spring in a trap. This energy is released for use by a cell's molecular machinery when the ATP splits into ADP (adenosine diphosphate) and phosphate.*

Cell respiration, *or the generation of energy-rich compounds, entails charging up ADP molecules to make ATP molecules. This takes place in a series of chemical reactions, mostly in the mitochondria. There are three distinct phases: glycolysis, the Krebs cycle and the electron transport system. Together they break down glucose molecules (each containing six carbon atoms) into carbon dioxide and water, producing more than 30 ATPs per glucose molecule.*

Glycolysis, which takes place in

Glucose molecule with six carbon atoms

Glycolysis

Krebs cycle

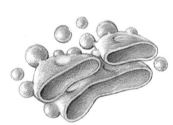

CO_2

NAD

FAD

the cytoplasm, breaks down the 6-carbon glucose into two 3-carbon fragments, releasing a small number of ATPs. The main ATP production shifts to the mitochondria where, in an altered form, the carbon fragments are fed into a cycle of reactions, the Krebs cycle. It makes carbon dioxide and joins hydrogen atoms on to transfer molecules NAD and FAD. These hydrogens drive the ATP-making machinery of the electron transport system on the knobs on the cristae in the mitochondria. Once ATP is made, the hydrogens link with oxygen to form water.

The endoplasmic reticulum (below) *consists of folded sheets of membrane. It is found in the cytoplasm (the region inside the cell membrane but outside the nucleus) of almost all cells. In places its membranes may merge with those of the envelope around the nucleus and with the cell membrane.*

Much of the reticulum carries rounded granules, or ribosomes, made of RNA and protein. Ribosomes are the protein-making machinery of the cell and they translate messenger RNA (mRNA), from the nucleus, into the proteins for which the RNA carries the code. Newly made protein is held initially in transfer vesicles – small bags of reticulum membrane.

The Golgi apparatus (above) *is a stack of flattened sacs of membrane closely associated with the endoplasmic reticulum. It gathers the protein-containing transfer vesicles from the reticulum and passes them across the stack and out the other side in the form of secreted packets of protein. During this transfer the Golgi sacs add sugars to the proteins to convert them into glycoproteins.*

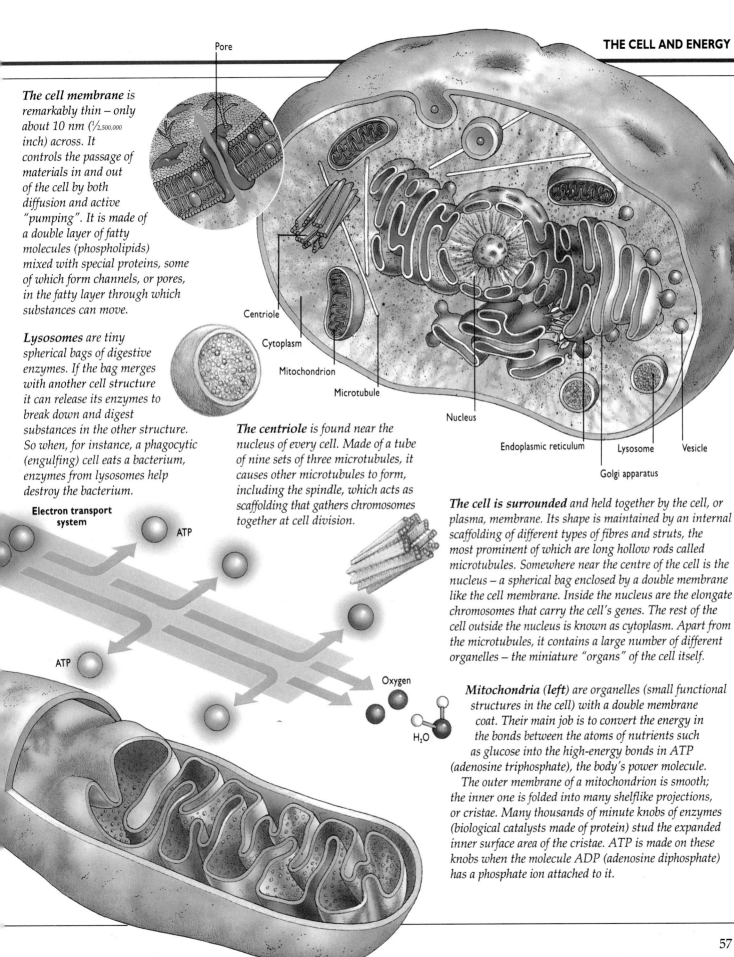

Pore

The cell membrane is remarkably thin – only about 10 nm ($\frac{1}{2,500,000}$ inch) across. It controls the passage of materials in and out of the cell by both diffusion and active "pumping". It is made of a double layer of fatty molecules (phospholipids) mixed with special proteins, some of which form channels, or pores, in the fatty layer through which substances can move.

Lysosomes are tiny spherical bags of digestive enzymes. If the bag merges with another cell structure it can release its enzymes to break down and digest substances in the other structure. So when, for instance, a phagocytic (engulfing) cell eats a bacterium, enzymes from lysosomes help destroy the bacterium.

Electron transport system

ATP

ATP

Oxygen

H_2O

Centriole

Cytoplasm

Mitochondrion

Microtubule

Nucleus

Endoplasmic reticulum

Lysosome

Vesicle

Golgi apparatus

The centriole is found near the nucleus of every cell. Made of a tube of nine sets of three microtubules, it causes other microtubules to form, including the spindle, which acts as scaffolding that gathers chromosomes together at cell division.

The cell is surrounded and held together by the cell, or plasma, membrane. Its shape is maintained by an internal scaffolding of different types of fibres and struts, the most prominent of which are long hollow rods called microtubules. Somewhere near the centre of the cell is the nucleus – a spherical bag enclosed by a double membrane like the cell membrane. Inside the nucleus are the elongate chromosomes that carry the cell's genes. The rest of the cell outside the nucleus is known as cytoplasm. Apart from the microtubules, it contains a large number of different organelles – the miniature "organs" of the cell itself.

Mitochondria (left) are organelles (small functional structures in the cell) with a double membrane coat. Their main job is to convert the energy in the bonds between the atoms of nutrients such as glucose into the high-energy bonds in ATP (adenosine triphosphate), the body's power molecule.
The outer membrane of a mitochondrion is smooth; the inner one is folded into many shelflike projections, or cristae. Many thousands of minute knobs of enzymes (biological catalysts made of protein) stud the expanded inner surface area of the cristae. ATP is made on these knobs when the molecule ADP (adenosine diphosphate) has a phosphate ion attached to it.

See also
ENERGY
▶ The speed of life 36/37

▶ Cells at work 58/59

SUPPORT AND MOVEMENT
▶ The living framework 16/17

▶ Muscles at work 26/27

CIRCULATION, MAINTENANCE AND DEFENCE
▶ Waste disposal 74/75

▶ Routine replacement 82/83

REPRODUCTION AND GROWTH
▶ Language of life 102/103

▶ Building bodies 104/105

▶ The sexual advantage 106/107

BUILDING THE BRAIN
▶ Food for thought 188/189

Cells at work

The majority of the body's cells have identical genes, yet each cell type has its own specific structure and shape.

All the different cell types use energy for different reasons to perform their major functions. Yet almost all, whether skin cells, nerve cells or muscle cells, use the same energy-rich molecules, such as ATP (adenosine triphosphate), during energy exchange. Although the various cells' reasons for using energy are diverse, there are three major patterns of energy use common to many of them.

The first of these is in the building up of complex molecules from simpler ones – a secretory cell, for instance, uses most energy in manufacturing its secretory products from chemical sub-units and then exporting them from the cell. In the pancreas there are two main types of secretory cells: one type makes the hormone insulin and releases it into the blood, the other synthesizes digestive enzymes which are passed into the duodenum.

The second pattern of energy use concentrates on producing changes in cell shape; inside muscle cells highly ordered arrays of actin and myosin fibres slide past one another to produce muscle contraction. The myosin molecules need an energy source of ATP to achieve this. The third is in the pumping of materials across cell membranes, which may involve taking

By using energy to "pump" *charged particles, or ions, from the inside to the outside of the cell membrane, and vice versa, many types of cells generate tiny differences in voltage, or potentials. Nerve cells, for instance, have ion pumps that create a potential across their membranes so they are ready to pass on nerve impulses. An impulse is a sudden change in the distribution of ions between the inner and outer surfaces of the cell's membrane. After an impulse has passed, ions are pumped across the membrane to restore the potential.*

When a cell needs to take up a useful substance such as a nutrient from its *surroundings, it has two alternatives: it can do it without use of energy, by diffusion; or in an energy-using way, by active transport. If the substance the cell needs is at a higher concentration outside the cell than it is inside, and if the cell membrane is permeable to it, the substance moves in by diffusion. But with the concentrations reversed the cell must use energy to work a molecular pump in its membrane to draw the desired molecule in.*

up useful materials such as nutrients into a cell, pushing out unwanted ones or, in the case of excitable cells like nerves, maintaining an electrical potential difference between the inside and the outside of the cell. For example, a cell in the wall of the proximal convoluted tubule of a kidney nephron expends great amounts of energy pumping sodium ions from the newly formed urine back into the bloodstream to maintain the correct level of sodium in the blood.

Flagellum

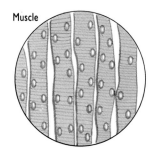

Muscle

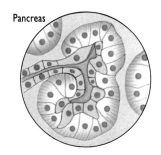

Pancreas

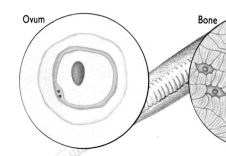

Ovum

Bone

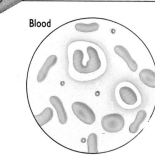

Blood

THE RANGE OF CELLS – THE GENOME IN ACTION
Almost every single cell among the billions in a single human body has the same genome – the same set of genes. The only obvious exceptions to this, at least in a healthy body, are the sex cells – eggs and sperm – each of which contains only a random 50 percent of a person's total genome. But if all the cells have the same genes, why

are there so many different sorts of cells in the body? How, for instance, can the same genes form products as disparate as elongated, metre-long nerve cells, free-floating rounded white blood cells only a fiftieth of a millimetre across and star-shaped bone cells embedded in the solid mineral matrix of bone in tight-fitting chambers? The answer is to be found in the unfolding pattern of cell differentiation during the

A human sperm burns up energy on its mission to find an egg and fuse with it to fertilize it. To do this the sperm must swim through the cervical mucus at the top of the vagina, through the fluids in the uterus then along a Fallopian tube. The minute sperm cell thus has to swim many centimetres through the female reproductive tract, which it achieves by beating its tail, or flagellum.

   Enzymes in the sperm's mitochondria break down sugar fragments to form ATP, which is then used to generate shape changes – and thus movement – in the flagellum. ATP-powered bending movements in the filaments of the tail drive the sperm forward in a head-first direction. The base of the region containing the mitochondria – the powerhouse of the cell – is marked by a structure called the annulus.

Nucleus

Annulus

Axial filaments

Mitochondria

Cells use energy to generate shape changes. The most obvious examples of this are the movements generated by muscles where individual cells contract in concert. Other cells that use energy to change shape are those with cilia and flagella – cell appendages that wave to and fro either to move the cell (flagella) or move liquid past the cell (cilia). In all cases ATP is used as the immediate energy source.

To manufacture a complex molecule a cell needs an energy source. So when, for instance, a protein is built by linking its individual component amino acids together with peptide bonds, this requires an input of chemical energy. Only reactions that break chemical bonds and form simpler molecules out of complex ones release energy rather than taking it in – energy from such reactions powers protein building.

Liver

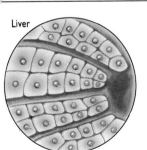

Heart

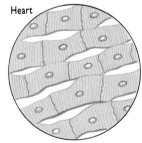

Lung

Kidney

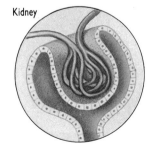

Brain

development of an early embryo in the mother's womb. As development progresses, different subsets of role-determining genes in the total genome are switched on in different groups of cells, turning them into different cell types. Thus there are heart muscle cells that spontaneously and rhythmically contract and lining cells of the alveoli of the lungs which

form the respiratory surface for gas exchange. This story of different end points emerging from the same genome is no more surprising than the fact that a cabbage white butterfly caterpillar, the pupa it turns into and the butterfly that emerges from the pupa all have the same genes – same genes, different gene sets in operation.

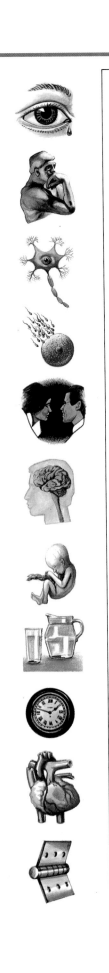

Circulation, Maintenance and Defence

T he blood circulating in veins and arteries is not the only transportation system in the body. It is, perhaps, the most important, but there are other types of transportation at work, including systems that mop up fluid between tissues and those that send wastes out via the body's disposal routes.

Other systems maintain the structure of the body, routinely replacing and repairing cells that die due to wear and tear. And still others are concerned with its defence; they exist at both macro and micro levels – from the skin barrier to the tiny hunter-killer cells borne in the blood. And they can deal with almost any invading germ, reacting fast to mount a devastating counterattack.

*Left (**clockwise from top**): anti-vaccination propaganda; titanium – safe inside; killing tears; skin, the outer barrier. **This page (right**): the microscopic marvels of the immune system; (**left**) a bacterium – know the enemy.*

Transport systems

Much of the activity in the body depends on moving materials around it, as well as in and out.

If an animal is small enough – only a few millimetres across – it can depend on purely passive physical processes to solve its internal transport problems. The main such process is diffusion, in which molecules – which are always in motion, jostling each other about – move, on average, from a region where they are in high concentration to areas of lower concentration until the concentrations even out. Over the distances in tiny animals diffusion works well enough to let oxygen in and carbon dioxide out without the need for a circulatory system. And nutrients and other key molecules can move into the creature – and around inside it – by diffusion alone.

Any large animal, though, requires specialized transport systems to move materials and cells around when simple diffusion cannot do the job. These systems can be closed loops, as in the circulatory system which allows blood to flow continuously around the body through the same tube; unidirectional, as in the urinary system; or two-way, as happens with the in and out movement of air in our lungs.

Whatever the direction of the movement or the type of channel, there are only a few driving forces for the transport of bulk materials. The main mechanisms are muscle contraction, secretion pressure, the beating of cilia (tiny hairs) and the force of gravity.

Breathing and the movement of food through the digestive tract use muscle action. The production of a secretion in a gland forces the secretion to move outward from the gland like toothpaste being squeezed from a tube. For instance, the sebaceous (oily) secretions in skin are squeezed on to the skin and hair by the pressure of secretions behind them.

The waving to and fro of microscopic hairs on cell surfaces, or ciliary beating, can move liquids and objects. The mucus lining the airways of the lungs is moved along like a conveyor belt by cilia, taking airborne pollution such as dust particles out of the lungs. Similarly, rows of ciliated cells in a woman's Fallopian tube move an egg along the tube to where it can be fertilized. Gravity is a driving force for internal transport. For example, part of the flow of blood back to the heart through veins in the head and neck region depends on gravity.

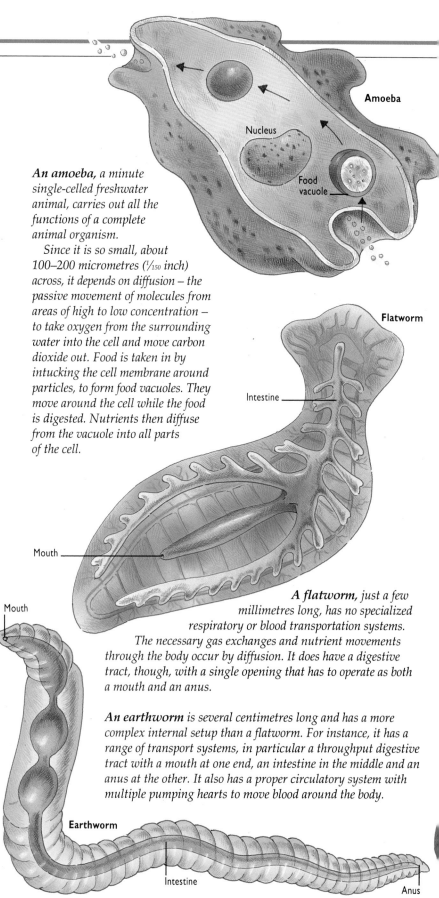

An amoeba, *a minute single-celled freshwater animal, carries out all the functions of a complete animal organism.*

Since it is so small, about 100–200 micrometres (1/150 inch) across, it depends on diffusion – the passive movement of molecules from areas of high to low concentration – to take oxygen from the surrounding water into the cell and move carbon dioxide out. Food is taken in by intucking the cell membrane around particles, to form food vacuoles. They move around the cell while the food is digested. Nutrients then diffuse from the vacuole into all parts of the cell.

A flatworm, *just a few millimetres long, has no specialized respiratory or blood transportation systems. The necessary gas exchanges and nutrient movements through the body occur by diffusion. It does have a digestive tract, though, with a single opening that has to operate as both a mouth and an anus.*

An earthworm *is several centimetres long and has a more complex internal setup than a flatworm. For instance, it has a range of transport systems, in particular a throughput digestive tract with a mouth at one end, an intestine in the middle and an anus at the other. It also has a proper circulatory system with multiple pumping hearts to move blood around the body.*

WAVING PUMPS

The sea anemone belongs to the major division of animals known as the coelenterates – invertebrates (spineless creatures) with saclike bodies and just one opening to the gut. It has no circulatory system, so depends on diffusion for the exchange of gases, such as oxygen and carbon dioxide, and the absorption of nutrients. The molecules diffuse through easily since its body wall is extremely thin.

To keep its shape, the sea anemone relies on a system similar to the transport system in the human lungs. When it takes in water and closes its gut opening, grooves full of cilia (tiny waving hairlike cell extensions) down its length pump water into the anemone's gut space to bulk the animal up into its normal shape.

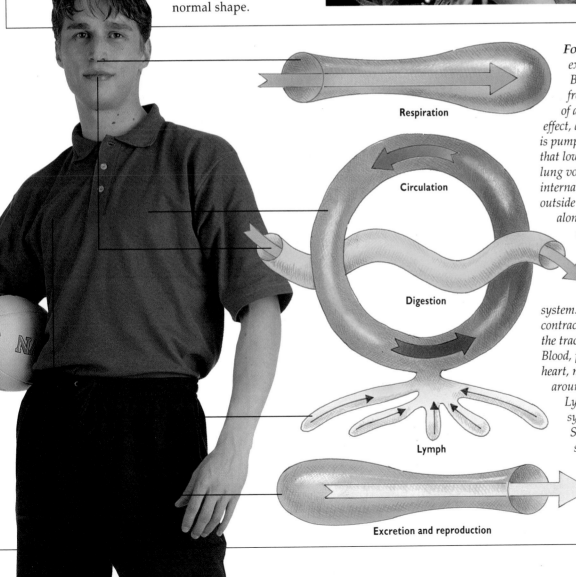

Respiration

Circulation

Digestion

Lymph

Excretion and reproduction

Four types of flow patterns exist in our transport systems. Breathing shows the to and fro, or oscillatory, movements of air in and out of what is, in effect, a blind-ended tube. The air is pumped in by muscle movements that lower the diaphragm, increase lung volume and thus reduce internal pressure, causing air from outside to rush in. Air is forced out along the same path when the diaphragm moves up again. The digestive tract shows the unidirectional movement of food through an open-ended system. Peristalsis – sequential contraction of the muscles lining the tract – forces matter along. Blood, pumped by the muscular heart, moves unidirectionally around a closed, circular system. Lymph fluid from the lymphatic system flows into the blood. Secretions such as excreted sweat, urine and reproductive products move in a single outward direction along their own specialized ducts.

The living pump

*Beating steadily in your chest, your heart
sends blood coursing to all parts of your body.*

A pump about the size of a clenched fist, the heart
sends blood around the body's circulatory system –
a closed, tubular system of arteries, veins and capillaries.
It is like a hot water central heating system: the piping
and radiators correspond to the blood vessels, while the
water pump, which drives hot water through the pipes,
is the equivalent of the heart. All living tissue has to be
supplied with blood – it delivers nutrients and oxygen
and takes away waste products. If blood flow to a part
of the body stops – even for just a few minutes – that
region will be seriously damaged and may die.

To force blood through the blood vessels the whole
heart contracts, squeezing blood out of its internal
chambers. The heart is, in fact, a double pump with two
pairs of pumping chambers. Specialized flap valves in the
internal spaces of the organ mean that each side of the heart
allows blood to move in only one direction.

Each side of this double pump has its own role. The right
side pumps oxygen-depleted blood from the rest of the body
to the lungs, where it gains a new oxygen supply. The
reoxygenated blood then moves to the left side of the heart,
from where it is pumped back to the remainder of the body.
Part of the output from the left side supplies the heart muscle
itself via the coronary arteries.

The four chambers of the heart, two atria and two ventricles,
are built of muscle – cardiac muscle. It is a specialized type of
muscle in which individual barrel-shaped muscle-cell sections

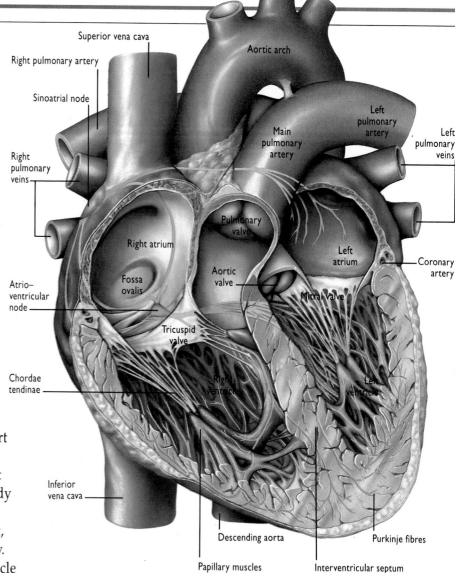

Like a foot pump, the heart contains one-way
valves to ensure flow is unidirectional. But unlike
the heart, a foot pump does not have built-in
muscles to help it force
out its contents.

*The muscle that makes up the left
ventricle of the heart, which includes
the interventricular septum (the wall
separating the two lower chambers),
is thicker than that of the right – the
left ventricle has to be stronger
since it pumps at higher pressure.
Blood coming from the left ventricle
is fed via the aorta – the body's main
artery – to every part of the body, which
demands high-pressure output. Blood
from the right ventricle only has to go
via the pulmonary arteries to the lungs.*

*The sinoatrial node, atrioventricular
node and Purkinje fibres are part of the
heart's own pacemaking and internal
nerve signal transmitting apparatus.*

are linked together end to end at junctions known as intercalated discs. These tie the cells together and ensure that there is synchronized contraction of heart muscle.

Certain regions of cardiac muscle are modified to form a type of living pacemaker, which spontaneously beats out the rhythm of the heart's regular contractions and transfers that tempo to the rest of the heart muscle. These pacemaker regions are connected to the body's nervous system to ensure that the speed, strength and capacity of the heart's pumping is matched to the body's moment to moment needs. So when you run upstairs your heart rate is increased to push more blood both to your muscles, which require glucose and oxygen, and to the lungs to pick up oxygen more quickly.

HEART FACT FILE

The heartbeat can be monitored by sounds (with a stethoscope). An unusual heart sound is called a murmur and is often caused by a valve leaking.

Av. size of heart		12 x 9 cm (4¾ x 3½ inches)
Weight of heart		250–390 g (8–14 ounces)
No. of valves		4
Av. beats per	minute	70
	day	100,000
	lifetime	2.5 billion
Av. blood pumped per	beat	75 ml (2½ fl. ounces) at rest
	day	7,500 litres (1,650 gallons)
	year	2.5 million litres (550,000 gallons)
Blood sent at rest to	heart	250 ml/min (8¾ fl. ounces/min)
	muscles	1,200 ml/min (2 pints/min)
Ventricular pressure	left	120 mm/Hg on contraction
	right	20 mm/Hg on contraction

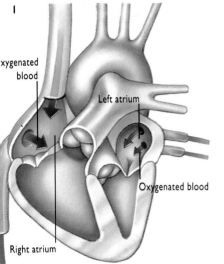

1

Oxygenated blood

Left atrium

Oxygenated blood

Right atrium

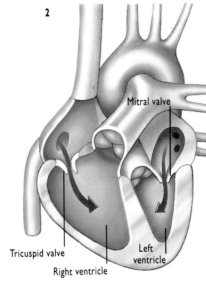

2

Mitral valve

Tricuspid valve

Right ventricle

Left ventricle

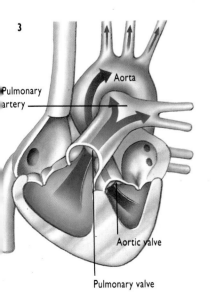

3

Pulmonary artery

Aorta

Aortic valve

Pulmonary valve

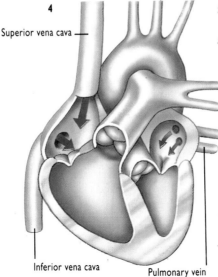

4

Superior vena cava

Inferior vena cava

Pulmonary vein

Each beat of the heart (contraction or systole) is *a carefully orchestrated sequence of events. But even when the heart is not undergoing contraction there is still plenty happening. In its resting phase (diastole) the two smaller chambers, the atria, are filling with blood (1). The right atrium fills with "spent" deoxygenated blood returning from the body, the left with freshly oxygenated blood coming back from the lungs. A beat starts when muscle in the atria contracts from the top down, forcing blood into the main chambers, or ventricles (2). Blood from the right atrium is squeezed into the right ventricle through the interconnecting tricuspid valve, which is forced open by the pressure in the atrium. Similarly, blood in the left atrium is forced through the mitral valve into the left ventricle.*

The contraction continues in the ventricles. The muscle starts to contract from the bottom, so blood in them is squeezed upward (3), but the two interconnecting one-way valves close so blood does not flow back into the atria. Blood from the right ventricle moves under pressure into the pulmonary artery through the pulmonary valve, and on to the lungs where it is oxygenated. Likewise, blood from the left ventricle is forced through the aortic valve into the aorta. When the power stroke finishes, the aortic valve and the pulmonary valve slam shut to stop blood flowing back in to the ventricles. The heart enters its resting phase again when all four valves are closed. Meanwhile the cycle starts again: the right atrium fills with blood from the superior and inferior venae cavae and the left atrium fills with blood from the pulmonary veins (4).

Growing heart

The first fully functioning system to form in a foetus is the heart and circulation.

By just 30 days after an egg has been fertilized by a sperm, there is a working blood-transporting system in the baby-to-be. It takes oxygen and nutrients to all parts of the foetus's 0.2-cm ($\frac{1}{12}$-inch) long body.

The final fully formed heart is a four-chambered muscular pump for moving blood around the body. Its right side receives deoxygenated blood back from the body and pushes it into the lungs where it is oxygenated. Oxygenated blood from the lungs then passes to the left side of the heart, from where it is pumped around the body to supply the tissues.

A heart with almost all of the adult components is in place about eight weeks after fertilization. There is one key difference, however – since the foetus is in the uterus, its lungs do not contain any air and so cannot oxygenate blood as they do after birth. The foetus's blood is oxygenated instead in the placenta and passes from there to the right atrium of the heart. Some of this blood passes to the right ventricle and then on to the lungs to provide them with oxygen and nutrients for growth and development.

Most of the oxygenated blood either shunts from the right to the left atrium through a hole between the two atria – a special foetal feature known as the oval window – or from the pulmonary arteries into the aorta, the main artery that comes from the left ventricle, through the ductus arteriosus, again specific to the foetus. Both these shunts enable oxygenated blood to be pushed around the developing foetus's body by the left ventricle, which is, in the foetus and in later life, the heart's most powerful chamber.

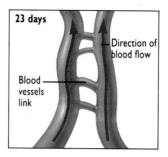

In the extraordinarily tiny embryo *23 days after it has been fertilized (shown **below** at actual size), two minute and primitive blood vessels have grown adjacent to each other. Cross linkages between these two vessels start to form. This is the first stage in the construction of what will become the heart.*

From this point on, over a period of about four weeks, this primitive structure develops to become a heart that is fully formed, albeit in miniature.

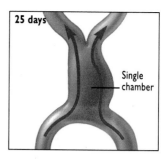

Shortly after the blood vessels form links, *they draw together and fuse to make a single chamber. This occurs about 25 days after fertilization.*

The blood vessels and the single-chambered "heart" that they form are surrounded by a sheath of muscle. This sheath will later grow into the muscular walls of the heart which, when they contract, will tirelessly pump blood around the circulatory system.

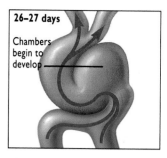

The single chamber, *made by the fusing of the two vessels, now bulges and twists, forming an S-shaped object that is less than 0.1 cm ($\frac{1}{25}$ inch) long. This marks the start of the process of forming more chambers.*

Even at this early stage, the proto-heart beats, or pulses. But since there are no valves in the heart at this time, the blood ebbs and flows and does not have the one-way flow of the fully developed organ.

Actual size at 23 days

Actual size at 25 days

Actual size at 26–27 days

WHEN THE GAPS DON'T CLOSE

There are three defects that occasionally occur in newborn babies' hearts. In all of them deoxygenated blood is mixed with oxygenated blood and sent around the arterial system. Since the oxygen content of the blood is lowered, an infant with one of these defects may have a bluish tinge because deoxygenated blood is blue and oxygenated is red. If the gaps fail to close on their own, all three conditions can be cured with surgery.

In the defect known as patent ductus arteriosus, the channel that allows blood to bypass the lungs in the foetus does not close fully after the baby is born. This leaves a link between the aorta and the pulmonary artery and allows deoxygenated blood from the pulmonary artery to mix with oxygenated blood in the aorta.

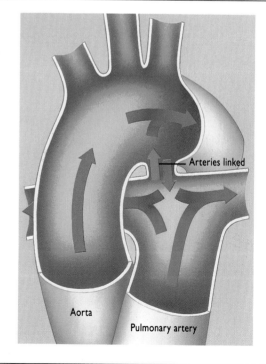

Arteries linked

Aorta

Pulmonary artery

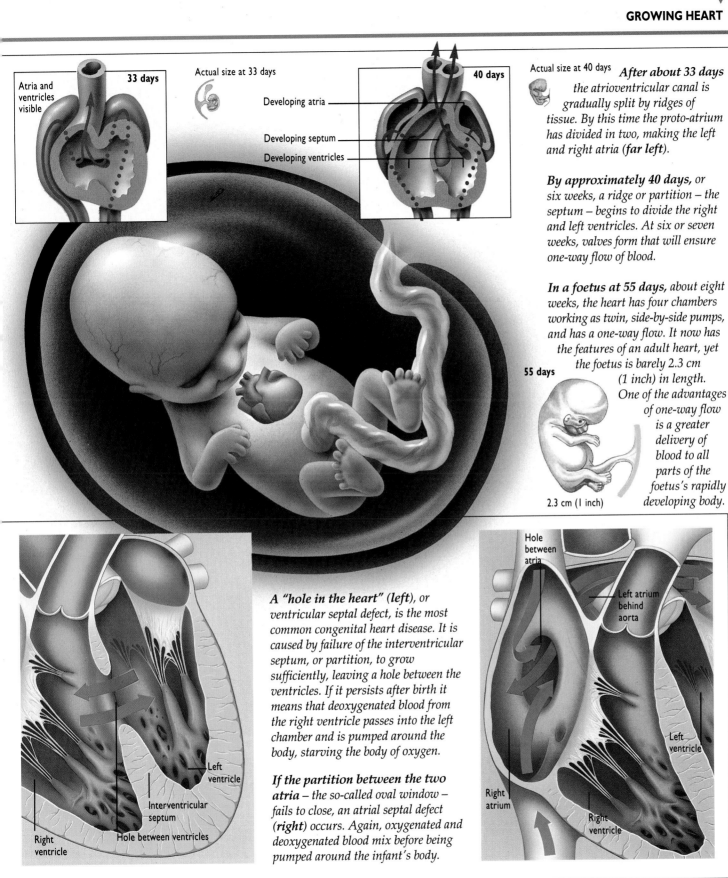

33 days

Atria and ventricles visible

Actual size at 33 days

40 days

Developing atria

Developing septum

Developing ventricles

Actual size at 40 days

After about 33 days the atrioventricular canal is gradually split by ridges of tissue. By this time the proto-atrium has divided in two, making the left and right atria (**far left**).

By approximately 40 days, or six weeks, a ridge or partition – the septum – begins to divide the right and left ventricles. At six or seven weeks, valves form that will ensure one-way flow of blood.

In a foetus at 55 days, about eight weeks, the heart has four chambers working as twin, side-by-side pumps, and has a one-way flow. It now has the features of an adult heart, yet the foetus is barely 2.3 cm (1 inch) in length. One of the advantages of one-way flow is a greater delivery of blood to all parts of the foetus's rapidly developing body.

55 days

2.3 cm (1 inch)

A **"hole in the heart"** (**left**), or ventricular septal defect, is the most common congenital heart disease. It is caused by failure of the interventricular septum, or partition, to grow sufficiently, leaving a hole between the ventricles. If it persists after birth it means that deoxygenated blood from the right ventricle passes into the left chamber and is pumped around the body, starving the body of oxygen.

If the partition between the two atria – the so-called oval window – fails to close, an atrial septal defect (**right**) occurs. Again, oxygenated and deoxygenated blood mix before being pumped around the infant's body.

Left ventricle

Interventricular septum

Right ventricle

Hole between ventricles

Hole between atria

Left atrium behind aorta

Left ventricle

Right atrium

Right ventricle

In circulation

Arteries deliver blood to the capillaries, where it does its work, then veins return it to the heart for recycling.

Blood truly circulates – it passes continuously around the body, returning to its starting point again and again. In one complete tour of the system, blood goes in turn around each of the body's two circulation tracks: from the heart, through the lungs and back to the heart; and from the heart to the rest of the body and back.

In both tracks thick-walled arteries carry blood under relatively high pressure away from the heart, and thinner-walled veins carry blood under much lower pressure back again. Linking the arterial and venous blood vessels are networks of increasingly fine arteries and veins (arterioles and venules) which eventually join up in a mesh of the thinnest blood vessels – capillaries. These are so narrow that red blood cells, which are only 0.0007 cm ($\frac{1}{3,600}$ inch) across, have to pass through them in single file. The capillary walls consist of a single, ultrathin layer of tissue made of flattened cells. The thinness of this layer allows wastes, nutrients and gases, such as oxygen and carbon dioxide, to pass between the cells in the body's tissues and the blood in the capillaries. The capillary networks of all the organs are the exchange zones of the blood system – the rest of the system merely distributes the blood.

CIRCULATION FACT FILE

The largest blood vessels are more than 3,000 times the width of the smallest blood vessels.

Diameter	largest vein or artery	2.5–3 cm (1–1⅕ inch)
	smallest capillary	0.0008 cm ($\frac{1}{3,200}$ inch)

Percentage of blood in	
veins	75
arteries	20
capillaries	5

Amount of blood in circulation	
av. man	5–6 litres (8¾–10½ pints)
av. woman	4–5 litres (7–8¾ pints)

Time taken for blood to circulate through	
lungs	4–8 seconds
body	25–30 seconds

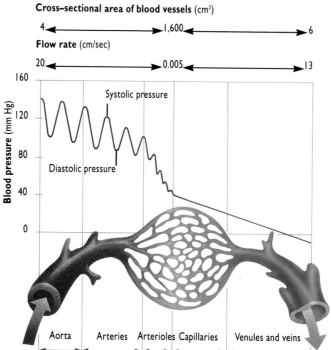

Cross–sectional area of blood vessels (cm²)

4 ⟷ 1,600 ⟷ 6

Flow rate (cm/sec)

20 ⟷ 0.005 ⟷ 13

Blood pressure (mm Hg)

160 — 120 — 80 — 40 — 0

Systolic pressure

Diastolic pressure

Aorta | Arteries | Arterioles | Capillaries | Venules and veins

Surface veins in the skin of this exercising body builder stand out because they are inflated by the large volume of blood returning to the heart from his muscles.

Blood pressure rises and falls in the arteries according to the contractions (systoles) and relaxations (diastoles) of the muscles of the heart's left ventricle, which force the blood around the body. Overall, this pulsating pressure drops with increasing distance from the heart until there are no variations in the capillaries and veins. Just before the veins return to the heart, pressure can drop so low that the blood must be sucked in by the atria. Blood thus moves fastest in the arteries and slowest in the capillaries, picking up speed again in the veins.

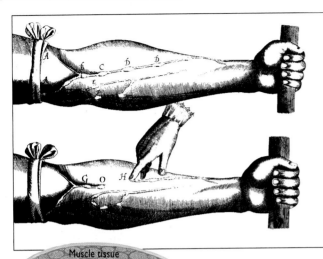

HARVEY AND THE VALVES

In 1628 British physician William Harvey (1578–1657) published *On the Motions of the Heart and Blood*, a small book in which he cleared up the hitherto mysterious nature of the flow of blood. He showed beyond doubt that blood circulated. These lithographs from the book show the effects of non-return valves in veins just beneath the skin in the arm.

The incredible highway of blood vessels carries blood to and from almost every part of the body. Only specialized regions, for instance the cornea of the eye, the enamel of the teeth and the dead outer layers of the skin, hairs and finger- and toenails, are without blood vessels.

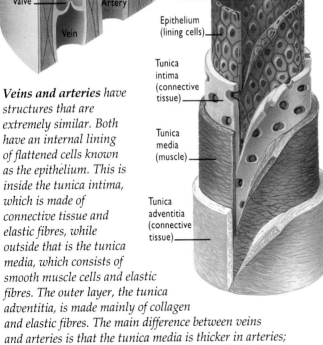

Muscle tissue
Open valve
Closed valve
Contracted muscle
Artery
Vein

Vein
Lumen
Epithelium (lining cells)
Tunica intima (connective tissue)
Tunica media (muscle)
Tunica adventitia (connective tissue)

Many veins and arteries run through muscles (**left above**). With low pressure in some veins, muscle contractions help to massage blood along the veins, aided by the one-way valves which ensure that the blood flows only in the correct direction.

Artery
Lumen
Epithelium (lining cells)
Tunica intima (connective tissue)
Tunica media (muscle)
Tunica adventitia (connective tissue)

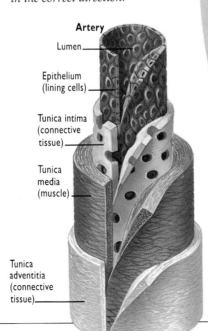

Veins and arteries have structures that are extremely similar. Both have an internal lining of flattened cells known as the epithelium. This is inside the tunica intima, which is made of connective tissue and elastic fibres, while outside that is the tunica media, which consists of smooth muscle cells and elastic fibres. The outer layer, the tunica adventitia, is made mainly of collagen and elastic fibres. The main difference between veins and arteries is that the tunica media is thicker in arteries; these thicker walls are "designed" to cope with the higher pressures of blood from the heart.

In many parts of the arterial network, the smooth muscles of the tunica media can contract under the control of the nervous system to alter blood pressure.

Superior vena cava
Carotid artery
Jugular vein
Cephalic vein
Brachial artery
Inferior vena cava
Aorta
Femoral artery
Femoral vein

Blood: supplying the body

The whole body depends on a constant supply of blood to sustain, nourish and protect its tissues.

Blood is the central transport facility of the body and is as important to human activity as road, rail and airline systems are to the workings of a modern industrialized state. Our blood is like a rich soup of many ingredients and, like a soup, the most plentiful ingredient is water. In blood the watery background, or plasma, has materials dissolved in it; it also has a wide range of free-floating blood cells suspended in it. Most of these are oxygen-transporting red blood cells, or erythrocytes. The others are white blood cells, or leucocytes, of many types, most of which have functions to do with body defence, repair and immunity.

The blood is, in fact, a liquid tissue that, like any other type of tissue, has a range of roles. For instance, its respiratory job is to carry oxygen to all body tissues. The oxygen is bound to haemoglobin, an iron-containing protein in the red blood cells. At the tissues, the haemoglobin gives up its vital gas in regions where oxygen concentration has become lowered. The waste product carbon dioxide, mainly in the form of bicarbonate, is carried by the blood away from respiring body cells for transport to the lungs and removal in exhaled air. Blood also has nutrients dissolved in it, including sugars, amino acids, fatty acids, fats, minerals and vitamins, and is a vehicle for transporting information in the form of hormones.

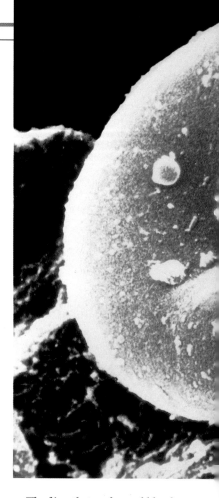

Blood cells are continually made to replace those that die in the normal course of events. Red cells, platelets and some white cells – all made in bone marrow – originate from one type of cell (*left*) but differentiate and follow separate paths, some with many intermediary cell types.

Haemocytoblast

Rubriblast

Prorubricyte

Megakaryoblast   Myeloblast   Rubricyte

The line that makes red blood cells (erythrocytes) has six steps. Along the way the cells repeatedly divide to increase numbers.

Metarubricyte

Progranulocyte

Promegakaryocyte

Basophilic myelocyte

Neutrophilic myelocyte   Eosinophilic myelocyte

One development line makes huge metamegakaryo-cyte cells. These cells fragment to give vast numbers of tiny platelets which have a crucial role in blood clotting.

Neutrophilic metamyelocyte

Megakaryocyte

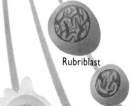

BLOOD FACT FILE

Blood in arteries gets its redness from oxygenated haemoglobin in red cells; deoxygenated haemoglobin gives blood in veins a bluish colour. Blood from a cut vein looks red because as soon as blood contacts air, haemoglobin takes in oxygen and becomes red.

| Volume of blood | man | 5–6 litres (8¾–10½ pints) |
| | woman | 4–5 litres (7–8¾ pints) |

No. of red blood cells in body	25 trillion (25 x 10¹²)
Red cell dimensions*	width	7 micrometres (¹/3,600 inch)
	thickness	2 micrometres (¹/12,500 inch)
Lifetime of red cell	80–120 days
Ratio of red to white blood cells	1,000:1
pH of blood	7.35–7.45

*About 30 red blood cells placed side by side would stretch across the full stop at the end of this sentence.

Blood is half water and nearly half red cells. Other matter suspended or dissolved in blood, including white cells and platelets, makes up ¹/20.

Water 50%

Plasma substances 4%

White blood cells and platelets 1%

Red blood cells 45%

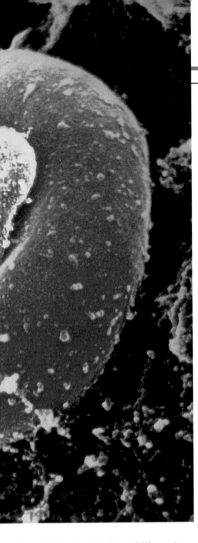

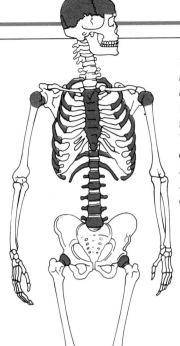

The white cells made in lymph system tissue develop into lymphocytes (B-cells and T-cells) or monocytes. Lymphocytes are key players in immune responses, the body's defence against invading foreign substances or organisms. The B-cells, for instance, are the origin of cells that secrete antibodies. Monocytes can transform into large phagocytic (engulfing) cells called macrophages.

Lymphoid progenitor cell

Lymphoblast

Monoblast

In lymph tissue

Lymphocyte

Lymphocyte

Promonocyte

B–cell lymphocyte

In blood

T–cell lymphocyte

Monocyte

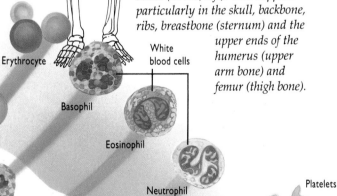

In adult life red blood cell production (erythropoiesis) takes place in the bone marrow of certain bones (in red, left). This happens particularly in the skull, backbone, ribs, breastbone (sternum) and the upper ends of the humerus (upper arm bone) and femur (thigh bone).

Red blood cells

White blood cells

Erythrocyte

Reticulocyte

Basophil

Eosinophil

Neutrophil

Platelets

In blood

Thrombocytes

A red blood cell, shaped like a ring doughnut with no hole, is adapted to have maximum surface area for gas exchange, specifically the oxygen it transports around the body. The yellow object on the cell is a platelet.

Basophilic band cell

sophilic etamyelocyte

Eosinophilic metamyelocyte

Eosinophilic band cell

Neutrophilic band cell

The white blood cells produced in bone marrow come in three forms: neutrophils, eosinophils and basophils.

In bone marrow

Neutrophils can attack bacteria. Eosinophils and basophils have complex functions that are linked with the allergy response and inflammation.

Blood cells are formed either in the bone marrow or in the tissues of the lymphatic system, such as the lymph nodes, tonsils and spleen. Red blood cells (erythrocytes), white cells known as granulocytes (neutrophils, basophils and eosinophils) and platelets are all made in bone marrow; other white cells are made in lymph tissue.

In each of the two sites, an early cell type undergoes multiple sets of cell division to make hundreds, then millions, of daughter cells. As they multiply, different sets of these cells become progressively differentiated into the various specialized cell types that are ultimately found in the blood.

Metamegakaryocyte

See also

CIRCULATION, MAINTENANCE AND DEFENCE
▶ Transport systems 62/63

▶ The living pump 64/65

▶ In circulation 68/69

▶ The water balance 76/77

▶ Inside the kidney 78/79

▶ Damage repair 84/85

ENERGY
▶ The gas exchange 54/55

▶ The cell and energy 56/57

▶ Cells at work 58/59

REPRODUCTION AND GROWTH
▶ Baby in waiting 116/117

▶ Being born 118/119

BUILDING THE BRAIN
▶ Food for thought 188/189

The body's drain

Not only does the lymphatic system drain excess fluid from tissues, it is also in the first line of immune defence.

A drainage ditch in an agricultural system is as vital as the irrigation channel that brings water to the crops. The drain takes waste water from the land to prevent waterlogging. In the human body the lymphatic system acts, among other things, as the drainage canal network, removing excess fluid from all the body tissues and returning it to the blood system. To do this it has collecting vessels throughout the body and this means that as a system it is excellently equipped to monitor problems in the areas that it drains. It also functions, therefore, as a rapid response section of the body's immune system.

There is always fluid – known as interstitial, or extracellular, fluid – in and around the body's tissues and thus between the cells that the body is made of. It leaks out of the blood capillaries and passes in and out of the cells as they perform their metabolic processes. There are other substances in the fluid as well as water – dissolved chemicals, molecules and stray items such as disease-causing microorganisms that have found

Dead-end lymphatic capillaries collect fluid from between the cells. The fluid enters through one-way valves, called flap valves, that line the lymph capillaries. Inside the capillaries more flap valves ensure a one-way flow of fluid away from the tissues through the lymphatic system. Larger flap valves in the lymphatic ducts maintain the direction of flow into filtering lymph nodes. From there the lymph returns to the blood system through the thoracic duct, which joins the left subclavian vein.

LYMPHATIC SYSTEM FACT FILE

Unlike blood, which is moved by the heart, lymph is not pushed along by a special pump. Movements of surrounding organs push it through the system.

Amount of lymph fluid in body	1–2 litres (1¾–3½ pints)
Percentage of body weight	1–3
Largest lymphoid body	spleen
Size of spleen	12 cm (4¾ inches) across
No. of lymphocytes in body	2 trillion (2 x 10¹²)
Max. rate of increase of lymph flow during exercise	15 times

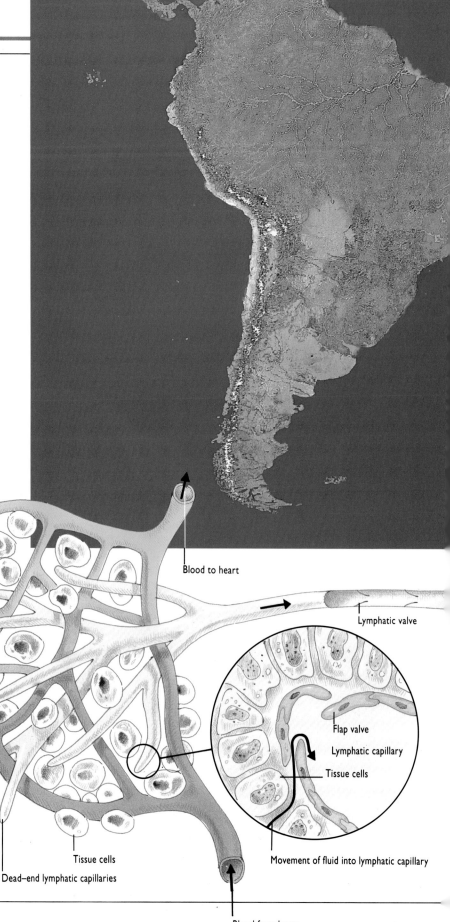

Blood to heart

Lymphatic valve

Blood capillaries

Flap valve

Lymphatic capillary

Tissue cells

Tissue cells

Movement of fluid into lymphatic capillary

Dead–end lymphatic capillaries

Blood from heart

their way into the body, perhaps through a cut.

The lymphatic system starts as a series of dead-end tubes – lymphatic capillaries – close to the blood capillaries in tissues. Extracellular fluid passes into the lymphatic capillaries, which eventually join together to form larger ducts, or lymphatics. At intervals these pass through "way stations", the lymph nodes, where foreign material, including invading microorganisms drained from the tissues, is filtered out.

There are also larger lymphatic organs, including the tonsils, thymus gland and spleen. The fluid moving through them, now known as lymph, comes into contact with large numbers of the immune system's white blood cells which are on the lookout for matter foreign to the body. Finally, lymph is returned to the blood system where a large lymphatic vessel – the thoracic duct – joins the left subclavian vein taking blood to the heart.

Just as the myriad tributaries of the Amazon come together as they drain a large part of South America, so the lymphatic capillaries of the lymphatic system merge in a branching network to drain the body tissues of excess extracellular fluid.

Cervical nodes
Lymphatic ducts
Subclavian veins
Axillary nodes
Thoracic duct
Intestinal nodes
Iliac nodes
Inguinal nodes

The lymphatic system extends throughout the body. Major lymphatic vessels pass through lymph nodes before lymph fluid is returned to the blood for circulation.

Lymph node

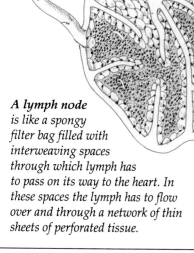

A lymph node is like a spongy filter bag filled with interweaving spaces through which lymph has to pass on its way to the heart. In these spaces the lymph has to flow over and through a network of thin sheets of perforated tissue.

Blood supply to node

Space containing white blood cells

Subclavian vein

The tissue sheets in lymph nodes have large numbers of white blood cells on them. These include the cells that play crucial roles in the body's immune defences. There are phagocytes that engulf and destroy, and lymphocytes that recognize invading matter and prime the immune system for action.

This screen of white blood cells – acting like lookouts for the immune system – effectively filters the lymph of pathogens (dangerous microorganisms) and monitors the fluid for foreign material of all sorts. This filtering out explains why, when infection starts, the lymph nodes are often swollen with the activity of the immune system swinging into action.

Waste disposal

Toxins and wastes, wherever they come from, must be dealt with by the body.

One basic process – energy generation in cells – creates waste water and carbon dioxide. Water is sweated, breathed, urinated and excreted in faeces. Carbon dioxide can be breathed out or combined with other chemicals and passed out in urine. A by-product of another basic process – digestion – is roughage, the parts of food including the cell walls of plant material that cannot be digested. It is passed out of the body as faeces.

Another type of waste is ammonia, which is highly toxic. The liver changes it into the less poisonous waste urea, which exits the body in urine. Ammonia conversion is an example of the vital process known as detoxification, which happens mostly in the liver. Batteries of enzymes in liver cells turn toxic chemicals into less toxic ones that are easy to remove, usually in urine or bile. The toxins made harmless in this way are produced by the body itself or are poisons: pollutants and drugs taken in from outside.

Benzene (C_6H_6) – *a volatile minor part of petrol – is highly toxic and if inhaled is a health hazard. If small amounts enter the body they are rapidly detoxified by liver cells in a two-stage process. First, enzymes called mixed function oxidases change the benzene to phenol.*

On most marine oil-producing platforms *waste gases from the oil production process are burned off as a flare at the end of a long exhaust pipe away from the rig. All complex manufacturing processes – including those inside the body – produce wastes that have to be disposed of.*

Second, another enzyme, glucuronidase, adds glucuronic acid – a sugar acid – to the hydroxyl group.

Glucuronic acid

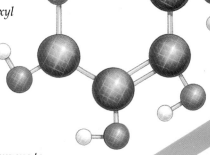

Phenol is benzene to which an oxygen atom is added to give it a hydroxyl (-OH) group.

Phenol

Oxygen

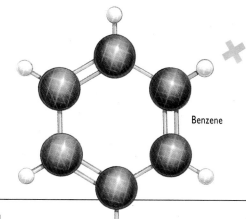

Benzene

There are five major sources of body waste products: toxins from outside; internally produced chemicals such as hormones that are no longer needed; food; nitrogen-containing waste left over from protein re-use; and energy production. After processing, the resulting products are eliminated from the body along one of the five disposal routes. Indigestible fibre, for instance, moves through the intestine to make the bulk of solid faeces. Water exits in all outputs.

Source / **Process**

Toxins — Detoxification in liver
Hormones — Metabolism
Food — Digestion
Nitrogenous wastes — Deamination and urea product
Energy production — Cellular respiration

Phenylglucuronide – the hybrid molecule formed in the two-step process in the liver – is much less toxic to the body than either benzene or phenol. It also dissolves in water for excretion in solution in bile or urine.

Hydrogen

Carbon

Oxygen

Nitrogen

Output

Sweat

Sweat pore

Feces

Gall bladder

Urine

Intestine

Urinary system

Breath

Lungs

Phenylglucuronide

Disposal route

Product

Detoxified toxins

Hormones and hormone metabolites

Cellulose and lignins

Urea

Water (H_2O) and carbon dioxide (CO_2)

Ammonia, the by-product of deamination, is combined with carbon dioxide to form urea and water. This detoxification process, like many others, occurs in the liver. By joining together ammonia and carbon dioxide, two important wastes are conveniently dealt with at once, forming a relatively non-toxic waste that is easily excreted in urine.

WASTE PROTEIN

One of the major sources of waste material in the body is ammonia. It is produced when proteins, from which the body's tissues are constructed, are broken down and recycled. In this process proteins are first split up into their constituent building blocks of amino acids. Deamination enzymes then cut off an amine group ($-NH_2$) from each amino acid to form ammonia (NH_3) and a keto acid. The keto acids are re-used either to produce energy or to form stored fats. Ammonia is toxic, however, and has to be processed before being excreted.

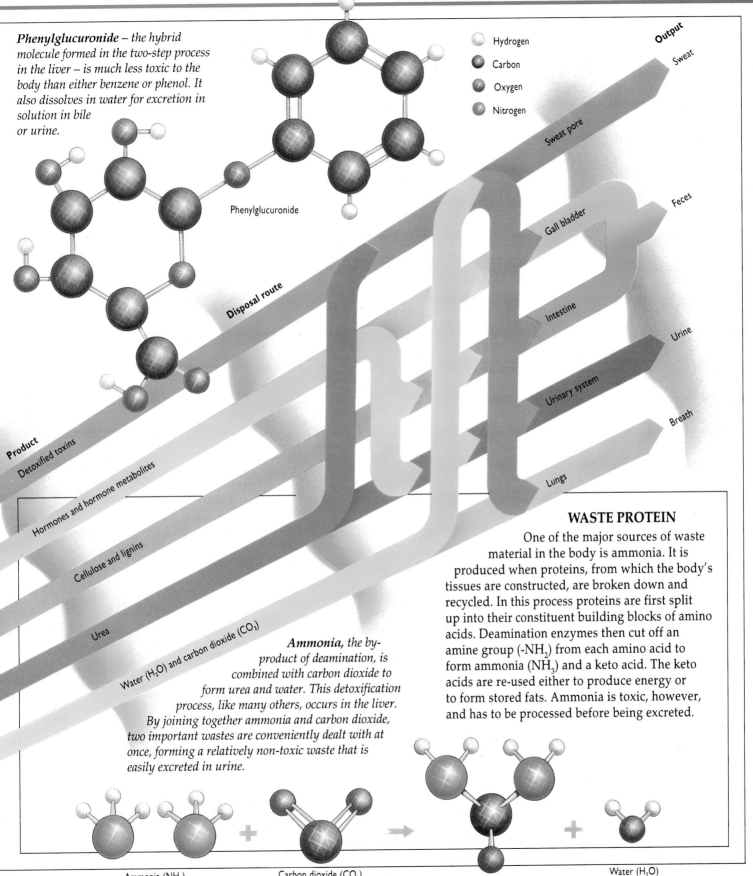

Ammonia (NH_3)   Carbon dioxide (CO_2)   Urea ($CO(NH_2)_2$)   Water (H_2O)

The water balance

Our bodies are almost two-thirds water. So where is all that liquid and how are fluid levels controlled?

Each and every cell in the human body contains water and is bathed in water. Indeed, there is more water in the body than any other substance. And since water transports all the sustaining substances that the body's cells require, it is no wonder that for a healthy existence the total volume of water in the body and the concentrations of materials dissolved in it have to be kept within extremely tight limits.

At the heart of the physiological machinery that manages the body's water balance are the kidneys. They work by first filtering water and a wide range of soluble molecules from the blood and then reabsorbing useful molecules and rejecting unwanted waste materials, which are expelled from the body in solution in urine. They are so important that untreated kidney failure leads to death within days. Modern medicine provides a solution to failure in the form of dialysis – the filtration of the blood by artificial kidneys – or kidney transplant.

Urine is formed in the kidneys by filtration of plasma – the liquid in which blood cells are suspended. This entails the removal of large quantities of water and all soluble materials from it. Useful substances and water are then selectively returned to the blood, while unwanted materials, such as urea (a waste product of the breakdown of proteins), stay in the filtrate. In 24 hours the kidneys filter out 150 litres (33 gallons) of water from the blood but return an average of 99 percent of it, keeping only 1.5 litres (2½ pints) to form a day's worth of urine.

By contrast, of the 50 g (2 ounces) of urea filtered out daily by the kidneys, almost half is excreted dissolved in the urine. There are many other soluble substances in the blood, all of which pass through the kidneys. Each is returned to the blood or excreted in urine in a particular proportion. Glucose, for instance, is usually all reabsorbed, except in a disease such as diabetes, when some is lost.

Some 60 percent of our body weight is water – only 40 percent is made up of solid material. In an average-sized adult man that 60 percent of water makes up about 40 litres (68 pints). The water inside cells, or intracellular water, makes up about two-thirds of the total body water. All the remaining water, about 15 litres (26 pints) in an average person, is extracellular. It is found in a variety of body fluids. Most is present in the so-called interstitial fluid – the liquid medium which immediately surrounds all cells. Most of the rest is in lymph fluid in the lymphatic vessels, liquid in brain and spinal spaces (cerebrospinal fluid) and blood plasma.

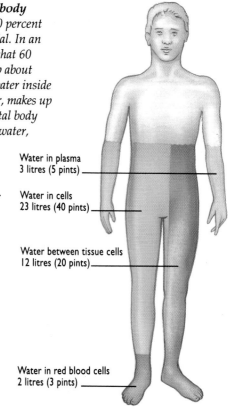

Water in plasma
3 litres (5 pints)

Water in cells
23 litres (40 pints)

Water between tissue cells
12 litres (20 pints)

Water in red blood cells
2 litres (3 pints)

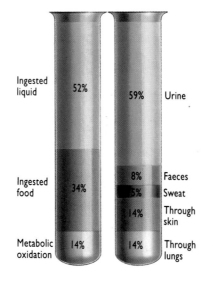

Ingested liquid	52%	59% Urine
Ingested food	34%	8% Faeces
		5% Sweat
		14% Through skin
Metabolic oxidation	14%	14% Through lungs

The amount of water taken in plus that made internally by the conversion of glucose (the body's fuel source) to energy matches that lost by various means. The average daily intake, and thus output, is about 2.7 litres (4¾ pints).

KIDNEYS FACT FILE

Blood enters the kidneys at 20–25 percent of the rate at which it leaves the heart – they receive proportionately more blood than any other organ.

Dimensions	length	11 cm (4⅓ inches)
	width	6 cm (2⅓ inches)
	thickness	3 cm (1⅕ inches)
Weight of kidney		140 g (5 ounces)
No. of nephrons per kidney		1 million
Total length of nephron tubules		80 km (50 miles)
Kidney blood flow per hour		72 litres (16 gallons)
Pressure of blood entering kidney		75 mmHg
Time to filter total blood plasma		30 minutes
Length of	ureter	30 cm (12 inches)
	urethra (man)	20 cm (8 inches)
	urethra (woman)	4 cm (1½ inches)
Water content of	body	60%
	blood (most)	83%
	fat (least)	10%
Solids excreted in urine		50 g (2 ounces) per day
Av. urine passed on urination		300–400 ml (½–⅔ pint)
pH of urine		4.8–7.8

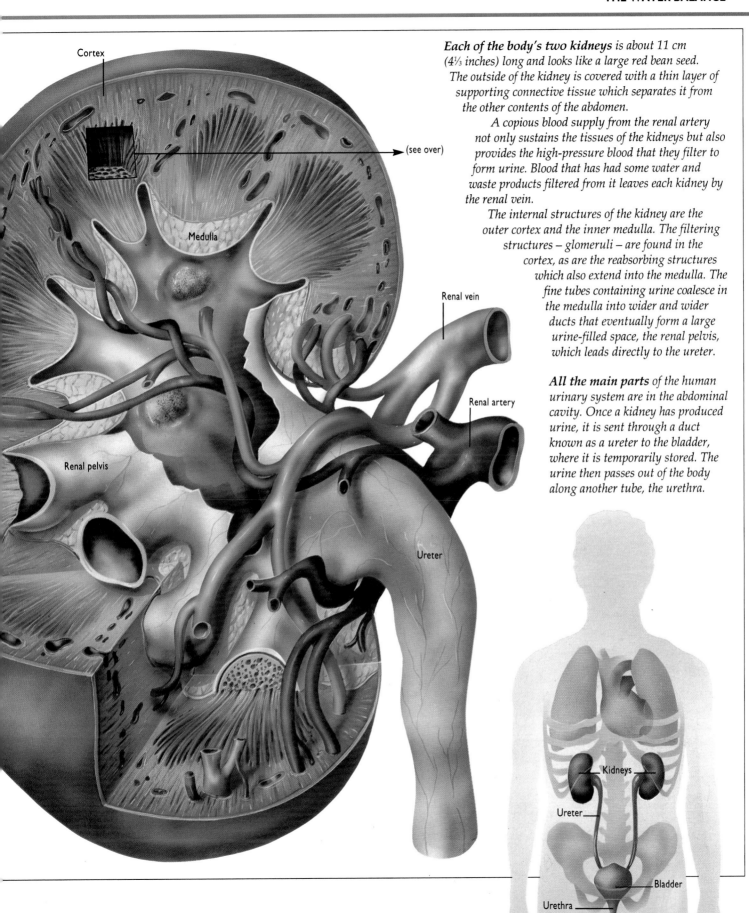

Cortex

Medulla

Renal vein

Renal artery

Renal pelvis

Ureter

Each of the body's two kidneys *is about 11 cm (4⅓ inches) long and looks like a large red bean seed. The outside of the kidney is covered with a thin layer of supporting connective tissue which separates it from the other contents of the abdomen.*

A copious blood supply from the renal artery not only sustains the tissues of the kidneys but also provides the high-pressure blood that they filter to form urine. Blood that has had some water and waste products filtered from it leaves each kidney by the renal vein.

The internal structures of the kidney are the outer cortex and the inner medulla. The filtering structures – glomeruli – are found in the cortex, as are the reabsorbing structures which also extend into the medulla. The fine tubes containing urine coalesce in the medulla into wider and wider ducts that eventually form a large urine-filled space, the renal pelvis, which leads directly to the ureter.

All the main parts *of the human urinary system are in the abdominal cavity. Once a kidney has produced urine, it is sent through a duct known as a ureter to the bladder, where it is temporarily stored. The urine then passes out of the body along another tube, the urethra.*

(see over)

Kidneys

Ureter

Bladder

Urethra

Inside the kidney

Urine is the end product of a sophisticated process involving millions of tiny filtration units.

Although each kidney looks like a single entity, it consists of more than a million micro organs, or nephrons. Each one produces its own tiny output of urine to yield a combined output of about 1.5 litres (2½ pints) per day. Urine production is a convoluted process, reflected in the structure of the nephron.

Blood under high pressure enters a nephron through a glomerulus, a tangled knot of capillaries fed by one of the renal arteries. The plasma of the blood is filtered through the specialized wall of the glomerular capillary and the inner lining of the pocket in which the glomerulus sits. This pocket is known as a Bowman's capsule. Almost all the water and dissolved substances, such as glucose and sodium, found in plasma pass from the glomerulus into the Bowman's capsule, and from there into the nephron tubule.

The tubule and its contents take a highly complex, meandering track through the kidney. Most, if not all, of the substances that are useful to the body, for example glucose, are reabsorbed back into the plasma via the intricate network of capillaries that hug the sides of the tubule. This is achieved in a number of ways, including passive diffusion (where molecules in solution move from regions of high to low concentration), osmosis (where water passes through a semipermeable membrane from a weak solution to a strong solution), and active transport of molecules across the tubule membrane. By the end, all that remains in the tubule is urine – a mixture of waste products such as urea and some salts and water. This passes into the renal pelvis and ultimately, via the ureter, to the bladder.

Reabsorption of salt and water is under complex hormonal control. A key factor that can influence the rate of water and salt loss by the kidneys is the state of the body's water balance. For instance, if you become dehydrated in a hot climate, hormonal changes ensure that water reabsorption rates in the tubule are increased so you lose less fluid.

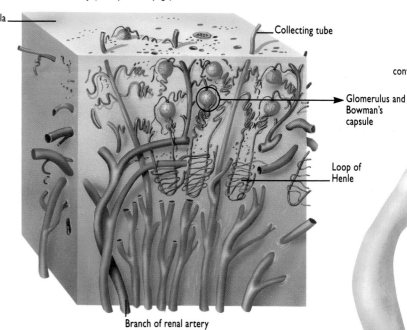

Detail of kidney (from previous page)

Medulla

Collecting tube

Dist convolute tub

Glomerulus and Bowman's capsule

Loop of Henle

Branch of renal artery

Within kidney tissue a glomerulus – enclosed in a Bowman's capsule and supplied by a branch of the renal artery – is found at the outer end of each nephron. The nephron tubule leaves the glomerulus and dips down – in the loop of Henle – into the medulla, where it is surrounded by a mesh of fine blood vessels. The tubule finally joins with the collecting tube which carries urine to the renal pelvis.

Collecting tube

Grounds are filtered from coffee to make a palatable drink. In the same way, the glomerulus and Bowman's capsule filter out larger molecules and the blood cells, allowing only small molecules – including water – to pass into the nephron tubule.

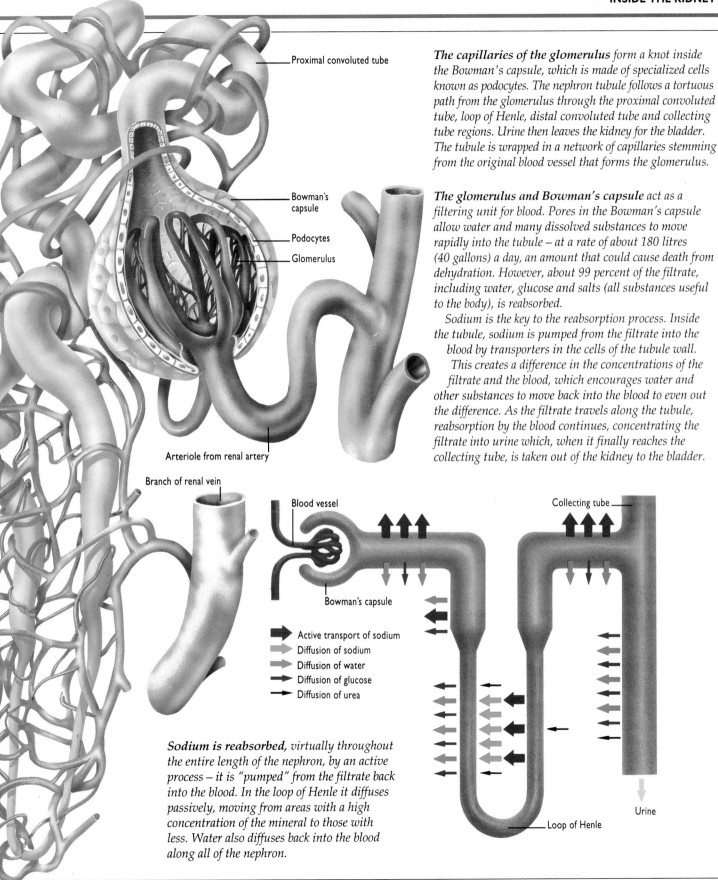

Proximal convoluted tube

Bowman's capsule

Podocytes

Glomerulus

Arteriole from renal artery

Branch of renal vein

Blood vessel

Bowman's capsule

Collecting tube

→ Active transport of sodium

→ Diffusion of sodium

→ Diffusion of water

→ Diffusion of glucose

→ Diffusion of urea

Urine

Loop of Henle

The capillaries of the glomerulus form a knot inside the Bowman's capsule, which is made of specialized cells known as podocytes. The nephron tubule follows a tortuous path from the glomerulus through the proximal convoluted tube, loop of Henle, distal convoluted tube and collecting tube regions. Urine then leaves the kidney for the bladder. The tubule is wrapped in a network of capillaries stemming from the original blood vessel that forms the glomerulus.

The glomerulus and Bowman's capsule act as a filtering unit for blood. Pores in the Bowman's capsule allow water and many dissolved substances to move rapidly into the tubule – at a rate of about 180 litres (40 gallons) a day, an amount that could cause death from dehydration. However, about 99 percent of the filtrate, including water, glucose and salts (all substances useful to the body), is reabsorbed.

Sodium is the key to the reabsorption process. Inside the tubule, sodium is pumped from the filtrate into the blood by transporters in the cells of the tubule wall. This creates a difference in the concentrations of the filtrate and the blood, which encourages water and other substances to move back into the blood to even out the difference. As the filtrate travels along the tubule, reabsorption by the blood continues, concentrating the filtrate into urine which, when it finally reaches the collecting tube, is taken out of the kidney to the bladder.

Sodium is reabsorbed, virtually throughout the entire length of the nephron, by an active process – it is "pumped" from the filtrate back into the blood. In the loop of Henle it diffuses passively, moving from areas with a high concentration of the mineral to those with less. Water also diffuses back into the blood along all of the nephron.

See also

CIRCULATION, MAINTENANCE AND DEFENCE
▶ Transport systems 62/63

▶ In circulation 68/69

▶ Blood: supplying the body 70/71

▶ The water balance 76/77

BUILDING THE BRAIN
▶ Food for thought 188/189

INPUTS AND OUTPUTS
▶ Keeping control 238/239

▶ Dealing with drives 240/241

Loop of Henle

Maintaining the system

The body maintains, repairs and protects itself with an astounding array of systems – and directing them all is the brain.

A house has to be intrinsically strong and resilient to withstand the ravages of weather, decay, subsidence, woodworm, beetles and burglars. The physical robustness of the house – its frame, roof, bricks, cement, doors and windows – provides the first line of defence against these potential problems. The body has equivalent defences to protect it against attack by viruses, bacteria, fungal infections and poisons. These range from the protective outer covering of the skin to complex physiological and chemical defences inside the body.

Wear and tear mean that different parts of the house also need repair and replacement. The body likewise requires running repairs, almost all of which are carried out by cells that have the capacity to divide, producing new cells to replace the old ones. In addition, damaged organs such as broken bones and cut blood vessels can also be mended.

Deliberate attacks on a house and its contents provide the most severe tests. An attempted break-in by an intruder requires sophisticated defences because the strategy and cunning of the invader must be overcome. It is much the same when the body has to confront attacks by disease-causing organisms, whether they are viruses and bacteria that are invisible to the naked eye or large parasites such as tapeworms. Since harmful invaders (pathogens) have active mechanisms to help them breach the body's layers of protection, countering infection requires precise and flexible defensive weaponry. The cells and antibodies of the immune system are the physiological equivalents of surveillance cameras, burglar alarms and detectives with long memories.

BRAINS INSIDE THE SYSTEM

In addition to the body's brilliant array of automated defence, repair and maintenance systems, there is another dimension to the maintenance of the human system – human brain power and problem-solving abilities. This means that defence against invading disease agents also has an overriding and unique human dimension, equivalent in some ways to the architect whose skills and intellect plan a house in the first place. Thus, through health education, we can change our behaviour to minimize disease risks. We can purify water before drinking it, sleep under mosquito nets to avoid infection by the bite of malaria-infected insects, and make sure that foods are cooked appropriately to kill germs in them. Beyond such preventative measures we have also developed vaccines to protect us from infections and drugs to eliminate them if they have managed to establish themselves.

Like the walls of a house, the skin provides the outermost physical protective barrier. Tough and flexible, with a surface built from dead skin cells packed with keratin (a fibrous structural protein), the skin can stop invasion by disease-causing microbes. Its crucial role is seen in severe burn injuries, which are almost always fatal because it is impossible to stop bacterial infection without the outer skin layers.

The lining of the mouth, throat, lungs and reproductive system is constructed from layers of cells that secrete large amounts of watery fluid known as mucus. The mucus traps invading microbes, and the antibacterial enzyme lysozyme in the mucus helps to keep microorganisms under control. From the lungs the mucus, containing foreign particles, is moved outward toward the throat as a cleaning mechanism.

Like a house, the human body must be maintained and defended. Even a house as brilliantly designed as Fallingwater (**above**), built in 1936 at Bear Run, Pennsylvania, and designed by American architect Frank Lloyd Wright (1867–1959), will survive only if it is looked after and protected.

DEFENDING THE BODY

The symbols (**right and above**) identify functions of the body's defence system. Like a house, the body has an in-built passive defence system – walls, a roof and a damp-proof course, keeping weather and intruders out – shown here by the wall and brick symbols. It also has repairers, analogous to painters, glaziers and builders (paint pot symbols), and an active defence system, like a security alarm with a direct line linked to the police (alarm bell symbols).

A static defence system waiting passively in the stomach is high acidity caused by secretion of hydrochloric acid by the stomach lining. Conditions are such that almost all disease-causing organisms taken in accidentally with food or drink are killed in the stomach by the acid.

The complement system – a complex mixture of proteins in the liquid part of the blood (the plasma) – is normally in a non-activated state. However, when these proteins are "switched on" by contact with bacteria, they are able to destroy invading bacterial cells.

Damage repair systems have to deal with the failure of major structural components. For instance, if bones are put under enough strain, they crack and fracture. When this happens new cells are formed in a blood clot at the broken bone ends. These cells transform into bone cells that knit the bone together again.

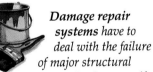

Regular maintenance involves replacing worn out or dead cells. In the skin, for instance, the dead outer layers constantly fall off. They are replaced by new cells that were formed in the living lower layer, where rapidly dividing cells produce a constant supply of replacement cells. A similar process occurs in the hair follicle in each hair "root" so hairs constantly grow at their bases.

Repairing the wall of a damaged blood vessel as quickly as possible is important so that the flow of blood can be stemmed. This is done first with a quick-setting temporary patch made from platelets. A longer term repair is then made with fibrin – an insoluble blood protein. Finally, new cell growth makes a permanent repair in the vessel wall.

Active defences that react to invaders include antibodies – specialized proteins of the immune system which are secreted by white blood cells. They recognize and stick to foreign molecules which have invaded the body. This "brands" the invading molecules as targets for attack. Once an invader has been recognized, more and more antibodies are made to counter it. When the invader has been defeated, the immune system is ready for it the next time it invades.

An attacking part of the immune system is the population of phagocytic cells which "eat" and digest invading microbes. Once antibodies have identified the microbes, the phagocytes, including cells such as macrophages, consume and digest the invaders, in the process killing them.

Some of the body's white blood cells (lymphocytes) can recognize and react to cancer cells in the body as well as to body cells which have been infected with an invading virus. These lymphocytes are called natural killer cells – they attach to altered body cells and kill them by secreting deadly chemicals which make the cell's contents leak out.

Routine replacement

The body is a community of countless cells which, like any community, sees both death and birth.

When a piece of machinery breaks down or wears out, someone, usually a skilled engineer, has to diagnose the problem and fix the machine. By contrast, the human body does not need some outside agency – save in exceptional circumstances – to come along and mend it or replace a worn-out part. Our bodies are self-repairing and self-replenishing. In fact, almost all the living parts of the body are in a state of constant flux. It has been estimated that during each hour almost 200 billion cells die – but in a healthy body these dying cells are simultaneously replaced by new ones. So although individual cells become ineffectual and then die, the body replaces its worn-out parts seamlessly and continuously.

So where do these new cells come from? They are formed by the division of previously existing cells into pairs of daughter cells. This division, or splitting apart, is a phase of the cell cycle. In this continuous cycle of changes, both to the cell nucleus and to the cytoplasm region outside the nucleus, the chromosomes – containing the gene-carrying DNA molecules – first copy themselves so the nucleus has a double set. Then, in a process known as mitosis, the two sets of chromosomes are

Early prophase

Interphase

Chromosome

Late prophase

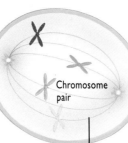
Chromosome pair

Spindle fibre

Cell turnover in the body is like the seemingly constant appearance of a waterfall. A fall looks the same from moment to moment even though at every successive instant it is made of different droplets.

When a cell divides to copy, or replicate, itself, the nucleus divides in two, and each new nucleus has an identical set of the cell's genetic information, or genes. This division of the nucleus is called mitosis. Before this happens, in the interphase stage (above) the genetic material copies itself. In early prophase, the genetic material becomes condensed to form short pairs of chromosomes.

Metaphase

Early anaphase

In late prophase chromosome pairs attach to the fibres of the spindle apparatus that is formed by two organelles, or centrioles. The nuclear envelope breaks down at this time. In the stage called metaphase, the chromosomes line up around the equator zone of the spindle.

Late anaphase

THE LIFE SPAN OF DIFFERENT CELLS

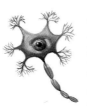

Nerve cells are the body's longest cells – they can have a complex, elongated and branched shape. Once a nerve cell attains this shape during development in the womb or in early childhood it cannot divide further. This means that some nerve cells live for as long as the person they are part of. Another implication of this is that once a cell of the nervous system dies it is not replaced, whether in the brain itself or elsewhere in the body.

Liver cells, or hepatocytes, in the lobules that make up the bulk of the liver lobes are metabolically complex cells that often carry out many processes simultaneously. So great is their ability to divide – and therefore multiply – that even if an entire liver lobe is removed by surgery, the remaining liver cells can slowly replace the lost liver tissue. The approximate life span of a liver cell is 500 days.

carefully and accurately separated from one another in a perfectly orchestrated set of microscopic movements which carry identical sets of chromosomes to opposite ends of the cell. After the newly reproduced chromosomes have separated like this they form two new nuclei and then the cell itself splits in two – each half with an identical set of genes in its nucleus.

In this way, one turn of the cell cycle transforms one cell into two. Carefully regulated multiplication of this sort can exactly compensate for the dying and dead cells in a healthy body. This balanced loss and birth of cells means that although a person's body does not seem to change, it is made of new cells day by day. So even though all the cells in the skin of your face can be replaced, your face still retains its characteristic looks.

The life of an individual cell can end in one of two ways: the cell can divide, forming two identical daughter cells; or it may become diseased or worn out, so that it dies before it is able to duplicate itself. Different cell types have characteristically varying life spans linked either to the rapidity with which they divide or to the time during which they are able to work properly. Some cells cannot replicate themselves, notably the neurons in the brain and nervous system.

Interphase

Late telophase

Early telophase

During anaphase and telophase the two chromosome sets move to opposite ends of the cell, driven by the action of fibres in the spindle. At the end of telophase two new nuclei have formed and the cell itself splits in half with a new nucleus in each daughter cell.

New red and some white blood cells are formed by the actively dividing cells that are found in the bone marrow of many large bones. Their phenomenally active rate of cell division means that bone marrow cells have one of the shortest life spans of any human cell. They divide every 10 hours or so – about 900 times a year. About 200 billion red blood cells are made a day.

Once formed, red and white blood cells move from the bone marrow into the bloodstream. Red blood cells, which do not possess nuclei and therefore cannot undergo mitosis, live for about 120 days in the blood before dying. Nucleated white blood cells last for an average of only 13 days before dying or dividing.

83

Damage repair

If you are unfortunate enough to get hurt, you can rely on your body to look after you.

The human body has self-regulating methods for replacing the cells in tissues that wear out and die. New skin cells, hair cells and blood cells are made in a ceaseless and precisely controlled fashion to take the place of those that are lost in cellular ageing. In addition to this process of continuous repair and replacement, the body has dramatic capacities to repair itself when more catastrophic types of damage occur.

These large-scale abilities for emergency repair are clearly shown in one of the most crucial organ systems in the body, the blood-carrying circulatory system. When blood vessels are ruptured, "first-aid" responses happen almost instantaneously to minimize the immediate risks. Then a step-by-step, longer-term set of changes begins to repair the damage.

Since the whole circulatory system is pressurized, a hole in the wall of a blood vessel is potentially fatal. Unless the hole is rapidly sealed, the internal pressure will mean that blood continues to flow from the opening. The body has a three-phase set of emergency responses to deal with this "red alert" situation. First, the muscles in the blood vessel wall contract to minimize the hole size. Second, platelets in the blood stick together to make a soft clot over the hole. Third, blood clotting, or coagulation, produces a much more solid patch over the breakage.

Damage is also repaired in other parts of the body. Broken bones can grow back together – and be as strong as before the break. Dislocated or sprained joints are immobilized by fluid in the tissues and held in place while healing takes place. Even severed nerves can join up to restore feeling and control of muscles to a limited extent. And in the brain, the network of neurons can rewire itself so that damage can be minimized.

One of the body's prime "emergency services" enables it to stop an open wound from losing too much blood. For instance, when you cut your finger, breaking blood vessels, a sequence of events comes into play which slows down – and then stops – the potentially dangerous loss of blood.

The damage to the blood vessel directly stimulates involuntary, or smooth, muscles in the wall, causing them to constrict. This reduces not only the size of the break or wound but also the amount of blood flowing toward it.

Specialized cells in the blood – thrombocytes or platelets – also respond quickly to any trauma. They release chemicals that further stimulate muscles to contract, aiding the direct constrictive mechanism working in the blood-vessel walls. The muscles may stay contracted for up to 20 minutes, giving immediate protection against excessive blood loss.

Platelets

Under normal circumstances, platelets in the blood slide past each other and other blood cells – their shape is relatively smooth and they

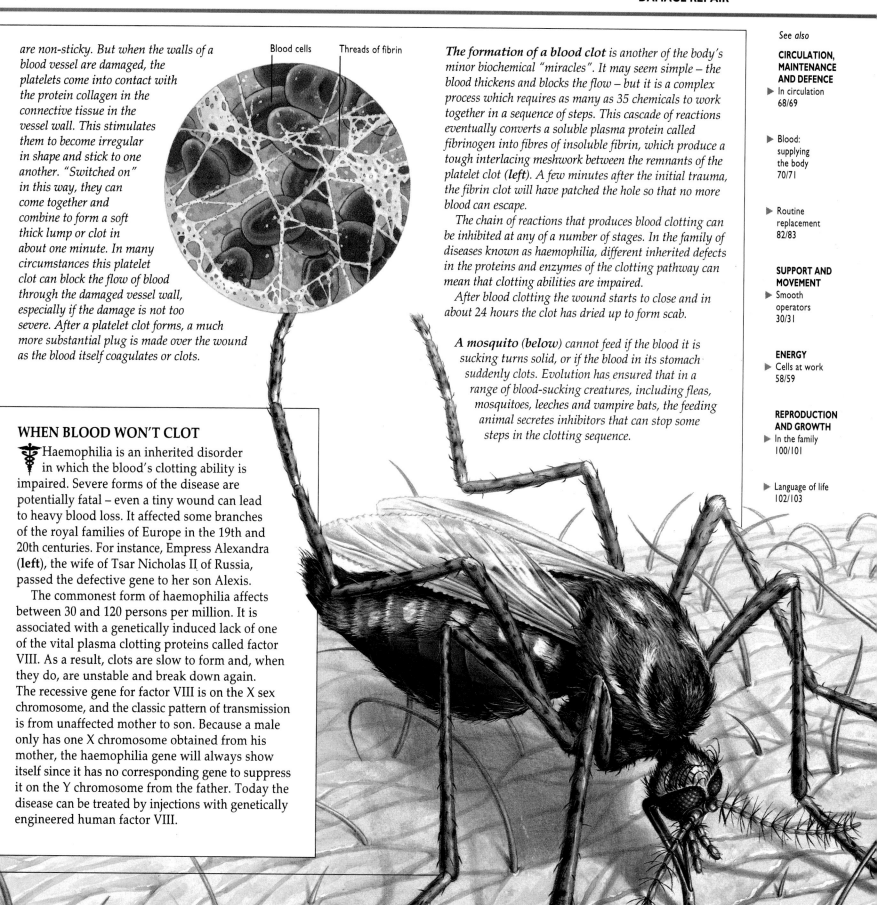

Blood cells   Threads of fibrin

are non-sticky. But when the walls of a blood vessel are damaged, the platelets come into contact with the protein collagen in the connective tissue in the vessel wall. This stimulates them to become irregular in shape and stick to one another. "Switched on" in this way, they can come together and combine to form a soft thick lump or clot in about one minute. In many circumstances this platelet clot can block the flow of blood through the damaged vessel wall, especially if the damage is not too severe. After a platelet clot forms, a much more substantial plug is made over the wound as the blood itself coagulates or clots.

The formation of a blood clot is another of the body's minor biochemical "miracles". It may seem simple – the blood thickens and blocks the flow – but it is a complex process which requires as many as 35 chemicals to work together in a sequence of steps. This cascade of reactions eventually converts a soluble plasma protein called fibrinogen into fibres of insoluble fibrin, which produce a tough interlacing meshwork between the remnants of the platelet clot (*left*). A few minutes after the initial trauma, the fibrin clot will have patched the hole so that no more blood can escape.

The chain of reactions that produces blood clotting can be inhibited at any of a number of stages. In the family of diseases known as haemophilia, different inherited defects in the proteins and enzymes of the clotting pathway can mean that clotting abilities are impaired.

After blood clotting the wound starts to close and in about 24 hours the clot has dried up to form scab.

A mosquito (*below*) cannot feed if the blood it is sucking turns solid, or if the blood in its stomach suddenly clots. Evolution has ensured that in a range of blood-sucking creatures, including fleas, mosquitoes, leeches and vampire bats, the feeding animal secretes inhibitors that can stop some steps in the clotting sequence.

WHEN BLOOD WON'T CLOT

Haemophilia is an inherited disorder in which the blood's clotting ability is impaired. Severe forms of the disease are potentially fatal – even a tiny wound can lead to heavy blood loss. It affected some branches of the royal families of Europe in the 19th and 20th centuries. For instance, Empress Alexandra (**left**), the wife of Tsar Nicholas II of Russia, passed the defective gene to her son Alexis.

The commonest form of haemophilia affects between 30 and 120 persons per million. It is associated with a genetically induced lack of one of the vital plasma clotting proteins called factor VIII. As a result, clots are slow to form and, when they do, are unstable and break down again. The recessive gene for factor VIII is on the X sex chromosome, and the classic pattern of transmission is from unaffected mother to son. Because a male only has one X chromosome obtained from his mother, the haemophilia gene will always show itself since it has no corresponding gene to suppress it on the Y chromosome from the father. Today the disease can be treated by injections with genetically engineered human factor VIII.

See also

CIRCULATION, MAINTENANCE AND DEFENCE
▶ In circulation 68/69

▶ Blood: supplying the body 70/71

▶ Routine replacement 82/83

SUPPORT AND MOVEMENT
▶ Smooth operators 30/31

ENERGY
▶ Cells at work 58/59

REPRODUCTION AND GROWTH
▶ In the family 100/101

▶ Language of life 102/103

Outer defences

Surrounding our fragile insides is a thin yet strong covering that protects us from the outside world.

It is easy to think of bare skin as being soft and vulnerable. In fact, human skin forms a remarkably effective outer defence for the body. It is tough, resilient, self-replenishing, self-healing when damaged, excludes invading microorganisms, generates hairs and nails and is the location of the sense of touch. And all these functions are packed into a layer of tissue that is usually only a millimetre or two thick.

The main protective function of the skin is provided by the layers of dead cells that form the outer part of the epidermis. Each new cell, produced by cell division at the base of the epidermis, moves outward toward the surface. As it does so its cytoplasm, the fluid portion of a cell's interior, is transformed into a tough, sulphur-rich protein known as keratin, and in the process the cell dies. Keratin is robust and is difficult to break down with normal digestive enzymes because of the sulphur–sulphur bonds linking the chains of amino acids that make up the keratin. This strength means that potentially invading bacteria and fungi find it difficult to gain a purchase on the outer layer of the skin.

Outer dead keratinized cells are continuously falling from the skin surface. In fact, a large proportion of household dust is made up of dead human skin. Where whole collections of skin cells fall off together in flakes from the scalp the flakes are called dandruff. As cells are lost in this way they are replaced by new ones coming up from beneath, so maintaining a virtually impenetrable barrier.

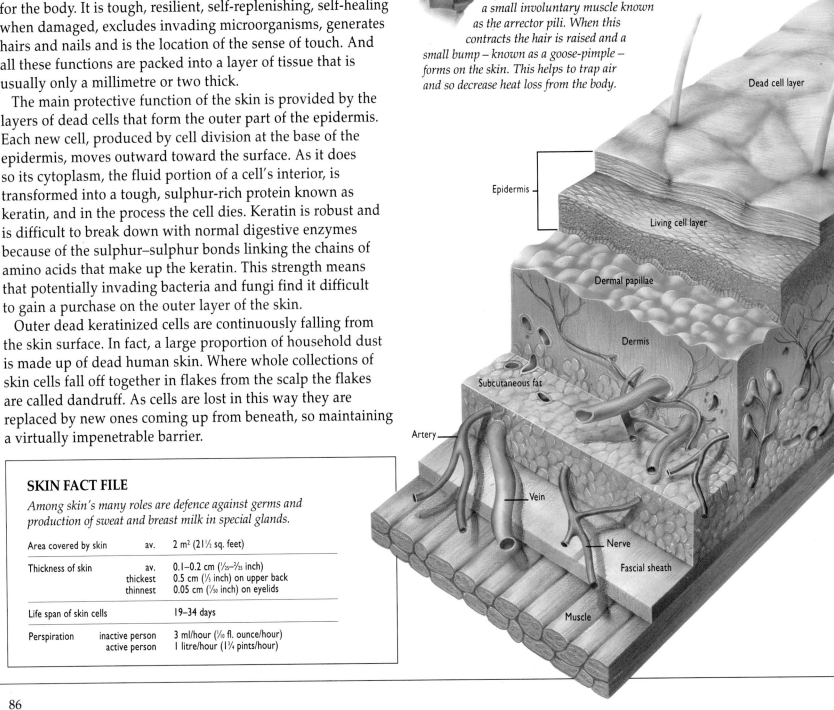

Hairs project from hair follicles – specialized pockets of actively dividing cells at the base of the dermis. Like the skin surface, as well as finger- and toenails, hairs are made of cells that have turned into keratin and died. Each hair is a solid cylinder of dead, keratinized skin cells which are organized into layers known as the cortex, medulla and cuticle. Only areas like the soles of the feet, palms, nipples, lips and the tip of the penis are without hair. Situated deep within the hypodermis of the skin, the hair root is joined to a small involuntary muscle known as the arrector pili. When this contracts the hair is raised and a small bump – known as a goose-pimple – forms on the skin. This helps to trap air and so decrease heat loss from the body.

Cortex
Medulla
Cuticle
Dead cell layer
Epidermis
Living cell layer
Dermal papillae
Dermis
Subcutaneous fat
Artery
Vein
Nerve
Fascial sheath
Muscle

SKIN FACT FILE

Among skin's many roles are defence against germs and production of sweat and breast milk in special glands.

Area covered by skin	av.	2 m² (21½ sq. feet)
Thickness of skin	av.	0.1–0.2 cm (¹⁄₂₅–¹⁄₁₂ inch)
	thickest	0.5 cm (⅕ inch) on upper back
	thinnest	0.05 cm (¹⁄₅₀ inch) on eyelids
Life span of skin cells		19–34 days
Perspiration	inactive person	3 ml/hour (¹⁄₁₀ fl. ounce/hour)
	active person	1 litre/hour (1¾ pints/hour)

The skin contains three distinct layers even though it is only as thick as a piece of card. The outermost layer, the epidermis, is a sheet of self-replacing cells; beneath that is the dermis, a thicker layer of fibrous connective tissue. Lastly, a layer of looser connective tissue, which often contains a great deal of fat, forms the hypodermis. Underneath lie the superficial muscles.

A person's skin colour depends on how much melanin – a black-brown pigment – is concentrated in the skin. Melanin is found in melanocytes, cells in the lower part of the epidermis. These cells have pigment-filled projections which weave between other skin cells. Melanocytes are present in all areas of the body, with higher concentrations in the external genitals, the nipples, the anal region and the armpits. Melanin is also responsible for the colouring of hair and eyes.

Melanin plays a vital role as an ultraviolet (UV) radiation screen, stopping excessive amounts of UV in sunlight from reaching the genetic material in cell nuclei. Too much UV radiation can mutate the genetic material and turn ordinary skin cells into cancerous cells. Prolonged exposure to UV rays increases melanin secretion, producing a tanned skin that is less sensitive to sunlight. But UV light does play a useful role by converting a substance in the skin called 7-dehydrocholesterol into vitamin D, which is vital for laying down calcium salts in bones and teeth.

Sebaceous glands are found on all surfaces of the body that grow hairs. They are connected to the sides of hair follicles and produce sebum, an oily secretion. Sebum is made when the interior skin cells break down, producing an oily liquid. It coats hairs and the skin's surface with a waterproofing and softening film which also discourages the attachment of harmful bacteria and fungi. If a gland opening becomes plugged with sebum, inflammation occurs and a blackhead results, which could develop into a pimple. Pimples and blackheads are especially common during sexual maturation when sebum secretion levels are high.

Melanin

Melanocyte

Sweat pore

Sweat
duct

Sebaceous
gland

eat
nd

Hair follicle

Sebum

*Sweat provides
enough nutrition*
to support an average
of 10,000 bacteria for
every square centimetre
of the human body.

Sweat

Bacteria

LIVING WITH THE SWEAT EATERS

Perspiration secreted from sweat glands in the skin performs a variety of roles. In addition to cooling the body through evaporation it provides nutrients for certain bacteria and fungi that live on the skin's surface and produce acidic waste products such as lactic acid, thus reducing the pH of the skin's surface. This surface acidity creates a microenvironment that invading, harmful bacteria find difficult to inhabit.

These beneficial microorganisms are said to be symbiotic. Symbiosis is a state in which both organisms benefit from the relationship. In this case the bacteria are able to survive off human secretions, while we benefit from the protective qualities of their waste products.

Repelling invaders

A range of reflexes and killer chemicals are among the hazards facing foreign bodies that invade the body.

To fight successfully against unwelcome and actively dangerous disease-causing microbes and parasites, the human body has to employ sophisticated defences. Although the protective mechanisms are diverse, they can be fitted into two broad categories – innate and adaptive, which is generally known as the immune response.

The innate defences such as the skin and sneezing are fixed defences – ones which are always available at the same degree of readiness. They are relatively unselective and can be used against many different types of invader. Adaptive defences, such as antibodies, are more subtle. They are usually selective and specific in their action, operating against only a very narrow range of disease-causing agents. They are adaptive in the sense that, in using them, the body reacts to a particular attack in a responsive rather than a fixed manner.

The physical barrier of the skin is the first in line of the innate defences, but beneath it there are a range of physiological, cellular and biochemical weapons. These, acting alone or together, are usually capable of removing or destroying the invaders. The physiological weapons include unconscious reflex actions that can damage or remove harmful material or microbes – scratching, sneezing, coughing, vomiting and the production of tears.

Cellular defences include cleansing currents in the airways of the lungs which are driven by cilia (tiny waving hairs). The bronchioles, bronchi and trachea are all lined with waving ciliated cells that propel sticky mucus from the inner recesses of the lungs up to the throat. This stream of mucus, acting like flypaper, traps fine dust, pollen grains, fungus spores, bacteria, viruses and yeast cells from the inhaled air and transports these potentially dangerous particles to the throat. They are then swallowed to be destroyed by hydrochloric acid and digestive enzymes in the stomach, or coughed up. Smoking can destroy this protective flow of mucus, laying the smoker's lungs open to easy colonization by bacteria and viruses.

Among the most potent of the many biochemical innate defences are lysozyme, the antibacterial enzyme found in secretions such as tears, saliva and milk, and the so-called complement system in the blood. Complement proteins provide a generalized chemical defence against bacteria. When they are activated, either directly by contact with the outer surface of a germ or indirectly by antibodies, they shoot holes in bacterial cells. In a series of enzyme activations, non-active complement proteins are converted to active forms. The clusters of activated digestive enzymes then dissolve holes in the cell membrane of the targeted bacteria – killing and repelling the invaders.

LOCAL ACTION

The body responds to local irritation in many protective ways. Scratching, coughing, sneezing, crying and vomiting can all, in their own ways, help to remove dangerous materials or organisms from some part of the body.

Most of these actions, for example a cough or a sneeze, are involuntary – they are reflexes involving automatically coordinated muscle contractions. Conscious will is normally used only to inhibit these actions.

Itching is caused by low-grade damage to the body's surface layers. Scratching can protect against invasion by the scabies or itch mite which burrows into the skin's surface. It keeps the parasites under control by excavating their shallow skin burrows, causing them to dry out and die. When itching is due to infection, scratching can cause more soreness and more itching – a vicious circle.

A sneeze is a sudden exhalation like a cough, but directed through the nose. During a sneeze air leaves the nose at about 160 km/h (100 mph).

The cell lining of the passages in the nose is vulnerable to invasion by viruses and bacteria, which can give rise to respiratory infections. Local inflammation of these lining cells, with extra mucus production due to infection, results in irritation in the nasal cavity and the reflex response of a sneeze which can remove infected mucus. Sneezing is also brought on by irritants such as dust or pollen.

The coughing reflex is a rapid and strong exhalation through the open mouth caused by muscle contraction in the diaphragm. The expelled air forces particles and microbe-laden mucus out of the lungs and upper trachea.

A cough is triggered when particles of matter, such as inhaled foreign bodies or mucus resulting from increased secretion due to infection, stimulate the upper airways. The cilia-driven stream of mucus in the lungs, which delivers matter for coughing up, helps to protect the airways from inhaled particles and hostile microbes.

Bacteria look like dots even under powerful microscopes. Yet they are self-contained unicellular organisms. The bacterium E. coli (*right*) even has its own propulsion unit, a rotating flagellum. Bacteria can cause humans problems when their metabolic by-products are toxic.

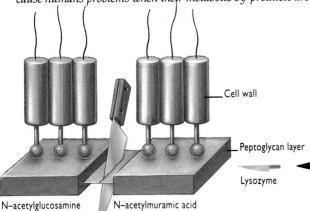

Cell wall

Peptoglycan layer

Lysozyme

N–acetylglucosamine

N–acetylmuramic acid

Cell membrane

Peptoglycan layer

Cell wall

Bacterium

Flagellum of bacterium

One of the innate defences present in the body all the time is the enzyme (protein catalyst) lysozyme. It is a protective enzyme that can be found in the secretions of all vertebrates – creatures with backbones. In people it is present in mucus secretions, tears, saliva and breast milk. These secretions are generally found at the open borders of the body where invading bacteria do not have to face the highly effective barrier of the skin. For instance, the saliva of the mouth has to deal with a large influx of bacteria every day.

Lysozyme is useful because of its ability to cut through a particular chemical bond found in one layer of the protective cell wall that surrounds most bacteria. In the so-called peptoglycan layer of the wall, lysozyme cuts the chemical link between two wall sub-units, N-acetylglucosamine and N-acetylmuramic acid. This breakdown is like removing all the mortar from a brick wall, causing the wall to collapse. With the bonding between the sub-units broken down, the bacterial wall falls to pieces and the bacterium is killed.

Tears are made in the lacrimal, or tear-producing, glands that lie above each eye. These glands constantly secrete tears which spread over the surface of the eyeball with each blink and then drain through tear ducts at the inner corner of each eye into the nose cavities.

Tear secretion keeps the eyes clean and moist, and lysozyme in the tears helps maintain the bacterial sterility of the eye surface. With intense irritation of the eye or pain localized elsewhere, the tear secretion rate increases and all the fluid cannot be handled by the tear ducts. Crying is the result – tears overflow the rim of the lower eyelids.

Vomiting happens when harmful substances in the stomach or duodenum are identified by receptors in the wall of the digestive tract.

The upper part of the stomach constricts and any movement down the digestive tract stops and reverses. Abdominal muscles contract, squeezing the stomach and pushing its contents past the sphincter at the bottom of the oesophagus and out through the mouth. The airway into the trachea is closed and the soft palate rises to shut off the nasal passages to stop vomit entering the lungs or nose.

Sentinels of immunity

Any disease-causing organism invading the body is in for a shock – the body's defences are ready for it.

In the front line of the immune system are our antibodies – and there are more than a million different types – watching out for any foreign material that enters the body. An antibody is a protein molecule that is able to recognize and stick onto a small, precisely defined part of another protein – normally only a protein fragment that is not part of its own body tissue. Once antibodies have recognized the alien proteins of invaders – the most important of which are disease-causing organisms, such as viruses, fungi, bacteria and parasites – the defensive machinery of the immune system goes into action. But why are there so many different antibodies, and why do they not recognize the proteins of their own body?

The cells that make antibodies are a class of lymphocyte (white blood cells formed in lymph tissues) known as B-cells. Each B-cell carries, on its surface, molecules of its own individual and specific antibody. During the early development of a baby in the womb, the genes that specify which antibody a B-cell will make undergo a type of

An individual B-cell makes copies of its own specific antibody and attaches them to the outer surface of its cell membrane. The antibodies extend outward like minute, highly tuned aerials waiting for contact with the specific bit of protein that they can recognize.

Antibodies

Variable region of light chain

Constant region of light chain

Constant region of heavy chain

Variable region of heavy chain

Antibody

Carbohydrate group

B-cell

Antigen-binding site

When a disease-causing organism gets into the body, its surface has proteins (antigens) that are different from those of the body's own tissues. There will thus be some B-cells whose antibodies recognize and stick to those antigens. When they do so the shape of the antibody's Y changes. Like a switch being turned on, this alteration activates the B-cell carrying the antibody and

causes it to divide. Huge numbers of cell "offspring" are produced as the cell divides; its progeny then divide, as do their progeny and so on. The copies have the same antibody-making ability as the parent B-cell. This means that the cell divisions rapidly increase the number of the body's B-cells that can respond to the invading organism.

Activated B-cells

Antigen

An antibody is made of two light and two heavy chains of amino acids (the sub-units of proteins) held together in a Y shape. The base of the Y is made of heavy chains; its arms are made of both light and heavy chains. The constant regions of chains are the same in many different types of antibodies. But the variable regions – the tips of the arms – each have a uniquely shaped cavity that fits exactly onto the shape of the antibody's "chosen" protein fragment.

When millions of copies have been made, most B-cells stop dividing and become plasma cells, a type of cell whose interior is packed with the apparatus to make one product – antibodies. These are not stuck to the surface of cells but are sent as free antibodies into the blood plasma, where they can come into contact with, recognize and bind to invading antigens.

Some of the dividing B-cells continue dividing indefinitely, keeping the population of cells that respond to the invading antigen "topped up" for a long period, usually many years. These cells are known as memory cells and are the basis of long-term immunity to a disease had in the past.

The shape of the "teeth" on a key fits only a specific lock. If the key is the wrong shape it will not work the lock. Like a key, an antibody must be the same shape as a fragment of protein on an invading antigen before it can recognize and stick to it. There are over a million different shapes of antibody, so there will always be at least one that will fit the shape of a piece of any antigen's protein.

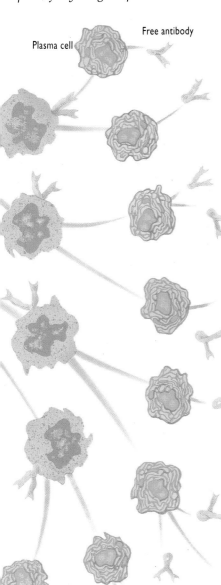

Plasma cell

Free antibody

Memory cell

IMMUNIZATION

The process of immunization artificially primes the immune system to repel disease organisms (pathogens) as soon as they come into contact with it. When the body is injected with antigens (foreign proteins) identical or very similar to those of the pathogen, B-cells are activated. They multiply, produce secreted antibodies and set up memory cells, even though the pathogen is not yet in the body. If the pathogen later invades the immunized person, the pre-existing antibodies and memory cells mount a massive, rapid attack, and the person does not succumb to the disease.

Often the material that is injected is a mild version of the real pathogen, which stimulates but does no harm. Alternatively, a close relative of the pathogen can be injected that induces immunity but does not cause the disease itself.

In immunization's early days, patients were injected with cowpox (a mild viral disease in humans). This switched on immune protection against the closely related and often lethal smallpox virus. Contemporary satirists lampooned the procedure.

Free antibodies manufactured in countless millions by plasma cells roam around in the blood and lymph fluid. When they bump into an invading antigen that they recognize, they bind onto it. Antigens with an antibody attached to them have been "branded" by the antibody in a way that means that other parts of the immune system know that the antigen should be attacked.

When an antibody binds onto its target antigen it changes shape. It is the shape change of the antibody that makes it "stick" to the outside of macrophages (large white blood cells that engulf and destroy foreign matter). A bacterium with an antibody adhering to it is easily engulfed and killed. This process by which invaders are made more "attractive" to macrophages by antibody attachment is known as opsonization.

genetic shuffling. The result of this is that each of the millions of early B-cells can make a different antibody – but only that one – each able to stick to a different protein fragment. But any B-cell that bumps into a protein that it recognizes, binds to it and dies. Since some of the antibodies will recognize proteins that are part of the foetus's body, this huge population of B-cells is reduced. By removing all the responding B-cells when the baby is in the womb – where there are no foreign proteins about – the body ensures that the remaining set of B-cells can only recognize foreign proteins, or antigens.

Macrophage

Helpers and killers

Moving into action against invading organisms is a deadly cocktail of cells that cooperate in the kill.

The immune system has many interlocking components, but its underlying sophistication and precision depend on two major weapon systems: antibodies and the cell-mediated immune system. The key players in cell-mediated immunity are the T-cells (lymphocytes, or white blood cells), but the process depends on a chain of interactions between various cell types.

First in the chain is an antigen-presenting cell (APC) that "eats" any foreign material in the body. Examples of APCs are macrophages – white blood cells found in most tissues that can engulf and destroy bacteria and other disease-causing agents (pathogens). They do this by taking them into a cavity, or vesicle, in their cytoplasm – the part of the cell outside the nucleus – and adding digestive chemicals to them. These chemicals break the bacteria into fragments of the proteins from which they were made, fragments that are now harmless, but which can also be utilized.

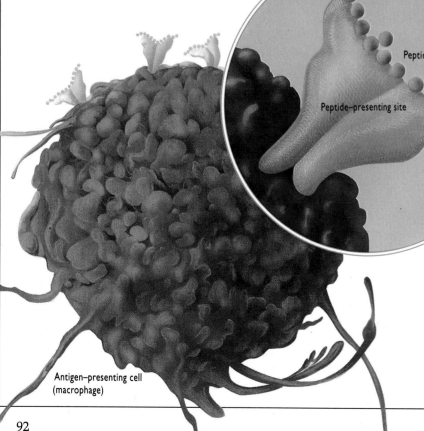

Antigen–presenting cell
(macrophage)

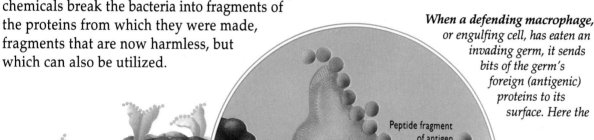

Peptide fragment
of antigen

Peptide–presenting site

When a defending macrophage, or engulfing cell, has eaten an invading germ, it sends bits of the germ's foreign (antigenic) proteins to its surface. Here the fragments, or peptides, are presented on the cell membrane stuck to a molecule of major histocompatibility (MHC) protein. Only when presented on an MHC molecule can the antigen fragment be recognized by a helper T-cell.

TISSUE TYPING

The major histocompatibility complex (MHC) proteins on the surface of human cells such as macrophages are extremely important in determining the "foreignness" of tissues during transplant surgery. Donor cells with identical MHC proteins to those of the recipient are least likely to be rejected after the transplant. This is why transplants between identical (genetically identical) twins are very rarely rejected.

When the transplant comes from a genetically non-identical donor it is important to match up MHCs as accurately as possible. This is done by "tissue-typing" the recipient and several possible donors. Once typing has been carried out, an organ from the donor with the closest match to the recipient is used for the transplant. If tissues are not very closely matched, it is highly likely that they will be attacked by the recipient's immune system, resulting in rejection.

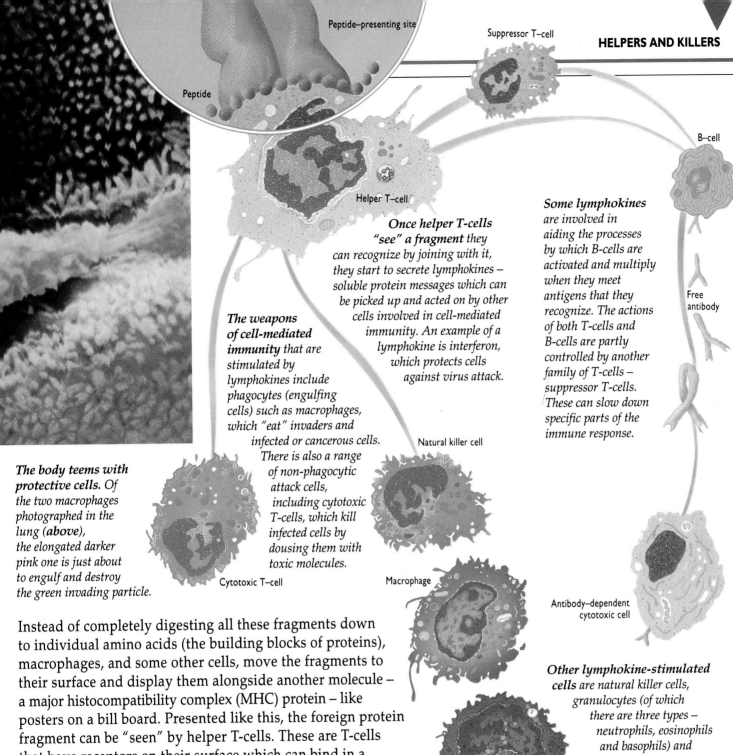

Peptide–presenting site

Peptide

Suppressor T–cell

Helper T–cell

B–cell

Free antibody

Natural killer cell

Cytotoxic T–cell

Macrophage

Antibody–dependent cytotoxic cell

Granulocyte

Once helper T-cells "see" a fragment they can recognize by joining with it, they start to secrete lymphokines – soluble protein messages which can be picked up and acted on by other cells involved in cell-mediated immunity. An example of a lymphokine is interferon, which protects cells against virus attack.

The weapons of cell-mediated immunity that are stimulated by lymphokines include phagocytes (engulfing cells) such as macrophages, which "eat" invaders and infected or cancerous cells. There is also a range of non-phagocytic attack cells, including cytotoxic T-cells, which kill infected cells by dousing them with toxic molecules.

Some lymphokines are involved in aiding the processes by which B-cells are activated and multiply when they meet antigens that they recognize. The actions of both T-cells and B-cells are partly controlled by another family of T-cells – suppressor T-cells. These can slow down specific parts of the immune response.

The body teems with protective cells. Of the two macrophages photographed in the lung (**above**), the elongated darker pink one is just about to engulf and destroy the green invading particle.

Other lymphokine-stimulated cells are natural killer cells, granulocytes (of which there are three types – neutrophils, eosinophils and basophils) and antibody-dependent cytotoxic cells that also kill infected cells. Neutrophils, in fact, make up over half of all white blood cells and they destroy invading cells by engulfing them. Cytotoxic cells secrete chemicals that make the contents of invading cells leak out, thus destroying them.

Instead of completely digesting all these fragments down to individual amino acids (the building blocks of proteins), macrophages, and some other cells, move the fragments to their surface and display them alongside another molecule – a major histocompatibility complex (MHC) protein – like posters on a bill board. Presented like this, the foreign protein fragment can be "seen" by helper T-cells. These are T-cells that have receptors on their surface which can bind in a "lock and key" fashion to the fragments. Each helper T-cell has a different receptor, so only some will respond to any particular displayed fragment.

Once they have bound to the fragments, helper T-cells are activated and they secrete proteins known as lymphokines. These act as chemical messages that enable other T-cells, B-cells and phagocytes (engulfing cells) to become active and fight against the foreign material in the body.

See also

CIRCULATION, MAINTENANCE AND DEFENCE
▶ Waste disposal 74/75

▶ Maintaining the system 80/81

▶ Repelling invaders 88/89

▶ Sentinels of immunity 90/91

▶ Knowing me, knowing you 94/95

ENERGY
▶ The cell and energy 56/57

BUILDING THE BRAIN
▶ Food for thought 188/189

STATES OF MIND
▶ Emotional states 276/277

Knowing me, knowing you

The immune system's ability to tell self from non-self, in terms of tissues, is not always a good thing.

Exquisitely precise, the defensive mechanisms of the human immune system are vital for our wellbeing. Antibodies, protective T-cells and phagocytes (engulfing cells) together provide defence against all types of invading pathogens and many types of cancer cells. But there are circumstances in which the system can cause problems: both in autoimmune diseases and following tissue and organ transplant, for example. Autoimmune diseases are ones in which our own tissues become damaged because our immune defences are inappropriately directed against them in a type of immunological "friendly fire". Examples of such diseases are multiple sclerosis and rheumatoid arthritis.

Tissue and organ transplants can be a potential problem for the immune system. Unless donor and recipient are one and the same person – in the case of a skin graft, for example – or the donor is an identical twin of the recipient, there is a strong possibility that some of the tissues of the transplant from the donor will be regarded as foreign by the immune system of the recipient. In such cases, with antibodies and T-cells targeting the transplanted tissue, their combined attack may cause the transplant to be rejected.

A number of approaches are used to overcome this problem. Some transplants, like the corneas of the eyes, contain no blood vessels or lymphatic vessels. This means that lymph- and blood-borne T-cells cannot get to the transplant, so it cannot be rejected. Because of this, cornea transplants between genetically non-identical people are usually successful.

When transplanted organs – a kidney, liver, lung or heart, for example – do have blood vessels, something has to be done to prevent rejection. Tissue typing is a checking procedure prior to the transplant to ensure that the donor's tissues are as similar as possible to the recipient's. This minimizes the "foreignness" of the transplant. Immunosuppressive drugs can also dampen down the rejection reaction. These drugs reduce the immune attack on the transplant in a number of ways. Some, like 6-mercaptopurine, inhibit the multiplication of white blood cells; others, such as cortisone, reduce inflammation; while cyclosporins reduce the activity of helper T-cells.

The body's immune defences attack matter made of proteins that are foreign to the body. A substance like Terylene (right) has no proteins in it so can be used to make artificial body parts.

A person donating blood is giving tissue to be transplanted. Blood is as much a tissue as the more obvious transplanted organs such as the heart, lungs and kidneys. It is also a tissue that can be donated easily. Most people can do it on a regular basis without feeling any ill-effects. Some people should not give blood, however, including those who have suffered from certain diseases such as hepatitis and those who are HIV positive.

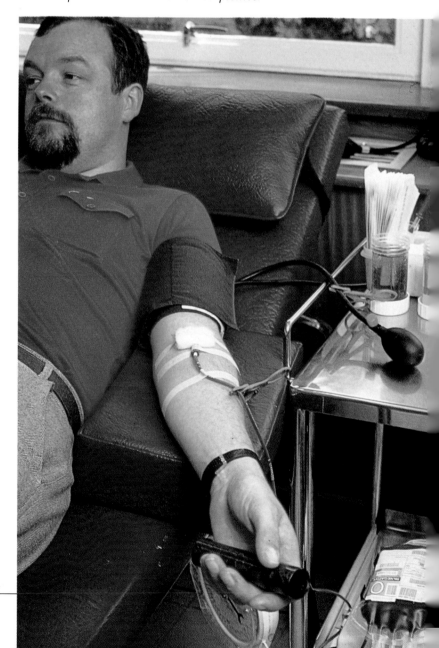

Non-living material can sometimes be successfully placed inside the body without the immune system attacking it. For this to occur the material introduced must be chemically inert, so that it does not react with substances in the body to corrode or break down.

It should also contain no organic substances that might be recognized as foreign by the immune system. Most of the materials used have surfaces that are ultra-smooth and chemically "uninteresting" to the immune system. Examples include stainless steel and titanium for bone prostheses, and the plastics Teflon and Terylene for heart valves and blood vessel walls.

The inert properties of these materials are also exploited in more everyday situations, like the non-stick Teflon coating of a frying pan and stainless steel in kitchen knives, the Terylene in clothing and the titanium of the outer case of a wristwatch.

Using such materials, scientists have been able to develop a number of artificial parts that can be used to replace human components. For instance, knee, hip, ankle, toe, finger and shoulder joints as well as inter-vertebral discs can be inserted where the body's own joints have become non-functional. Parts of the circulatory system, including major and minor arteries and the heart, can also be replaced. Testicular implants are available for cosmetic replacement of a missing testis. There is even a hydraulic implant available with a pump to inflate the penis where this is no longer possible by natural means.

THE CORRECT TYPE OF BLOOD

Often a life-saving procedure, the transfusion of donated blood into the circulatory system of a patient is the commonest type of tissue transplant. As with other types of tissue transplant, careful matching of the donor's and the recipient's blood types is necessary to ensure that transfused blood is not rejected.

In the early years of blood transfusion it was not understood why transfused blood was sometimes incompatible with that of the recipient. And by 1900, through the investigations of the Viennese pathologist Karl Landsteiner (1868–1943), it was realized that it was not possible to use blood safely from just any donor when giving blood to a particular patient. The reason for this is that there are many different blood types corresponding with the different types of proteins (antigens) on the surface of blood cells.

A person generally has one specific type of blood-cell antigen (the two main ones are termed A and B) and antibodies to the antigen or antigens they do not possess. This means, for instance, that someone with blood antigen type A has antibodies to B, those with blood type B have antibodies to A. People with both antigens, A and B, have antibodies to neither. Conversely, those with neither A nor B (the so-called O group) have antibodies to both. In transfusion, it is the antigens contained in the transfused blood that cause potential problems. If the recipient has antibodies to the transfused antigens, a dangerous immune reaction occurs, and the red cells clump together.

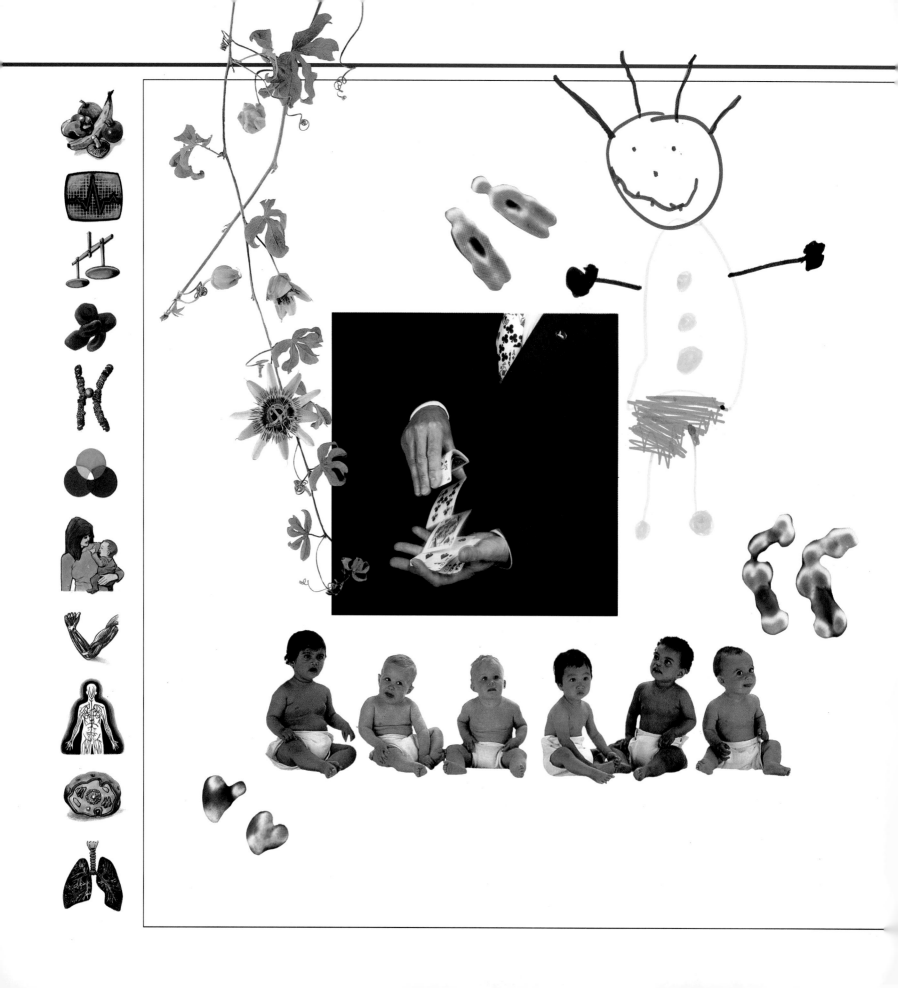

Reproduction and Growth

The cycle of life is repeated endlessly down the generations: people are born, mature, reproduce and, in the fullness of time, die. The story of human life from the fertilization of an egg by a sperm right up to adulthood is one of the most triumphant demonstrations of the complexity and precision of nature at work. And, as with most things to do with the human body, the crucial workings of the process take place at a cellular and molecular level. Despite its minute size, scientists have worked out how the information of heredity is stored, duplicated, passed on and then translated into the many types of tissue that make up a human. And this knowledge of genetics now places all of the stages and processes of reproduction and growth in a much clearer light.

Left (clockwise from top): *genetic material – the stuff of life; the learning process; starting out; the shuffling of genes; growing to a plan.*
This page (above): *nearly ready for the world;* **(right)** *DNA – instructions for life.*

Cradle to grave

The average human life span depends on a number of factors.

Extraordinary – and unpredictable – the story of a human life is altered and moulded by a range of far-reaching influences. For instance, the exact physical and intellectual development of individuals is influenced both by their genetic make-up and by the conditions – physical and cultural – in which they grow up. And while genes from parents certainly determine a great deal – from eye colour to the ability to roll the tongue into a tubelike shape – to a large extent they govern potentials rather than actual outcomes.

The effect of genetic traits is strongly modified by conditions in the environment that a person inhabits. Diseases, nutritional state, upbringing, social opportunities and a multitude of other factors all help to shape the final pattern of a person's life. For instance, the maximum height that people can attain is determined by their genes, but if they do not receive proper nutrition at the appropriate times in their life they will not reach it.

Maximum life span, like maximum height, would appear to be genetically programmed – the longest being about 110 years, although few people actually live to that age. But this too is highly influenced by environmental and social factors, as seen in the remarkable increase in life expectancy over the past 100 years, particularly in the developed, industrialized countries of the world. In the United States 100 years ago average life expectancy at birth was not more than middle age. In the last decade of the 20th century this has risen to almost 79 years for women and 71–72 years for men. Gradually, actual life spans are creeping toward the genetic potential.

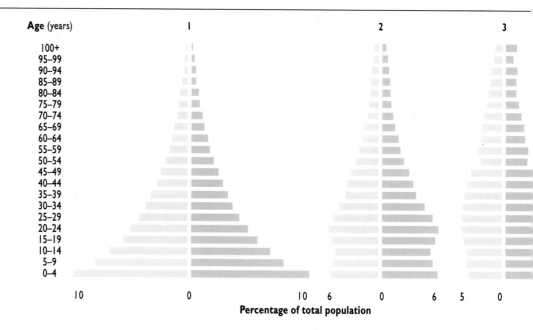

This increasing longevity is the result of a number of interlinked factors, including improved hygiene and clean water supplies. The introduction of sanitation systems and the use of immunization and drugs to control infectious diseases have also played a part. And better nutrition and an increased understanding of the effects of diet and the dangers of habits such as smoking have all contributed to the trend toward longer lives.

A bar chart showing percentages of people alive in five-year age ranges reveals the population structure of a country. A wide-based steeply tapering pyramid (1) is typical of an undeveloped country with high birth rates, high death rates generally and low life expectancy. The lower birth rate, lower death rates in childhood and large numbers of a considerable age in a developed country give a more even shape to the chart (3). A country in a mid-developmental stage (2) has an intermediate shape.

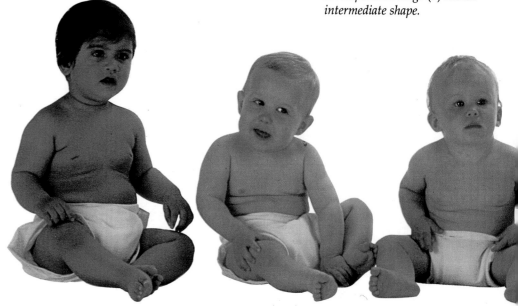

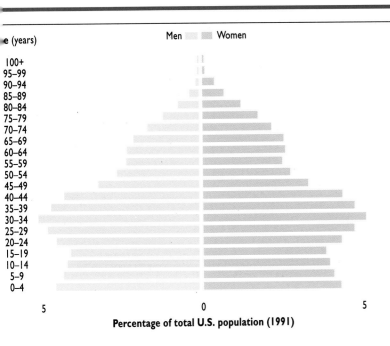

Men ☐ ☐ **Women**

e (years)

| 100+ |
| 95–99 |
| 90–94 |
| 85–89 |
| 80–84 |
| 75–79 |
| 70–74 |
| 65–69 |
| 60–64 |
| 55–59 |
| 50–54 |
| 45–49 |
| 40–44 |
| 35–39 |
| 30–34 |
| 25–29 |
| 20–24 |
| 15–19 |
| 10–14 |
| 5–9 |
| 0–4 |

5   0   5

Percentage of total U.S. population (1991)

The population chart for the United States of America in 1991 is typical of a developed country. It has some unusual features, however, including the bulge in the pyramid for people aged between about 20 and 45. Perhaps the most easily attributable cause of the bulge is the so-called baby boom that occurred after World War II. This accounts for the older people in the bulge, born shortly after their fathers returned from the war, and some of the people aged 20 or so, the children of the "baby boomers".

The faces of four people (right) photographed at three stages in their lives – childhood, adolescence and maturity – show how time brings about gradual changes in physical appearance. Despite obvious signs of ageing, each person is clearly identifiable at each stage, and his or her basic look – evidenced in facial structure and overall expression – remains remarkably and characteristically constant.

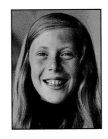

These six babies have their lives ahead of them. Already, though, their genetic inheritance, which gives them their potential abilities, is interacting with their environment to shape them into what they will become.

The babies, between five and nine months old, are embarked on the learning processes of childhood – already, for instance, they have learned how to sit up unaided. As the learning continues, growth and the accumulation of physical, communication and social skills will transform these totally dependent babies into self-reliant adults who might themselves have babies. How long they live will depend on what was programmed into them by their genes and on how their lives evolve. Some will reach close to their maximum life span and others will fall far short because of disease, perhaps caused by lifestyle or by factors imposed by the environment.

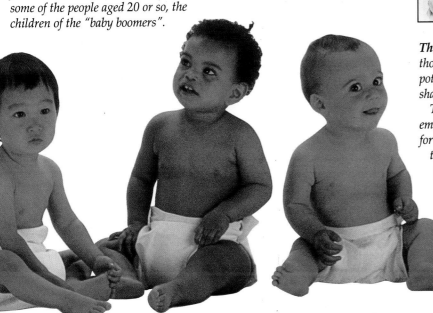
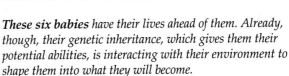

99

In the family

Similarities can be seen between parent and child, but everyone is unique.

Genes, made of DNA, determine height, skin, eye and hair colour, facial features and so on. We get these genes from our parents, and this simple fact explains the hereditary links between generations – children look like their parents because they share genes with them. A person's genes come together at the moment of fertilization and remain the same throughout their life. Half of the genes come from the father's sperm and half from the mother's egg.

In each body cell's nucleus, genes are arrayed along 46 chromosomes, which are arranged in 23 pairs. One chromosome in each pair is a replica of a maternal chromosome, the other a copy of a paternal one. Genes for specific functions are found at precise locations on particular chromosomes, and there are always two copies of any given gene, one on each chromosome of a pair. The two genes in a pair can be identical or different, and this arrangement influences a person's characteristics. A dominant gene is one that affects the body form even when it is paired with a different, or recessive, gene type. Only when a person has the same recessive gene on both chromosomes of a pair is the characteristic of the recessive gene apparent in their body.

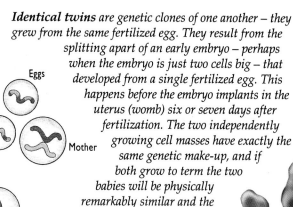

Two genetically identical embryos

Fertilized egg splits in two

Fertilized egg

Eggs

Mother

Sperm

Father

Identical twins are genetic clones of one another – they grew from the same fertilized egg. They result from the splitting apart of an early embryo – perhaps when the embryo is just two cells big – that developed from a single fertilized egg. This happens before the embryo implants in the uterus (womb) six or seven days after fertilization. The two independently growing cell masses have exactly the same genetic make-up, and if both grow to term the two babies will be physically remarkably similar and the same sex.

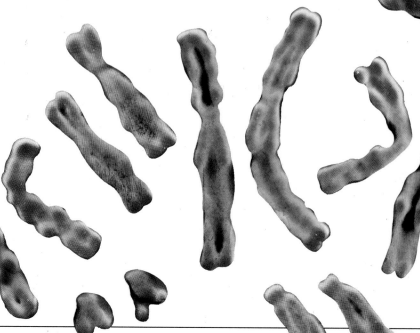

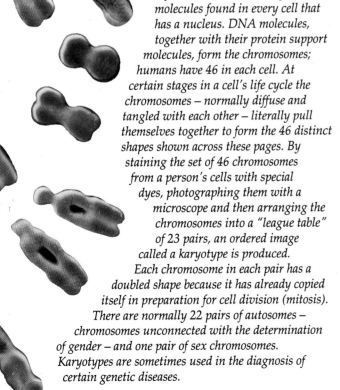

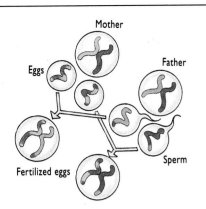

A woman's chromosomes are distinct from a man's, since there are two X sex chromosomes (**shown right**), instead of an X and a Y.

Sex chromosomes

Non-identical twins are born when two eggs, rather than one, are released at ovulation and both are fertilized. Since the two children that develop are the result of two different eggs being fertilized by two different sperm, they are not genetically identical. Indeed, they are no more alike than any two siblings. Non-identical twins may be of the same or different sex.

Each person's genetic information is carried by the DNA molecules found in every cell that has a nucleus. DNA molecules, together with their protein support molecules, form the chromosomes; humans have 46 in each cell. At certain stages in a cell's life cycle the chromosomes – normally diffuse and tangled with each other – literally pull themselves together to form the 46 distinct shapes shown across these pages. By staining the set of 46 chromosomes from a person's cells with special dyes, photographing them with a microscope and then arranging the chromosomes into a "league table" of 23 pairs, an ordered image called a karyotype is produced. Each chromosome in each pair has a doubled shape because it has already copied itself in preparation for cell division (mitosis). There are normally 22 pairs of autosomes – chromosomes unconnected with the determination of gender – and one pair of sex chromosomes. Karyotypes are sometimes used in the diagnosis of certain genetic diseases.

WHICH SEX?

A person's sex is determined when an egg from the mother is fertilized by a sperm from the father. Females have two X sex chromosomes (**see above**), while males have one X and one smaller Y chromosome. This means that a child's sex is specified solely by the nature of the sperm that fertilizes the egg from which the child develops.

The mother possesses no Y chromosomes so all her eggs will have only an X chromosome. By contrast, half of the man's sperm will possess an X chromosome, half a Y. If an X chromosome sperm fertilizes the egg, an XX, or female, embryo results. If a Y chromosome sperm is responsible for fertilization, this produces an XY, or male, embryo. The equal numbers of X and Y sperm in any population of sperm explains why, statistically, males and females are produced in almost equal numbers.

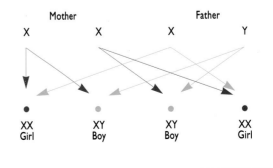

Language of life

The data of heredity is carried by a set of complex molecules that tells the body how to grow and live.

To build and run such an extraordinarily complex organic machine as a human being takes a vast set of instructions. And yet all the necessary knowledge is crammed into the nucleus of each and every human cell. The information is written in segments, or genes, of a set of huge deoxyribonucleic acid (DNA) molecules. In fact, the DNA molecules carry tens of thousands of genes, which are the instruction units of heredity. But DNA is not found on its own in a cell nucleus, it is linked to supporting protein molecules; the DNA molecules and their support proteins together make up chromosomes. The nucleus of each human cell has 23 pairs of chromosomes.

Each gene in a DNA molecule contains the coding for the manufacture of a specific protein – the molecules out of which our bodies are constructed. Each protein is made of a long, linear sequence of sub-units called amino acids; there are 20 different amino acids. The sequence of amino acids is defined by each gene in a list of instructions that spells out the structure of a protein.

The instructions are given in codes made up of four sub-units, or nucleotide bases, on the DNA molecule. There are four bases – adenine, thymine, cytosine and guanine – usually represented by the letters A, T, C and G. The codes consist of three-letter words. Every three-letter word that can be made using the four letters (such as AAT, GAT) either stands for an amino acid or is a signal to stop or start a protein chain.

All the information of human heredity – the instructions for how the body operates and the data for the construction, maintenance and everyday functioning of individual cells – is packaged into the nucleus of each individual cell, which itself is usually only a few thousandths of a millimetre across. This information, called the total human gene set, or genome, is carried on chromosomes – DNA molecules and protein support molecules. Each DNA molecule is made of an immensely long sequence of chemical sub-units, known as nucleotides. The genome contains around 6 billion nucleotides, divided between 46 DNA molecules.

Chromosomes, which can be seen when they are stained with dye and observed using high-power microscopes, spend most of their time as a diffuse network of extended filaments, known as chromatin. When a cell is dividing, chromosomes shrink down and form clearly recognizable paired units (*below*).

Chromosome pair

Coil of nucleosomes

Histone proteins

Nucleosome

For the DNA in the chromosomes to fit compactly into the nuclei, much of it is held in a complex coiled coil for most of the time. The basic double helix is wrapped around clusters of protein molecules known as histones to form a string of tiny "beads", or nucleosomes. Chains of nucleosomes are then coiled up.

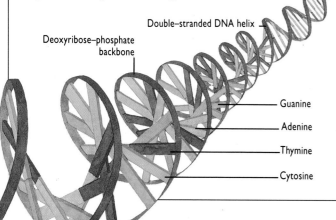

Double-stranded DNA helix

Deoxyribose–phosphate backbone

Guanine

Adenine

Thymine

Cytosine

DNA is a double spiral or helix shape, like a twisted ladder. It is made from the sub-units of DNA, called nucleotides. Each nucleotide is made up of a phosphate group, a sugar unit and one of four bases (adenine, guanine, thymine and cytosine). Each side of the ladder is made of a chain of alternating sugar and phosphate units. Two bases link between the sides to make the rungs.

MOLECULES OF HEREDITY FACT FILE

Written down, the genetic information in a cell's nucleus would be 3 billion words long, enough to fill 3,000 books of 1,000 pages with 1,000 words a page.

No. of		
	chromosome pairs	23
	nucleotides in DNA molecule	130 million (av.)
	base pairs in DNA molecule	65 million (av.)
	base pairs in total	3 billion (av.)
Possible 3-nucleotide permutations		64

Width of DNA helix 2 nm (80 billionths of an inch)
Gap between base pairs 0.34 nm (13 billionths of an inch)
Length of 1 twist of DNA spiral 3.4 nm (135 billionths of an inch)

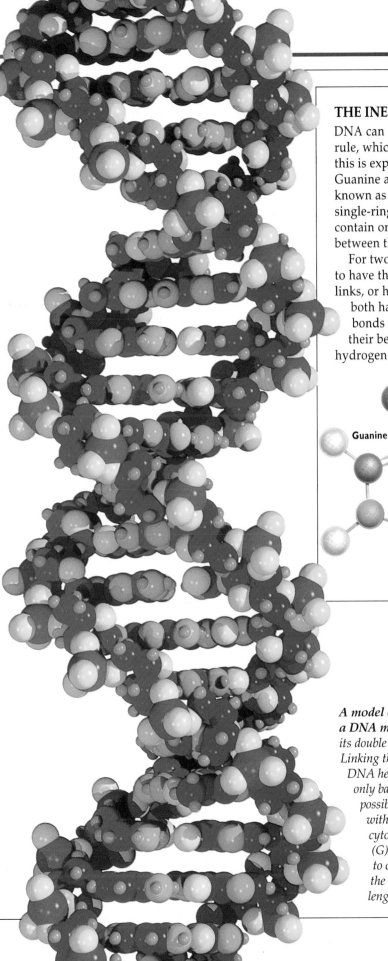

See also
REPRODUCTION AND GROWTH
▶ In the family
100/101

▶ Building bodies
104/105

▶ The sexual
advantage
106/107

▶ The growing
plan
114/115

▶ The future body
128/129

SUPPORT AND MOVEMENT
▶ Staying in shape
12/13

ENERGY
▶ The cell
and energy
56/57

CIRCULATION, MAINTENANCE AND DEFENCE
▶ Routine
replacement
82/83

INPUTS AND OUTPUTS
▶ The big picture
236/237

THE INEVITABLE LINKS

DNA can copy itself exactly because of the so-called base pairing rule, which states that A fits only with T, and C only with G; this is explained by the chemical structures of the DNA bases. Guanine and adenine are wider double-ring molecular sub-units known as purines, while cytosine and thymine are narrower single-ring units called pyrimidines. One rung of two bases has to contain one purine and one pyrimidine to be the right length to fit between the two strands of the DNA ladder.

For two bases to be able to "dock" with one another, they have to have the right arrangement of atoms to match the number of links, or hydrogen bonds, offered by the opposite base. A and T both have two bonds, so they can link; C and G both have three bonds and they, too, can link. But A cannot link with C, despite their being a purine–pyrimidine couple, because A forms two hydrogen bonds and C three – they are incompatible.

Carbon Nitrogen Hydrogen Oxygen

Guanine **Cytosine**

Hydrogen bond
between base pair

A model of a tiny section of a DNA molecule (left) shows its double helix construction. Linking the two sides of the DNA helix are the bases. The only base pairings which are possible are adenine (A) with thymine (T) and cytosine (C) with guanine (G). This enables DNA to copy itself when the molecule unzips lengthways down the middle, *since each base on each half can only link to one other base. Every A needs a replacement T and every G needs a C. Each strand of unzipped DNA thus picks up the missing bases (which are swirling around in the chemical "soup" of the nucleus) in the exact same order, creating two identical new DNA molecules. This capacity for molecular copying of genetic material underlies the reproduction of all life on Earth.*

Mitochondrion

Building bodies

How does the human genetic blueprint – written on molecules in the cell nucleus – become living tissue?

The structure and physical functioning of the different parts of the body are based upon the structure and functioning of tens of thousands of different proteins. Some of these, such as the digestive enzymes which break up the food we eat, perform specific metabolic jobs; others, like the proteins of muscle tissue, make up structural components of the body.

Proteins are made in the body's cells, and the instructions for their manufacture are stored in genes – segments of deoxyribonucleic acid (DNA) molecules which are found inside the nucleus of almost all body cells. Some genes carry plans for proteins with neither metabolic nor structural jobs. These are control proteins – they determine when other proteins should be made and when they should not. In effect their function is to switch on and off the genes that build specific proteins or groups of proteins. Some genes are switched on in all cells, but others only operate in specialized cells. For example, the genes that make digestive enzyme proteins are switched on in digestive system cells, and muscle-protein-making genes are switched on in muscle cells.

DNA thus contains the plans and instructions for the body. Under normal circumstances these plans not only do not change – if they

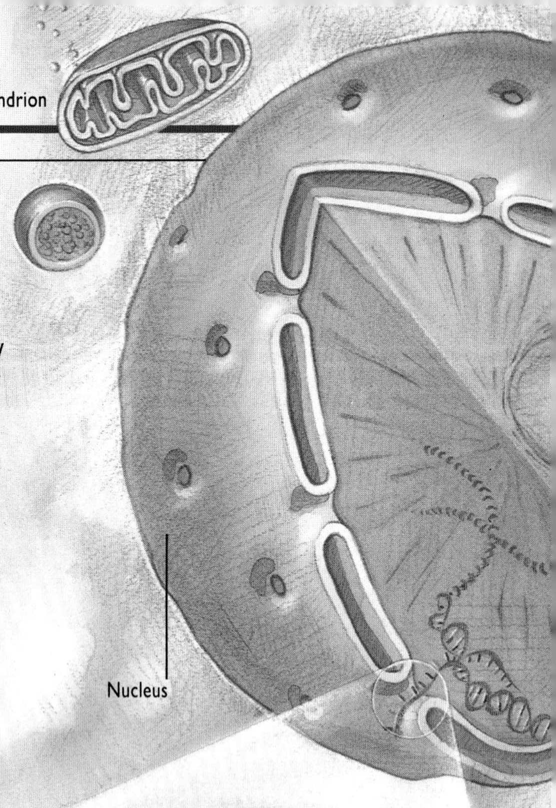

The nucleus of a cell holds genetic information carried by DNA molecules. On these are genes – sections of DNA which are instructions for the manufacture of an individual protein. When, for instance, a muscle cell makes the protein actin, which helps it contract, the gene that carries the instructions for actin making gets switched on. The DNA of the gene does not make the protein directly; the instructions are copied onto intermediary molecules of ribonucleic acid (RNA).

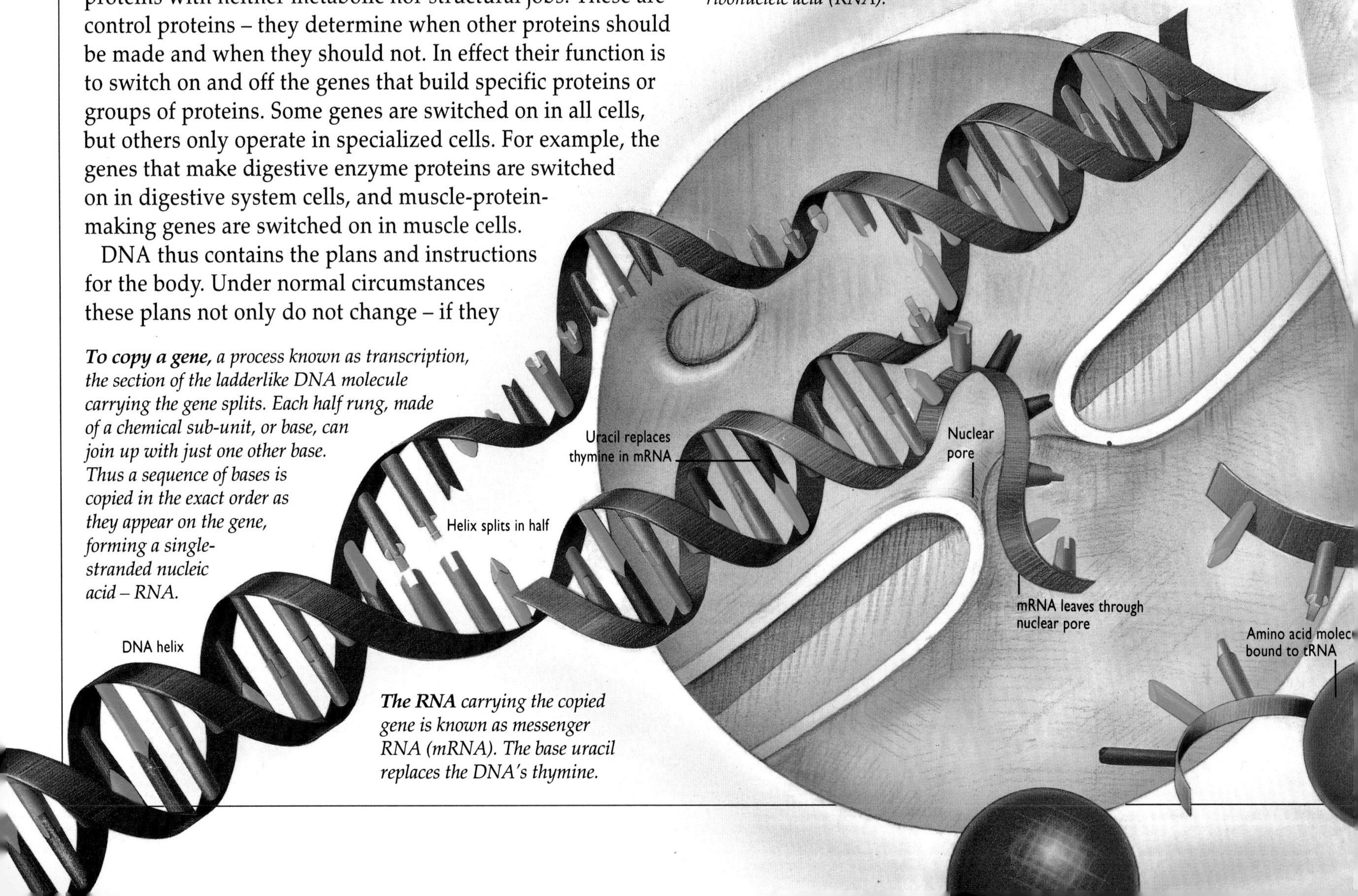

Nucleus

To copy a gene, a process known as transcription, the section of the ladderlike DNA molecule carrying the gene splits. Each half rung, made of a chemical sub-unit, or base, can join up with just one other base. Thus a sequence of bases is copied in the exact order as they appear on the gene, forming a single-stranded nucleic acid – RNA.

Uracil replaces thymine in mRNA

Nuclear pore

Helix splits in half

mRNA leaves through nuclear pore

Amino acid molec bound to tRNA

DNA helix

The RNA carrying the copied gene is known as messenger RNA (mRNA). The base uracil replaces the DNA's thymine.

Granular endoplasmic reticulum

Endoplasmic reticulum is an organelle, or structure, found in cells outside the nucleus. It is made of flattened sacs of membrane and it both circulates materials around the cell and acts as a store for enzymes (molecular catalysts) and proteins.

In some areas the outer surface of the reticulum is covered with thousands of tiny ribosomes, giving it a rough appearance. This is called granular endoplasmic reticulum.

Ribosomes are the actual sites of protein making.

They are hamburger-shaped structures, each consisting of a large and a small sub-unit, which contain roughly equal amounts of protein and a type of RNA known as ribosomal RNA (rRNA).

Ribosome

Large ribosomal sub–unit

Small ribosomal sub–unit

tRNA links with mRNA

Assembled protein chain

did the result would be mutation and chaos – but they also never leave the nucleus. So how does an activated (switched-on) protein-building gene bring about the manufacture of the protein for which it carries plans?

When a gene is activated in the nucleus, the first thing that happens is a process called transcription – a copy of that gene's instructions is made. The copy is created in the form of a molecule of messenger ribonucleic acid (mRNA). The mRNA moves out of the nucleus, through a nuclear pore, to a ribosome, a site where the information the mRNA carries is used to make the protein. In this process, known as translation, the chemical sub-units of the protein – amino acids – are brought together in the correct order and number with the help of molecules known as transfer ribonucleic acid (tRNA). After assembly the protein leaves the ribosome and goes to where it is needed.

Protein chain forms
actin fibre in muscle cell

After leaving the nucleus via nuclear pores, mRNA moves to a ribosome. Here the genetic code sequence in the mRNA is converted into the sequence of amino acids that make a protein molecule. Conversion of the mRNA code into a protein is known as translation. The process relies on the fact that every sequence of three bases along the DNA, and thus along the mRNA copy, is a code for an individual amino acid. For translation to occur, another type of

RNA, transfer RNA (tRNA), is needed. At one end of a tRNA molecule is a triplet of bases that corresponds to a code for an amino acid; at the other end of the tRNA is the amino acid itself.

On the ribosome, triplets of the mRNA base code are activated in sequence and link with the appropriate tRNA molecules which bring the amino acids. The many hundreds of triplet code words are rapidly changed into a sequence of amino acids to make a protein molecule, which then leaves the ribosome. In the case of actin, it forms part of the fibre in a muscle cell. Thus the DNA, which remains inside the nucleus, has been copied to make protein that makes part of a tissue.

The sexual advantage

All organisms of all species live by the same, inescapable, law of nature – reproduce or die out.

Every individual organism ultimately dies and the only way in which this can be partly overcome is to leave offspring that carry characteristics of the organism into the future. Many "simple" species reproduce asexually: individuals produce copies of themselves containing identical genetic information. But many species – humans included – reproduce sexually.

In humans the result of sexual intercourse is that an egg cell meets a sperm cell and a new, unique cell is made, a fertilized egg. Many cell divisions later, the egg becomes a baby. We take it for granted that a child shares some characteristics with its parents but has others that are unique to itself. In fact, apart from pairs of identical twins, each of the 5 to 6 billion people now alive is genetically unique. This is because of the two-part gene shuffling of sexual reproduction.

First, a human's genes are the result of the coming together of the gene sets of the egg and sperm, mixing together in one individual genes that were previously in separate individuals: the mother and father. Second, the production of the half gene set in each egg and sperm involves a type of shuffling, called meiosis, which precedes sperm and egg formation. In a normal cell there are 46 chromosomes (structures carrying the DNA molecules that spell out the genes) arranged in 23 pairs. Meiosis halves the chromosome number from 46 to 23 but each of the new 23 contains genes selected at random from one of the pairs. The assembling on one chromosome of genes that were previously on two separate parental ones is a process known as crossing over. The double shuffling of crossing over and egg–sperm union generates the almost infinite variety of humans.

But does sexual reproduction have any particular advantages over asexual reproduction? The answer, generally, is yes. While it may seem a less complicated way to replicate, asexual reproduction does have drawbacks. For instance, if conditions are favourable for identical organisms, all is well, but if a disease strikes to which they have no genetic resistance, they will all perish. By contrast, the chances are that at least some of the genetically varied offspring of sexual reproducers will be able to survive a disease that kills others, so the species as a whole will survive.

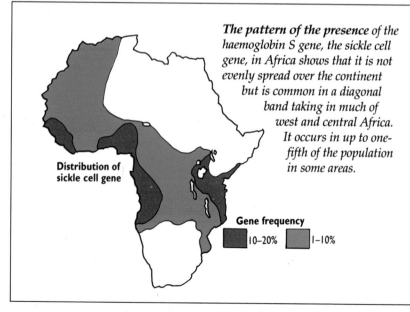

Distribution of sickle cell gene

The pattern of the presence of the haemoglobin S gene, the sickle cell gene, in Africa shows that it is not evenly spread over the continent but is common in a diagonal band taking in much of west and central Africa. It occurs in up to one-fifth of the population in some areas.

Gene frequency
10–20%   1–10%

Like the shuffling of genes in sexual reproduction, with each shuffle of a pack of 52 cards, a magician can deal out a different arrangement. We obtain half our genes from our mother and half from our father, and each half set has been just as well shuffled as the cards.

Sexual reproduction is not the only way to produce offspring. There are simpler non-sexual methods by which new plants or animals bud off from a parent. Since only one parent is involved in this process, it normally gives rise to offspring that are genetically identical with one another and the parent.

If a shoot, or cutting, is taken from a plant and placed in soil or water, a new plant will grow that is genetically the same as the parent plant. This method is vital for keeping the consistency of varieties of cultivated crop plants. The genetic make-up of particular types of apples (**right**) is originally formed by accidental or selective sexual breeding. Once a desirable form has been achieved it can be maintained indefinitely by non-sexual propagation techniques.

Malaria is a potentially lethal parasitic disease caused by rapidly multiplying protozoan parasites that live inside human red blood cells and destroy them. People become infected when they are bitten by an infected mosquito. But if the parasite enters a cell with sickle cell haemoglobin, the altered red blood cell cannot sustain the parasite, which dies instead of multiplying and causing malaria.

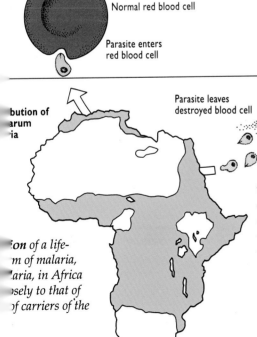

Parasite feeds on blood cell

Parasite multiplies

Normal red blood cell

Parasite enters red blood cell

Sickle blood cell

Parasite dies

Parasite leaves destroyed blood cell

bution of
arum
ia

ion of a life-
m of malaria,
aria, in Africa
osely to that of
f carriers of the

THE SICKLE CELL STORY

If a modified version of the gene that produces the haemoglobin molecule is inherited, sickle cell disease will result. The haemoglobin S gene, as it is called, differs sufficiently from the common gene to have profound effects on the red blood cells that contain haemoglobin S. They become stiff, less able to carry oxygen efficiently and often take up an irregular, crescent-moon shape, hence the name sickle cell. Altered red blood cells make the blood itself more viscous, thicker and prone to clog up small blood vessels. These changes can produce tiredness, pain and damage to tissues. The persistence of this apparently harmful gene in human populations is thought to be due to the protection it gives to people infected with the dangerous parasitic disease malaria. It seems that in areas of high malaria risk, the partial protection the gene provides for people infected with the disease offsets the disadvantages of the sickle cell disease.

Cycle of life

The sex organs – especially a woman's – are controlled and coordinated by subtle hormonal signalling.

Whether or not a woman of reproductive age becomes pregnant depends on two things above all. She cannot conceive if she has not produced an egg; neither can she conceive if there are no sperm around in her reproductive tract. Put simply, the male role in pregnancy is to produce and deliver sperm so one can meet the woman's egg and fertilize it. But the making of an egg is only part of a rather more intricate cycle of events that take place in the woman's body. For instance, the woman also has to provide a place for the fertilized egg to develop in her womb, or uterus.

The production of an egg or sperm takes place in a specialized form of cell division known as meiosis. Unlike mitosis, the ordinary type of division where an exact replica of a cell is made, in meiosis the genes on a cell's 23 pairs of chromosomes are first shuffled to produce genetic novelty. Then the number of chromosomes is halved as each half of a newly shuffled chromosome pair splits when the cell itself divides. The end result is cells with 23 instead of the usual 46 chromosomes. This happens so that when egg and sperm – each with a half set – combine at fertilization, the new cell has the full 46 chromosomes.

Men normally ejaculate between 300 and 500 million sperm at a time and can ejaculate many times each month. The level of the hormone responsible for sperm production – testosterone – remains relatively constant over time. Women, however, produce on average just one egg per month and the levels of the hormones responsible for egg production and the provision of a lining in the womb suitable for the nurturing of a fertilized egg change during the month.

Sperm (male sex cells) are made in the two testes, or testicles, which hang in a protective bag, the scrotum. Between each testicle and the penis is a system which first takes sperm up through the fine ducts of the epididymis into the vas deferens. There are two vasa deferentia – one from each testicle – which take sperm into the lower pelvic region. A number of accessory glands make nutritive and protective fluids with which the sperm are mixed to form semen. By far the bulk of semen is made of these fluids.

At the moment of ejaculation, muscles around the urethra contract involuntarily, squeezing semen out of the end of the penis in three or four rapid bursts, followed by a few less strong, irregular contractions.

There is more to semen – the fluid ejaculated on male orgasm – than sperm alone. The seminal vesicles and the prostate gland produce fluids that contain the sugar fructose, which provides energy for the swimming sperm, and alkaline substances that neutralize the acidic conditions in the vagina. The bulbourethral gland secretes a slippery fluid that leaks from the penis during sexual arousal to lubricate intercourse.

Vas deferens
Bladder
Ampulla of vas deferens
Seminal vesicle
Prostate gland
Bulbourethral gland
Epididymis
Efferent duct
Vas deferens
Urethra
Testis
Scrotum

Each testis – divided into lobules – holds nearly 1,000 tiny seminiferous tubules in which sperm are formed. A sperm takes two months to form, but the production rate is vast – up to 500 million are released per ejaculation.

Lobule
Seminiferous tubule
Sperm
Secondary spermatocyte
Primary spermatocyte
Spermatogonium
Basement membrane

Spermatogonia cells divide producing primary then secondary spermatocytes, which become sperm.

THE MENSTRUAL CYCLE

Female sex organs are more intricate than those of the male and they also fulfil a more complicated, multistage series of tasks. The two ovaries produce eggs – female sex cells, or secondary oocytes. These are normally released singly from alternate ovaries – in a process known as ovulation – in a monthly cycle, the menstrual cycle. At puberty a woman has about 200,000 oocytes but she only releases about 500 of them during her reproductive life span up to the menopause. The number of oocytes is determined during foetal development: a woman cannot "make" more eggs.

Egg development takes place in a follicle, a glandular sac, which has an important role. Not only does it contain and then release a matured egg but it also releases hormones that regulate several other processes. For instance, prior to egg release the follicle makes large amounts of the hormone oestrogen. This stimulates the lining of the uterus to make itself receptive to an egg, should one be fertilized. And after egg release, the follicle, now called the corpus luteum, continues to make oestrogen and starts to make progesterone, which maintains the uterus lining. If an egg is not fertilized, the prepared lining breaks down and is shed in a monthly process known as menstruation, or bleeding, which lasts a few days.

Hormones play the key role in the timing of events during the 28-day menstrual cycle. The start of bleeding is usually taken as the start of the cycle. In the first few days, raised levels of luteinizing hormone (LH) and follicle-stimulating hormone (FSH) – both made in the pituitary gland – cause follicles to develop in the ovaries. By about day six, one follicle – the most developed – is "selected". It starts making oestrogen, which rebuilds the lining of the womb in the pre-ovulatory phase.

A rise in oestrogen levels on about day 12 raises the LH and FSH levels, and this prepares the follicle and egg for release. On about day 14 ovulation happens. The corpus luteum formed from the follicle now makes high levels of oestrogen and progesterone to maintain the uterine lining in the post-ovulatory phase. But after 28 days the corpus luteum degenerates (unless the egg is fertilized), oestrogen and progesterone levels drop, the uterus lining breaks down and menstrual bleeding takes place.

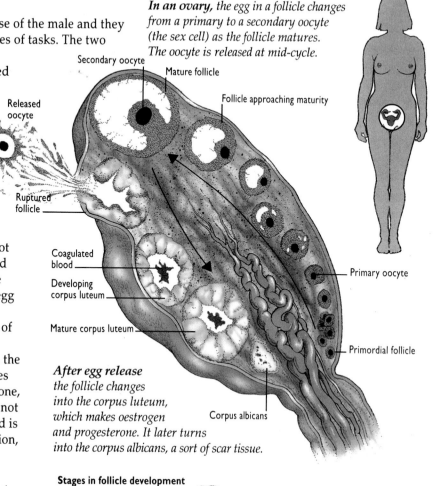

In an ovary, the egg in a follicle changes from a primary to a secondary oocyte (the sex cell) as the follicle matures. The oocyte is released at mid-cycle.

Secondary oocyte
Mature follicle
Follicle approaching maturity
Released oocyte
Ruptured follicle
Coagulated blood
Developing corpus luteum
Mature corpus luteum
Primary oocyte
Primordial follicle

After egg release the follicle changes into the corpus luteum, which makes oestrogen and progesterone. It later turns into the corpus albicans, a sort of scar tissue.

Corpus albicans

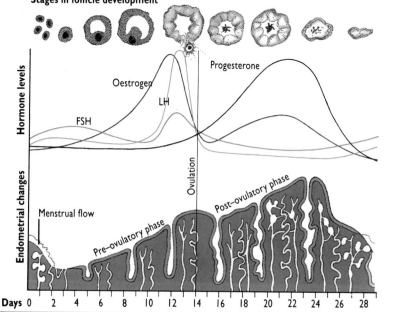

Stages in follicle development

Hormone levels

Oestrogen
Progesterone
LH
FSH

Endometrial changes

Ovulation
Menstrual flow
Pre-ovulatory phase
Post-ovulatory phase

Days 0 2 4 6 8 10 12 14 16 18 20 22 24 26 28

Fertilization

Each of us starts as a single microscopic cell – an egg fertilized by the winner of an amazing competition.

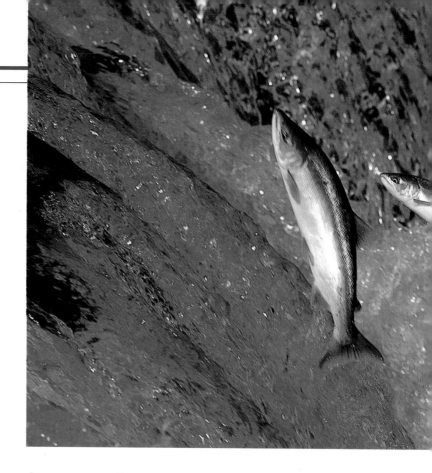

When fertilization takes place an egg from a woman and a sperm from a man meet and fuse, marking the beginning of the life of a human being. The fusion of the two cells normally takes place in one of the two Fallopian, or uterine, tubes that link a woman's ovaries to her uterus, or womb. This meeting in the right place at the right time is the result of two quite different journeys.

The journey of the egg – a relatively large spherical cell surrounded by a jellylike coat, or zona pellucida – starts when it is released from an ovary. The egg cannot move by itself. Instead, it is carried along by waving cilia – hairlike extensions of cells on the walls of the female reproductive tract. Cilia on the fingerlike fimbriae at the open end of each Fallopian tube waft the egg from the ovary into the tube. Additional cilia on the inner wall of the tube move the egg along the tube like a pearl on a conveyor belt.

Meanwhile, coming in the opposite direction are the sperm, delivered into the vagina when a man ejaculates during sexual intercourse. Not only do they have a longer journey than the egg but they also make it under their own steam. Hundreds of millions of sperm are released together during one ejaculation to become competitors racing to gain the prize of fertilizing the egg in the Fallopian tube some 15–20 cm (6–8 inches) away from the upper vagina. Only one sperm wins.

Each sperm is potentially capable of swimming to the top of the vaginal canal, through the mucus in the cervical canal that leads from the vagina to the uterus, up through the uterus itself and, finally, into the Fallopian tubes. This 20-cm (8-inch) journey is some 4,000 times the length of the 0.05-mm (1/500-inch) long sperm cell and is equivalent to a 1-m (3-foot) eel swimming 4 km (2½ miles). The trip probably takes between one and five hours for the fastest, most successful sperm. They swim through the fluid contents of the female tract by beating their propulsive tails (flagella). The long distance, the acid conditions in the tract and the cilia of

the uterine wall beating in the opposite direction to their own movement mean that the hundreds of millions of sperm in the vagina are reduced to a few hundred or even less in the region of the Fallopian tubes where fertilization occurs. At fertilization the genetic information in sperm and egg, from father and mother respectively, joins together and as the newly fertilized egg makes its first cell division, embryonic development begins. Approximately six or so days later the egg implants in the uterus and pregnancy begins.

On average about 400 million sperm are ejaculated into the vagina, of which some 350 million are actively swimming and viable. Only 10,000 or so make it through the cervical canal to the uterus. Of these perhaps 1,000 to 3,000 get to the upper parts of the uterus and then turn left or right into the Fallopian tubes. In the area of most likely fertilization, the upper region of a Fallopian tube, there may be only about 100 sperm in the vicinity of the egg.

400 million ejaculated

10,000 reach uterus

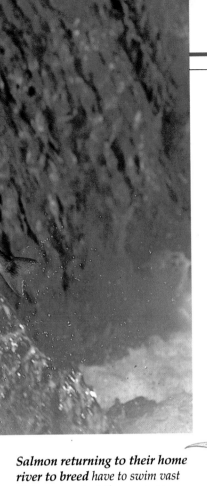

WINNER TAKES ALL

The head of the tadpolelike sperm has a nucleus and an acrosome – a region at its tip that helps it penetrate the ovum, or egg. Once the sperm reaches the egg cell membrane, the acrosome opens up to release enzymes which eat a path through the jellylike zona pellucida. The sperm nucleus leaves its propelling tail behind and merges with the nucleus of the egg to fertilize it. After fertilization, changes in the egg's cell membrane and zona pellucida stop other sperm entering.

Sperm nucleus

Acrosome and plasma membrane fuse

Acrosome releases acrosin

Ovum

Nucleus

Sperm

Zona pellucida

Nucleus

Plasma membrane

The sperm attaches head first to the outer surface of the zona pellucida via special binding proteins.

One sperm fertilizes ovum

Salmon returning to their home river to breed have to swim vast distances against the current to reach their upstream spawning grounds. "Shoals" of sperm have to make a similar hazardous journey from vagina to Fallopian tube where one successful sperm might fuse with an egg.

10 wear down zona pellucida

36 hours 2–cell stage

3 days 8–cell stage

4 days 64–cell stage

Fallopian tube

100 reach vicinity of ovum

Ovum

Ovary

Uterus

Implantation in uterus lining

Although only one sperm actually fuses with the egg, other sperm may help it by weakening the egg's jellylike coat (zona pellucida). Once fertilized, the egg travels down the Fallopian tube and embryonic development begins. When the embryo reaches the uterus, some four days after fertilization, it is a ball of 64 cells. By five or six days a hollow blastocyst has formed and the embryo attaches itself to the uterus wall in a process known as implantation.

2,000 reach Fallopian tube

5–6 days Blastocyst forms

The first month

Within just four weeks the entire foetal support system has formed in the womb.

For about six days after a human egg has been fertilized by a sperm, the resulting embryo develops as a free clump of cells. At this stage the minute embryo is not in direct contact with its mother's tissues but is floating in the fluid inside one of the Fallopian tubes (the tubes leading from the ovaries) or in the uterus (the womb).

At six days the early embryo is known as a blastocyst. It is a tiny hollow ball and has an inner cell mass, the embryoblast, concentrated at one end. This inner cell mass will become the new baby; the outer cells of the ball – the trophectoderm or trophoblast – will later help to form the placenta, which will nourish the growing foetus. Both the trophoblast cells and the embryoblast cells have come from the original fertilized egg which has by now divided many times.

This early stage of development in the womb already shows the subtle complexities of human embryology. The fertilized egg not only generates a baby, which will ultimately be an independent, unique human being, but is also responsible for the formation of the placenta, which is not part of the baby itself. In fact, the situation is even more complex. The trophoblast cells form four membrane systems – the foetal or extraembryonic membranes – none of which is part of the foetus itself. These membranes – the chorion, amnion, allantois and yolk sac – protect and support the developing baby. The chorion, together with uterine tissue, forms the placenta itself. The amnion provides the foetus with a protective, fluid-filled space for growth. And the allantois – part of the body stalk – and yolk sac eventually form the umbilical cord.

By day seven after fertilization the blastocyst has become attached to the inner lining of the uterus – the endometrium – in a process known as implantation. Eventually the blastocyst is entirely surrounded by uterine tissue, which brings the developing foetus into contact with sources of nutrients and oxygen and provides a means of removing waste products. Initially this happens through contact between the outer cells of the blastocyst – the trophoblast cells – and blood vessels in the endometrium; later it is through the placenta.

If fertilization and implantation do not occur, the womb lining is shed in a monthly process known as menstruation. A fertilized egg, however, is equipped to produce a special hormone – human chorionic gonadotrophin – which prevents this from happening. As a result, menstruation ceases from the moment of fertilization until a few weeks after the baby is born – the endometrium is not sloughed off and the embryo continues to develop.

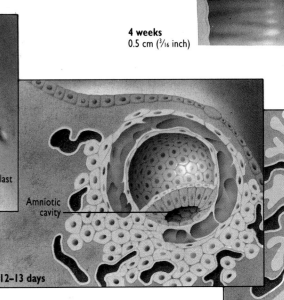

4 weeks
0.5 cm (³⁄₁₆ inch)

Labels: Amniotic cavity, Chorion, Uterine cavity, Chorionic cavity, Amnion, Placenta, Mucous plug, Cervix

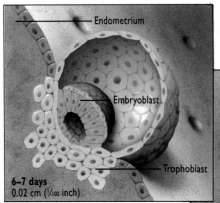

Labels: Endometrium, Embryoblast, Trophoblast

6–7 days
0.02 cm (¹⁄₁₀₀ inch)

At 6–7 days the trophoblast cells become attached to the endometrium – the lining of the uterus. A week later, at 12–13 days, the trophoblast is completely enclosed by uterine tissues and implantation is complete. The protective amniotic cavity starts to form.

Labels: Amniotic cavity

12–13 days

At 14–15 days chorionic villi reach uterine blood vessels. The body stalk (which will form part of the umbilical cord) and the primitive streak (which will form the baby) appear.

14–15 days
0.25 cm (¹⁄₁₀ inch)

The human embryo in position in the uterus about four weeks after fertilization is usually less than 0.5 cm (³/₁₆ inch) long, although it already has developing eyes and a functioning heart. The great thickness of the muscular wall of the uterus, together with multiple protective membranes and fluid in both the amniotic and chorionic cavities, cushion the embryo from knocks and shocks. The outer of these membranes, the chorion, has penetrated the surrounding uterine tissue to make contact with maternal blood vessels. In one area, the placenta, this contact becomes highly organized, so the embryo can gather oxygen and nutrients from its mother's bloodstream and discharge its waste products into her blood so that she can discard them. The cervix – the entrance to the uterus – is sealed by a plug of mucus.

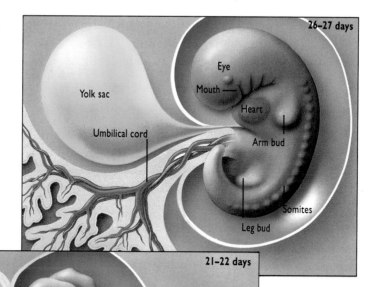

26–27 days

Eye
Mouth
Heart
Arm bud
Yolk sac
Umbilical cord
Somites
Leg bud

21–22 days

Somites

At 26–27 days the embryo has in miniature the beginnings of most organ systems – limb buds, a heart and a head with eyes and a mouth. The umbilical cord, linked to the placenta, provides a supply of blood and nutrients. This is just one of the life-support systems for the embryo established during the first month after fertilization.

18–19 days

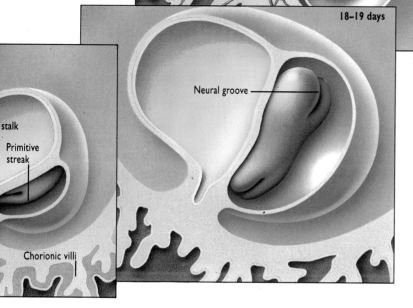

stalk
Primitive streak
Neural groove
Chorionic villi

At 21–22 days, just three weeks after fertilization, paired tissue blocks known as somites begin to form. These lay down a pattern of nerves and muscles in the body of the developing embryo. Proper blood vessels are now present in the umbilical cord, which connects the embryo to the placenta.

At 18–19 days a neural groove forms on the dorsal (back) surface of the embryo. This is the beginning of the development of the baby's nervous system. At this stage, growth is rapid, and cells in the embryo – nourished by blood from the maternal blood vessels – divide quickly to produce new tissue.

113

The growing plan

How do cells, which hold the genetic information to perform any role, specialize in structure and function?

In humans a single fertilized egg divides, then divides again and again, multiplying over and over until there are billions of cells. In a coordinated sequence, controlled by genes, these cells become organized into tissues, organs and organ systems. Most of this sorting out process, or cellular differentiation, happens when the human embryo is minute, buried among protective membranes and fluids deep in its mother's womb.

Genes are passed in identical form from the original fertilized egg to every subsequent cell. They carry a complete set of the genetic instructions for making the many tens of thousands of different human proteins. These are the building blocks, machine tools and control chemicals used to construct the body. What makes cells different is which of the many proteins they actually make. Muscle cells in the biceps, for instance, have to make contractile proteins, whereas cells in the adrenal glands must be able to secrete adrenaline.

Which genes are switched on – and thus which proteins are made – in a cell is a process that is itself controlled by genes. The control genes make proteins that activate sets of genes that in turn make the proteins that are appropriate for the type of cell.

The differentiation process starts a week or so after fertilization, when the early embryo – no more than a ball of cells – folds up into layers. Cells are programmed to move to a region of the early embryo that determines their range of differentiation possibilities. These regions are given the names ectoderm, mesoderm and endoderm because they correlate with cell layers (the names refer to outer, middle and inner cell layers).

Once committed to a layer, and thus to a particular range of possibilities, a

developing cell cannot normally change its fate by moving into a different set. An embryonic ectoderm cell, for instance, may eventually form a skin cell or a nerve cell but it cannot change into a muscle cell or a liver cell, which come, respectively, from the mesoderm and endoderm regions.

Scientists are beginning to identify the genes that first determine the range of possibilities of cells in the embryo and then further differentiate them into specific tissue types and organs. To the surprise of many, the controlling genes for major structural characteristics, such as head to tail differentiation in animals, are shared by almost all animals: very similar genes control the pattern of development in fruit flies, mice and humans. One family of these genes are the so-called homeobox genes which code for control proteins that help specify the position of organs in an animal. These proteins seem to act as signals to cells, making them switch on different subsets of the total gene set depending on their own positions in the body.

Studies of flowers *have thrown light on how cells differentiate. The sepals, petals, stamens and carpels of a typical flower – such as the passion flower (***below*** and ***right***) – are made of cells that are the descendants of cells that were once identical. The early cells of the flower bud switch on one of three control genes, depending on the distance from the bud's tips, with concentric rings of activation A, B and C. From then on, the fates of all the cells in the bud are set, because the protein products of the control genes switch on genes in bud cells that form different flower structures. Those cells that receive only an A signal make sepals at the base of the flower; those that get A and B together make petals; B and C signals mixed induce stamen formation; while C alone at the centre of the flower causes carpels to form.*

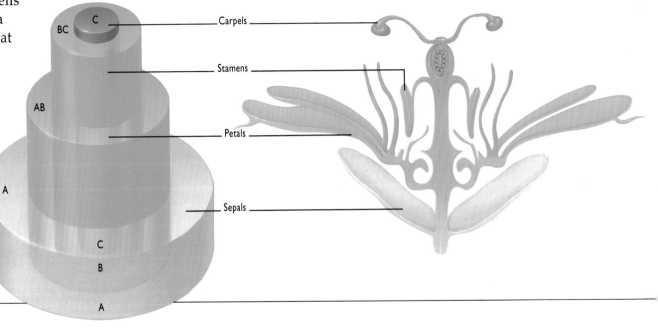

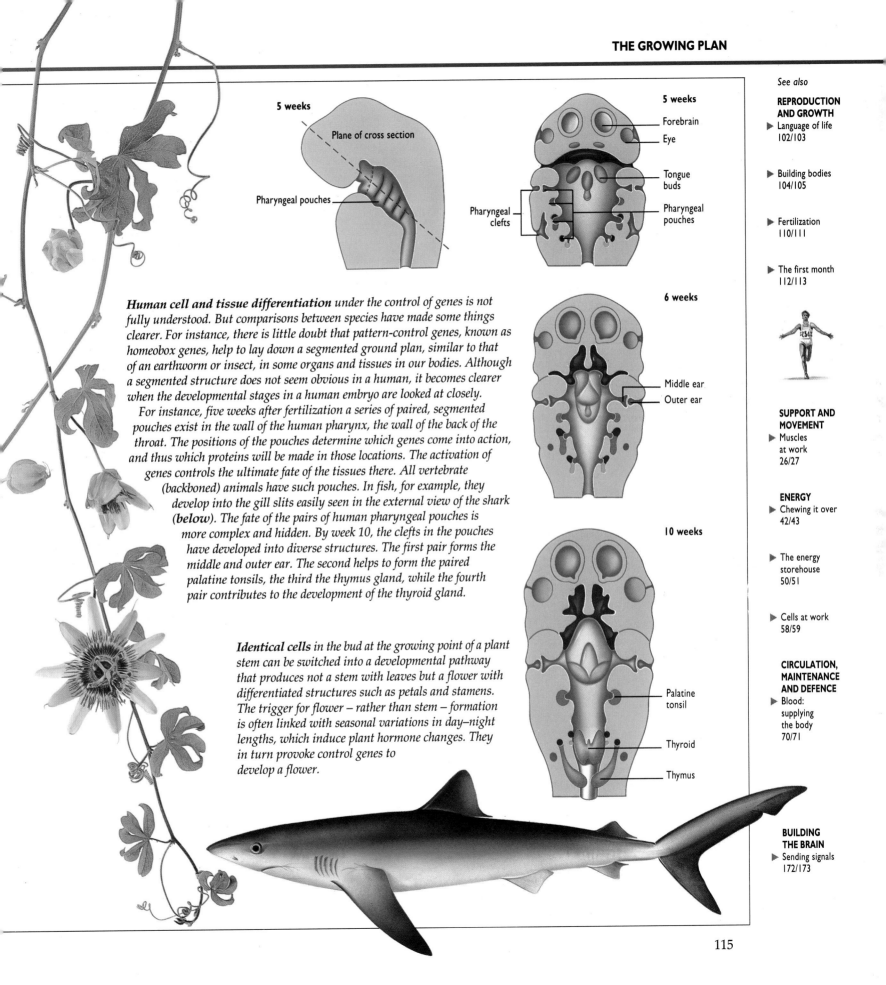

5 weeks

Plane of cross section

Pharyngeal pouches

5 weeks

Forebrain

Eye

Tongue buds

Pharyngeal clefts

Pharyngeal pouches

6 weeks

Middle ear

Outer ear

10 weeks

Palatine tonsil

Thyroid

Thymus

Human cell and tissue differentiation under the control of genes is not fully understood. But comparisons between species have made some things clearer. For instance, there is little doubt that pattern-control genes, known as homeobox genes, help to lay down a segmented ground plan, similar to that of an earthworm or insect, in some organs and tissues in our bodies. Although a segmented structure does not seem obvious in a human, it becomes clearer when the developmental stages in a human embryo are looked at closely.

For instance, five weeks after fertilization a series of paired, segmented pouches exist in the wall of the human pharynx, the wall of the back of the throat. The positions of the pouches determine which genes come into action, and thus which proteins will be made in those locations. The activation of genes controls the ultimate fate of the tissues there. All vertebrate (backboned) animals have such pouches. In fish, for example, they develop into the gill slits easily seen in the external view of the shark (**below**). The fate of the pairs of human pharyngeal pouches is more complex and hidden. By week 10, the clefts in the pouches have developed into diverse structures. The first pair forms the middle and outer ear. The second helps to form the paired palatine tonsils, the third the thymus gland, while the fourth pair contributes to the development of the thyroid gland.

Identical cells in the bud at the growing point of a plant stem can be switched into a developmental pathway that produces not a stem with leaves but a flower with differentiated structures such as petals and stamens. The trigger for flower – rather than stem – formation is often linked with seasonal variations in day–night lengths, which induce plant hormone changes. They in turn provoke control genes to develop a flower.

See also

REPRODUCTION AND GROWTH
▶ Language of life 102/103

▶ Building bodies 104/105

▶ Fertilization 110/111

▶ The first month 112/113

SUPPORT AND MOVEMENT
▶ Muscles at work 26/27

ENERGY
▶ Chewing it over 42/43

▶ The energy storehouse 50/51

▶ Cells at work 58/59

CIRCULATION, MAINTENANCE AND DEFENCE
▶ Blood: supplying the body 70/71

BUILDING THE BRAIN
▶ Sending signals 172/173

115

Baby in waiting

In just two-thirds of a year a fully formed human being grows from something the size of a fingertip.

About eight weeks after fertilization the embryo has the external characteristics of a recognizably human infant. It is, however, only about 2.3 cm (1 inch) long and is totally dependent on its umbilical link with the placenta and the protective fluid and membranes around it. At about this time it becomes known as a foetus rather than an embryo.

By now most of the different types of tissues that will make up the baby have already formed, so during the rest of the mother's pregnancy the foetus grows – remarkably fast. Fuelled by nutrients from the uterus, the foetus increases in weight from about 25 g (1 ounce) at eight weeks to more than 3 kg (7 pounds) at term – an increase of about 120 times in bulk in just seven months.

Item by item, the detailed modelling of the bodily features of a human occurs. Hair, eyebrows and eyelashes are in place in the 20th week. After that fingernails and toenails form. Downy hair, or lanugo, peculiar to the foetal period, soon covers the baby's torso and limbs. From 20 weeks onward, the foetus's heartbeat can be picked up using a sensitive stethoscope. Miniature lungs have now formed, but they are filled with fluid and cannot yet act as respiratory organs. The hands start to show the gripping reflex and a mother feels tiny kicks. By about 24 weeks the foetus is sufficiently developed to be able to stand a chance of survival outside the womb if it is intensively supported in a hospital incubator.

The body proportions of the growing foetus vary considerably. Six weeks after fertilization there is still a yolk stalk, a head as large as the rest of the body and a long tail beyond the legs. The foetus at eight weeks has a gigantic head, a small body and tiny limbs. As time passes, the foetal limb buds grow at a faster rate than the rest of the body until they reach their infant proportions; meanwhile the fingers and toes form. By 16 weeks, although the ever-vital umbilical cord joined to the placenta is still in place, the foetus's proportions are almost those of a baby at the end of pregnancy. It has proper ears, eyelids, fingers and toes.

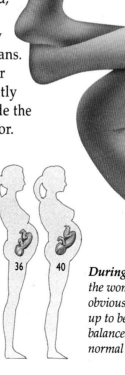

6 weeks
1.3 cm (½ inch)

8 weeks
2.3 cm (1 inch)

9 weeks
5 cm (2 inches)

16 weeks
14 cm (5½ inches)

Weeks after fertilization

4   8   12   16   20   24   28   32   36   40

During the 40 weeks of pregnancy there is a radical change in the size of the womb and of the baby inside. After about 16 weeks the "bump" becomes obvious and the woman looks pregnant. At 36 weeks the uterus has risen up to be level with the woman's ribs and she has to lean backward to stay balanced when standing up. After birth the uterus shrinks back to its normal non-pregnant dimensions in about six weeks.

Most babies are born head first and by 28 weeks after fertilization many are already positioned head down in the womb ready for birth. The baby is cushioned by amniotic fluid, and the neck of the womb, or cervix, is sealed by a plug of mucus.

Umbilical cord

Baby surrounded by amniotic fluid

Intervillus space

Villi in cross section

28 weeks
Actual size

Cervix

Mucous plug

External view of villi

Blood to baby
Blood from baby
Blood to mother
Blood from mother

The mother's blood seeps into the placenta's intervillus spaces. Nutrients, oxygen and waste products are exchanged between mother and baby via villi.

THE PLACENTA – LIFE-SUPPORT FOR A BABY

A temporary organ that supplies the growing foetus with all it needs to develop, the placenta (or afterbirth, as it is known when it is expelled from the uterus after a baby is born) grows until the fifth month of pregnancy. From its centre the umbilical cord connects it with the baby. A fully formed placenta weighs about 450 g (1 pound) and is close to 20 cm (8 inches) in diameter.

The placenta provides a huge surface area for contact between foetal and maternal blood vessels. The two bloodstreams never fuse but the two sets of capillaries lie so close to each other that glucose, amino acids and other nutrients, as well as oxygen, can diffuse from mother to baby, while carbon dioxide and organic wastes move in the other direction. The juxtaposition enables maternal antibodies to pass into the baby's system, providing some immunological protection from disease. But the close contact also means that infectious agents such as the rubella (German measles) and HIV viruses and drugs including alcohol can pass from the mother's bloodstream into the baby, causing it serious harm.

See also

REPRODUCTION AND GROWTH

▶ Cradle to grave
98/99

▶ Cycle of life
108/109

▶ Fertilization
110/111

▶ The first month
112/113

▶ The growing plan
114/115

▶ Being born
118/119

▶ The newborn baby
120/121

ENERGY

▶ The gas exchange
54/55

▶ The cell and energy
56/57

CIRCULATION, MAINTENANCE AND DEFENCE

▶ Growing heart
66/67

▶ In circulation
68/69

INPUTS AND OUTPUTS

▶ Food for thought
188/189

Being born

One of the shortest journeys in the world is also one of the most important – a baby's trip down the birth canal.

In the final month of a pregnancy the growing child in the uterus puts ever greater demands on its mother's body. Put simply, it is getting too big. In the last four weeks the mother's ribs have to spread out to provide space for her lungs since they are pushed upward by the increasingly huge uterus (womb). By week 36 the top of the uterus is up at the level of the lowest ribs. Most women at this stage have to stand and walk leaning backward to counterbalance the bulge at the front. The time for the baby to move into the outside world is approaching fast – if it grew much more its head might become too large to pass through the pelvic birth canal.

Contractions of the uterus – albeit weak ones – can be felt by the mother or a doctor as early as about week nine of pregnancy. But in the final month, as the time of birth draws nearer, uterine contractions become more powerful and frequent. Approximately 266 days after

a microscopic egg was fertilized, a baby – the result of that fertilization and now weighing some 3.2 kg (7 pounds) – is ready to be born.

Powerful contractions of the uterus stimulate the mother's pituitary gland to secrete the hormone oxytocin, which induces even stronger contractions. The positive feedback between contractions and a hormone that increases contractions seems to be an important part of the complex trigger that initiates labour and birth.

Sometimes, however, babies are born before the nine months are up. Babies born prematurely are small and are unable to control their body temperature effectively. They also have particular problems with efficient breathing, partly because the muscles in the chest wall and diaphragm are not yet strong enough to support powerful breathing movements. Poor breathing is also due to the fact that the spaces inside the lungs are still underdeveloped. In the last stages of foetal development, the baby's lung lining secretes large volumes of a natural detergent solution, or surfactant. It eventually reduces the liquid surface tension in the inner spaces of the lungs which holds back the movement of air into those spaces. A premature baby has not produced this surfactant, so its breathing is much more laboured until the lung lining has matured.

I

At the start of labour, contractions in the uterus push the baby down toward the cervix at the bottom of the uterus (1). Usually (in about 95 percent of deliveries) the baby's head becomes engaged in the cervical region. At the same time the cervical canal widens (dilates); when it reaches a maximum diameter of about 10 cm (4 inches) birth is imminent. Next the baby, guided by uterine contractions, passes through the birth canal and its head emerges (2, 3). At this point the baby is still attached by the umbilical cord.

2

LEAVING THE WOMB, ENTERING THE WORLD

There are three stages of labour, which takes anything from a few hours to three days in total. In the first, contractions of the uterus prepare the birth canal, and toward the end muscular contractions break the amniotic sac around the baby, and the liquid escapes through the vagina – the waters break. The second stage is the birth itself: the baby passes head-first down the birth canal. In the third stage the afterbirth is expelled.

3

While the baby is still attached to the placenta (**right**), its lungs are filled with amniotic fluid. Two shunts, one between the heart's atria (the oval window, or foramen) and one between the pulmonary artery and aortic arch (the ductus arteriosus), allow oxygenated blood from the placenta to pass directly to the heart's left side for pumping to the body.

At birth the oval window closes and the baby's first breath forces blood from the right side of the heart into the lungs via the pulmonary artery, and the baby receives oxygenated blood from its own lungs (**far right**). Within minutes the ductus arteriosus begins to close and is sealed 10 days after birth. Links to the umbilical cord soon shrivel.

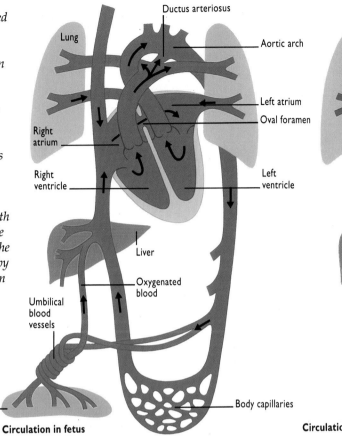

Circulation in fetus

Ductus arteriosus
Lung
Aortic arch
Left atrium
Oval foramen
Right atrium
Right ventricle
Left ventricle
Liver
Oxygenated blood
Umbilical blood vessels
Placenta
Body capillaries

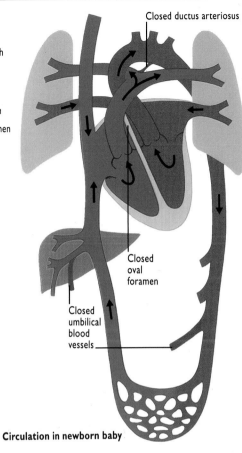

Circulation in newborn baby

Closed ductus arteriosus
Closed oval foramen
Closed umbilical blood vessels

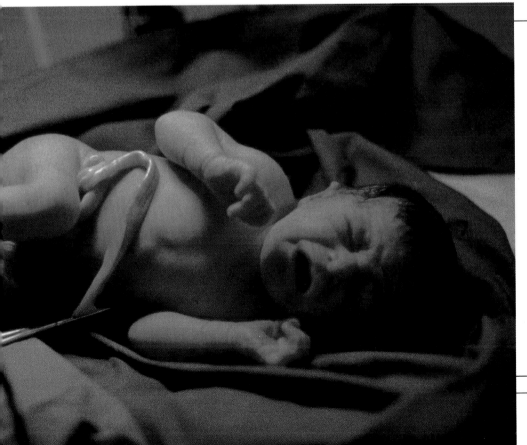

It is normal delivery practice to clamp and then cut the umbilical cord as the baby emerges. Soon after it enters the world the baby takes its first breath and utters its first cry. The baby must change from an "underwater" human (with lungs full of amniotic fluid and provided with oxygen via a life support blood system linked with the placenta) to a normal air-breathing human.

After the baby has been delivered, the third stage of labour begins. This usually takes only about 20 to 30 minutes and involves the painless continuing contractions of the uterus to expel the afterbirth – the remains of the amniotic fluid, cord and placenta.

The newborn baby

Despite being dependent on its parents, a new baby has some in-built abilities that help it along as it develops.

When a new baby enters the world, it is for the first time a separate human being, although it is still entirely reliant on its parents for warmth, protection and food. From the time of birth, the developing baby makes rapid advances toward becoming truly independent. By the age of 18 months or so most children can walk, talk, feed themselves and handle a whole range of practical everyday problems.

The newborn baby can see and hear the world around it and has an efficient sense of touch. But muscular coordination and strength are not well developed to begin with. It does, however, have some reflex movements that are valuable for survival. For instance, a baby cries when tired, uncomfortable or hungry, and parents find crying almost impossible to ignore. The suckling reflex is also vital – when a baby's cheek or lips are touched it at once turns toward the touch, grasps the object in its lips and begins sucking. This specific behaviour pattern allows efficient feeding from the mother's nipple or from a bottle teat.

More sophisticated movement (motor) skills, culminating in self-feeding and unaided walking, develop as the baby's muscles and nervous system mature. At birth, for instance, the nerves that control muscle contraction are not insulated by the usual fatty sheath of myelin. But by 12 months almost all nerves are encased in myelin, aiding walking and other feats of motor control. Repetition and practice help solve coordination problems.

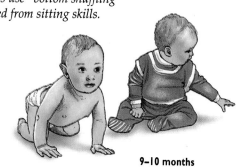

Milk to feed a baby is made in gland cells in the breasts under the influence of a hormone – prolactin – from the pituitary gland. When a baby sucks on a nipple, this provokes the pituitary to release a surge of another hormone, oxytocin. This has the effect of making the smooth muscles in the breast contract, moving milk toward the nipple and releasing it as the baby needs it. The release of milk in response to the baby's sucking is the "milk letdown" reflex.

There is no fixed timetable or even strict order in which a developing baby is able to perform particular activities. The exception is walking, in which stages are attained in a relatively set pattern and at fairly predictable times. After birth a baby is unable to lift its head, but four to six weeks later increasing muscle strength means it can raise its head from the horizontal.

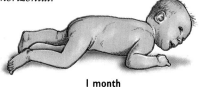

1 month

At four to five months a baby can lie on its front and lift its bottom up by pushing its knees forward or lift its shoulders from the ground by pushing up with the arms.

4–5 months

By nine or ten months many babies can crawl on knees and hands. Others use "bottom shuffling" derived from sitting skills.

9–10 months

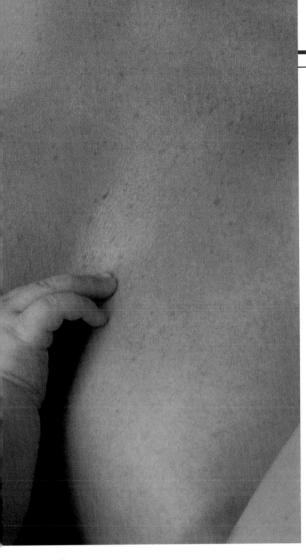

NOURISHMENT FOR THE NEWBORN

A new mother's breasts produce about 1 litre (1¾ pints) of milk a day, but for up to three days after birth the breasts give a protein-rich liquid – colostrum. This contains antibodies, to protect the baby from disease, and hormones that stimulate the lining of its digestive tract to digest milk.

Milk's composition varies from mammal to mammal. Human milk has the same fat content but much less protein and more sugar (lactose) than cow's milk. Seal milk has more than 10 times the amount of fat and protein found in human milk. This thick, rich milk enables a young seal to grow fast on its birth beach and lay down a thick layer of blubber before going to sea.

11.2 0.7
53.2
32.3
2.6
87.4
86.08
4.9
0.2
4.5 6.8
4.5
3.8
0.72

Fat
Protein
Lactose
Minerals
Water

Percentage of total volume

At around 11 months many children can pull themselves into a standing position, either with help from an adult or by hanging on to furniture or other supports.

But staying upright is difficult, and babies at this age tend to wobble and fall over if they attempt to move. Once a child is accustomed to the idea of taking all its weight on its feet, its confidence soon grows and standing, the preliminary to walking, becomes second nature.

However, at this stage a child might have trouble sitting down again. A child set down on the floor or in a cot will pull up to the standing position and then get stuck and cry for help. This stage only lasts for a few weeks and with help – a gentle lowering on to the floor – the child soon learns how to sit down again without a hard bump.

11 months

By about a year many babies are able to walk in a coordinated fashion by placing one leg in front of the other in a patterned way. Normally, though, they will need a mobile support, such as an adult's hand or a wheeled trolley, to do this without falling.

The first unaided step soon develops into a sequence of steps and the child becomes mobile. Some children seem to skip stages when learning to walk; it is not uncommon for a child to go from the pre-crawling stage straight to the standing stage.

12 months

Between 14 and 16 months, on average, a baby becomes a toddler, able to walk upright and unassisted. There is, however, considerable variation in timing from child to child. Some are up and running by 12 months, while others take their time and do not learn to walk until up to two years after birth. Whatever the case, in less than two years the child has come a long way – from a helpless almost immobile newborn baby to an active miniature adult. The attainment of the walking stage is matched by the development of the muscles and the nervous system that coordinates them. A child can now explore under its own steam.

14–16 months

The growing child

From learning to walk to reaching adolescence, a child undergoes an amazing series of changes.

By the end of its first dozen or so years a child is on the verge of sexual maturity and is able to walk, speak, write and communicate socially with sophistication and fluency. Reaching this point from the helplessness of infancy seems to happen with little apparent effort. The child seems programmed to learn new things easily, and the early years are a time when fresh knowledge and skills are absorbed. Thereafter learning new skills becomes increasingly difficult.

It is during the childhood years that humans develop the skills for understanding and manipulating the world around them – a world of objects, activities, social interactions and the consequences of action. But as well as the intellectual changes there are physical changes. The first 18 months or so of life see dramatic rates of growth; but these then slow down and body shapes alter more gradually. A stocky toddler becomes a taller five-year-old with longer limbs, making the child seem thinner. This thin look lasts until muscle growth catches up with the height gain. In the middle phase of childhood, between five and seven years, the first set of teeth, or milk teeth, start to be replaced by the permanent adult set. As the teenage years approach there is another growth spurt. This marks the beginning of adolescence – the coming of sexual maturity.

Between the ages of one and four children develop increasing motor skills and expand their intellectual accomplishments and their ability to see visual patterns in the world. This is demonstrated in the way a child draws.

At the age of one a child can hold a pen and make marks on paper. The lines produced are repeated curves generated by swinging movements of the whole hand and arm.

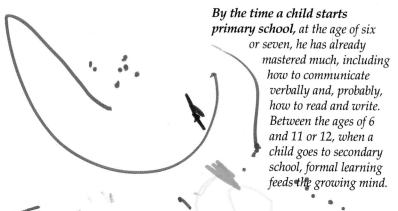

By the time a child starts primary school, at the age of six or seven, he has already mastered much, including how to communicate verbally and, probably, how to read and write. Between the ages of 6 and 11 or 12, when a child goes to secondary school, formal learning feeds the growing mind.

A two-year-old's marks are more deliberate. The lines have clear beginnings and ends, and the dots show more controlled, finer movements.

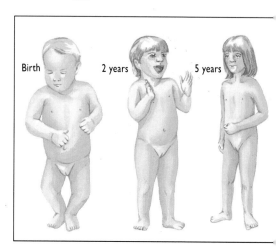

Birth   2 years   5 years

The stages in growth of a girl from birth to the age of 15 reveal a change in proportions. For each age the total body height has been drawn to the same scale so that relative body part sizes can be compared. The baby has a relatively huge head and short limbs, but by 15 the girl has a proportionately small head and limbs that are relatively much longer than the baby's.

By the time a child is three a picture (**left**) is an attempt to make an image of something. Each of the dense patches of scribbled lines represents a unit of the body – a hand, a nose or a pair of eyes.

The image drawn by a three-and-a-half-year-old (**below**) shows well-controlled lines. The body shape is plain and there are feet and a head with hair. Together with the dotted shading, this gives the image the beginnings of real representational qualities.

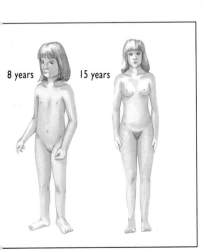

8 years   15 years

By the age of four a child can produce a fully stylized picture of a human. All the main body parts are in the right relationship with one another; two eyes, a nose and a mouth are in the correct position; and conventionalized hair, arms, hands, legs, feet and even trousers and buttons have been drawn. It is a great visual and motor achievement.

Sexual maturity

In the space of a few key years a person changes from a child into a sexually mature adult able to reproduce.

The changes of adolescence and puberty are controlled by a complex mix of interacting hormones. They bring about the enlargement and maturation of sex organs and the parallel development of a number of secondary sexual characteristics that are the external hallmarks of an adult. "Adolescence" refers to the period of general growth in boys and girls and the maturation of the reproductive organs while, strictly speaking, puberty is the time during adolescence when a maturing child becomes capable of reproduction. The onset of puberty is about 12 years for girls and about 14 for boys, although the age can vary by several years each way.

At the start of sexual maturation in both sexes, the hypothalamus region of the brain begins to secrete gonadotropin-releasing hormone (GnRH), which stimulates the secretion of follicle-stimulating hormone (FSH) and luteinizing hormone (LH) from the pituitary gland. In a boy these hormones prompt the testes (testicles) to grow further and stimulate them to produce the sex hormone testosterone. In a girl FSH and LH cause her immature ovaries to synthesize and release progesterone and oestrogen.

In childhood there is not much difference in athletic performance between boys and girls. But at about the age of 11 or so boys become better at activities that require speed and strength such as sprinting (**right**).

From the start of sexual maturation, testosterone brings about the development of typical male characteristics. Facial and body hair begins to grow, which can produce a thick beard or a hairy chest in young men. Hair also appears in the armpits and groin. Body reshaping reduces fat and increases muscle size. The Adam's apple (part of the larynx) enlarges and the voice breaks – drops to a lower pitch. The

testes start to produce sperm, and all the accessory glands of the male reproductive system, for example the prostate, begin to mature.

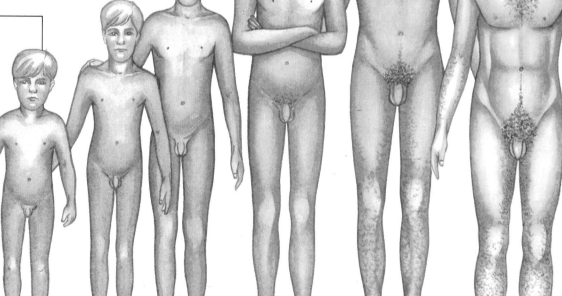

Yards per second | Meters per second — Male / Female — Age (years) 5 7 9 11 13 15 17

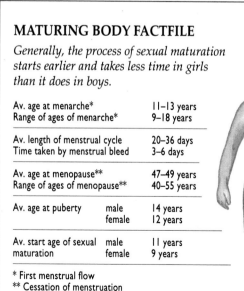

MATURING BODY FACTFILE

Generally, the process of sexual maturation starts earlier and takes less time in girls than it does in boys.

Av. age at menarche*		11–13 years
Range of ages of menarche*		9–18 years
Av. length of menstrual cycle		20–36 days
Time taken by menstrual bleed		3–6 days
Av. age at menopause**		47–49 years
Range of ages of menopause**		40–55 years
Av. age at puberty	male	14 years
	female	12 years
Av. start age of sexual maturation	male	11 years
	female	9 years

* First menstrual flow
** Cessation of menstruation

2 years   6 years   10 years   14 years   18 years   22 years

BREAST DEVELOPMENT

Humans are mammals, and one of the things that tells mammals apart from other creatures is that female mammals make milk to feed their young. Prior to the reproductive years milk production is not needed, so a girl's breasts are similar to those of a boy. But along with other changes of puberty, brought about by hormones which are preparing the human body for reproduction, the breast develops the capability to make milk.

Changes in the nipple are the first external signs of sexual maturation. They can begin as early as 8 and are usually obvious by 11. The nipple grows bigger and more prominent, and the tissues under the nipple form a small, cone-shaped enlargement. Next the breast itself enlarges and becomes smoothly curved. The area around the nipple, the areola, gets bigger and darker than the surrounding skin and the breast reaches its maturity in a young adult. During lactation, milk is made in the 15–20 lobes of milk-secreting (mammary) glands which increase in size to give the breast a more rounded shape. After lactation the breast returns to much the same shape as before. After the reproductive years the glands reduce in size, as does the breast.

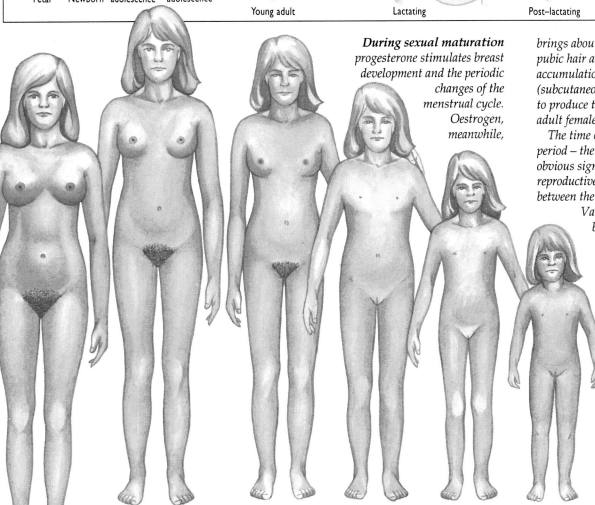

Fetal | Newborn | Early adolescence | Late adolescence | Young adult | Lactating | Post–lactating | Old age

Areola | Mammary glands

During sexual maturation progesterone stimulates breast development and the periodic changes of the menstrual cycle. Oestrogen, meanwhile, brings about the growth of a girl's pubic hair as well as the gradual accumulation of fat under the skin (subcutaneous fat) in specific areas to produce the typically rounded adult female body contours.

The time of the first menstrual period – the menarche – is the most obvious sign that a girl has reached reproductive age. It normally occurs between the ages of 11 and 13. Variations in timing between girls seem to be linked with body weight. In fact, menarche is more associated with reaching a weight of about 48 kg (105 pounds) than it is with a certain age. The lowering of menarche during the 20th century in many developed countries is thought to be due to improved nutrition and the threshold weight being reached at ever-younger ages.

18 years | 14 years | 10 years | 6 years | 2 years

22 years

Getting on

As time passes, the human body matures and reaches its prime. Inevitably, though, it changes with age.

In most individuals it is possible to discern some gradual yet obvious signs of the ageing process between the ages of 45 and 55. The skin slowly loses its youthful elasticity, the amounts of fat under the skin are reduced, and the skin – already showing wrinkles – begins to wrinkle more and sag. Muscles grow weaker, while sensory systems become less acute and the memory less reliable.

At some point between the ages of 45 and 55, for instance, women stop producing and releasing eggs from their ovaries and the cycle of the monthly menstrual bleed becomes irregular and then stops. This occurrence, which marks the end of their reproductive lives, is known as the menopause. The hormonal changes associated with the alterations in the way the ovary and uterus (womb) work sometimes have indirect effects, the most common of which are "hot flushes". The changed hormone balance may also bring about increased loss of structural mineral from bones, making them brittle and more liable to break – a condition known as osteoporosis. Some women use hormone replacement therapy to offset some of these postmenopausal symptoms and changes. Men normally experience reduced secretion of the sex hormone testosterone in later years but the consequences are not as extensive as those of the menopause.

But what exactly causes ageing? The body is a community of cells, most of which replace themselves on a regular basis by dividing. So why – if the cells are producing exact replicas of themselves – should the body not stay the same once adulthood has been reached? The signs of ageing show that cells are not functioning as well as they once did.

It seems there are a number of factors working together. For instance, as part of its normal activities a cell produces chemicals known as free radicals. These are highly toxic and can damage cells as time goes by. Other damage can be caused by mutation, or change, in the cell's DNA molecules, which control its genetic information. With changed DNA, the cell might not perform well. Another cause of ageing could be a process known as programmed cell death. It is thought that part of the genetic information held in cells is a signal to stop dividing after a certain time.

Whatever the actual causes of ageing, there is general agreement that stimulation and ongoing activity may slow some of the psychological and physical aspects. But although ageing can be influenced by lifestyle, the genetic make-up you inherit from your parents also affects your chances of living a long and healthy life. Like everything else about the body, the way in which it ages is an amalgam of the influences of genes and environment.

Keeping active keeps you young. In the past there was a feeling that after years of an active working life, the pattern of existence should be one of quiet and inactivity. But there is now evidence that many of the debilitating physical and emotional aspects of ageing can be slowed or reduced if an active and stimulating life is enjoyed.

An exercise such as swimming enhances cardiovascular health and lung function, strengthens weakening muscles and carries little risk of the sports injuries associated with more strenuous exercise. An active mental life is just as important as keeping on the go physically. If a person does not exercise the mind then it, too, becomes flabby. People who stay involved in life retain their faculties better and have more fun.

Marie Curie (1867–1934) was a Polish-born French physicist famed for her work on radioactivity. With Henri Becquerel and her husband, Pierre, she received the 1903 Nobel prize for physics. At the age of 43 she received a second Nobel prize, for chemistry.

Mao Zedong (1893–1976) was a key figure in China's communist revolution and in the first decades thereafter. He became leader of China in 1949, aged 55.

Charles Darwin (1809–1882) was the British naturalist who transformed ideas about the living world by setting out the idea of evolution caused by natural selection. He was 50 when On the Origin of Species *was published.*

Pablo Picasso (1881–1973), born in Spain, was arguably the most influential visual artist of the 20th century. He was a progressive and innovative force in all types of art, including painting, etching, sculpture and ceramics. He was still painting in the final year of his life, aged 91.

Benjamin Franklin (1706–90), born in Boston, Massachusetts, was a writer, a scientific researcher in the field of electricity, a politician and an inventor – he is credited, for instance, with the invention of the lightning rod and bifocal glasses. In 1787, aged 81, he was a key member of the Constitutional Convention which framed the Constitution of the U.S.

An incredible human resource exists among the older people in society as the ages and activities of the men and women here show. Talented people continue to succeed and be creative after the start of their fifth decade.

The wisdom and sophistication that develops in talented individuals through a lifetime of experiences and diversity can result in great achievement in any decade.

Nicolaus Copernicus (1473–1543), a Pole, was 70 when his **On the Revolutions of the Celestial Spheres** was published. It shook the world of astronomy by proposing that the Earth rotated and orbited the Sun.

Queen Victoria (1819–1901) reigned as the queen of Great Britain from 1837 until 1901. During this period she oversaw the pinnacle of the country's imperial power – at one time a quarter of the world was in the British Empire – and celebrated the Diamond Jubilee of her reign at the age of 78.

CHANGES THROUGH THE AGES

The weight, speed or function of various bodily attributes alters, on average, through a life span. The values for an attribute – for example metabolic rate, at ages 25 (red), 50 (mid-orange) and 70 (light orange) – are compared with the maximum value (100 percent). Lung capacity shows most decline between 25 and 70 years. Other attributes, including brain and liver weight and nerve-impulse transmission speed, hold up well. In fact, liver weight is at its maximum at age 50, not 25 as with all the others.

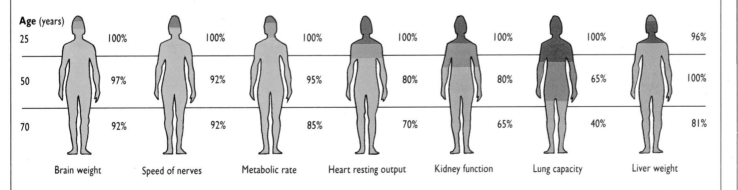

Age (years)	Brain weight	Speed of nerves	Metabolic rate	Heart resting output	Kidney function	Lung capacity	Liver weight
25	100%	100%	100%	100%	100%	100%	96%
50	97%	92%	95%	80%	80%	65%	100%
70	92%	92%	85%	70%	65%	40%	81%

The future body

Scientists now have the power to make changes to the very stuff of life – the genes of human heredity.

Since World War II the pace at which new therapies for human diseases have emerged has accelerated, and there have been several distinct waves of innovation. The first to have a profound impact was the discovery of antibiotics, natural microbe-killing substances derived from fungi and bacteria; new ones are still being found. Next came organ transplant techniques, and there is now an expanding range of body systems that can be replaced if they become diseased. The most recent boost to the explosion of new therapeutic ideas has come from the burgeoning field of molecular biology.

The structure and importance of the DNA molecule – the substance of heredity and the genes – was discovered in 1954. But it was not until the 1970s and 1980s that methods began to be developed to enable DNA to be altered at will in the laboratory. Scientists can now, in fact, directly manipulate the molecules of genes. They can remove a gene from a cell, describe it in minute detail, chop pieces out of it, insert new pieces and transfer working genes from one organism to another.

Thus it is possible to conceive of the direct treatment of genetic diseases by gene therapies. The life-threatening inherited disease cystic fibrosis, for instance, is caused by a defective gene that controls transport of certain materials across cell membranes. Attempts have recently been made to introduce the normal, functioning gene into the cells of patients with this disease by using harmless viruses carrying the "good" human gene as "gene infecting" agents.

Chemical plants are now able to produce, in reasonable quantities, therapeutic human proteins that once had to be laboriously extracted from dead tissues and purified. One such is human growth hormone, produced in the pituitary gland. It controls the rate of growth, especially in children and adolescents. The condition known as dwarfism, in which a person fails to grow tall enough, can occur if insufficient growth hormone is secreted. At one time growth hormone to correct dwarfism was obtained from the pituitary glands of dead bodies – it took many thousands to yield enough to treat a child. Now, however, the gene for growth hormone can be extracted from human cells and inserted into bacteria, which

In the past, *insulin was extracted from pig pancreases to treat human diabetes, a disease in which sufferers have to inject insulin to regulate their blood glucose levels, since they do not produce enough of their own. With modern genetic engineering techniques, however, it is now possible – and, indeed, standard practice – to make human insulin in a chemical plant. Bacteria implanted with the human insulin gene are grown in culture vats where they manufacture human insulin.*

are grown in culture vessels. The growth hormone that they make can then be isolated and used to treat dwarfism. Other genetically engineered bacteria make interferon and tumour necrosis factor for treatment of cancers and factor VIII for treatment of some forms of haemophilia.

These new powers over the workings of the human body have spawned a novel series of complex and troubling ethical and social issues. Is it wise to tinker with a person's genetic make-up? Should people be allowed to "choose" aspects of their offspring? What are the consequences of altering the genes that a person might pass on to future generations? The clinical benefits of many of the new therapies are obvious. The undoubted benefits, however, have to be carefully considered against the possible harm that human "genetic engineering" might cause.

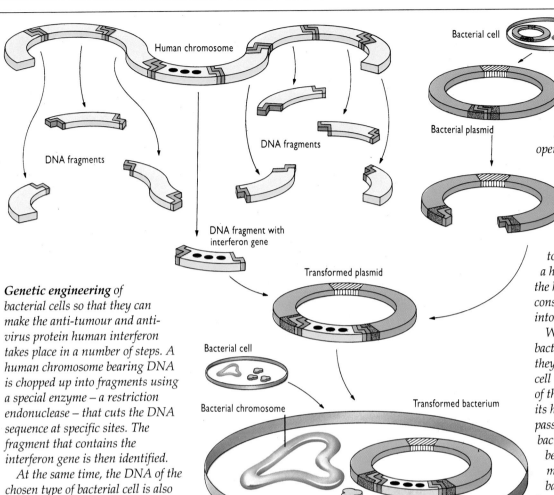

Human chromosome

DNA fragments

DNA fragments

DNA fragment with interferon gene

DNA fragments

Bacterial cell

Bacterial plasmid

Transformed plasmid

Bacterial cell

Bacterial chromosome

Transformed bacterium

Bacterial ribosome

variable numbers of small satellite chromosomes, or plasmids. One of the plasmids is removed from a bacterial cell and its circle is opened using the same enzyme that produced the interferon gene fragment. Because the cut ends of the human and plasmid DNA are produced by the same enzyme they can be spliced together perfectly. In this way a hybrid plasmid containing the human interferon gene is constructed. It is then put back into the bacterial cell.

When these genetically altered bacteria are grown in culture vessels they multiply by cycle after cycle of cell division. At each division, copies of the human gene, safely housed in its hybrid plasmid, are made to be passed on to the new generations of bacteria. Limitless quantities can be made. The human interferon manufactured by the transformed bacteria can be extracted from the bacterial culture and used as a drug in cancer treatment.

Genetic engineering of bacterial cells so that they can make the anti-tumour and anti-virus protein human interferon takes place in a number of steps. A human chromosome bearing DNA is chopped up into fragments using a special enzyme – a restriction endonuclease – that cuts the DNA sequence at specific sites. The fragment that contains the interferon gene is then identified.

At the same time, the DNA of the chosen type of bacterial cell is also manipulated. Bacteria have one large circular chromosome plus

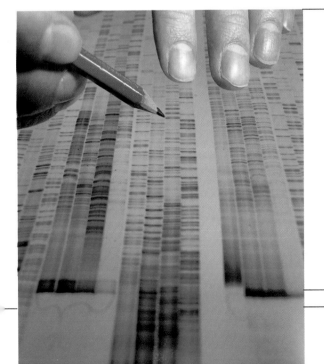

THE HUMAN GENOME – MAPPING OUT HEREDITY

"Sequencing gels" (**left**) are the basic technology used to map the genetic base sequences of human genes. Each gel has four rows of "ladder rungs" with each row standing for one of the four DNA nucleotide bases – adenine (A), thymine (T), cytosine (C) and guanine (G). The order of the bases along the DNA molecule provides the instructions for a particular protein.

When a human gene is appropriately chemically manipulated and then spread along the gel, the sequence of "ladder rung" bands on the gel can tell a researcher the order of bases on the gene. A huge international research programme, the Human Genome Project, is now in operation. Its aim is to list the entire base sequence of all the DNA molecules of the human genome – several billion bases. When completed, the project will have discovered the genes for the making of every protein in the human body.

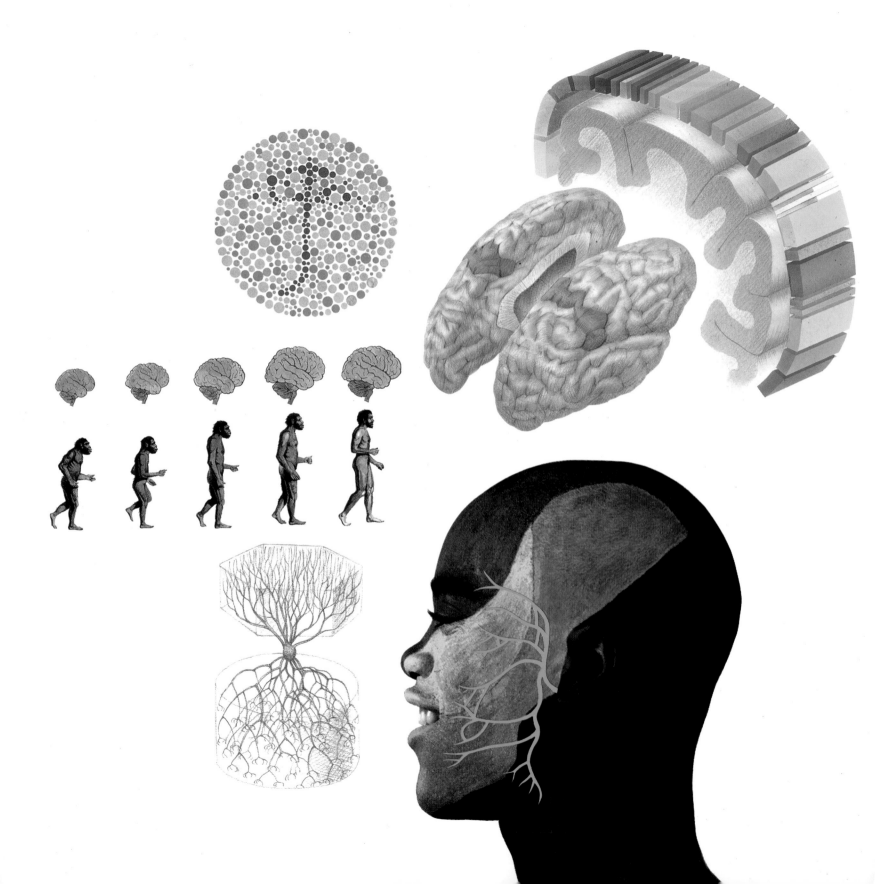

How Your Brain Works

The human brain presents the ultimate riddle: how can a slurry of tissue with the consistency of raw egg be responsible for your "mind", your thoughts, your personality, your memories and feelings, and even your actual consciousness? Until recently this was still a conundrum, but the last 25 years have witnessed the most astonishing progress in facts, clues and ideas.

An organ like any other in the body, the brain is nonetheless tantalizingly different. Whereas transplants of hearts, kidneys and lungs are now well established and widely accepted, the brain remains the essence of the individual. All our experiences of the outside world are dependent on the workings of this creamy mass of cells as numerous as the trees in the Amazon rainforest, and all crammed into the skull. The brain processes information from the senses about sound, light, touch, taste and smell and can initiate action, coordinating movements ranging from running and climbing to whispering and piano playing. These powers enable us to interact with a changing environment and to convey our thoughts and ideas to others; without these abilities we would each be a prisoner in our own private world.

Over the years scientists and thinkers have tried to fathom the mysteries of the mind. Here are some of the techniques they have used, along with observations of patients with different types of brain malfunction. We see what is known about how the brain works, how it processes information and how it controls the body. We look at thoughts, emotions and memories and how they are modified by drugs, therapeutic and otherwise, and by other types of clinical treatments. Empowered by our incredible mind, we explore what drives us, constrains us and inspires us.

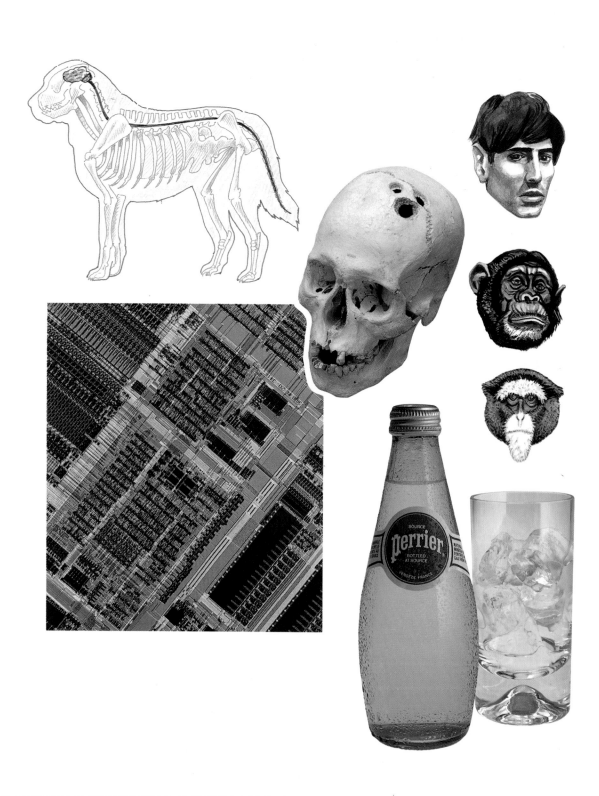

Surveying the Mind

Millennia ago, at about the time when people started attempting to explore and explain the world around them, they also began to consider thought itself. Generation after generation of great thinkers came up with theories as to what the brain did and how the mind worked – a process that continues today, for we seem irresistibly drawn to investigate ourselves.

We are unique among species in that as well as performing everyday functions, we are able to study these actions and our behaviour. We also examine thought processes and how the brain works. For many years work in this field was often inaccurate and based largely on guesswork but the advance of science has opened many avenues of enquiry, whether by experiment, comparison or observation. Tools to examine the brain systematically have now become available, enabling us to probe its innermost workings and set out detailed maps of its anatomy and function.

Left (clockwise from top): are bigger brains best?; thought processes in something as simple as getting a drink; how human and silicon brains measure up; the advancing animal brain; letting out spirits through a hole in the head.
This page (top): changing personality the hard way; (right) what animals can do that we cannot and vice versa.

What is a brain?

Why do we – and most other creatures living on Earth – have brains? And how did they evolve?

Inside the head of every person is one of the most astonishing objects in the universe: the human brain. It looks like a rather squidgy overgrown walnut and is little bigger than two clenched fists. Yet it enables us to think, feel and act – to read books and build televisions and to be human.

Humans are far from unique in possessing a brain – nearly every animal on Earth has one. What all brains have in common is that they enable creatures to respond to a situation – whether that situation is simply an obstacle in its path or the problem of finding food or fleeing from an enemy. Via the nerves, a brain both receives information (from the rest of the body and the outside world) and sends out orders (to control body functions and initiate action).

Without a brain to direct them, creatures that need to move and find food would find it hard to survive. The brain is thus a command and control centre in which the specialized cells that interpret and process data and then send out orders to the body are grouped together. Grouping makes the command and control process much more efficient than it would be if these cells were scattered around the body.

Single-celled organisms were the first to appear, perhaps 3,800 million years ago. They still exist today and while some of them, such as the amoeba, can move, they have no nerves. Next to evolve were multicelled organisms, such as sponges, again with no nerves. Specialized nerve cells first appeared in such creatures as jellyfish.

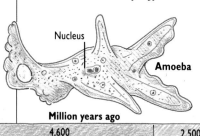

Nucleus

Amoeba

Million years ago

Segmented worm

Cerebral ganglion

Ventral nerve cord

A segmented worm, like its ancestors that evolved over 500 million years ago, has a cerebral ganglion – a cluster of nerve cells in its head – and a ventral nerve cord.

A brain is a device that enables an organism to control its response to the world. When a cat stalks its prey and then charges, its brain is being fed data concerning sight, hearing, smell, taste and touch from its sense organs. The brain decides how to respond to this information and sends out appropriate commands to the body to crouch, move and pounce.

Cerebrum

Fish

Olfactory bulb

Cerebellum   Spinal cord

Insect

Cerebral ganglion

Nerve cord

Ganglion

Separate brain areas came with the early fish like Dartmuthia. *Today's fish also have a cerebrum, cerebellum, olfactory bulb and a spinal cord – all features found on most vertebrates (creatures with backbones).*

Insects such as Collembola, *like other invertebrates, have brains and nervous systems, but the structure is more varied than with vertebrates. Insects have more sense organs, for example antennae and leg hairs.*

Cerebellum
Cerebrum

Olfactory bulb

Repti

In early reptiles, Hylonomus *and* Hypsognathus *for example, brain structures grew larger and distinct hemispheres developed.*

Collembola   Hylonomus

Dartmuthia

Million years ago						
4,600	2,500	570	500	440	410	365
Pre–Cambrian era	Pre–Cambrian era	Cambrian	Ordovician	Silurian	Devonian	Carbo

THE CREATURE THAT EATS ITS BRAIN

Only an organism that moves from place to place requires a brain. An organism that stays still responds automatically to changes in its environment, but has no need to direct its movements. Plants often have sophisticated reactions – like turning their leaves to face the sun – but they do not have to move, so possess no brain.

The relationship between a brain and mobility is illustrated by a tiny marine creature, the sea squirt. It swims about like a tadpole when young. But when it matures it attaches itself permanently to a rock and feeds by filtering plankton out of the water. It then consumes its own brain because it does not require it any more.

In the early part of its life the sea squirt Ascidian *has a brain and nerve cord to control its movements* (**right top**). *As it reaches its sedentary mature form, these structures are gradually absorbed and digested, leaving only those needed for filter feeding* (**right bottom**).

Nerve cord · Stomach · Eye · Brain · Mouth · Heart · Mouth · Heart · Ganglion · Stomach

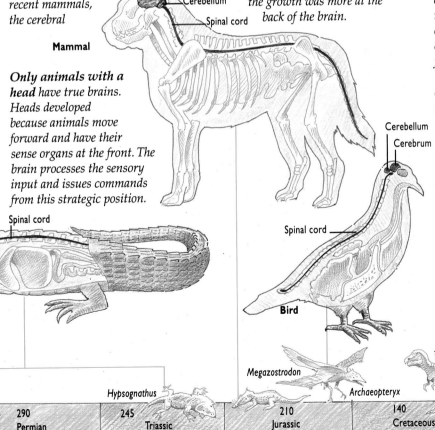

In early mammals, like Megazostrodon, *the cerebrum developed dramatically, creating a frontal lobe on each hemisphere. In more recent mammals, the cerebral* hemispheres swelled enormously taking over all but the most basic automatic responses, such as control of breathing and heartbeat. *In birds,* like Archaeopteryx, *the growth was more at the back of the brain.*

Cerebrum · Cerebellum · Spinal cord

Mammal

Only animals with a head have true brains. Heads developed because animals move forward and have their sense organs at the front. The brain processes the sensory input and issues commands from this strategic position.

Spinal cord

Cerebellum · Cerebrum · Spinal cord

Bird

Our brain and nervous system have much the same layout as those of all other vertebrates (creatures with backbones), from fish to dogs. At the heart of all vertebrate nervous systems is the central nervous system (CNS), which consists of the brain, including the cerebellum and cerebrum, and the spinal cord – the bundle of nerves running up to the brain through the backbone. All the other nerves in the body converge on the CNS. Some carry sensory data to the CNS; others carry commands from the CNS to the rest of the body.

The human brain is a product of gradual evolution. Like the brain of every other vertebrate, it has been created by adaptation to changing conditions over hundreds of millions of years. Only in the last few million years of this evolution has it been the brain of a "hominid", a humanlike creature such as our ancestor Australopithecus afarensis. Before that, its ancestry can be traced back through apelike creatures such as Ramapithecus, primates, small mammals, reptiles and fish. As the brain evolved, it grew outward in successive layers. Even today its structure reveals its ancestry, with the most primitive feature – the brain stem – at the centre, and the most modern – the cerebrum with its highly developed outer layer, the cortex – on the outside.

Human
Cerebrum · Cerebellum · Spinal cord

Megazostrodon · *Tyrannosaurus* · *Australopithecus afarensis* · *Hypsognathus* · *Archaeopteryx* · *Ramapithecus*

| 290 Permian | 245 Triassic | 210 Jurassic | 140 Cretaceous | 65 Tertiary | 2 Quaternary |

Discovering the brain

For millennia great thinkers have applied their minds to the problem of how, and with what, we think.

Thinking and the brain are, to us, inextricably linked, but this link was not always so clear. One of the first to realize that thoughts occur in the brain was the Greek physician Hippocrates (*c*.460–377 B.C.), who believed that the mind was in the brain and controlled the body, but was something intangible. Unlike his contemporaries, he also believed that disease and head injuries, not demons, caused madness and affected coordination.

This split between mind and body, or between mind and brain, became known as mind–body dualism. The opposite argument, that the mind and brain or mind and body are one – that all thoughts are basically physical processes in the brain cells – is called monism. The dualism–monism debate has dominated thinking about the mind since the theories were first mooted.

We now know that all thought occurs in the brain and, indeed, where specific processes, such as perception or language, take place. Yet there is still no agreement as to where consciousness – our awareness of ourselves and our identity – fits in. Some argue that mind and brain are the same thing, that consciousness is a physical, mechanical entity and that one day we may be able to fashion a mechanical mind which experiences consciousness as we do. Others suggest that our minds and consciousness are very different from the mere mechanical activity of brain cells. Yet others steer a middle course, arguing that consciousness is a mechanical process of the whole brain, rather than individual brain cells.

VITALISM, OR THE ROMANTIC DILEMMA

Ever since it became clear that the brain was the seat of thought, many have resisted the idea that the mind is simply a machine. Antoni van Leeuwenhoek (1632–1723), who was the first to study nerve cells with a microscope, believed that the brain contained a special vital animal spirit or fluid that embodied our life force and consciousness. Members of the late 18th-century Romantic movement, led by German writer Johann Wolfgang von Goethe, argued that the brain contained an active life force – an animating energy that turned its tissue into something living and dynamic. Although this idea was long ago discredited by scientists, it is not so different from some modern ways of looking at consciousness.

From prehistoric times until quite recently certain peoples carried out trepanning – the drilling of a hole in the skull. The theory behind this practice was that the sufferer's mind had been taken over by demons or evil spirits which had to be let out. But it may in fact have helped alleviate certain physical symptoms.

The ancient Greek philosopher Plato *(428–348 B.C.) agreed with Hippocrates that the mind was in the head, but believed that the mind and body are separate, and that we reach the truth not via our senses but through our thoughts – by logic and reasoning.*

Aristotle *(384–322 B.C.), Plato's student and rival, thought the mind – and the seat of our feelings – was in the heart. He also argued that the mind and brain were one and that the mind is entirely physical, with the result that we can only understand the mind by studying the body.*

René Descartes *(1596–1650), the French philosopher, perpetuated Plato's mind–body dualism by insisting that the human body and the senses were entirely mechanical and material – but the mind was something else, and that the seat of this nonmaterial mind was the pineal gland.*

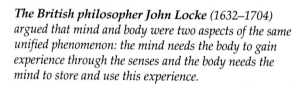

The British philosopher John Locke *(1632–1704) argued that mind and body were two aspects of the same unified phenomenon: the mind needs the body to gain experience through the senses and the body needs the mind to store and use this experience.*

James Mill *(1773–1836), the Scottish philosopher, argued in his book* Analysis of the Phenomenon of the Human Mind *that the mind is merely a machine and can be explained entirely in physical terms.*

Immanuel Kant *(1724–1804) tried to resolve the mind–body debate with the idea of faculties (mental powers) of sense, understanding and reason which integrate the mind and body. This German philosopher also argued that we are born with some knowledge (a priori knowledge) but learn through experience (a posteriori knowledge).*

The Greek physician *Erisistratus* (304–250 B.C.) divided the brain into two regions: big (the cerebrum) and small (the cerebellum). He also noticed how many more wrinkles the human brain had compared with those of animals and deduced, correctly, that they indicate greater brain power.

At much the same time, from his dissections made in Alexandria, the Greek anatomist Herophilus (born 320 B.C.) worked out that there were two kinds of nerves: sensory nerves, which receive sense impressions; and motor nerves, which stimulate motion.

In the 1700s many people still believed that the nerves were tubes containing a mysterious vital fluid. Then the Swiss physiologist Albrecht von Haller (1708–77) showed they were simply the carriers of impulses that stimulated muscles or created a sensation and that all nerves lead to the brain and spinal cord – which must, therefore, be where the senses are perceived and responses initiated.

The German physiologist Johannes Müller (1801–58) took a crucial step in showing that the perception of the senses takes place in the brain when he demonstrated that each of the sensory organs responds to stimuli in its own way. For instance, if the optic nerve leading from the eye to the brain is stimulated, we see a flash of light, regardless of whether light was the stimulus.

Galen (A.D. 129–199), the Graeco–Roman physician, is seen by many as the founder of experimental physiology.

He learned his trade by tending to gladiators' wounds. He believed cerebrospinal fluid was the psychic fluid, the fluid of the mind. When he discovered the ventricles in the brain where this fluid collects, he believed that he had found the seat of the mind.

The German physician Franz Gall (1758–1828) believed, rightly, that different parts of the brain are linked to different parts of the body. He also believed, wrongly, that personality and the relative development of particular regions of the brain could be read from the pattern of bumps on the skull, so initiating the pseudo-science of phrenology.

Frenchman Paul Broca (1824–80) was one of the first modern brain surgeons, treating an abscess on the brain, for instance, by trepanning (cutting through the skull). He also showed through post mortems how damage to a certain area on the left frontal lobe impaired speech – establishing for the first time a link between a particular area of the brain and a particular ability.

The Flemish anatomist Andreas Vesalius (1514–64) refused to accept Galen's work in its entirety, but built on it through study and dissection. In addition, Vesalius finally discredited Aristotle's idea that the mind, and the seat of our feelings, was in the heart, insisting that it was in the brain. Such was his standing and the authority of his book on anatomy, De Humani Corporis Fabrica, first published in 1543, that no one has since doubted this assertion.

In this drawing of the brain which appeared in Vesalius's great work, the membranes have been stripped from the brain to disclose the cerebral hemispheres connected by the corpus callosum.

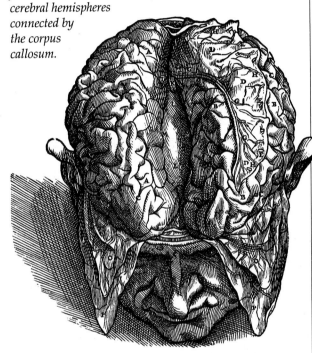

Hermann von Helmholtz (1821–94), the German scientist and philosopher, was a pupil of Johannes Müller at the Medical Institute in Berlin. Helmholtz was a pioneer in the study of both the eye and the ear and invented both the ophthalmoscope, which is used to examine the interior of the eye through the pupil, and the ophthalmometer, with which faulty vision is measured, so allowing the correct spectacles to be prescribed. He also showed that sensory conduction by the nerves (and thus the "speed of thought") was measurable. By demonstrating that the mind was thus limited by the physiology of the nerves, he opened the way to the experimental study of the mind.

The working mind

Numerous theories of how the mind works have arisen from the drive to know more about ourselves.

For thousands of years, only the brain was studied by scientists; the mind was seen as the realm of philosophers. But by the mid-1800s, scientists had found that sensations, at least, were the result of nerve impulses that could be analysed and measured. If this were so, might not science tackle perceptions, feelings and memories as well as the brain itself? The German physiologist Wilhelm Wundt (1832–1920) believed it could and opened the first psychological laboratory at the University of Leipzig in 1879.

Wundt tried to study the mind by "introspection" – the analysis of one's own thoughts as they occur – but by the early 1900s many psychologists seriously questioned this approach. The American John B. Watson (1878–1958), for instance, argued that with introspection results can never be proved or disproved. He maintained that a more valid approach was to study the way people behave and what they actually do and to analyse how people or animals respond to a particular stimulus. But this method – behaviourism – had its critics too, and it is now seen as just one of the many ways of studying the mind and hypothesizing about how it might work.

VOICES FROM THE PAST

 A man sought advice because he was troubled by voices (inaudible to anyone else) which took the form of supernatural messages. He was counselled to listen hard to the voices and pay them the attention they deserved since the gods did not waste their time with unimportant communications. Reassured by this the man went about his business, heeding the gods, and lived a prosperous life, eventually dying in a shipwreck not far from the thriving city of Troy.

This might have been the scenario about 3,000 years ago if one interesting – if not widely accepted – theory of the nature of the human mind is to be believed. Psychologist Julian Jaynes has put forward the theory that a sense of self, a coherent consciousness or ego, only developed about 3,000 years ago. Before that he maintains that the mind was two-chambered, or bicameral, referring to the left and right hemispheres which were, he claims, not integrated. One hemisphere "spoke" and the other followed its orders, attributing the "voice" to the gods. Today a man who sought advice because he was hearing voices would probably be diagnosed as schizophrenic and be prescribed powerful drugs to treat the symptoms.

*One theory of the mind was phrenology, developed by German physician Franz Gall in the 19th century. He believed the shape of the brain correlated with many emotional and temperamental qualities and that its shape could be worked out from the form of the skull. Character could thus be assessed by feeling the bumps on a person's head. Phrenological heads (**above**) were made, which mapped out where a particular quality might be felt on the head. Today the theory has no currency.*

The discipline of ethology studies the behaviour of animals in the natural environment, rather than in laboratory conditions. The ethological approach has been recognized by psychologists as a valuable way of understanding human behaviour by comparing it with the way animals behave. It emerged in Europe and reached its height with the work of Konrad Lorenz and Niko Tinbergen in the 1970s.

Ethology tries to show how an animal's innate behaviour could have evolved so as to fulfil a function and be useful for its survival. It also seeks to explain the rituals of animal courtship and aggressive behaviour.

An ethological approach to sexual attraction between humans might look at it in the light of instinctive behaviour patterns.

The cognitive approach originated during the 1950s and '60s when some psychologists were inspired by computers to look at the way people think or process information, that is, the sequence of mental events. Using this method a psychologist might ask, for instance, if people perceive things in the same way that computers are programmed to. The problem is that it is difficult to get inside the human mind to prove or disprove the cognitive psychologists' theories.

A cognitive psychologist who was looking at sexual attraction would try to analyse the mental processes taking place – taking reaction times and the subject's own analysis into account and, perhaps, creating computer simulations.

The biological approach is one of the most fruitful ways of studying the mind. Much has been learned by examining the physical substance and processes of the brain, rather than its mental processes or behaviour. Neuroscientists, for instance, have revealed how certain chemicals work in the brain to affect our behaviour and that different parts of the brain are linked to special tasks and abilities.

A neuroscientist studying sexual attraction might look for evidence of the effects of hormones on the brain or use scanners to monitor what is going on in particular regions when an attractive person is seen.

Behaviourism was the dominant approach to psychology from about 1920 to the mid-1950s and it still has many advocates. It concentrates entirely on how people (and animals) behave and tries to analyse all behaviour in terms of a stimulus and a response. Behaviourism was made famous by the Russian physiologist Ivan Pavlov (1849–1936), who showed how dogs could be "conditioned" to give a specific response to a particular stimulus, such as a ringing bell, which they associated with food.

B.F. Skinner (1904–90), one of its most extreme proponents, argued that all human behaviour could be explained by stimulus–response relationships. In his novel Walden Two he showed how a few powerful people could keep everyone "happy" by creating a world in which they were stimulated in the right way.

A behaviourist considering sexual attraction would look at the detail of physical response when an attractive person is seen – the way the people involved move or what happens to the eyes, for instance.

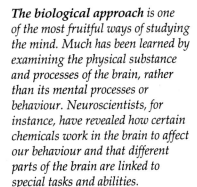

The psychoanalytic approach was pioneered by Sigmund Freud (1856–1939). The essential idea behind it is that people's psychological history explains to a large extent both the make-up of their character and their current behaviour. Freud suggested that we have "conscious" thoughts of which we are aware and "unconscious" thoughts of which we are unaware, but which have a great influence on the conscious mind. He emphasized the role of childhood experiences, particularly during the first five years of life, and the importance of sexuality in forming the adult personality.

A psychoanalyst studying sexual attraction might try to analyse a person's childhood and relationship with the parents to find the origin of sexual feelings.

Gestalt psychology was a reaction in the 1920s and '30s by many Austrian and German psychologists, notably Max Wertheimer (1880–1943), against behaviourism and the way it broke everything down into units of stimulus and response. Gestalt psychologists were interested in the mind's Gestalt – its entire, integrated form – believing that the whole is greater than the sum of the parts. They were concerned with understanding mental experience and development, and concentrated on people's awareness of the world and their surroundings.

Whereas a behaviourist studying sexual attraction might try to analyse the minutiae of a person's reactions, a Gestalt psychologist would look at what the whole experience of attraction means.

Comparing brains

Animal studies have revealed much about how brains work and give some insights into human thinking.

Physicians and anatomists have long realized that there was a great deal to be learned about the human body by studying animals. Since they have the same or similar senses and nervous systems, and even their brains have the same basic arrangement, animals have been the subjects of countless experiments. Anatomists and, more recently, neuroscientists have used animals to learn about the human brain and nervous system. Much of our knowledge about learning and memory, for instance, comes from studies of white rats.

It was only gradually accepted, however, that animals may be able to teach us something about the human mind. Early this century, psychologists developed the idea of behaviourism, which showed that learning in both humans and animals can be studied without worrying whether they think in the same way. It entails simply observing how a person or animal behaves in response to a particular stimulus.

Much of the research was geared to explaining how behaviour is learned. But many scientists argued that some kinds of behaviour were not learned but inborn, and "ethologists" studied animals' natural behaviour to see if they could identify any patterns. One noticed, for instance, that newly hatched goslings will "imprint" – form an immediate attachment – to the

first moving object they see nearby. Others have discovered different forms of inborn behaviour, such as "fixed-action patterns" – patterns of behaviour that are repeated seemingly automatically whenever certain events occur. Although it is important to remember that such animal experiments do not teach us about human behaviour directly, they provide many ideas which can guide research.

Termites live in a tightly regulated community with different castes that have specific roles in the nest. Humans, too, live in societies but – unlike termites, whose role seems genetically predetermined – are, in principle, able to move between roles.

Dogs have a good sense of smell and can track prey over long distances, since their noses are packed with scent receptors. They also communicate using smell – by scent marking their territories with urine.

Smell receptors

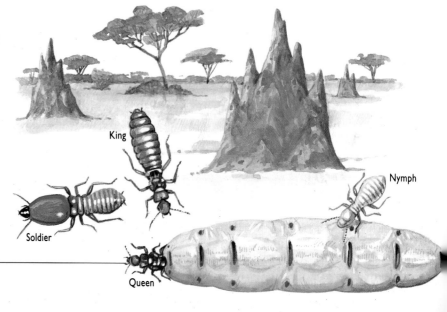

King

Nymph

Soldier

Queen

140

A spider has a tiny brain but this does not mean that it cannot perform feats that humans find impossible. The delicate tracery of a spider's web is an example of animal engineering at its finest. Not only can the spider instinctively make the web – accurately positioning the supporting strands and the infill threads – but it can also tell by the vibrations made when an object hits the web whether that object is a prey insect or a useless bit of fluff.

Only in the 20th century have humans managed powered flight. But birds have been doing it for millions of years. By studying how birds use air currents, how their wings are shaped and how they navigate, scientists and engineers have learned much about the principles of flight.

The cortex is the part of the brain where higher functions take place, so a large cortex relative to body size is seen as a sign of intelligence. If the areas of the cortices of various animals are shown by different sized pieces of paper, a rat's cortex is the size of a postage stamp; a monkey's the size of an envelope; a chimpanzee's the size of a sheet of A4 paper; and the human cortex the size of four sheets of A4. However, the cortex of an elephant is four times as big as a human's and that of a whale is six times greater. But the human cortex is large in relation to the size of the body, while the whale's and the elephant's are both much smaller in comparison to their bulk.

Some snakes can sense heat radiation. This lets them find prey in the dark by its body heat. They use a part of the spectrum not visible to humans called the infrared because it comes beyond the red end of the rainbow of colours that we are able to see.

Many bats navigate and hunt by means of a high-frequency echolocation system that uses sounds too high-pitched for us to detect. While the human ear can at best hear sound frequencies between 20 and 20,000 Hz (Hertz, or waves per second), some bats use sound frequencies of up to 200,000 Hz, when hunting insects, for instance.

141

Inside the mind

We think all the time, whether we are aware of it or not.
But what does the process of thinking really involve?

Psychologists can easily study our behaviour, the external result of our brain at work. Neuroscientists can also study the anatomy and neurochemistry of the brain, but it is far harder to see the mind in action. Experiments on animals, modern scanning techniques and experience with computers are slowly helping to build up at least a vague picture of what goes on.

Even something as simple as deciding to sit down involves a complex sequence of events. The brain receives a continual flow of information from the senses and the rest of the body – via the nerves and hormone system – which it analyses before sending instructions out to the body. All the time the analysis and orders are modified by feedback of more data. Thus the eyes will scan the room to look for a chair, messages go to the brain and a seat is chosen. Motor impulses, or nerve signals, from the brain stimulate muscles to make us move across the room. Then we have to assess the angle of the chair, how far to bend, how to keep our balance. Simultaneously we could be talking to a friend, daydreaming or rerunning a memory of a past event. Usually all this goes on without our realizing it, yet a unique facet of the human mind is that we can be self-aware – we know we are thinking – so aspects of the process can be studied.

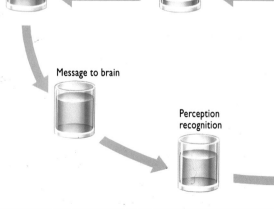

Action → Sensation ← Action

Message to brain

Perception recognition

The action of directing your gaze to a glass gives a visual sensation of the glass at the back of the eye. This is coded into nerve signals sent to the thalamus by retinal receptor cells. The thalamus passes this nerve signal pattern to the visual cortex, where the image of the glass is perceived and recognized. It is then stored as short-term sensory memory which holds things in the mind for a second or two even while new sensations are flooding in.

Just seeing ice cold water can make you lick your lips in anticipation, and a cascade of mental activity is set off. As you reach for the bottle, pick it up and pour, a stream of signals feeds back from the eye to the brain, which coordinates your movements and sends motor impulses to the muscles to keep you moving in the right way. As you sip, many new sensations flood your brain – the taste of the water, its cool feel.

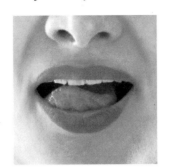

Associations spring to mind when you start thinking about what a glass of water means. The water may remind you of swimming in a clear pool, drinking cool lemonade, easing a parched tongue. Even seeing part of a bottle or its outline can trigger associations; they can be about almost anything in your experience and do not have to be directly about water. You may think, for example, about lack of water in a drought-stricken landscape.

Association comes only when the glass has been perceived and recognized. When the visual cortex "sees" the glass, the mind does a rapid check of its qualities – its shininess, its transparency, the way the water in it moves – to see if it can be identified. The idea is held in the mind for a while; like letters drawn in the air with a sparkler, the pattern of every visual image persists in the brain for a moment.

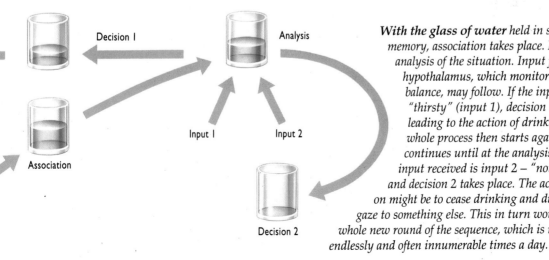

Sensory memory

Association

Decision 1

Analysis

Input 1   Input 2

Decision 2

With the glass of water held in sensory memory, association takes place. Next comes analysis of the situation. Input from the hypothalamus, which monitors water balance, may follow. If the input is "thirsty" (input 1), decision 1 is made, leading to the action of drinking. The whole process then starts again and continues until at the analysis stage the input received is input 2 – "not thirsty" – and decision 2 takes place. The action decided on might be to cease drinking and direct the gaze to something else. This in turn would spark a whole new round of the sequence, which is repeated endlessly and often innumerable times a day.

Electronic minds

Human brains and electronic computers seem to have some things in common. But just how alike are they?

Computers that talk and have all manner of human frailties, like the chirpy R2D2 in *Star Wars* and the sinister HAL 9000 in *2001*, are, so far at least, just science fiction. But the idea that computers might one day have minds and personalities like humans is the subject of fierce scientific controversy. Equally controversial is the idea that the human brain is simply a complicated computer.

Some argue that the brain is just a biological machine – albeit a complex one. If this is so, there is no reason why we cannot, ultimately, build an equivalent electronic machine that works in exactly the same way – and because electronic impulses can travel a million times faster than nerve impulses, this computer brain could be far superior to ours. Others argue that the brain is fundamentally different from a computer. Consciousness, intuition and things we take for granted, such as our ability to come up with ideas or use common sense, are all things that a computer will never be able to mimic, because these faculties do not work mechanically, but in a fundamentally different (as yet unknown) way.

Nonetheless, there are certainly similarities between computers and brains, and research into the parallels has helped both those working in Artificial Intelligence (AI, the theoretical basis for a thinking computer) and neuroscientists studying the brain. But so-called bottom-up comparisons between computers and brains at the level of individual cells and transistors have actually taught us little about the brain.

The real interest in computer–brain comparison at the moment is in the top-down approach – that is, comparisons between their overall functioning. Both computers and brains involve networks of connections, so AI experts have worked with the idea of neural networks – groups of connections that mimic particular brain functions. The idea is to come up with theoretical models of networks of neurons that, for instance, learn things the same way the brain learns them. But many scientists still feel that neural networks may ultimately only help in the development of computers and not in the understanding of the brain, and especially not in the understanding of qualities of the mind such as imagination.

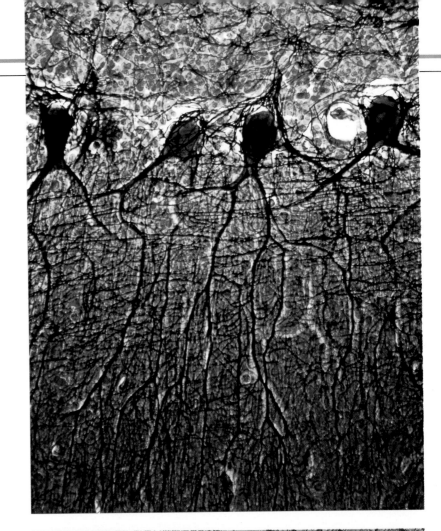

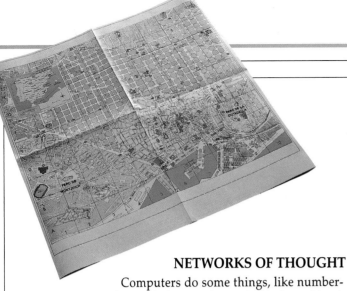

A map enables us to find out how to get from one place to another. A set of instructions using a limited set of rules can be worked out, such as first left, second right, straight ahead at the junction and then fork left. These are not unlike the components of an algorithm, a set of rules that if applied will lead to the solution of a problem.

NETWORKS OF THOUGHT

Computers do some things, like number-crunching and playing chess – indeed anything involving rigid logic – better than humans. Yet there are things like recognizing a good picture, laughing at a joke or cooking a meal that we find effortless that even the most sophisticated computers fail miserably at. In attempting to understand why, scientists have tried to find some logic in the brain's activity by creating neural networks.

Neural networks are designed using algorithms – sets of mathematical rules that rigidly guide the network's operation, so a particular data input will produce a particular output. A neural network is basically a way of arranging a computer's connections that will make it follow a particular algorithm. The idea is that the neural network mimics some brain function precisely, giving the same output for a given input. An important element in many is the ability to learn, and some networks can teach themselves.

One of the problems with neural networks is that it is difficult to find a single brain function that a network might mimic, since so many things in the brain work together and interact. Moreover, only rarely does the brain give an unvarying, inevitable output to a particular input in the way that a neural network must. Usually, each of the myriad inputs into the brain is mixed in with all the rest and stored for the future rather than producing a particular instant response.

Machines can be made to look similar to humans but they cannot do many humanlike things. The mannequin above has an articulated body and can sweat and breathe, but it would have trouble playing soccer against a human.

*At the basic cell level, brains initially seem similar to computers. Computers, for instance, are basically a series of tiny switches that can be set at either on or off. Neurons, or brain cells, (**left, above**) also seem switchlike because they either "fire", sending an electrochemical signal, or do not. However, neurons are never simply on or off; their level of excitation and their shape dramatically alter the way they communicate with one another. Attempts to create electronic versions of neurons have* *not worked well. In simpler computers, which use chips (**left**), circuits are connected in series – connections are made rapidly one after the other, so a signal runs through a single circuit. In the brain, however, neurons are connected in parallel – thousands or even millions of connections are made at the same time, and the signal divides and runs through huge numbers of circuits simultaneously, giving phenomenal power.*

Discovering through damage

Sometimes the behaviour changes of a patient with brain damage give insights into the mind's workings.

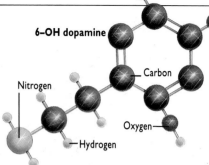

Tragic as they may be for those involved, the effects of tumours, strokes, gunshots, poisonings and other forms of brain damage have been valuable sources of information about which parts of the brain do what. Before the invention of modern imaging techniques, the region of damage could only be discovered after a patient's death. Researchers therefore had to wait for autopsy results before they could relate changes in behaviour or function to the place in a person's nervous system where there was a lesion.

The process of uncovering which functions and abilities are located in specific regions of the brain gained momentum from an observation by Parisian doctor Paul Broca. In 1861 he described a patient who, because of damage to a small region of the left side of the motor cortex, now known as Broca's area, had lost the power of speech. Research continues today into all sorts of damage, including, for example, that to the parietal lobe, which causes curious gaps in the victims' knowledge or abilities. One patient with damage on the right side lost all sense of the left of his body, ignoring anything on that side. He once drew a watch with all the numbers crammed into the right side.

6-OH (hydroxy) DA (dopamine) – similar to the neurotransmitter dopamine – is taken in by dopamine receptors, producing some of the symptoms of Parkinson's disease. Since 6-OH DA is taken up selectively into dopamine cells it can be used to research their functioning.

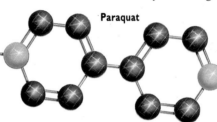

Paraquat is similar in structure to MPTP. It is found in certain types of weedkiller and if ingested causes fatal lung damage. There is no known antidote for paraquat so once enough has been absorbed it will kill. In areas where paraquat is used, there is a small statistical rise in the numbers of cases of Parkinson's disease. Its structural similarity to MPTP may account for this.

In the 1970s a group of people in their 20s started to develop the symptoms of Parkinson's disease. They were brought on by the impurity MPTP, in a compound made by people attempting to synthesize heroinlike drugs. MPTP selectively destroyed the dopamine cells of the substantia nigra region of the basal ganglia.

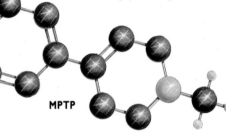

GAGE THE DAMAGE

American railway construction worker Phineas Gage was a member of a blasting crew. One day in 1848, while he was ramming dynamite into a hole drilled in rock, a blast occurred which sent his iron tamping rod – a metre long and 4 cm (1½ inches) wide – through his left cheek and out of the top of his head. Amazingly, he survived.

But when Gage had recovered from his injuries his behaviour had altered. He suffered a dramatic change of personality: from being a man described as shrewd, well balanced and persistent he became moody, difficult, given to bad language, unable to plan ahead and inconsiderate of other's feelings.

The rod had seriously damaged the frontal lobes of his cortex, thus providing good evidence that the frontal lobes control our sense of self and ability to carry out long-term plans. Surprisingly, in view of its drastic effects, about a century later deliberately destroying the frontal lobe briefly became a treatment for some intractable psychiatric illnesses.

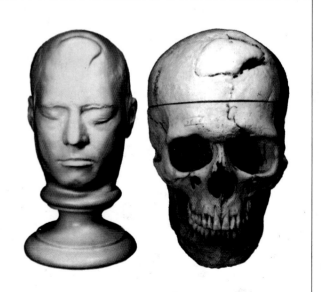

Phineas Gage's death mask and his skull show where the metal rod that injured him entered and left his skull.

❶ Prefrontal lobe damage – as in the case of Phineas Gage – alters the ability of people to execute plans and can make them inconsiderate. It can also pacify them.

❷ Frontal lobe damage affects movement since this area contains the pre-motor and motor cortices.

❸ Damage to the parietal lobe of the cortex interferes with perception of touch and pain, as well as some visual functions and the knowledge of where the body is in space.

❹ Posterior parietal lesions can have bizarre effects, one of which is referred to as "neglect". When the left posterior parietal lobe is damaged, "right neglect" occurs. Typically, a patient treats the right side of the body and the world around it as if they did not exist. This is because each side of this region of the brain integrates inputs from the different senses to form a coherent picture of what is happening in the opposite side of the body, where the signals originated.

❺ Damage to any of the areas marked with diagonal lines can cause blindsight – a person can detect something visually, but cannot acknowledge that he or she can see it.

❻ Injury in the V5 visual (occipital) region, which is thought to play a part in the perception of motion, causes some odd symptoms. For instance, following a stroke there, a patient might see the world only as a series of static images.

❼ People with damage to Wernicke's region, an area in the left temporal lobe, can speak fluently but make no sense. A typical reply to a question about a holiday might run: "Oh, yes, we have done it, could be different, but nevertheless done. Go, go, gone, and however successful it still fails". The area deals with sense and comprehension of language.

❽ A range of symptoms is evident in patients with damage to the temporal lobe. The right temporal lobe is involved in controlling spatial tasks, and damage to a specific part of it can render someone unable to recognize faces, even those of close family members. A farmer with damage to much the same area could recognize his family, but lost the ability to recognize his sheep. Damage to other parts of the temporal lobes can result in dramatic hallucinations or a loss of memory for any subsequent events.

❾ Patients with lesions in Broca's area can sometimes speak, but the speech is laboured and halting. Ask them about a holiday and they might reply "Ho, ho, holiday, like . . . eat turkey . . . people . . . good". This region controls grammar and vocalization.

See also

SURVEYING THE MIND
▶ Discovering the brain
136/137

▶ Probing the mind
148/149

▶ Brain maps
152/159

BUILDING THE BRAIN
▶ Recovering from damage
186/187

▶ The ageing brain
198/199

INPUTS AND OUTPUTS
▶ Levels of seeing
214/215

▶ Active vision
216/217

FAR HORIZONS
▶ The infinite store?
252/253

▶ Parallel minds
260/261

STATES OF MIND
▶ Emotional states
276/277

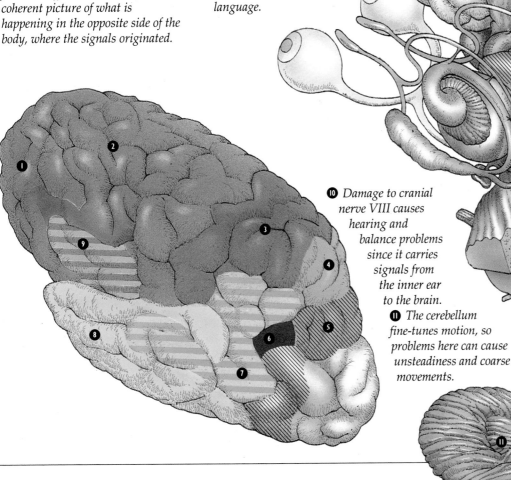

❿ Damage to cranial nerve VIII causes hearing and balance problems since it carries signals from the inner ear to the brain.

⓫ The cerebellum fine-tunes motion, so problems here can cause unsteadiness and coarse movements.

Probing the mind

Investigating the physical properties of the brain reveals much about how it works.

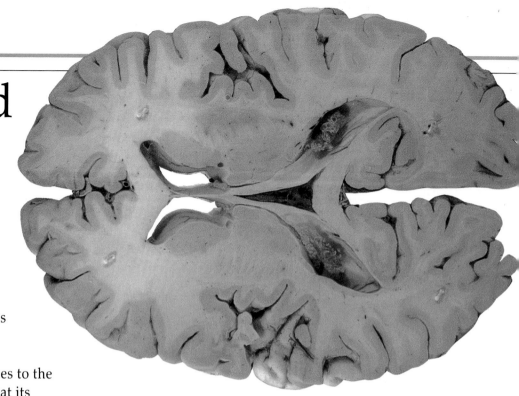

Only comparatively recently has the true scale of the complexity of the human brain emerged. It has around 100 billion nerve cells, or neurons, each connected to hundreds, sometimes thousands, of other cells. Unravelling how this vast network operates has been one of the great challenges of the 20th century. And today scientists have a number of techniques at their disposal.

Until individual neurons were first stained and directly observed using powerful microscopes, clues to the brain's workings could be gained only by looking at its anatomical structure. But scientists can now use techniques, such as the electroencephalogram (EEG) machine, first developed in the 1930s, that measure the minute fluctuating wavelike electrical signals that result from circuits of neurons firing in unison.

Using laboratory animals, researchers can remove parts of the brain or damage them to see the effect on the behaviour or function of the living animal. Or by inserting tiny recording electrodes deep into living tissue they can home in on individual neurons and record their electrical activity. By keeping thin slices of brain alive outside of the body, scientists can use electrical probes to examine the brain's workings. They can control the environment of isolated populations of neurons and, for example, measure their response to drugs that they would not normally come into contact with. The responses are frequently registered using an electrode placed inside the neuron.

If you had never seen a basketball game before, looking at just one player on his own would make it difficult to work out what he was doing, what the rules are and what his role was.

Similarly, techniques that study the activity of just one brain cell can tell something about the way an individual cell reacts to a stimulus but give no idea of the

big picture. For instance, only truly vast numbers of brain cells working together as a unit can process our visual inputs of the outside world on the way to perception, or make our muscles work. And some of the more complicated brain functions, such as making decisions, involve precisely coordinated networks of cells from half a dozen different brain areas.

MAKING WAVES

Using electroencephalogram (EEG) machines, the tiny voltage changes (around 10 microvolts) that result from the synchronized firing of large groups of neurons can be picked up by electrodes placed on the scalp. Because the current involved is so small it is amplified before being traced out on a sheet of paper where the voltage changes appear as a series of waves. There are a number of wave patterns – actually a record of the difference in potential between two points on the scalp – which are named after letters of the Greek alphabet.

So alpha, with a frequency of 9 to 11 waves per second, appears when our eyes are shut and we are relaxed. Beta is faster and indicates alertness; delta and theta are slower and linked with stages of sleep. EEG readings can show what stage of sleep a person is in and, some claim, if the subject is lying. They can also distinguish types of epilepsy.

EEG waves produce their typical wave pattern because of the way that groups of neurons alternately excite and inhibit one another. If one group of neurons is excited by a stimulus, they fire when it appears, triggering a nearby group whose job it is to reduce activity; as things quieten down the inhibitory neurons turn themselves off, allowing the excitatory ones to fire up again. The size of an EEG wave reveals how many cells are synchronizing their impulses; a larger wave indicates more synchronization.

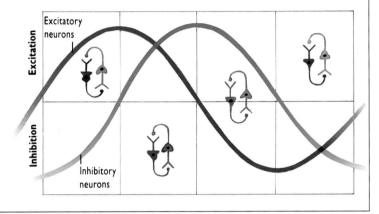

Recordings from individual neurons form the basis of our understanding of the brain. Typically these recordings – obtained by placing a small electrode outside the neuron – detect the tiny pulses of electricity that it produces when it "fires", sending messages to other neurons. Much has been learnt, for instance, about the different sensory systems in the brain – especially the visual system – by monitoring what individual neurons do in response to different external sensory stimuli.

*from the brain of an animal such as a rat can be used in several ways. It can be stained so that individual neurons and their connections show up. Or it can be kept in a special solution that sustains the cells for a few hours; this enables researchers to experiment on living brain tissue. In autoradiography, a radioactively tagged substance is injected into the animal before the slice is taken. An image (**left**) obtained using a film sensitive to the radiation shows how that substance is used by regions of the brain.*

Taking a slice of brain and then experimenting on it is a favourite technique for researchers. The slice

Surgical operations have provided many insights into brain functions. If the corpus callosum, the net of 100 million nerve fibres linking the two cerebral hemispheres is cut to relieve epilepsy, for example, two half-brains are created, each governing the opposite side of the body. By studying these "split-brain" patients, doctors have been able to determine the differing roles of the two sides of the brain.

If the hippocampus is destroyed, when a tumour is being removed for example, the ability to lay down new memories is lost, although people can remember details of their past life and, indeed, how to speak. But they do not recognize people they have met only hours earlier and can read a page repeatedly without knowing they have seen it before.

Scientists can not only detect signals of the electrical pulses of individual brain cells but they can also see how electricity is involved in minute parts of the cells themselves. In a technique known as patch clamping, micro-fine glass pipettes are used to record the activity of a single ion channel in the wall of a brain cell, responsible for the flow of electricity. The tip of the pipette is placed against the cell membrane and a tight seal created. The movement of the ions through the channel can be measured in terms of the current that this creates.

The view from outside

Modern imaging techniques cannot tell what you are thinking but they can tell where it happens in the brain.

A human brain is a delicate thing, and the challenge to researchers studying it is to discover what it is doing without causing it any damage. The first pictures of the living brain were taken with X-rays in 1917 but they gave only general information about structure since X-rays are not able to show much detail in soft tissues such as those that make up the nervous system. Only about 50 years later, with the arrival of the computerized axial tomography (CAT) scanner, could X-rays be used to produce the first detailed images of the brain.

But CAT images cannot show the brain in action. Today, however, there are a number of alternative techniques that make this possible. These include positron emission tomography (PET), functional magnetic resonance imaging (fMRI) and magnetoencephalography (MEG). None of these uses potentially harmful X-rays. Currently PET scans can give information on what is happening at 30-second intervals over

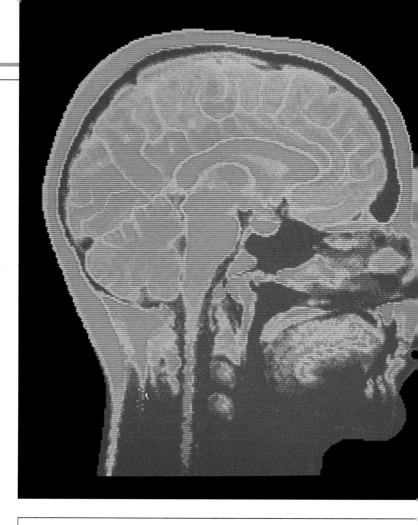

Positron emission tomography (PET) involves injecting into the blood a tiny amount of a radioactive substance, attached to molecules that are absorbed during brain activity. This gives off gamma rays that can be recorded by sensors and analysed by computers to build up a picture of where in the brain increased use of the molecules is taking place.

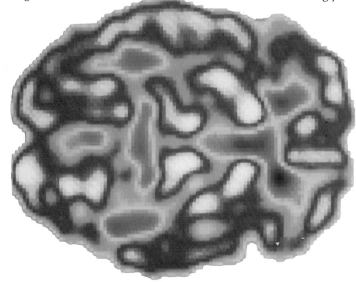

ROENTGEN'S REVEALING RAYS

Discovered by German physicist Wilhelm Roentgen in 1895, X-rays made it possible to obtain images of structures inside the body without surgery. Although this was a breakthrough, X-rays do have limitations. They can only show large-scale features such as tumours, since the minutiae of soft tissues like the brain do not show up well, and they cannot indicate depth or the different layers within an organ. They also cannot always differentiate between healthy and diseased tissues.

Another limitation of ordinary X-rays is that they can reveal only what is in the path of a single burst of radiation. The same is not true of CAT scans, which provide detailed images of the brain's soft tissues. And by putting a number of CAT scan "slices" together, a 3-D image can be assembled. However, although CAT scanning is a great advance, like all X-ray techniques it can only take snapshots of structure and does not show changes in the brain's activities.

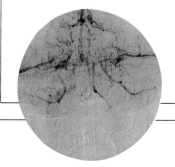
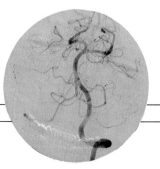

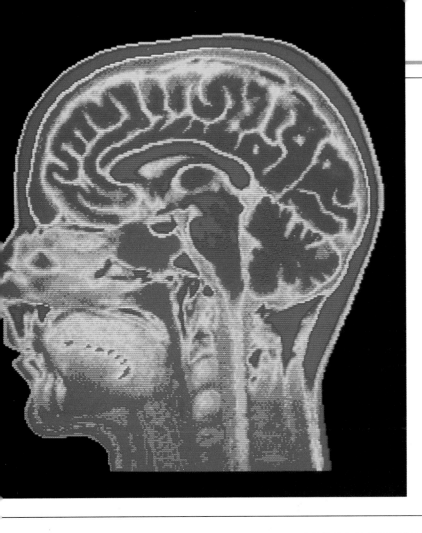

Magnetic resonance imaging (MRI) works because atoms in body molecules can be made to behave like tiny magnets if they are put in a strong magnetic field. A beam of radio waves fired at them will make them resonate and give off radio signals of their own. Sensors detect these signals and the information can be made into an image by a computer.

an area of about 2 mm (¹/₁₃ inch). But this is still not enough to detect brain changes that may last only a fraction of a second. While fMRI is somewhat better than PET, it still cannot show the extremely fast-moving events that take place in the brain. However, the new MEG technique makes this possible to some extent. Active groups of nerve cells generate tiny electric currents, which can be shown in electroencephalogram (EEG) recordings; MEG works by detecting the magnetic fields these tiny currents generate. The computer-processed images produced make it possible to record the site of brain activity by the millisecond.

See also

SURVEYING THE MIND
▶ Discovering the brain 136/137

▶ Probing the mind 148/149

▶ Brain maps 152/159

BUILDING THE BRAIN
▶ Support and protection 164/165

▶ Recovering from damage 186/187

▶ Food for thought 188/189

FAR HORIZONS
▶ Word power 258/259

STATES OF MIND
▶ The failing mind 298/299

Computerized axial tomography (CAT) scans combine X-rays and computer technology to show details of the brain itself. Information from a number of X-ray sources placed around the head is digitized and then reconstructed to give a cross-sectional view of the brain in any plane that is wanted (right).

The blood supply to and within the brain can be seen using cerebral arteriography (bottom left and centre). A radio-opaque dye – which does not allow X-rays to pass through it and so shows up on an X-ray image – is injected into a main artery supplying the brain. As it diffuses into the blood, X-rays are taken. They reveal the distribution of the dye, which shows the size and shape of the vessels. The X-rays can be used to find the site of any narrowing, blockage or displacement in blood vessels. By contrast, a simple X-ray of the head (bottom right) shows little about the brain structure since bone absorbs most of the X-rays.

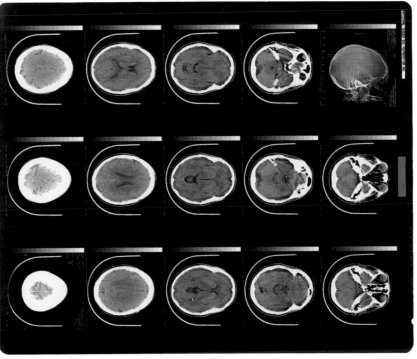

Brain map 1

There is far more to the convolutions of the brain than meets the eye.

We all know where the brain is and have a rough idea of what it looks like. But once we start exploring the brain closely, everyday knowledge soon proves inadequate. This is the case especially when the outer layers of the brain are stripped away to reveal the maze of internal structures.

Anatomists have identified numerous individual regions that are distinct from one another in any number of ways, in terms of both appearance and function. They may, for example, vary in colour, have a different texture or be encased in a self-limiting membrane, or they may be responsible for one highly specific brain function.

The 12 pairs of cranial nerves, which branch directly from the brain itself, can be seen when the brain is viewed from below. Several of these nerves take signals from the sense organs to the brain, but others connect the brain with body organs such as the heart and lungs.

When the brain is viewed from above, *the wrinkled mass of the cerebral hemispheres is revealed. The hemispheres are slightly narrower at the front than at the back.*

The brain is dominated *by the cerebrum, with the cerebellum (little brain) below. It connects with the body via the spinal cord, together with its nerves, and via the cranial nerves.*

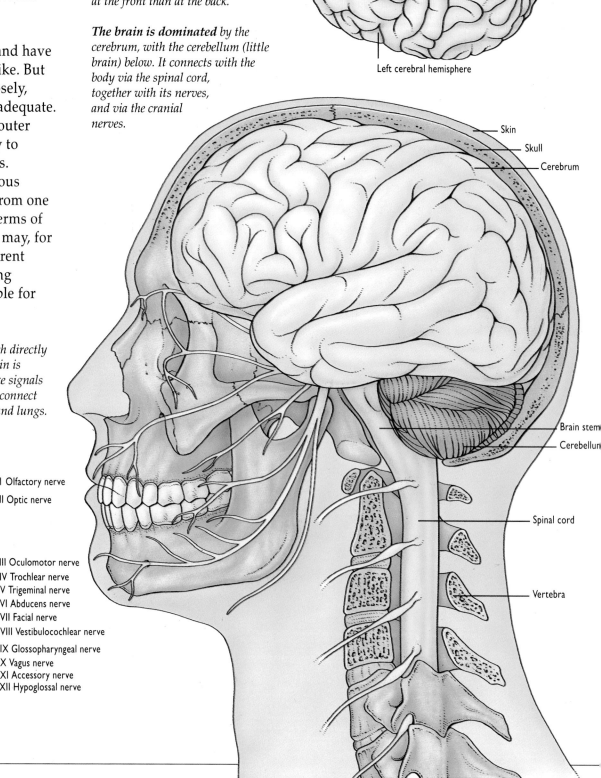

Right cerebral hemisphere

Front · Back

Left cerebral hemisphere

Skin
Skull
Cerebrum
Brain stem
Cerebellum
Spinal cord
Vertebra

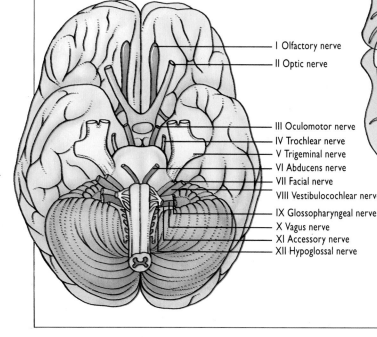

I Olfactory nerve
II Optic nerve
III Oculomotor nerve
IV Trochlear nerve
V Trigeminal nerve
VI Abducens nerve
VII Facial nerve
VIII Vestibulocochlear nerve
IX Glossopharyngeal nerve
X Vagus nerve
XI Accessory nerve
XII Hypoglossal nerve

In the map on the right, the central region shows a cross section more or less through the centre line of the brain, from front to back, as far out as the corpus callosum. The outer region represents a slightly off-centre cross section, cut in the same direction.

The relatively thin outer layer of each cerebral hemisphere is the cerebral cortex, which is packed with the cell bodies of nerve cells and their many local interconnections. Beneath that the cerebrum consists of the message-carrying fibres, or axons, of nerve cells. Regions of the cortex are linked to each other by short association fibres, which take signals to and from adjacent areas, and by long association tracts, which take signals from lobe to lobe of the cortex. Projection fibres take signals between the left and right hemispheres via the corpus callosum, and from the outer cortex down to inner brain regions such as the thalamus and hypothalamus and on to the body.

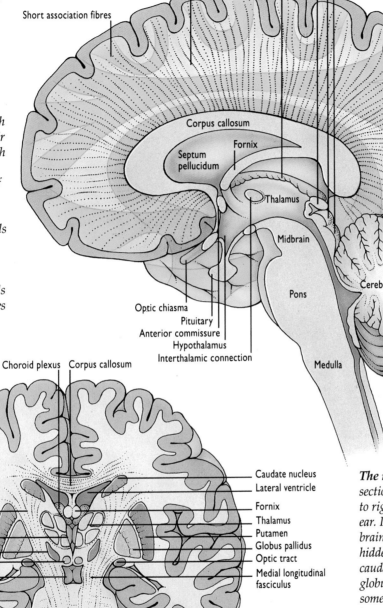

Projection fibres
Short association fibres
Choroid plexus
Pineal gland
Superior colliculus
Inferior colliculus
Long association tract
Cerebral cortex
Corpus callosum
Fornix
Septum pellucidum
Thalamus
Midbrain
Cerebellum
Pons
Optic chiasma
Pituitary
Anterior commissure
Hypothalamus
Interthalamic connection
Medulla

Choroid plexus
Corpus callosum
Internal capsule
Third ventricle
Substantia nigra
Mammillary body
Fourth ventricle
Pons
Caudate nucleus
Lateral ventricle
Fornix
Thalamus
Putamen
Globus pallidus
Optic tract
Medial longitudinal fasciculus
Olivary body
Pyramidal decussation

The map on the left shows a cross section of the brain taken from left to right approximately from ear to ear. It reveals many of the inner brain structures which are normally hidden, including the thalamus, caudate nucleus, putamen and globus pallidus. Also shown are some of the fluid-filled cavities known as ventricles.

The nerve fibres connecting the two cerebral hemispheres are in the corpus callosum, and the fibres that link the cortices to other brain regions and the body are in the internal capsule and the medial longitudinal fasciculus. Most nerve fibres from the brain cross over from one side to the other at the pyramidal decussation at the top of the brain stem.

See *also*

SURVEYING THE MIND
▶ Discovering through damage 136/137

▶ The view from outside 150/151

▶ Brain maps 152/159

BUILDING THE BRAIN
▶ Support and protection 164/165

▶ The brain's cells 166/167

▶ The brain plan 190/191

INPUTS AND OUTPUTS
▶ Body links 202/203

▶ The long junction 204/205

▶ Guided motion 208/209

▶ The big picture 236/237

▶ Dealing with drives 240/241

FAR HORIZONS
▶ Parallel minds 260/261

Brain map 2

Explore the details of the brain's core and cortex.

The naming of parts of the brain can at first seem confusing, particularly since much of the terminology is either in Latin or Greek (or derived from them). This is because these languages provide universal terms which can be used by scientists regardless of their mother tongue. However, once you have mastered the meaning of the most common words, it becomes much easier to understand the terms.

Ten important Latin words are used as directional terms: superior means above or toward the top; inferior means below or toward the bottom; ventral means underneath or lower; dorsal means upper or higher; anterior and rostral both mean toward the front; posterior and caudate mean toward the back; medial means toward the middle; and lateral away from the middle. Three other words are also often used. Septum describes a wall between two cavities; a gyrus is a ridge on the cerebral cortex; and a sulcus is a groove – on the cerebral cortex sulci are the grooves between gyri. Many words describe shape, hence the hippocampus (from the Greek words for horse and sea monster), which resembles a sea horse in cross section.

***With the overlying cerebral hemispheres removed,** the regions in the interior of the brain become visible. For clarity (**right**) the two structures labelled lentiform nucleus have been pulled away from the thalamus, which they surround. The eyes are shown since they are effectively outstations of the brain: they house the retinas which contain nerve cells, or neurons. They send partly processed signals back to the brain via the optic nerves, chiasma and tract, and these arrive at the lateral geniculate bodies, or nuclei, of the thalamus.*

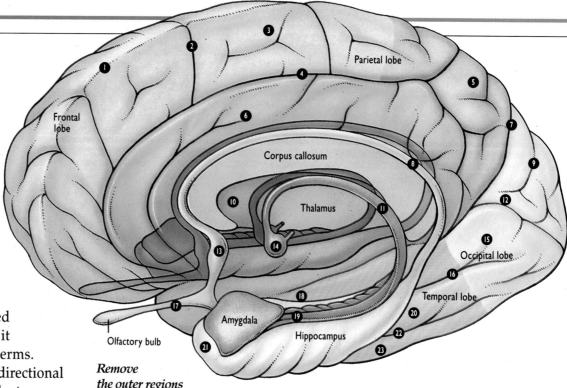

***Remove
the outer regions***
*of one cerebral hemisphere, and normally hidden inner structures are revealed. They include some of the components of the limbic system, which is involved in emotion: the parahippocampal gyrus (**18**), the cingulate gyrus (**6**), the hippocampus, the amygdala, the fornix (**11**), the mammillary body (**14**), and parts of the thalamus, septum pellucidum (**10**) and lower frontal lobe.*

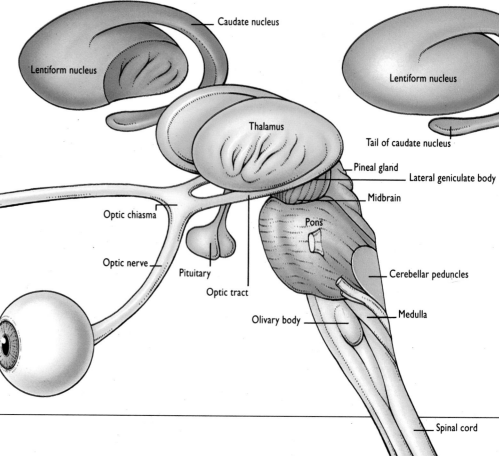

1. Medial frontal gyrus
2. Central sulcus
3. Paracentral lobule
4. Cingulate sulcus
5. Precuneus
6. Cingulate gyrus
7. Parietal occipital sulcus
8. Dorsal fornix
9. Cuneus
10. Septum pellucidum
11. Body of fornix
12. Calcarine sulcus
13. Paraterminal gyrus
14. Mammillary body
15. Lingual gyrus
16. Collateral sulcus
17. Olfactory tract
18. Parahippocampal gyrus
19. Dentate gyrus
20. Medial occipital temporal gyrus
21. Uncus
22. Occipital temporal sulcus
23. Lateral occipital temporal gyrus
24. Superior frontal gyrus
25. Superior frontal sulcus
26. Medial frontal gyrus
27. Precentral sulcus
28. Precentral gyrus
29. Central sulcus
30. Postcentral gyrus
31. Postcentral sulcus
32. Angular gyrus
33. Inferior frontal gyrus
34. Inferior frontal sulcus
35. Lateral cerebral sulcus
36. Transoccipital sulcus
37. Lateral occipital sulcus
38. Medial temporal sulcus
39. Superior temporal gyrus
40. Superior temporal sulcus
41. Medial temporal gyrus
42. Medial temporal sulcus
43. Inferior temporal gyrus

The sulci and gyri of each person's brain are often in unique positions, so any labelling is therefore approximate.

See also

SURVEYING THE MIND
▶ Discovering through damage 146/147

▶ The view from outside 150/151

▶ Brain maps 152/159

BUILDING THE BRAIN
▶ Support and protection 164/165

▶ The brain's cells 166/167

▶ The brain plan 190/191

INPUTS AND OUTPUTS
▶ Body links 202/203

▶ The long junction 204/205

▶ Guided motion 208/209

▶ The big picture 236/237

▶ Dealing with drives 240/241

FAR HORIZONS
▶ Parallel minds 260/261

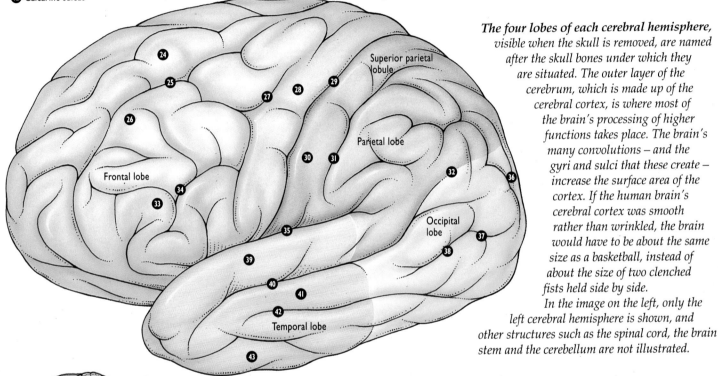

Superior parietal lobule

Parietal lobe

Frontal lobe

Occipital lobe

Temporal lobe

The four lobes of each cerebral hemisphere, visible when the skull is removed, are named after the skull bones under which they are situated. The outer layer of the cerebrum, which is made up of the cerebral cortex, is where most of the brain's processing of higher functions takes place. The brain's many convolutions – and the gyri and sulci that these create – increase the surface area of the cortex. If the human brain's cerebral cortex was smooth rather than wrinkled, the brain would have to be about the same size as a basketball, instead of about the size of two clenched fists held side by side.

In the image on the left, only the left cerebral hemisphere is shown, and other structures such as the spinal cord, the brain stem and the cerebellum are not illustrated.

Cerebellar peduncles

Cerebellum

The cerebellum – which means, literally, "little brain" – is a distinct structure found tucked away at the rear base of the whole brain. It is attached to the brain stem by the stalklike cerebellar peduncles. Like the cerebrum, the cerebellum has a lobed structure with an outer layer of grey matter made up of nerve cell bodies and their interconnections. This outer layer is called the cortex and it includes nuclei (bunches of neuron cell bodies and synapses) and nerve tracts (groups of fibres or axons). The basic structure of the cerebellum is evolutionarily conservative – that is, it has changed little through millions of years of evolution. The cerebella of different vertebrates – creatures with backbones – thus bear a strong resemblance to one another, unlike the cerebra which can look extremely different.

155

Map of functions

Each part of the brain contributes to the overall working of the whole.

Some brain functions are neatly sited in a clearly defined region, as is the case with the hypothalamus, which is known to control certain autonomic (or automatic) body processes. But other brain functions seem to be spread across many areas, which is especially true of the cerebral cortices.

The corpus callosum (below and below right) is a bundle of nerve fibres linking the cerebral hemispheres. The caudate nucleus along with the putamen and the globus pallidus, which together make up the lentiform nucleus, have a role in the control of movement.

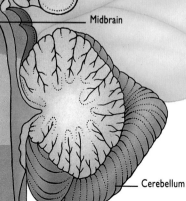

Parietal lobe
Frontal lobe
Occipital lobe
Temporal lobe

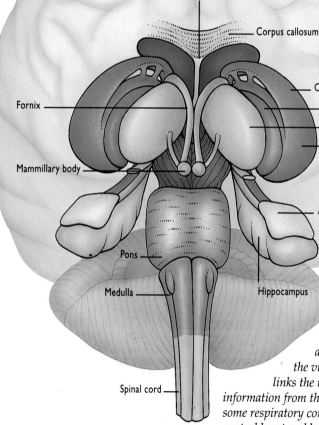

Septum pellucidum
Corpus callosum
Caudate nucleus
Globus pallidus
Thalamus
Putamen
Fornix
Mammillary body
Amygdala
Pons
Hippocampus
Medulla
Spinal cord

The hippocampus and mammillary body, linked by the fornix, have a role in emotional behaviour, learning and motivation. The amygdala coordinates autonomic and endocrine (hormonal) responses with emotional states and is involved with emotions generally. The septum pellucidum merges into the septal nucleus, which is thought to govern the level of emotional responses. Autonomic body functions, such as temperature regulation and water balance, are handled by the hypothalamus which also links with the pituitary and, through this gland, controls the body's endocrine system.*

The midbrain helps control sensory and motor functions such as eye movement and coordination of the visual and auditory reflexes. The pons links the medulla and the midbrain, conveys information from the cerebrum to the cerebellum and has some respiratory control. The medulla has centres that control heart and breathing rates and blood pressure, as well as coughing, sneezing, swallowing and vomiting.

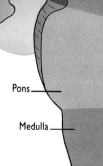

Corpus callosum
Septum pellucidum
Thalamus
Hypothalamus
Midbrain
Pituitary
Pons
Medulla
Cerebellum
Spinal cord

The cerebral cortex can be divided by function into various regions, as shown in the coloured and numbered areas on these views of the brain (**left** and **below**).

The blue dotted lines trace out Brodmann's areas, which are based on differences in nerve cell arrangement and structure in the cortex.

❶ This region is mainly involved with motor functions. Toward the rear is the primary motor cortex where precise muscle-moving signals originate. Toward the front is the premotor cortex, which is devoted to initiating and sequencing movements.

❷ The sensations of touch, pain and temperature are dealt with here. The receiving area for incoming signals is sited toward the front; at the rear, in the somatosensory association cortex, these somatosensory perceptions are integrated to produce an understanding of the location of the body in space.

❸ Some of the higher intellectual functions, along with planning and intention, are thought to be found here. The wish to move might originate in this area, which then activates the motor regions directly behind it·to carry out the detailed work of coordinating all the many muscles in the right order to initiate action.

❹ Association areas are some of the many areas in the brain that have no specific role or clear function.

❺ This scattered collection of regions plays a part in emotion, mood and general behaviour. The areas at the front of the frontal lobe are instrumental in the higher intellectual functions, while the region at the front of the temporal lobe is probably involved in imaging and in complex memories. Areas at the base of the frontal lobe are thought to inhibit emotions and those above the corpus callosum could add appropriate emotional responses to sensory experiences.

❻ This area not only deals with olfactory functions, but also has a role in emotion and mood. The part in the temporal lobe is important in memory and olfaction, or detecting smells.

Parietal lobe

Frontal lobe

Occipital lobe

Temporal lobe

❼ This cortical region deals with sensory functions of touch, taste and sight, and also has a role in olfaction and in emotions and behaviour.

❽ This region deals with the sense of vision. It contains the primary motor cortex, which processes "raw" incoming signals from the ganglion cells of the retina, and the visual association areas, which handle color, motion and form and bring the visual world toward conscious perception.

❾ Several interlinked functions are housed in this region, which copes with hearing and language but is also implicated in memory, especially auditory memory.

The cerebellum (right) has a role in movement, balance and eye movements handled by the flocculonodular lobe. The vermis and intermediate part of the hemisphere deal with the execution of movements, while the lateral part is instrumental in planning them.

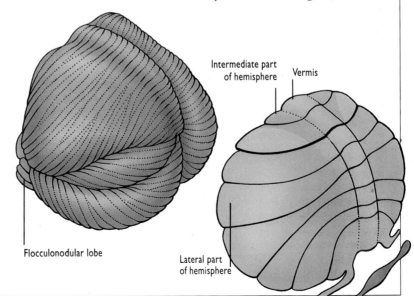

Intermediate part
of hemisphere   Vermis

Flocculonodular lobe

Lateral part
of hemisphere

Flocculonodular lobe

Map of chemicals

A range of chemicals – neurotransmitters – play key roles in the functioning of the brain when it comes to passing nerve signals.

Neurotransmitters are chemicals that take a nerve signal across the so-called synaptic gap between a sending nerve cell, or neuron, and a receiving one. On the receiving neuron are receptors into which the neurotransmitters fit like a key in a lock. Once a neurotransmitter is bound to its specific receptor this affects the likelihood of the receiving cell "firing" to send its own message. Some neurotransmitter–receptor systems make receiving cells more likely to fire (they are excitatory), whereas others make them less likely to fire (they are inhibitory).

A sending nerve cell releases neurotransmitters from the end of its axon, a signal-carrying fibre. The axon can link with receiving cells locally or extend to more remote receiving cells. So a nerve cell might have its cell body in the brain stem but fibres that reach cells in the cerebral cortex. The location in the brain of the nerve cell bodies and projection fibres of six important neurotransmitters is shown here.

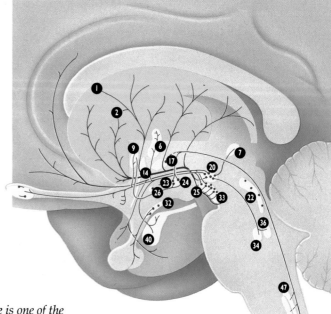

Dopamine is one of the amine group of neurotransmitters. It is involved in arousal levels and in motor activity. In the brain it can be a modulatory neurotransmitter – it can bias the response of nerve cells when it is released. Dopamine is thought to play a major role in the illness schizophrenia, since drugs that block the action of dopamine reduce the symptoms of the illness, and drugs that enhance its action can induce symptoms similar to those of schizophrenia.

❶ Caudate nucleus
❷ Putamen
❸ Fornix
❹ Stria terminalis
❺ Stria medullaris
❻ Nucleus interstitialis striae terminalis
❼ Habenula
❽ Subthalamic nucleus
❾ Septum
❿ Mammillothalamic tract
⓫ Globus pallidus
⓬ Superior colliculus
⓭ Midbrain gray matter
⓮ Anterior commissure
⓯ Preoptic nucleus
⓰ Dorsal diagonal nucleus
⓱ Paraventricular nucleus
⓲ Habenulo-interpeduncular tract
⓳ Dorsal longitudinal fasciculus
⓴ Ventral tegmental area
㉑ Hypothalamus
㉒ Raphé nuclei
㉓ Cell group A13
㉔ Cell group A11
㉕ Substantia nigra
㉖ Cell group A14

㉗ Meynert's nucleus
㉘ Ventral diagonal nucleus
㉙ Interpeduncular nucleus
㉚ Anterior olfactory nucleus
㉛ Olfactory tubercle
㉜ Infundibular nucleus
㉝ Retrorubral area
㉞ Locus coeruleus
㉟ Dorsal tegmental nucleus
㊱ Lateral parabrachial nucleus
㊲ Superior central nucleus
㊳ Suprachiasmatic nucleus
㊴ Supraoptic nucleus
㊵ Amygdala
㊶ Hippocampus
㊷ Pons
㊸ Lateral lemniscal nuclei
㊹ Vestibular nucleus
㊺ Trigeminal nerve nucleus
㊻ Cochlear nerve
㊼ Nucleus solitarius
㊽ Dorsal vagal nerve nucleus
㊾ Parabrachial nuclei
㊿ Spinal nerve
51 Olivary nucleus

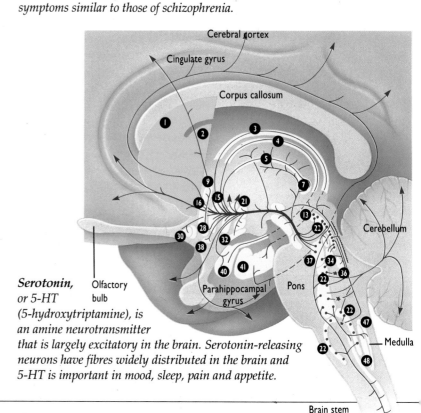

Serotonin, Olfactory *or 5-HT* bulb *(5-hydroxytriptamine), is an amine neurotransmitter that is largely excitatory in the brain. Serotonin-releasing neurons have fibres widely distributed in the brain and 5-HT is important in mood, sleep, pain and appetite.*

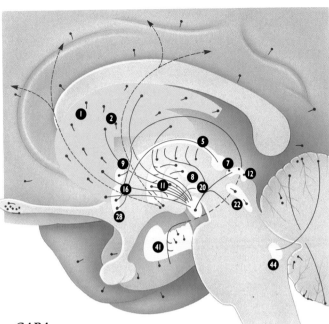

GABA, or
gamma-aminobutyric acid, is one of the
amino acid group of neurotransmitters. In
the brain it is inhibitory – its release makes
nerve cells less likely to "fire". Drugs that
enhance the action of GABA are used to treat
anxiety. By suppressing the action of neurons
involved specifically in the emotions, these drugs
bring anxiety levels down.

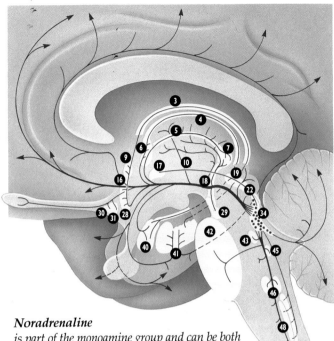

Noradrenaline
is part of the monoamine group and can be both
excitatory and inhibitory. In the brain, nerve
cells that release noradrenaline are clustered in
the locus coeruleus of the brain stem, with their
message-carrying axons projecting to many brain
regions. Noradrenaline is involved in arousal levels,
as well as autonomic (automatic) control of body
functions such as temperature regulation.

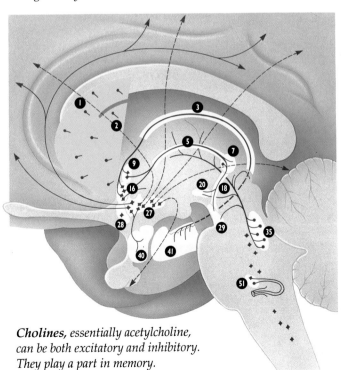

Cholines, essentially acetylcholine,
can be both excitatory and inhibitory.
They play a part in memory.

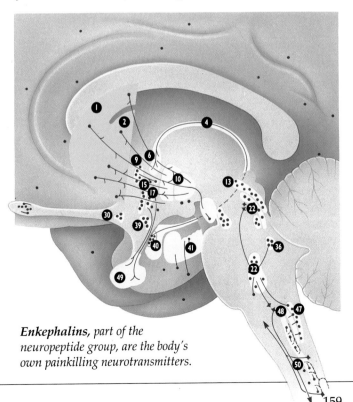

Enkephalins, part of the
neuropeptide group, are the body's
own painkilling neurotransmitters.

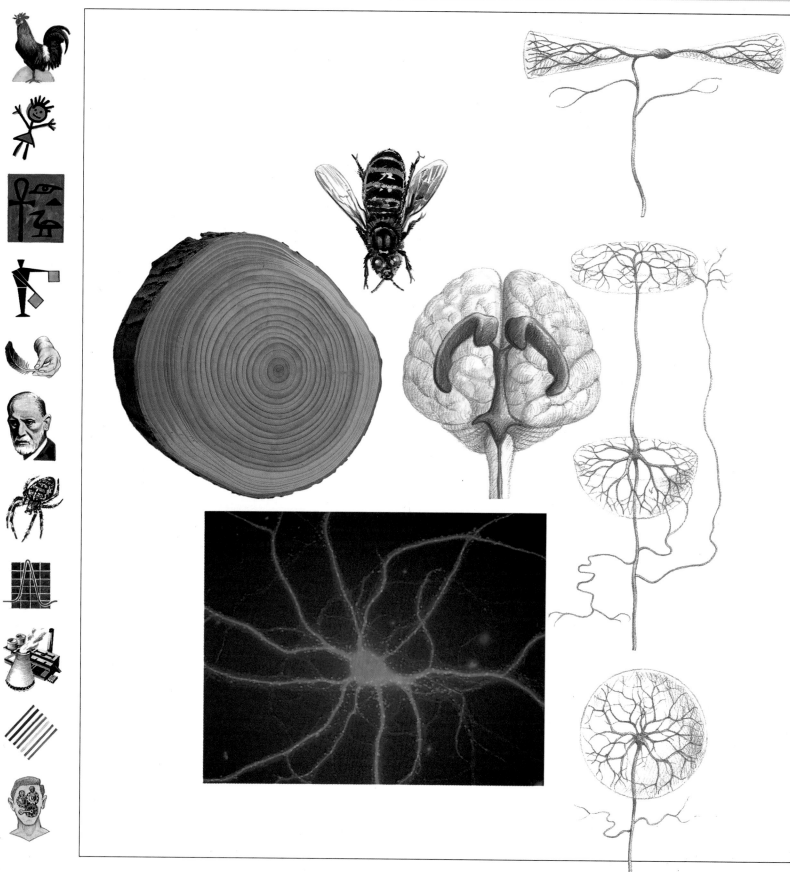

Building the Brain

O n delving into the workings of the brain it is possible to be overwhelmed by its layers of complexity. There are, for instance, as many as 100 billion individual neurons, each one connected to thousands of others. They constantly communicate with each other, sending up to 300 signals a second, which undergo transformations from electrical to chemical and back to electrical again. A neuron can receive messages simultaneously from thousands of other neurons; it can be bombarded with dozens of different messenger chemicals, each of which may have a different effect. All the time the brain is changing as it adapts to new inputs, learns new skills and lays down memories. Certain key principles can be applied across this bewildering mass of information. They apply in particular to how brain cells communicate with one another, and they are the key to understanding the brain.

*Left (**clockwise from top**): neuron shapes; close-up on the neuron; cells like tree rings; neurons link like a bee finds its way; brain bath.* ***This page (top):*** *learned links;* ***(left)*** *the brain's beginnings.*

Building blocks

The brain contains nerve cells, highly specialized members of the body's vast cellular community.

Life is based on the cell. This microscopic entity, averaging 20–50 microns (thousandths of a millimetre) across, is the smallest unit that can be defined as "alive". An organism such as an amoeba has all the features of life packed into just one cell, enabling it to feed, move, grow and reproduce. A roundworm the size of a scrap of cotton thread is composed of a few thousand cells but, unlike the amoeba's single cell, these cells cannot survive alone. They are specialized – they differ in structure and function, with each type carrying out a particular task. They depend on each other to keep the whole organism, the worm, alive.

The human body is far more complex still – it is made up of more than 50,000 billion cells, of at least 200 main kinds. The different body cells work together as a vast living cooperative. To delve into the human mind, it is necessary to focus on one type of cell in particular – the nerve cell, or neuron. This is the characteristic cell of nervous tissue, including the brain – and so it could be regarded as the building block of the mind.

While neurons have most of the basic parts that other cells have, their specializations lie in their spidery shape – which allows them to connect and thus communicate with one another – and their excitable nature. Their excitability means that under certain conditions neurons can generate and

*The brain is built from cells but having more cells – a bigger brain – does not, on average, make someone cleverer. If you could compare the brains of yourself, a great thinker such as Albert Einstein (**left**), and one of your less bright friends, you would probably see no difference in size or outward appearance. Average brain weights are 1.35 kg (3 pounds) for men and 1.25 kg (2¾ pounds) for women. Since men are generally larger than women, the brain to body ratio weight is slightly greater in females.*

convey tiny pulses of electricity along their membranes. These pulses are nerve signals, also referred to as action potentials. If neurons are the cellular building blocks of the brain and nervous system, nerve signals are the data – the information carried around and stored in the system.

Little of this would be understood were it not for generations of research in the areas of anatomy, microscopy, physiology and medicine. A major breakthrough came in 1873, when Italian physician and medical researcher Camillo Golgi (1844–1926) discovered that stains, or dyes, containing silver showed up nerve cells clearly under the microscope. Previously, no one had been able to follow the twists and turns of their spidery projections as they snaked between other cells and tissues – they were too fine and impossible to see, even at high magnification.

The silver stains showed the neurons as dark lines and began to reveal the hitherto secret details of the nerve net. Neurology, the study of the brain and nerves, took a leap forward. In recognition of his efforts, Golgi was awarded the Nobel prize in 1906, and the Golgi apparatus, a structure in the cell body, was named after him. More than 100 years after Golgi's discovery, neurology continues to be one of the most exciting and progressive areas in the life sciences as still more secrets of the neuron are unravelled one by one.

A fly trapped in amber has every tiny detail of its body, legs, wings, head and hairy covering encased and supported by fossilized conifer-tree resin. A nerve cell, or neuron, is an even more complex and convoluted shape, with many thin, delicate, curving projections thousands of times longer than its main body. It too has support, both physical and chemical, from the cells around it. Of course, the fly in its resin is long dead and hardened into a fossil. But neurons in their supporting framework are alive and flexible, and remain able to change their connections over the years.

The "typical" body cell does not exist as such, but the cell below left shows the basic parts that most ordinary cells contain. The plasma membrane is the outer wrapping and controls what enters and leaves the cell. It is folded inward to form other structures such as the endoplasmic reticulum, where proteins are assembled from amino acids. These proteins are combined with sugar and packaged for export by the Golgi apparatus. Mitochondria liberate the energy from energy-rich sugars to drive the cell's processes. Lysosomes are ball-shaped bags of digestive enzymes; vesicles are membranous sacs that store and transport materials. Microtubules form the cell's internal scaffolding, while centrioles assist in cell division. All the components are suspended in cytoplasm and the whole is controlled by genetic information in the form of molecules of DNA in the nucleus.

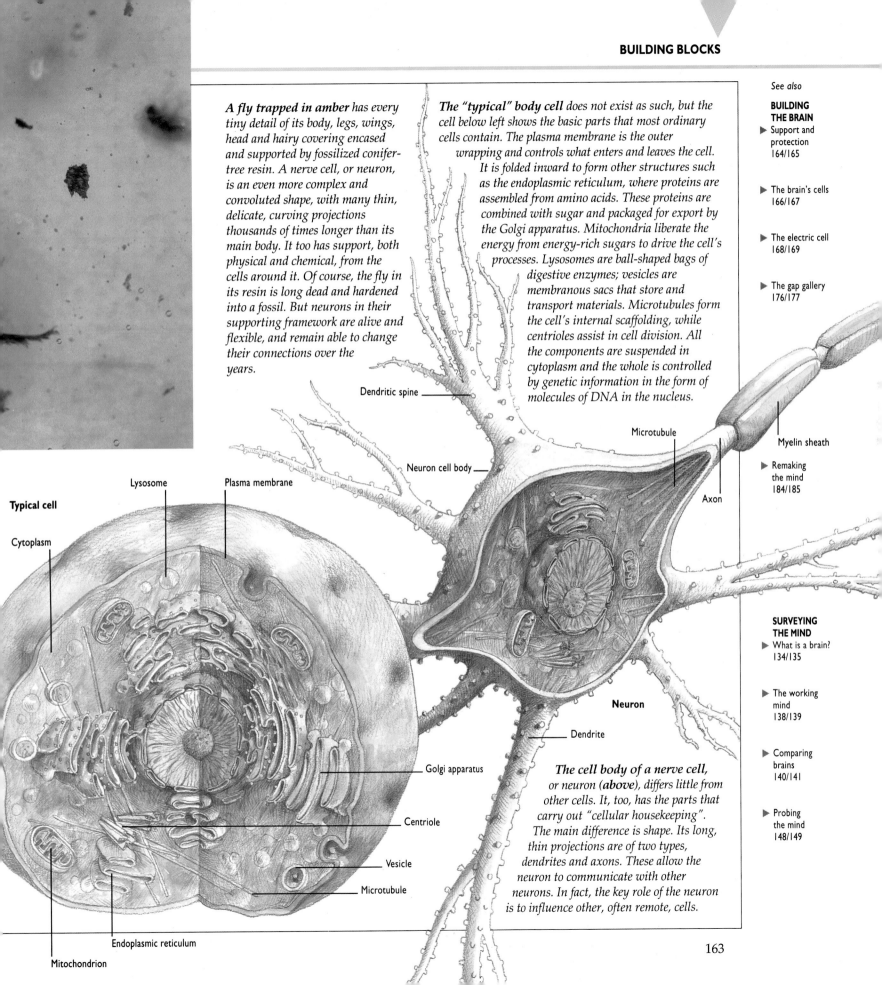

Typical cell

Cytoplasm

Lysosome

Plasma membrane

Dendritic spine

Neuron cell body

Microtubule

Myelin sheath

Axon

Golgi apparatus

Centriole

Vesicle

Microtubule

Endoplasmic reticulum

Mitochondrion

Neuron

Dendrite

The cell body of a nerve cell, or neuron (**above**), differs little from other cells. It, too, has the parts that carry out "cellular housekeeping". The main difference is shape. Its long, thin projections are of two types, dendrites and axons. These allow the neuron to communicate with other neurons. In fact, the key role of the neuron is to influence other, often remote, cells.

163

Support and protection

Evolution has provided a suitably secure system to cradle the delicate parts of that most precious organ, the brain.

The brain has the consistency of set yogurt. It is cradled within the rigid protective casket of the cranium, or "brain box". This box is formed by the firmly jointed curved bones of the skull. Layers of muscle, fat, skin and (in most people) hair on the outside of the skull act as a shock-absorbing cushion for minor knocks and jars. Hair can also protect against extreme temperatures. Directly inside the skull bones are the three layers, or membranes, of the meninges, with cerebrospinal fluid (CSF) between the inner two. With this support, the brain "floats" within the skull and is shielded from shocks and vibrations.

At the microscopic level, the brain's neurons have a cellular scaffolding of supporting cells, or neuroglia ("nerve glue"). Indeed, neuroglial cells form up to 90 percent of all cells in the brain and about half of the brain's total volume. Specialized capillary blood vessels create a "blood–brain barrier" – one that prevents invasion of the brain by potentially harmful chemicals from the blood. Finally, the brain is protected by a person's behaviour: the head is moved quickly to duck a fast-moving ball, for example, or hazardous situations are avoided.

Cerebrospinal fluid (CSF) protects the brain in many ways. Outside, it occupies the subarachnoid space between the middle and inner meninges and provides hydraulic cushioning. Within, it flows slowly through a system of four interconnected branching cavities – the ventricles – supplying nutrients and removing wastes.

A network, or choroid plexus, of blood capillaries lining each ventricle produces CSF, which moves through the ventricles and into the subarachnoid space through openings in the fourth ventricle. Some flows down the spinal cord, but most seeps through arachnoid granulations to rejoin the blood in the superior sagittal sinus on top of the brain.

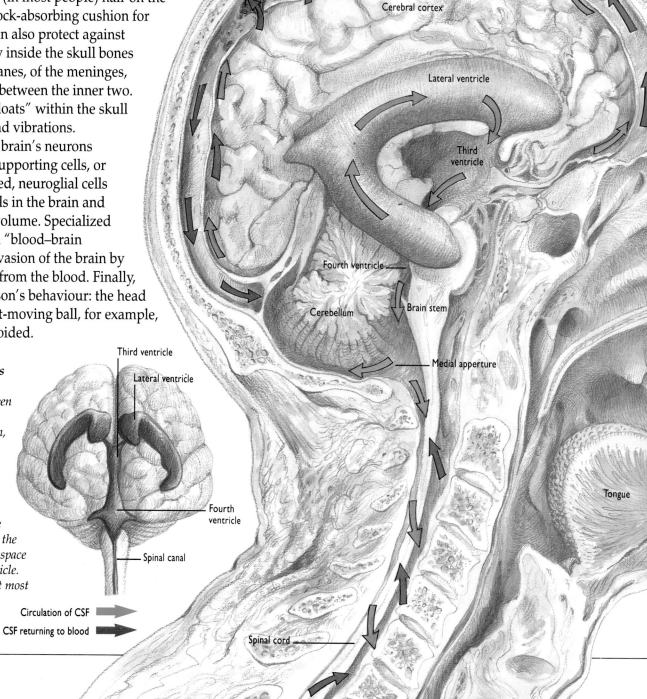

Skin

Skull

Dura mater
Arachnoid granulation
Superior sagittal sinus
Subarachnoid space

Cerebral cortex

Superior sagittal sinus
Arachnoid granulation
Skull

Cerebral cortex

Lateral ventricle

Third ventricle

Fourth ventricle

Cerebellum

Brain stem

Medial apperture

Tongue

Third ventricle

Lateral ventricle

Fourth ventricle

Spinal canal

Circulation of CSF

CSF returning to blood

Spinal cord

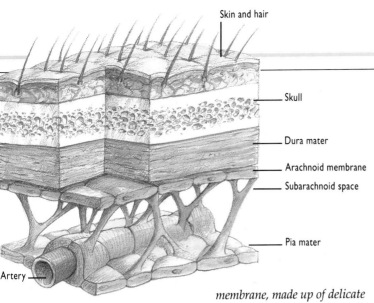

Skin and hair

Skull

Dura mater

Arachnoid membrane

Subarachnoid space

Pia mater

Artery

A buffer of several layers shields the brain from the outside world. Hair and skin cover the hard bony skull and act as shock absorbers. The inside of the skull is lined by the dura mater, the outer of the three meninges, which is a relatively thick and tough membrane. The arachnoid membrane, made up of delicate connective tissue, separates the dura mater from the subarachnoid space, which contains vital cerebrospinal fluid. The thin innermost pia mater, rich in blood vessels that supply some of the blood to the brain, follows every contour of the brain's surface.

Debris-scavenging microglial cells are usually found between neurons and along blood vessels in the central nervous system. They are not true glial cells, but are part of the group of white blood cells known as macrophages – they patrol between neurons and neuroglia, searching for debris to engulf and destroy. Microglia are one of the four types of neuroglia, along with ependymal cells, astrocytes and oligodendrocytes. The microglia above, in bright yellow, are from a cranial nerve of a rat.

Star-shaped astrocytes insulate neurons, provide nutrients and form their cellular supporting framework, especially during early development of the embryo. They also recycle neurotransmitter chemicals, and some can transmit their own electrical signals. With oligodendrocytes, astrocytes form the group of neuroglial cells called macroglia.

Nose

Ependymal cell

Ependymal cells line the ventricles and the spinal canal. They are covered with fingerlike microvilli and allow certain molecules from the brain to pass into the CSF.

Protoplasmic astrocyte

Blood cell

Pericapillary
end foot

Capillary

The blood–brain barrier protects the chemical environment of neurons and neuroglia in brain tissue, keeping it within precise limits. Blood vessels and capillaries in the brain are lined with a closeknit layer of cells that restrict the movement of substances between them. The cells themselves also have limited permeability, so only a few highly selected types of molecules can pass through them, from the blood into the brain.

Oligodendrocytes are neuroglial cells that make myelin in the brain. Spiral layers of this fatty substance insulate the axons of some neurons. (In the peripheral nervous system, Schwann cells do this task.)

Axon

Neuron

Oligodendrocyte

Subpial end foot

Fibrous
astrocyte

Microglial cell

Myelin sheath

Pia mater

Perineuronal end foot

Synapse ⸺

The brain's cells

Nerve cells come in an extraordinarily wide range of shapes and sizes.

Neurons, or nerve cells, are the basic units of the entire nervous system. There are probably about 100 billion neurons in the brain itself and at least the same number again in the rest of the nervous system. In its cell body, or soma, the typical neuron is much like any other cell. It is average in size, at 15–25 micrometres ($\frac{3}{5,000}$–$\frac{1}{1,000}$ inch) across, and has a cell nucleus, or control centre, and other parts, or organelles, found in most types of cells.

So what makes the neuron special? Two main features. The first is that a neuron's outer layer – the plasma membrane – is specialized to convey nerve signals as electrochemical pulses. The second is its overall shape – the average neuron is not a sphere or cylinder like so many other cells. It has numerous projecting parts

known as neurites, which are like long tentacles or wires. They snake through the tissues to make connections with other neurons, so that nerve signals can pass between them. There are two main types of neurites: axons and dendrites. Axons are usually long, and each neuron has only one, which may branch; dendrites are shorter and have multiple branches.

In most neurons, especially those in the brain, the dendrites are so numerous and branching that they represent 90 percent or more of the neuron's total surface area. The geometry of its neurites determines the physical shape of a neuron and the connections it can make, which in turn determine its role and function.

Stellate neurons, found in the cerebral cortex and some regions of the brain stem and spinal cord, have neurites that occupy an approximately spherical volume. In the cortex their role is to deal with local processing, and they send messages to other cells that are in their immediate vicinity.

Stellate neurons

Golgi neuron

Pyramidal neuron

Bipolar neuron

Unipolar neuron

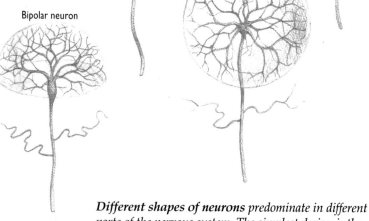

Different shapes of neurons predominate in different parts of the nervous system. The simplest design is the unipolar neuron found mainly in the sensory systems. Its cell body (dark circle) does not take much part in signal conduction. The bipolar neuron collects signals from other cells via its dendrites, which all merge at the cell body, and passes its own signal along one main axon. The pyramidal neuron – the most common type in the cerebral cortex – has a roughly pyramid-shaped cell body. It has two widely separated sets of dendrites, as well as axon branches that may link back to them. The large Golgi neuron is found in the cerebellum, the part of the brain that has a role in fine movement.

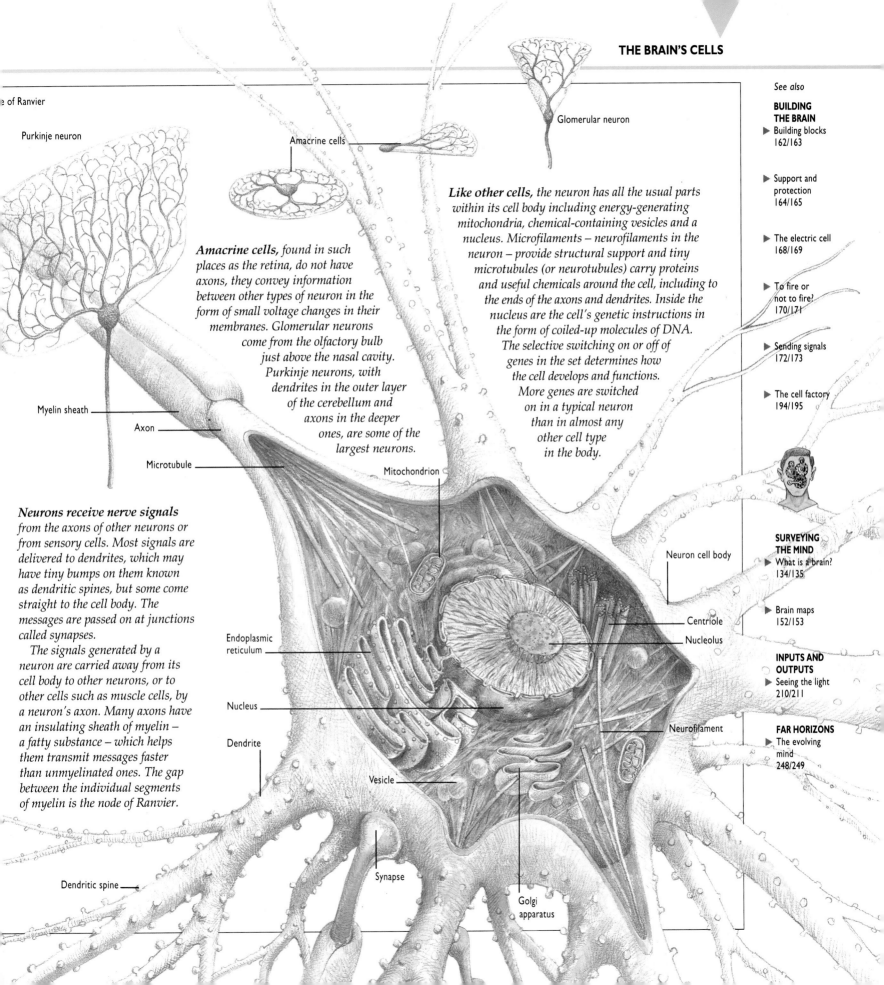

e of Ranvier

Purkinje neuron

Glomerular neuron

Amacrine cells

Like other cells, the neuron has all the usual parts
within its cell body including energy-generating
mitochondria, chemical-containing vesicles and a
nucleus. Microfilaments – neurofilaments in the
neuron – provide structural support and tiny
microtubules (or neurotubules) carry proteins
and useful chemicals around the cell, including to
the ends of the axons and dendrites. Inside the
nucleus are the cell's genetic instructions in
the form of coiled-up molecules of DNA.
The selective switching on or off of
genes in the set determines how
the cell develops and functions.
More genes are switched
on in a typical neuron
than in almost any
other cell type
in the body.

Amacrine cells, found in such
places as the retina, do not have
axons, they convey information
between other types of neuron in the
form of small voltage changes in their
membranes. Glomerular neurons
come from the olfactory bulb
just above the nasal cavity.
Purkinje neurons, with
dendrites in the outer layer
of the cerebellum and
axons in the deeper
ones, are some of the
largest neurons.

Myelin sheath

Axon

Microtubule

Mitochondrion

Neurons receive nerve signals
from the axons of other neurons or
from sensory cells. Most signals are
delivered to dendrites, which may
have tiny bumps on them known
as dendritic spines, but some come
straight to the cell body. The
messages are passed on at junctions
called synapses.

The signals generated by a
neuron are carried away from its
cell body to other neurons, or to
other cells such as muscle cells, by
a neuron's axon. Many axons have
an insulating sheath of myelin –
a fatty substance – which helps
them transmit messages faster
than unmyelinated ones. The gap
between the individual segments
of myelin is the node of Ranvier.

Endoplasmic
reticulum

Nucleus

Dendrite

Vesicle

Dendritic spine

Synapse

Golgi
apparatus

Neuron cell body

Centriole

Nucleolus

Neurofilament

See also

**BUILDING
THE BRAIN**
▶ Building blocks
162/163

▶ Support and
protection
164/165

▶ The electric cell
168/169

▶ To fire or
not to fire?
170/171

▶ Sending signals
172/173

▶ The cell factory
194/195

**SURVEYING
THE MIND**
▶ What is a brain?
134/135

▶ Brain maps
152/153

**INPUTS AND
OUTPUTS**
▶ Seeing the light
210/211

FAR HORIZONS
▶ The evolving
mind
248/249

The electric cell

Nerve cells have outer membranes with extraordinary properties vital to their ability to send messages.

Electricity is a natural part of living and is involved in every cell in the body. The myriad biochemical reactions and pathways that make up life processes take place in solution, with substances dissolved in water. When a substance such as common salt dissolves, it no longer exists as the usual atoms and molecules – in the case of salt, sodium chloride. The atoms lose or gain electrons to become free-floating particles known as ions. These have a positive or negative charge, and since electricity is the movement of charge, the movement of charged ions inside a living cell is electricity. In a typical cell, certain ions are kept in specific positions on either side of the cell membrane. But ions tend to drift around so that they become evenly spread out and balanced – they will diffuse until their concentration is equal, and any charge difference has been eliminated. Keeping ions separated out against their tendency to equalize charge and concentration uses up energy, which the cell has to expend.

By means of a pump, a neuron's so-called excitable cell membrane is able to restrain ions from passing freely

Sodium and chloride ions

An atom is made up of a positively charged central nucleus and particles called electrons which spin around it and which between them have an equivalent negative charge, so the whole atom is electrically neutral. In solution, an atom loses or gains one or more electrons. The result is a particle, or ion, that has charge. In crystals of common salt, sodium chloride (NaCl), the sodium and chlorine atoms are joined, or bonded, by sharing one electron. In solution they

Sodium chloride (NaCl)

Positively charged sodium ion (Na$^+$)

via channels into or our of the cell. Thus a neuron that is "on standby" keeps an excess of positive ions, or cations, just outside its cell membrane, and an excess of negative ions, or anions, inside. This separation of particles with opposite charges produces a potential difference, an electrical difference, between the inside and the outside of the membrane. It is known as the resting potential and can be measured with sensitive scientific equipment at around – 70 millivolts, with the inside of the cell negatively charged.

When the neuron comes "off standby" and actually sends its signal, ions cross the membrane for a split second to make the inside momentarily positive by about 50 millivolts. This rise in voltage is an action potential. The shift in charge as the ions move is an electrochemical event and produces an electrical pulse – the nerve signal.

separate. Sodium loses the electron and becomes a positive ion, Na$^+$; chlorine gains one to make a negative ion, Cl$^-$. These, along with the potassium ion K$^+$, are the main ions involved in nerve impulses.

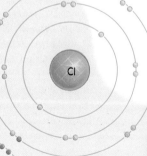

Negatively charged chloride ion (Cl$^-$)

Water (H$_2$O)

An archer draws the bowstring and holds it steady, using muscle power to maintain enforced equilibrium. A small movement will release the bow's stored (or potential) energy. The neuron also uses energy to maintain the resting potential by separating charged particles across its cell membrane. Just a small

change will cause the enforced equilibrium of the resting potential to give way as the particles move through the cell membrane to balance out the artificially maintained potential difference. This movement causes an action potential.

Inside the membrane there is an overall excess of negative ions (anions); outside an excess of positive ions (cations). Since opposite charges attract, positive and negative ions line up on either side of the membrane.

Sodium (Na+)

Potassium (K+)

Chloride (Cl-)

Protein anions

Axon

Membrane

The ions on either side of the axon's cell membrane are dissolved in the fluid (mostly water) that is found both inside and outside all body cells.

The cell membrane enables the cell to generate a resting potential. This is done using energy-consuming pumps in the membrane which make sure that ions stay segregated against their natural tendency to spread out and equalize their electrical charges and chemical concentrations. Sodium ions are pumped out of the cell, and potassium ions pumped back in.

A battery, or electric cell, is a device designed to make electricity by separating positive from negative charge – usually by separating negative electrons from the rest of their now positive atoms. In an alkaline dry battery, zinc powder is dissolved in potassium hydroxide. When connected into a circuit, the zinc gives up electrons to the manganese dioxide. These flow around the conductor as an electric current. A living cell, a type of "biological battery", also separates charge across its membrane.

Positive terminal

Insulation and cover

Steel sheath

Seal

Manganese dioxide with graphite

Only electrons pass through separator

Battery–driven device

Paste of zinc and potassium hydroxide

Direction of electron flow

Metal nail collects electrons

Seal

Negative terminal

To fire or not to fire?

Every fraction of a second, each nerve cell in the brain and body decides whether or not to send a signal.

What prompts a nerve cell, or neuron, suddenly to fire a nerve signal, or action potential, along its axon? The answer depends largely on the signals that the neuron has itself received. These signals can be coming in at the rate of tens of thousands every second from other neurons which have connections (synapses) with the neuron in question. A neuron may have up to 100,000 synapses, tiny gaps crossed by signalling chemicals (neurotransmitters) which cause an electrical change when they arrive. This takes the form of a postsynaptic potential (PSP), a tiny strength change in the electrical potential – the difference in voltage – across the cell's membrane. Each PSP moves out from its synapse by a process called passive spread, fading with time and distance.

Every instant waves of PSPs pass around the neuron's cell membrane. But they can trigger a signal only at the cone-shaped axon hillock where the axon joins on to the neuron's cell body. If the combined PSPs reaching the hillock push the potential there over a threshold level, an action potential of a fixed strength is fired and this travels along the axon.

But an absence of inputs does not mean that a cell will not fire. Some neurons are autorhythmic – they can generate their own action potentials repeatedly (through oscillation in their membrane potential). Inputs to these neurons modulate their inherent rate of firing, turning it up or down. In other cases a neuron will be quiescent until excited by an input. Information is coded in the brain and nervous system in the frequency of action potentials, the gaps between them and the total numbers of neurons involved. For example, suppose a few neurons fire at a slow rate and then a large number fire in rapid succession. If these two extremes represented signals from skin touch sensors, they might enable you to tell the difference between being hit by a table tennis ball or a football.

Separate small explosive charges set at different places yet detonating together or in sequence can bring about the fall of a building. One small charge on its own would not have much effect. It is the adding, or summation, of the charges that works. A neuron works by a similar simple principle. Many small and variable events – incoming nerve signals – add together to tip the balance and trigger a large outcome, the outgoing nerve signal, or action potential.

When a neuron receives a signal from another neuron via one of its communication points, or synapses, neurotransmitter chemicals from the sending neuron diffuse across the synaptic gap and bind on to receptors in the membrane of the receiving neuron. These receptors either directly or indirectly cause tiny channels in the receiving cell's membrane to open, allowing ions (charged particles) into or out of the cell. This movement of ions creates a postsynaptic potential (PSP), which changes the potential of the neuron's membrane locally and generates a so-called electrotonic current which spreads passively through the neuron and the fluid surrounding it. The electrotonic current of a PSP travels to the axon hillock of the neuron where it alters the potential across the membrane, which has an influence on whether or not the neuron sends its own action potential.

Electrotonic currents

Synapse

Axon

Neuron

Dendrite

Cell membrane

Inside the cell Outside the cell

Inactivating particle

Activation gate

Voltage-gated ion channel

Axon hillock

Sodium ion (Na⁺)

Myelin sheath

At the axon hillock the potential across the cell membrane changes polarization according to the effects of all the various PSPs that take place in the neuron. PSPs can add, or combine, their effects if they occur closely spaced in time, a feature known as temporal summation. In the graph below, a sequence of PSPs – each one caused by the flow of ions through an ion channel, which takes a certain length of time – have occurred close enough together for the effects to accumulate.

The ensuing depolarization at the axon hillock has been sufficient to trigger an action potential. PSPs also add their effects if they are physically near to one another on the neuron or its dendrites, a feature known as spatial summation. Any single PSP usually has to interact with many PSPs from other synapses. Some are not stimulatory, but inhibitory; the two types work to cancel each other out.

A single action potential is an all-or-nothing event of a fixed amplitude. It comes about when the tens of thousands of special ion channels clustered at a neuron's axon hillock open in concert. These are voltage-gated ion channels and they stay closed until the local voltage (potential) at the hillock reaches the threshold – typically 10–20 millivolts depolarized from the resting potential of about –70 millivolts inside the membrane compared to outside. Temporarily the potential changes by 120 millivolts to around +50 millivolts. Once triggered, the action potential proceeds at this strength along the length of the axon.

At rest a voltage-gated ion channel is closed (**1**). When the polarization threshold is crossed an activation gate on the inside of the channel swings open (**2**) and sodium ions flood inside (**3**), making the cell more positive. After a short while a so-called inactivation particle swings shut, blocking the channel (**4**). When the polarization returns to normal the activation gate resumes its closed position (**5**).

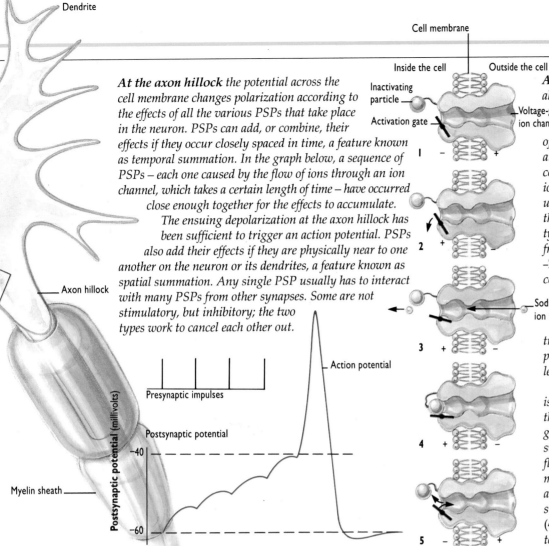

Action potential

Presynaptic impulses

Postsynaptic potential

Postsynaptic potential (millivolts)

–40

–60

Time

HOMING IN ON THE NERVE CELL'S SECRETS

Since 1976, researchers have had the means to study those parts of the nerve cell that are responsible for its remarkable characteristics. The technique that has made this possible – patch clamping – has allowed them to isolate and study single ion channels in the cell membranes of neurons. Indeed, this technique has proved so valuable that its main developers – Erwin Neher and Bert Sakmann – received the Nobel prize for medicine in 1991.

An incredibly fine glass pipette (tube) is placed on the cleaned membrane of a cell, and slight suction is applied up it. This seals the pipette's mouth, which may be 50,000 times finer than a human hair, against a small area, or patch, of membrane. The patch is isolated physically, electrically and chemically. Wires in the pipette and in other parts of the cell either stimulate it or measure electrical changes that result, as ion channels in the isolated patch open and close. Various chemicals can also be introduced via fluid in the pipette, and their effects followed. Or the patch of membrane can be torn away from the cell for further study in isolation.

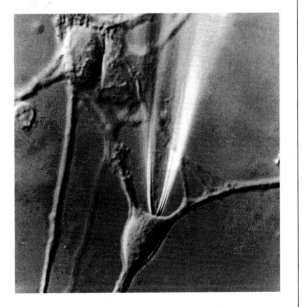

Sending signals

Tiny fibres carry signals from one nerve cell to another. Some are carried quickly, others more slowly.

When a neuron, or nerve cell, sends a message down its wirelike axon to another neuron, the signal moves along as a travelling electric pulse. The pulse is carried along by the sequential opening and closing of tiny pores in the axon's membrane. These pores, known as voltage-gated ion channels, respond to voltage changes, or depolarization. Below a certain threshold voltage they stay closed; above that level they open to allow charged particles (ions) to flow through them.

Since a flow of charged particles is, in effect, an electric current, this flow locally pushes the voltage of the axon membrane over the threshold and causes channels next to the ones that have just opened to open in turn. Thus a pulse, or action potential, travels along the axon.

Many axons are insulated with a spiral wrapping of myelin, a fat-rich substance formed by a special type of cell. Typically, each segment of myelin sheath is about 1 mm (¹⁄₂₅ inch) long and it may have up to 100 layers. The myelin segments are arranged along the axon like a string of sausages. But they

*A **nerve signal starts** in the axon hillock of a nerve cell (**below left**). Here, negative inhibitory potentials and positive excitatory ones from elsewhere in the nerve cell coincide, and when the potential rises above a certain threshold, it causes voltage-gated ion channels in the initial segment of the axon to open. This sends a wave of depolarization, or an action potential, along the axon.*

*The **runners in a relay race** do not complete the course but the baton does. Each runner passes it in turn to the next runner in the sequence, for energy input and a fresh burst of speed. Similarly, a nerve signal jumps along the insulated sections of a myelinated axon, receiving a fresh burst of energy at each uninsulated section to speed it along.*

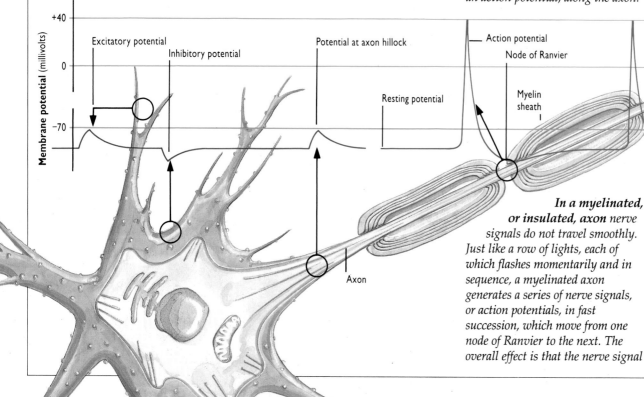

In a myelinated, or insulated, axon nerve signals do not travel smoothly. Just like a row of lights, each of which flashes momentarily and in sequence, a myelinated axon generates a series of nerve signals, or action potentials, in fast succession, which move from one node of Ranvier to the next. The overall effect is that the nerve signal

flashes along the axon. Because of this, myelinated axons conduct their signals faster and more efficiently than neurons whose axons lack a myelin sheath. Signals move along myelinated axons at speeds of 4–120 m/sec (13–394 feet/sec) – the thicker the axon the faster the signal. In non-myelinated axons, speeds are much slower – 0.5–4 m/sec (20 inches–13 feet/sec).

MULTIPLE SCLEROSIS

In a myelinated axon – the wirelike extension of a neuron (nerve cell) that carries messages from the cell body – the fatty myelin sheath is a good electrical insulator. It prevents the electrochemical charges of a nerve signal from leaking away into the cells and fluid around the axon and conducts signals rapidly and energy efficiently.

Some medical conditions are caused by problems with the myelin sheaths, and this can have a great impact on the way that neurons communicate. One of these is multiple sclerosis, or MS, in which myelin is progressively destroyed, possibly due to the body's immune defence system mistakenly attacking itself. The demyelinating sites become inflamed and affected by non-functioning scar tissue (sclerosis and plaque formation).

Layers of myelin

Axon

This prevents the damaged neurons from sending messages. Symptoms generally develop slowly and depend on the nerves affected. They may include numbness or tingling in the hands and feet, visual disturbances, muscle weakness, slow movements and clumsiness, bladder and bowel problems, and personality changes. The symptoms tend to come and go but, in general, they progress over years. There is no cure for MS – treatment focuses on symptom relief, and helps and aids for daily life.

MS usually begins around 20 to 25 years, but it can develop at any age from 10 to 50. It is relatively common in certain (mainly white) ethnic groups, affecting as many as 1 in 350 people. Yet it is almost unknown in other groups, such as some black Africans and Inuits.

are not quite in contact with each other – there is a small gap between one segment of myelin sheath and the next. This gap is known as a node of Ranvier and it acts like a "booster station" to the nerve signal, just as booster stations at regular intervals along a telephone cable amplify and resend fading signals.

Between these nodes, the myelin coating prevents contact between the axon membrane and the extracellular fluid, which contains the various ions needed for changing the voltage. This means that the depolarizing effects of the action potential spread passively along the membrane itself and inside it until a node of Ranvier is reached. Here the axon's membrane has extracellular fluid and ions on the outside and is very excitable, so the full action potential can be reconstituted and refired, making it appear to leap from node to node along the axon. It is known as saltatory conduction (from the Latin *saltare*, to jump). Axons that do not have a myelin sheath conduct their signals more slowly than insulated myelinated axons.

As a nerve signal, or action potential, travels along an axon's membrane, electrically charged sodium ions (Na^+) rush to the inside of the membrane through voltage-gated channels. This temporarily changes the difference in voltage between the inside and the outside of the membrane from its resting potential of -70 mV to as much as +40 mV. This change is known as depolarization and it makes adjacent Na^+ channels open and a wave of depolarization travels along it. After Na^+ floods in, potassium ions (K^+) move out as the cell repolarizes. To restore the resting potential, pumps in the membrane remove the Na^+ and import K^+.

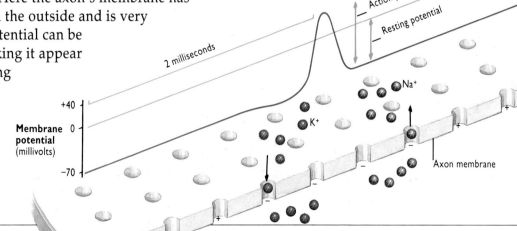

Direction of impulse

Action potential

Resting potential

2 milliseconds

+40
Membrane 0
potential
(millivolts)
−70

K^+

Na^+

Axon membrane

Ion channel

173

Crossing the gap

For one nerve cell to communicate with another, it has to transmit its signal across a small gap.

When a nerve signal, or impulse, reaches the end of its axon, there is a fundamental change in its nature. Along the axon, the nerve signal has travelled as an action potential – a pulse of electricity. But between one neuron and the next there is no cellular continuity; there is a gap called the synapse. The membranes of the sending and receiving cells are separated by the fluid-filled synaptic gap.

Although the gap is only 20–25 nanometres across ($\frac{1}{600}$ the width of a hair), the signal cannot leap it electrically. So chemicals, or neurotransmitters, are released by the presynaptic "sending" membrane and seep across the gap to receptors on the receiving neuron's postsynaptic membrane. The binding of neurotransmitters to these receptors has the effect of allowing ions (charged particles) to pass in and out of the receiving cell. This amounts to a transient change in potential difference (that is, an electrical signal). This signal is not large enough on its own to be a full action potential but contributes to the possible initiation of one at the axon hillock, the start of the receiving neuron's axon.

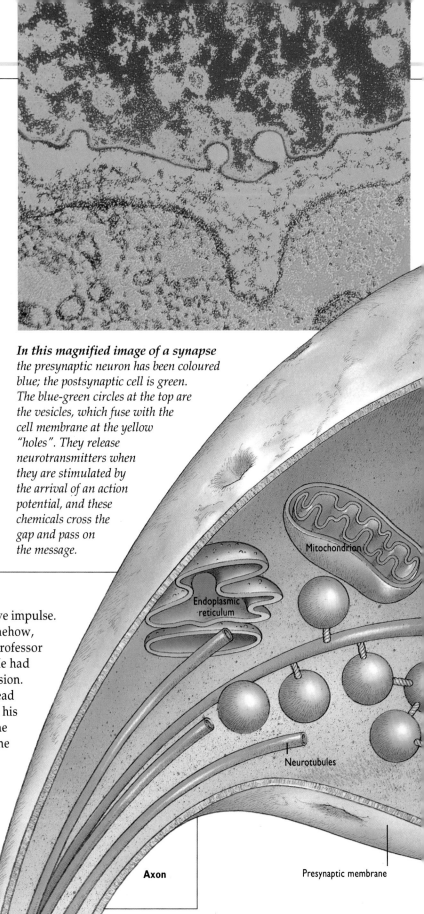

In this magnified image of a synapse the presynaptic neuron has been coloured blue; the postsynaptic cell is green. The blue-green circles at the top are the vesicles, which fuse with the cell membrane at the yellow "holes". They release neurotransmitters when they are stimulated by the arrival of an action potential, and these chemicals cross the gap and pass on the message.

Mitochondrion

Endoplasmic reticulum

Neurotubules

Axon

Presynaptic membrane

A REWARDING EASTER

In the early 1900s much research was carried out into the nature of the nerve impulse. Some scientists suspected that it was not solely an electrical process; somehow, chemicals were involved. In 1921 physiologist Otto Loewi (1873–1961), professor of pharmacology at Graz, Austria, woke in the night of Easter Sunday. He had an idea to demonstrate chemical involvement in nerve-impulse transmission. He scribbled some notes and slept on, but in the morning he could not read his handwriting! The next night he woke again and immediately went to his laboratory and did the experiment. He used dissected frog hearts with the vagus nerve, which controls heart rate, still attached. Loewi immersed one frog heart in a fluid, Ringer's solution, and stimulated its vagus – which would normally slow the heartbeat. As expected, the beating rate reduced. When a second heart was put in the solution its beat also decreased – without stimulation. Loewi reasoned that a chemical from the first heart had seeped through the solution and affected the beating of the second heart. After two hours he had shown for the first time that chemicals – now called neurotransmitters – were involved in nerve-impulse transmission. In 1933 the chemical involved, acetylcholine, was isolated. Dozens of neurotransmitters have since been discovered.

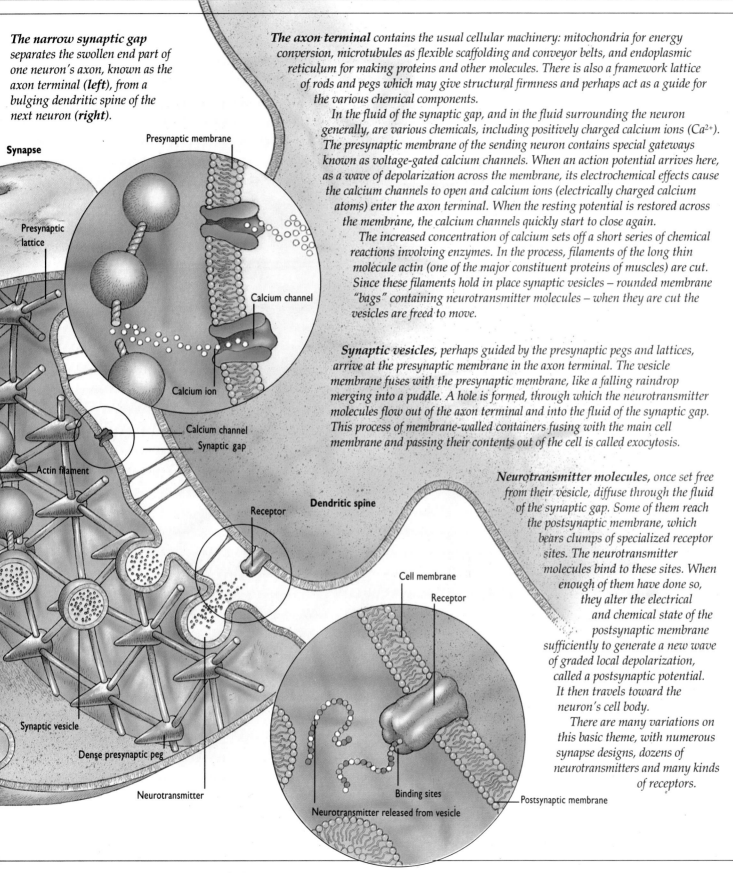

The narrow synaptic gap separates the swollen end part of one neuron's axon, known as the axon terminal (**left**), from a bulging dendritic spine of the next neuron (**right**).

Synapse

Presynaptic membrane

Presynaptic lattice

Calcium channel

Calcium ion

Calcium channel

Synaptic gap

Actin filament

Receptor

Dendritic spine

Synaptic vesicle

Dense presynaptic peg

Neurotransmitter

Cell membrane

Receptor

Binding sites

Neurotransmitter released from vesicle

Postsynaptic membrane

The axon terminal contains the usual cellular machinery: mitochondria for energy conversion, microtubules as flexible scaffolding and conveyor belts, and endoplasmic reticulum for making proteins and other molecules. There is also a framework lattice of rods and pegs which may give structural firmness and perhaps act as a guide for the various chemical components.

In the fluid of the synaptic gap, and in the fluid surrounding the neuron generally, are various chemicals, including positively charged calcium ions (Ca^{2+}). The presynaptic membrane of the sending neuron contains special gateways known as voltage-gated calcium channels. When an action potential arrives here, as a wave of depolarization across the membrane, its electrochemical effects cause the calcium channels to open and calcium ions (electrically charged calcium atoms) enter the axon terminal. When the resting potential is restored across the membrane, the calcium channels quickly start to close again.

The increased concentration of calcium sets off a short series of chemical reactions involving enzymes. In the process, filaments of the long thin molecule actin (one of the major constituent proteins of muscles) are cut. Since these filaments hold in place synaptic vesicles – rounded membrane "bags" containing neurotransmitter molecules – when they are cut the vesicles are freed to move.

Synaptic vesicles, perhaps guided by the presynaptic pegs and lattices, arrive at the presynaptic membrane in the axon terminal. The vesicle membrane fuses with the presynaptic membrane, like a falling raindrop merging into a puddle. A hole is formed, through which the neurotransmitter molecules flow out of the axon terminal and into the fluid of the synaptic gap. This process of membrane-walled containers fusing with the main cell membrane and passing their contents out of the cell is called exocytosis.

Neurotransmitter molecules, once set free from their vesicle, diffuse through the fluid of the synaptic gap. Some of them reach the postsynaptic membrane, which bears clumps of specialized receptor sites. The neurotransmitter molecules bind to these sites. When enough of them have done so, they alter the electrical and chemical state of the postsynaptic membrane sufficiently to generate a new wave of graded local depolarization, called a postsynaptic potential. It then travels toward the neuron's cell body.

There are many variations on this basic theme, with numerous synapse designs, dozens of neurotransmitters and many kinds of receptors.

The gap gallery

Synapses – their design, structure and position – are the key to how nerve signals are transmitted.

Between two nerve cells (neurons), one sending and one receiving a signal, there is a synapse, or synaptic gap, that can take many forms. The synapse's sending part is usually the terminal of an axon, the signal-carrying "wire" of a neuron. The receiving part may be on the shaft of a neuron's dendrite; on the cell body – or soma – of the neuron; or on a bulge, or "spine", projecting from the dendrite or the soma.

When a signal is received, the voltage in the membrane of the receiving neuron changes the polarization locally. This passes like a current in a wire to the axon hillock, a part of the receiving cell close to its body. Each millisecond, a neuron is subjected to waves of polarization changes coming in from up to 100,000 synapses. If these changes are strong enough and/or occur close enough together to take the voltage at the axon hillock over a threshold level, the receiving cell in turn sends a signal and transmits a message down its own axon.

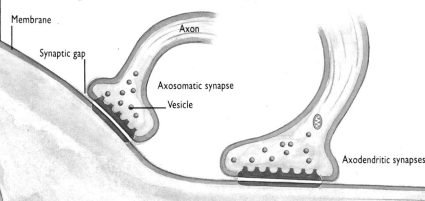

Membrane
Axon
Synaptic gap
Axosomatic synapse
Vesicle
Axodendritic synapses
Cell body
Dendrite
Dendritic spine

Axospinodendritic synapse

An axosomatic synapse (far left) has a powerful effect because it is so close to the nerve cell body. The closer a synapse is to the cell body, the greater its effect. So if the two axodendritic synapses below sent a signal simultaneously, the one on the left would have more influence on the receiving cell.

In most large companies decision making depends on many sources of information. Some input – like that of department chiefs or board members – carries more weight. But some influence is exerted at all levels, from staff on the factory floor to those in accounts. On the way to the boardroom, where final corporate decisions are made, ideas and proposals are filtered, coordinated, added and integrated.

Similarly, the neuron is subjected to myriad influences when it comes

Synapses are named after their component parts. Thus the synapse (left) is termed axospinosomatic since it has an axon from a sending neuron on one side of its gap and a spine projecting from a receiving nerve cell body, or soma, on the other side.

At an axospinodendritic synapse (right) an axon forms a synapse with a spine on the dendrite of a receiving neuron. They are the most common, forming 60 percent of all synapses in the human brain. Axodendritic synapses (above) make up 30 percent, axosomatic ones 6 percent.

A STAGGERING POTENTIAL

The human brain has about 100 billion nerve cells, or neurons. Each neuron can have tens of thousands of links with other neurons. The number of possible routes for nerve signals through this vast maze defies contemplation. The permutations are greater in number than all the fundamental particles – electrons, protons, neutrons and so on – in the universe. Our brain's complexity, plus limited study opportunities, means that scientists often look to smaller, simpler creatures to try to discover its principles of operation.

A grasshopper has around 16,000 neurons in the main nerve ganglia that function as its "brain". This is a fraction of the number of human neurons.

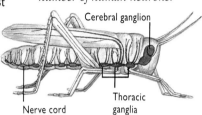

Cerebral ganglion

Nerve cord

Thoracic ganglia

to its "corporate decision": whether to fire its own signals, or action potentials. Potentials of different strength arrive at the cell body from the thousands of synapses on its dendrites. Synapses that make important contributions are generally those closest to the neuron's main cell body. Potentials from the more remote dendrites have faded by the time they reach the cell body, just like the decisions in the more remote parts of a company, far from head office.

There are two main types of synapses, excitatory and inhibitory. Excitatory synapses generate polarization changes that are more likely to make the cell fire (send a signal); inhibitory ones are less likely to make the cell fire. In the axospinodendritic synapses below, the inhibitory synapse counteracts the excitatory. If both axons try to send a signal across the synapse at the same time, there may be no overall change. If one axon becomes active while the other is quiet, its influence is passed on.

In an axoaxonic synapse (below), the axon from one neuron synapses with an axon from a second neuron; this second axon also synapses with a third neuron, for instance on a dendritic spine. The first axon can modulate the action of the second – if it has an inhibitory effect, it might stop the second axon from passing its message to the third neuron. This is known as presynaptic inhibition. In presynaptic excitation, the first axon works with the second to create more excitatory activity in the third neuron. At an electrical synapse, the axon and dendrite actually touch, with no gap between them.

Axospinodendritic synapses

Inhibitory synapse

Excitatory synapse

Axoaxonic synapse

Electrical synapse

Axon

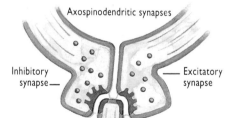

Synapse

Bulge in axon

Axon

A synapse does not always occur at the end of an axon; it can, in fact, form part of the way along the axon's length (**left**). This can only happen where the axon is not covered by an insulating myelin sheath. Typically, the axon bulges at this type of synapse.

Dendrodendritic synapse

At a dendrodendritic synapse (above) a dendrite forms a functional contact with another dendrite. This type of synapse is relatively rare.

Dendrite

On or off

A nerve cell's rate of signalling is governed by a complex control system with competing on–off inputs.

The effect of a nerve signal after it crosses the synapse – the gap across which messages pass from one neuron to the next – is vital to the workings of the brain and nerves. Along the axon of a sending neuron it travels as an action potential, a wave of depolarization. After crossing the synapse in chemical form, it is not big enough to constitute an action potential but continues in the receiving neuron as a smaller depolarization, a postsynaptic potential (PSP), which fades with distance and time. This signal is integrated with other PSPs from other axons.

The neurotransmitter that crosses the synaptic gap and the target receptor that binds it govern what happens in the receiving cell. Some neurotransmitters pass across the synapse to receptors and cause depolarization. This depolarization excites the receiving neuron, so it is more likely to fire its own action potentials. It is known as an excitatory postsynaptic potential (EPSP), the "on" side of the system.

Other neurotransmitters produce inhibition – the "off" side of the system. This involves not depolarization but hyperpolarization. The inside of the postsynaptic membrane briefly becomes more negative than normal with respect to the outside. This inhibitory postsynaptic potential (IPSP) damps down the receiving neuron by working against the effects of EPSPs and makes it less likely that the neuron will fire its own action potentials. Still other neurotransmitters can produce

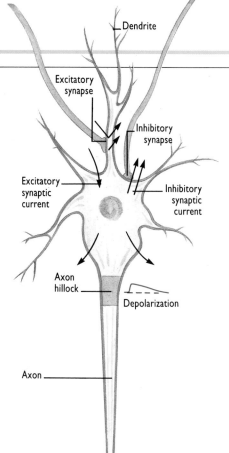

Dendrite

Excitatory synapse

Inhibitory synapse

Excitatory synaptic current

Inhibitory synaptic current

Axon hillock

Depolarization

Axon

The neuron integrates both "on" and "off" inputs. On signals are received from synapses where an excitatory postsynaptic potential (EPSP) is produced and off signals come from synapses where an inhibitory postsynaptic potential (IPSP) is made. These potentials move as currents to the axon hillock of the cell. The EPSPs cause depolarization, the IPSPs hyperpolarization and these two conflicting currents tend to cancel each other out.

The final addition and subtraction of depolarizations and hyperpolarizations (and there are thousands of each from a cell's many synapses) takes place at the neuron's axon hillock. If the potential here reaches its threshold, the neuron is excited enough to fire its own action potential, sending a signal along its axon.

either inhibition or excitation, depending on the receptors that are waiting for them. One of the principal inhibitory ones, gamma-aminobutyric acid (GABA), is found at about one-third of all brain synapses and inhibits neuronal firing in such parts as the brain stem, cerebellum and cerebral cortex.

THE ELECTRICAL STORM

Once seen as a form of supernatural possession, epilepsy is now recognized as a malfunction of brain neurons. It appears to have various causes and involve different parts of the brain, so each type has distinct symptoms. Grand mal epilepsy affects motor areas, causing the jerky, spasmodic movements of a seizure. The petit mal form involves sensory brain areas, making sufferers experience strange sights, sounds, smells and thoughts. Symptomatic epilepsy is due to an underlying condition such as a brain abscess or tumour. Idiopathic epilepsy has no obvious cause.

EEG traces of epilepsy sufferers show a mass of random signals that have temporarily lost their natural peaks, troughs and rhythms. The cells seem to be superexcited, with no inhibitions, and are set off by the slightest event. This may affect just one area of the brain, a partial seizure, or spread through the brain as a generalized seizure.

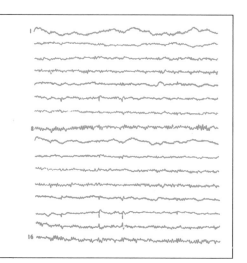

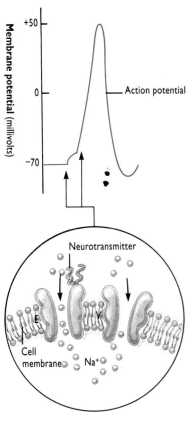

Membrane potential (millivolts)

+50

0

−70

Action potential

Neurotransmitter

Cell
membrane

Na⁺

Excitation is produced by EPSPs. Neurotransmitters cause an excitatory receptor (E) to allow sodium ions (Na⁺) into the cell across the postsynaptic membrane, creating a depolarizing postsynaptic potential that passes to the axon hillock. Here, if it reaches its threshold level the voltage-gated ion channel (V) opens, allowing sodium ions to flood in and triggering an action potential (**left**). Usually it takes a number of EPSPs to produce the waves of depolarization that make the neuron fire its own action potential.

Inhibition is caused by IPSPs. An IPSP arises when neurotransmitters make an inhibitory receptor (I) open its ion channel. The inhibitory receptor right allows positive potassium ions (K⁺) to leave the cell. Other typical inhibitory receptors allow negative chloride ions (Cl⁻) to enter the cell. The effect in each case is to cause hyperpolarization – the inside of the cell becomes more negative with respect to the outside. This counteracts the effect of EPSPs, making firing less likely, since the necessary threshold level will not be reached and so the voltage-gated channel will not open (**right**).

E —Excitatory receptor

I —Inhibitory receptor

V —Voltage-gated ion channel

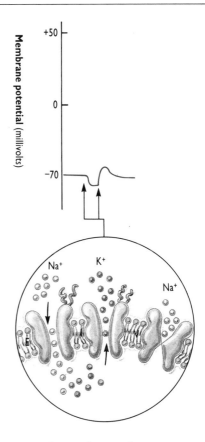

Membrane potential (millivolts)

+50

0

−70

Na⁺   K⁺

Na⁺

A racing car has two important foot-pedal controls – accelerator for "go" and brake for "stop". Without brakes, the car is far more difficult to control. The driver can only coast and slow down by letting natural resistance take its effect, such as friction with the air and in the engine and gears. Compared to braking, this is a more lengthy and less precise process.

Neurons in the brain also have accelerators and brakes. Excitatory synapses press the accelerator and encourage the receiving neuron to fire its own signals, and fire them more rapidly. Inhibitory synapses apply the brakes and have a slowdown effect, adding another layer of control and precision to the overall functioning.

Unlocking the gate

Like locks opened by chemical keys, tiny receptors are essential parts in the transmission of nerve signals.

Neurotransmitters are the molecules responsible for the chemical transmission of nerve signals across synapses. They act like keys that fit into the locks of receptors – protuberances of protein in the cell membrane of a neuron. When a receptor accepts a specific neurotransmitter, it either directly or indirectly opens channels through which ions (charged particles) flow. This has the effect of causing electrical changes in the membrane of the cell receiving the signal, which result in a postsynaptic potential (PSP).

There may be as many individual types of receptors as there are neurotransmitters – more than 60. Our knowledge of receptors has lagged behind that of neurotransmitters, but recent research is revealing their secrets. It seems that in the human brain and spinal cord receptors fall into two broad groups. These are the neurotransmitter-gated ion channels (NGICs) and the G-protein linked receptors (GPLRs).

Detail of M2 segment

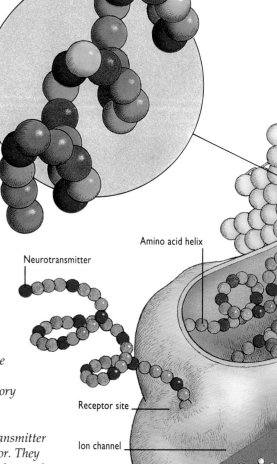

Neurotransmitter molecules activate a neurotransmitter-gated ion channel (NGIC) when they bind on to receptor sites on sub-units of the NGIC (four of which can be seen as bulges in the large diagram). This alters its shape, opening a channel in the middle.

The tunnel is lined by five coiled M2 segments (see below). The shapes and electrical charges on these segments draw ions through the channel into the cell. In this NGIC the ions are positive, making the cell more positive inside and so contributing to its depolarization – an excitatory postsynaptic potential.

Amino acid helix

Neurotransmitter

Receptor site

Ion channel

Like a baseball *in a baseball glove, a neurotransmitter molecule fits precisely with its intended receptor. They are truly made for each other. The shape of the glove makes catching the correct ball easier and surer. A basketball would not fit in the glove at all and a golf ball would rattle around loosely. Likewise, the characteristics of a neurotransmitter molecule – its size, shape, electrical charges, bonding sites and other features – are exactly fitted to a certain receptor or receptor group and no others.*

A neurotransmitter-gated ion channel *(NGIC) is effectively one large doughnut-shaped protein structure, 12 nanometres ($\frac{1}{2,000,000}$ inch) long. It is set in the "receiving" part of the synapse, the postsynaptic cell membrane of the neuron. Most of it projects out of the cell membrane, into the synaptic gap where it can come into contact with neurotransmitters.*

The NGIC is made of five sub-units, each of which consists of four coils, or helixes, of amino acids (building blocks of proteins). The coils are named M1 to M4. Five M2 helixes – one for each sub-unit – form the centre, or "ring", of the doughnut. They control the flow of ions through the NGIC.*

To activate a postsynaptic receptor, an action potential arrives at the presynaptic membrane and causes the release of neurotransmitters, which drift across the synaptic gap. In an NGIC the neurotransmitter-receiving sites and ion channel are part of the same structure, so this type of receptor works relatively fast.

Section through neurotransmitter-gated ion channel

Ion

The first type of NGIC to be studied – in a type of fish, the electric ray – was the nicotinic receptor for the neurotransmitter acetylcholine. Similar types of these doughnut-shaped receptors have now been found in other animals and humans. The various designs of NGICs work with other neurotransmitters such as GABA, glycine, glutamate and serotonin. Some of these chemicals are excitatory and others inhibitory, so the design of the ion channel must be adapted to suit both positive ions, such as sodium and potassium, and negative ions such as chloride. GPLRs work in a different, more complex, way, using a "second messenger" system. They are also more widespread and variable than NGICs. They include receptors for noradrenaline, dopamine and serotonin.

Cell membrane

REMOTE CONTROL

The G-protein linked receptor (GPLR) has an indirect action on ion channels. It has its effect through a series of biochemical steps using the second messenger molecule known as G-protein (short for GTP-binding protein). A typical GPLR is a single protein molecule in the form of a long, concertina-shaped chain. Its sections cross through the cell membrane a characteristic seven times as though it has been stitched in place. When a molecule of the relevant neurotransmitter arrives, it binds to the GPLR (green) and changes the receptor's shape. This has the effect of attracting the G-protein complex (yellow) to it. The alpha sub-unit, one of several sub-units in the G-protein, moves to a target in the cell body or membrane, where it triggers more reactions. When the GPLR loses its neurotransmitter the alpha sub-unit joins the G-protein again, which then detaches from the GPLR.

G-protein complex

G-protein linked receptor

Alpha sub-unit

Cell membrane

Target

When an ion channel is the target of a G-protein, the net effect – the opening of the channel to allow ions in or out – is much the same as for an NGIC, but as the system is more long-winded, it takes longer. There are various types of G-protein; they can have excitatory or inhibitory effects on different targets; and different G-proteins set free by different neurotransmitters may even compete for the same target.

G-proteins can home in on enzymes as well as ion channels. An enzyme (the green coil) activated by a G-protein can bring about still more reactions, producing new chemicals. These might not necessarily be involved in the opening or closing of ion channels in the receiving cell's membrane. For instance, the G-protein known as Gq leads – via a cascade of reactions – to changes in protein levels in the cell.

Discovering transmitters

Nerve-signal transmission between neurons – using messenger chemicals called neurotransmitters – is exquisitely varied and complex.

In order to jump the gap between a sending, or presynaptic, neuron and a receiving, or postsynaptic, neuron, a nerve signal makes use of chemicals – neurotransmitters. There are at least 60 different ones and more are being discovered all the time. Some are generally excitatory, making receiving neurons more likely to fire; others are inhibitory, damping down their activity. Some can be either, depending on the part of the nervous system involved, the receptors waiting for them, and the ways that these receptors are linked into the machinery of the postsynaptic membrane. Different neurotransmitters may activate receptors which are all "wired" to one type of ion channel, so they cause one type of electrochemical response. This is known as convergence. Or, the same neurotransmitters can stimulate receptors that are connected to different ion channels, producing several responses, or divergence.

Researchers are finding ever greater levels of sophistication, and their work is having immense practical consequences, too. This is because the chemistry of neurotransmitter-receptor systems is one of the few stages in the process of brain and nerve function that is amenable to outside manipulation – using drugs. Some drugs work against neurotransmitters by disrupting their production or release, or by attaching to them as they cross the synaptic gap, so that they cannot fit into their tailor-made receptors. Others mimic

*When neurotransmitters are released from their vesicles at the presynaptic membrane in response to the arrival of an action potential, they enter the synaptic gap. Some diffuse across the gap and reach their target receptors, but many do not. Whether they hit their target or not they have to be cleared away or broken down to prevent them interfering with signals conveyed by subsequent releases of neurotransmitters. Some just leak away from the synapse into the fluid that surrounds nerve cells; while others are actively broken down by enzymes (**right, above**); and still others are reabsorbed for reuse (**far right**).*

*In order to minimize the risk of running out of neurotransmitters they have to be made constantly. One site of manufacture is in the cell body where they are assembled under control of instructions from genes held in the DNA in the nucleus. Instructions are first copied on to an RNA molecule (**below**) which leaves the nucleus for an assembly site – a ribosome – on the endoplasmic reticulum. Another site of manufacture is in the axon terminal, where sub-units of neurotransmitters are put together.*

DNA

Dendrite

RNA

Like water from a mop and bucket, some neurotransmitters are released to do their work then collected up again for reuse.

NEUROTRANSMITTERS: DECADES OF DISCOVERY

Since neurotransmitters were first discovered, each decade has seen the investigation of a different group. First came acetylcholine, a major one in peripheral nerves. It excites at synapses where motor neurons connect to muscles, making them contract, but inhibits at heart muscle synapses, reducing the heart's activity. In the 1950s, amine-group neurotransmitters were found, including noradrenaline (excites and inhibits muscle and internal-organ function), dopamine (muscle movements, arousal, excitatory in the brain), histamine (excitatory in the brain) and serotonin (mood, appetite, pain, sleep). In the '60s, some were found to be amino acids or similar chemicals, including GABA and glycine (inhibitory in the brain) and glutamate and aspartate (excitatory in the brain). In the '70s neuropeptides – such as endorphins and enkephalins, somatostatin, substance P and CCK – were investigated. In the '80s came simple gases, such as nitrous oxide, and the energy molecule ATP.

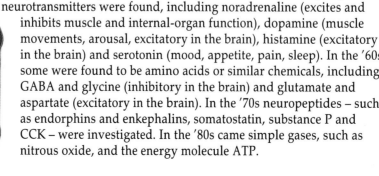

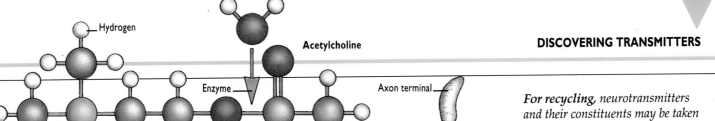

Hydrogen

Acetylcholine

Enzyme

Nitrogen Carbon

Oxygen

Axon terminal

Transmitter

Vesicle

Cell membrane

Enzymes help to break neurotransmitters *into
their simpler constituents in the synaptic cleft and
around the postsynaptic membranes. For example,
the enzyme acetylcholinesterase breaks down the
neurotransmitter acetylcholine (above) into
choline and acetic acid, which then become
available for general cell chemistry. The
breaking down of neurotransmitters by
enzymes means they have no further
effect on nerve signals. It also helps
to limit the time that any single
receptor is "engaged" with
a certain neurotransmitter
so that the receptor
soon becomes "vacant"
again, ready to respond
to the next wave.*

For recycling, *neurotransmitters
and their constituents may be taken
back into the axon's end by a process
known as endocytosis, in which they
are enclosed by vesicles that fuse with
the presynaptic membrane. Some
drugs work by blocking this re-uptake.
One such is fluoxetine, or Prozac,
the antidepressant that prevents the
re-uptake of serotonin.*

**Neurotransmitters made
in the main cell body** *are
carried along the axon to
its terminal by axonal flow.
Various raw materials,
nutrients, neurotransmitter
sub-units, vesicles and
organelles such as mitochondria
move along the axon at a rate of
about 1 mm (1/25 inch) a minute.
These items are moved by specialized
neurotubules (bottom) that work
like micro-conveyor belts. Waste
substances and materials for
rebuilding and recycling are carried
the other way, from the terminals
to the cell body.*

Mitochondrion

Neurotubule

Nucleus

Vesicle

Neuron

Ribosome

Endoplasmic
reticulum

neurotransmitters by simulating their response, or even produce enhanced
responses by fitting into and activating the receptors. Still others block
neurotransmitter action by being similar enough to fit into the receptors,
but not similar enough to trigger a response.

From the evidence of drugs used for research and treatment,
neurotransmitters are implicated in many conditions of the nervous
system. For example, serotonin is thought to be involved in depression,
and dopamine in both schizophrenia and Parkinson's disease. However,
the overall complexity of the neurotransmitter-receptor
systems in different parts of the central nervous system
means that it is rarely possible to assign a single
disease to problems with a single neurotransmitter.

Vesicle

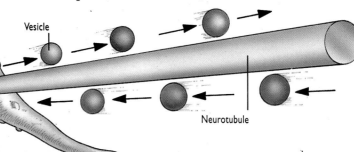

Neurotubule

See also
**BUILDING
THE BRAIN**
▶ To fire or
not to fire?
170/171

▶ Crossing
the gap
174/175

▶ On or off
178/179

▶ Unlocking
the gate
180/181

▶ Remaking
the mind
184/185

**SURVEYING
THE MIND**
▶ Brain maps
152/159

**INPUTS AND
OUTPUTS**
▶ Feeling pain
226/227

▶ Rhythms of
the mind
242/243

**STATES OF
MIND**
▶ The resting
mind?
282/283

▶ Physical cures
288/289

▶ Feeling low
290/291

▶ Anxious states
294/295

Remaking the mind

The brain changes itself throughout life, as it thinks, controls the body, learns and makes memories.

A living, changing, evolving entity, the brain adapts itself continuously according to its inputs, internal processing and outputs. These changes occur within and between neurons, in various ways and over various timescales. Neurons can alter the strength of their connections and thus the way they respond to or send messages. These messages are transmitted in the form of neurotransmitter molecules released into the synapses – the gaps where signals are passed between neurons.

The change in strength can be short term when, for instance, the amount of neurotransmitter released into the synapse by the sending cell rises during a burst of signalling. A change can also be longer term when a given amount of neurotransmitter arriving at the receiving cell has a greater effect than originally. Long-term changes occur over periods ranging from a few hours to weeks and can involve changes between the connecting structures of neurons.

Grains of sand are rearranged in their billions as they are blown by the wind, endlessly reshaping the dunes and altering the desertscape. Similarly, the billions of neurons in the brain continually make and remake their connections on many levels, in response to their individual histories and current activities, to reshape the landscape of the mind.

THE SHRINKING SEA SNAIL

You shrink away if something possibly harmful touches you. So does *Aplysia*, a type of marine snail. Touch it lightly on its siphon (breathing tube) and its sensory neurons pick up the signal; the message passes via axons and synapses to neurons controlling the gill muscles, and the gill is withdrawn for safety. But after a few touches the snail habituates, no longer reacting to the touch.

If an electric shock is then applied to its tail, the snail is sensitized for some time, and even a gentle touch to the siphon brings about an increased withdrawal. The nerve signals travelling along axons from the tail's sensory neurons pass via intermediate interneurons to facilitate (increase the effect of) signals coming from the siphon's neurons. This change in the way a set of neurons works is called presynaptic facilitation, since the effect takes place before the signal reaches the synapse that conveys the withdrawal message.

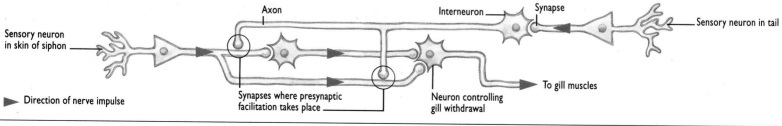

Sensory neuron in skin of siphon

Axon

Interneuron — Synapse

Sensory neuron in tail

Direction of nerve impulse

Synapses where presynaptic facilitation takes place

Neuron controlling gill withdrawal

To gill muscles

Some synapses can change the strength of their connection. When a regular number of firings, or action potentials, travel along a neuron's axon, they induce a corresponding postsynaptic potential in the receiving neuron's membrane. But when a very rapid burst of firings arrives, as in a burst of nerve signals, the resultant postsynaptic membrane potential changes overall, rising in strength, due to an increase in neurotransmitter release. For a while, perhaps up to a few minutes or even hours, the postsynaptic potential – and thus the likelihood of the receiving neuron itself firing – is increased even after a return to a regular rate of firing. The synapse has been potentiated.

Presynaptic firing rate

Low | High | Low

Potentiation

Time

Postsynaptic membrane potential (millivolts)

2.5

1

0

Postsynaptic potentials in the membrane of a receiving neuron are low when the presynaptic firing rate is low. If the rate rises, the resulting postsynaptic potentials can rise. This effect may last so that after the rate has dropped, each firing still gives a higher postsynaptic potential.

The most common excitatory neurotransmitter in the brain is glutamate, a chemical that activates several subtypes of receptors. These occur in large numbers in the hippocampus, part of the brain involved in memory and learning. Among them are NMDA (N-methyl-D-aspartate) receptors, which, like other such receptors, need both glutamate and an agonist, or "helper", chemical to generate local postsynaptic potentials – in this case glycine. In a presynaptic neuron (**below left**) that is quiescent, some activity takes place, but the neuron fires action potentials only occasionally, like a clock ticking in the background. These generate corresponding but low-level depolarizations in the postsynaptic membrane. The main depolarization changes are due to the inflow of sodium ions (Na^+). The NMDA receptor is non-operational under these conditions.

When, like a clock setting off its alarm, the presynaptic neuron sends a rapid burst of signals to the synapse (**right**),

a build-up of local depolarization results. The NMDA receptor, being voltage-dependent, responds. A magnesium ion (Mg^{2+}) "plug" which blocks its channel is driven out. This allows both sodium ions and calcium ions (Ca^{2+}) to flow through, giving a stronger depolarization in the receiving cell. This effect can last some time. Inside the postsynaptic neuron, calcium may also be involved in microstructural changes that underlie long-term potentiation.

This is just one of the vast array of processes whereby neurons alter and adapt their activities, changes which underlie thinking, learning and other mental processes in the brain.

Axon

Few firings

Axon

Many firings

Glutamate

Glutamate

Glutamate

Mg^{2+}

Mg^{2+}

Glycine

NMDA receptor

Ca^{2+}

Na^+

Na^+

Na^+

Weak depolarization

Strong depolarization

Recovering from damage

Once an adult loses a brain cell it has gone for ever. But unless the injury is severe, the brain can restore at least some function.

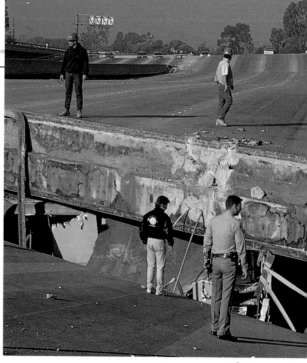

Most organs, such as the skin or liver, can usually repair damage because the cells in their tissues are all similar and can proliferate and replace those lost. But the fully developed brain presents problems, because every neuron is unique and so specialized in form and function that the cells can no longer proliferate. With its snakelike axon and thousands of dendrites synapsing with the other neurons, its individual three-dimensional architecture is impossible to replace. So repairing brain damage, when possible, is a slow and difficult process.

Since neurons in the brain cannot be replaced, people with brain damage who undergo rehabilitation have to try to "retrain" undamaged neural circuits to take on new roles, such as controlling the muscle movements of walking. This involves the growth of axons and dendrites on existing neurons, to make new connections as they rewire themselves. Such activity is the basis of the developing brain. But in a mature brain it is a more modest process. There are, for instance, the supporting glial cells, or astrocytes, which form fibrous tissue at the damage site, creating an impenetrable microscopic thicket for any axons and dendrites trying to grow. Yet there can be progress. Vacant synapses are thought to produce a substance that stimulates nearby axons to sprout new branches and grow toward them. Growth usually stops after a few micrometres because of the hostile conditions, so larger-scale repair may have to take place in a series of short steps as the brain commandeers some of its neural circuits for new uses.

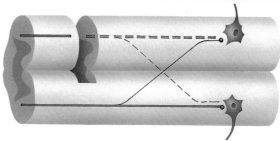

In the spinal cord there are many axons crossing from one side to the other that appear to have no function. However, if one side of the cord is damaged, they come into their own and can restore contact to a neuron below the site of the damage and some function can be regained.

To get around the effects of damage, the strength of synapses can change. If a neuron is linked to four axons from other neurons (**right**) and two of them die (**below**), the amount of neurotransmitter in each of the two remaining axons can increase so that when they fire, releasing their neurotransmitter into the synapses, the effect of the two remaining axons is almost the same as the original four.

The receiving part of a neuron (above) can become more sensitive after the loss of an axon. The number of receptors can increase in response to a lower stimulation from just a single axon (**below left**). With more receptors, the receiving neuron is able to make up for the effect of reduced neurotransmitter release.

A neuron might be connected to two axons, each splitting into two (**below left**). If one of the axons is destroyed, another axon can, in some circumstances, grow new terminals as replacements (**below right**).

When an axon has been severed (dotted line) it can put out a so-called regenerative sprout to link up with another neuron close by and thus restore some function. It will never be quite as good as new, however.

Receptor

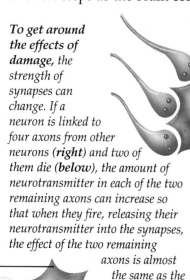

Neuron

Defunct axon

Neurotransmitter

Synapse

Axon

An earthquake shatters the landscape and breaks lines of communication and transport, especially roads. The blockage can be passed by diverting along rough tracks through less damaged areas. In the long term it may be worth developing these temporary tracks into permanent roads, rather than repairing the original routes.

When its neurons are damaged the nervous system also establishes diversions and bypasses, sending nerve signals along them – either until the original damage is repaired or on a permanent basis.

The process of overcoming damage in the brain can be slow in adults, and full recovery is unlikely. The same is not true of children, however. This is because the brain is still developing in children – its neurons are all established before birth, but the axons and dendrites continue to grow, forming new connections all the time. So a young child's brain can cope with relatively severe damage, not only rerouting its links to avoid that damage, but actually regrowing some of the connections. The adult brain is unable to do this because it is already fully formed and cannot continue its growth.

A CASE OF DAMAGE

A man was accidentally hit hard on the head with a cricket ball and was unconscious for a short while but seemed to recover. He was taken to hospital where an X-ray showed he had a fracture. A few hours later he developed a headache, felt nauseous, vomited and became drowsy. He was quickly given a computer tomography (CT) scan which revealed an epidural haemorrhage.

In an epidural haemorrhage the blood vessels in the dura mater, the outermost of the three layers (meninges) covering the brain, rupture. When these large vessels bleed, blood rapidly fills the space between the brain and skull (as shown in the red oval feature at centre left of the CT scan below). This is a dangerous complication that quickly puts the brain under pressure and which can starve it of oxygen from its own blood supply. The patient recovered after an operation to relieve the pressure and repair the blood vessels.

Apart from such accidents, the most common condition in which the brain is starved of blood is stroke, when the blood supply to part of the brain is cut off or blood leaks from its vessels into the brain tissue. The symptoms include slurred speech, loss of muscle control, numbness, paralysis, confusion and disruption of the senses such as touch or sight. Among the more common causes are cerebral thrombosis, a blood clot that forms in an artery supplying the brain; cerebral embolism, a blood clot, fatty lump or other object that lodges in an artery supplying the brain; aneurysm, a weak spot in the arterial wall that can burst; and damage caused either by disease or by an injury.

If the stroke affects only one side of the brain, then only the other side of the body is affected. With time and physiotherapy the stroke victim who survives the initial trauma can recover much lost function as the brain finds alternative pathways around the damaged regions.

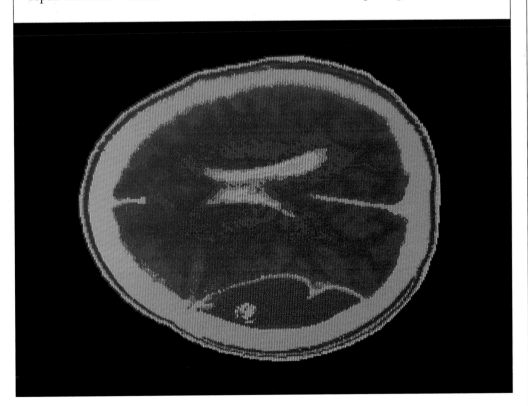

Food for thought

Like the body's other organs, the brain depends on two vital substances, brought to it by circulating blood.

Along with the glucose, or blood sugar, from digested food which powers life processes we also need oxygen from the lungs. It is an essential ingredient in the chemical pathways of cellular respiration, the process of extracting energy from glucose in a form that cells can use. The brain is by far the body's "hungriest" part – the major consumer of glucose and oxygen. Weight for weight, it requires 8 to 10 times more glucose and oxygen than other organs. Indeed it uses almost 20 percent of the body's oxygen intake, despite being only 2 percent of total body weight. But why?

Unlike an obviously contracting muscle or our writhing intestines, the brain does not look outwardly active. Its activities are at the electrochemical and molecular levels, as its billions of neurons constantly maintain resting potentials, alter them to fire nerve signals and synthesize neurotransmitters. The various ion pumps and other cellular machinery involved in these processes use large amounts of energy – and they need it continually, whether the body is running a sprint or fast asleep. They receive it at a constant rate – blood flow to the brain along the cerebral arteries is 750 ml (1⅓ pints) each minute. An equivalent amount of electrical energy would run a 10-watt light bulb – perhaps not very bright, but in bodily terms a huge amount. And to maintain this steady supply of energy, if glucose levels in the blood drop, other organs reduce their consumption of it, leaving more fuel for the brain.

Blood flow to organs fluctuates greatly according to their needs and general body activity: when we are resting they require less blood, during physical activity they need more. But the brain's need for blood is different. It remains almost constant, flowing through at 750 ml (1⅓ pints) per minute no matter what the brain or body is doing – from resting to intense thought, such as reading a book, or hard physical exercise.

The brain needs this constant supply because unlike the liver, which can store energy as glucose and starch, and the muscles, which can store oxygen as myoglobin, it cannot store its fuel. And just 5 to 10 seconds without oxygen flowing to the brain causes a person to lose consciousness. A further 10 seconds and body muscles begin to twitch convulsively as the brain's motor centres lose control of them. After four minutes, serious damage begins in the neurons and other brain cells. Just 10 minutes after the initial loss of supply this damage is usually irreversible – and fatal.

Like a leaky boat in which the crew constantly bails out water to keep it afloat, the brain uses most of its energy – about 80 percent – to pump sodium ions out of nerve cells and potassium ions in, against their natural concentration levels. The pump uses the energy molecule ATP which turns to ADP and phosphate (P_i) in the process.

Potassium ion (K^+)

Sodium ion (Na^+)

Detail of sodium pump

Cell membrane

$ADP + P_i$

Neuron

The brain is protected from natural body wastes, drugs and other toxins which might seep through the walls of its capillaries by a special barrier – the blood–brain barrier. This is formed by tight, secure junctions between the endothelial cells in its capillary walls. But the barrier might also keep out useful nutrients and chemicals. So special proteins in the cell membranes of the endothelial cells recognize such nutrients and transport them from the capillary out to neurons and other brain cells.

Endothelial cell

Capillary in brain

Nucleus

Mitochondrion

Vesicle

Glycolysis

2 ATP

Red blood cell

Tight junction

Astrocyte end foot

Dendrite

Nucleus

Mitochondrion

Axo

WHEN THE FUEL SYSTEM BREAKS DOWN

Generally perfectly healthy and sane, a man found that he was experiencing extremely peculiar thoughts and moods. Things came to a head when he became abnormally fascinated with a drill which he was using to put up some shelves, to the extent that his terrified wife believed he was about to harm himself and telephoned for a doctor. It turned out that he was suffering from a condition known as hypoglycaemia, in which glucose in the blood drops to a dangerously low level, thus effectively starving the brain of fuel.

If the brain is starved in this way, loss of consciousness quickly results – just as is the case with a failure in the oxygen supply. What this man was experiencing was a state that occurs between consciousness and unconsciousness, in which sufferers commonly report aggressive feelings and loss of self-control, free will and the ability to follow any sort of reasoning – symptoms not unlike those of schizophrenia.

There is a simple cure, however. By monitoring levels of glucose in the blood, sufferers can tell if they are falling too low and thus prevent an attack by eating something that will raise them again. Sufferers need to be aware of such things as when they last had a meal, how much they ate and whether they exercised after eating.

In all body cells, including neurons, glucose – a sugar with energy locked up in its chemical bonds – is broken apart and the energy released in a series of biochemical stages. At each stage energy is "captured" by adding a phosphate group (P_i) to the substance ADP (adenosine diphosphate) to make ATP (adenosine triphosphate), a high-energy molecule that powers many cell processes.

In the glycolysis stage, there is a net gain of two ATPs. In the citric acid (Krebs) cycle, which takes place inside the mitochondria, two more ATPs are gained. In the electron transport system stage, powered by energy from hydrogen ions (H^+) released in glycolysis and the citric acid cycle, the gain is 32 ATPs. These activate F1 particles – enzymes that add P_i to ADP – on the mitochondrion's inner membrane.

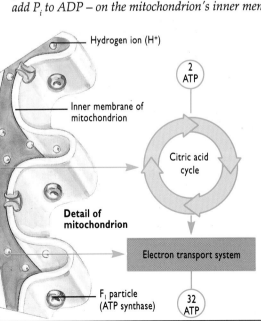

Hydrogen ion (H⁺)

Inner membrane of mitochondrion

Detail of mitochondrion

F₁ particle (ATP synthase)

2 ATP

Citric acid cycle

Electron transport system

32 ATP

Different organs use blood at varying rates depending on the level of activity in the body, as these figures show (all are per minute).

Blood used by brain
At rest 750 ml (1⅓ pints)
Exercising 750 ml (1⅓ pints)
Digesting 750 ml (1⅓ pints)

Blood used by muscles
At rest 1.2 litres (2 pints)
Exercising 12.5 litres (22 pints)
Digesting 1 litre (1¾ pints)

Blood output/used by heart
At rest 5.8 litres (10 pints) / 250 ml (9 fl. oz)
Exercising 17.5 litres (31 pints) / 250 ml (9 fl. oz)
Digesting 7.3 litres (13 pints) / 300 ml (10½ fl. oz)

Blood used by intestines
At rest 1.4 litres (2½ pints)
Exercising 600 ml (1 pint)
Digesting 3.5 litres (6 pints)

The brain plan

Along with the rest of the body, the brain grows and matures under the control of the genetic blueprint.

If you could look back at yourself when you were a day-old fertilized egg, you would see a tiny dot of living tissue, only just visible to the unaided eye. You would be a single cell about 0.1 mm ($\frac{1}{250}$ inch) across, formed when an egg cell from the mother joins with a sperm cell from the father. Fertilization marks the time when genes from both parents form the complete genetic make-up of a new individual.

Genes provide the instructions for the development and functioning of a human body in its entire and intricate detail. There are between 100,000 and 200,000 of them in the full gene set, the human genome. Each individual gene takes the form of a functional section, or sub-unit, of one of the 23 pairs of DNA molecules contained in the nucleus of every body cell.

After a short time, the fertilized egg divides into two cells, then four, and so on. Amazingly, each time a cell divides, the entire set of DNA molecules is copied, so that each of the new daughter cells receives the full gene set. At first the cells all look the same but, gradually, as the number increases, they differentiate. Differentiation is achieved when only certain genes in a cell are activated, such as the genes needed to make a nerve cell, and the rest of the set remains quiescent. Groups of cells take on their own structure and function, as muscle cells, skin cells, nerve cells (neurons) and so on. In the embryo the process of cell differentiation determines the order and position in which structures appear. It takes place "top-down", with the brain leading the way, followed by the head, face and special sense organs, then the heart, intestines and other internal organs, the arms and, finally, the legs.

We all start out with the same potential, in theory, but we do not stay the same. Thus one person may end up an architect and another a manual worker. Similarly, every cell in an embryo has a full set of genes and so the same theoretical potential, yet the end result is a wide range of specialized cell types.

At about two weeks the body of the embryo is a two-layered plate of cells, with the yolk sac on one side and the protective fluid-filled amniotic cavity on the other. A week later the embryonic disc is evident.

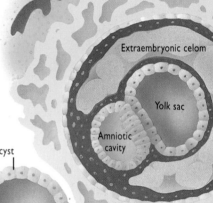

2 weeks

Uterine wall

Extraembryonic celom

Yolk sac

Amniotic cavity

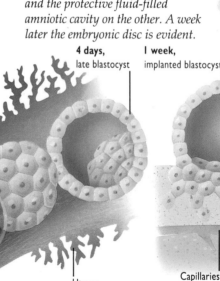

4 days, late blastocyst

1 week, implanted blastocyst

As a fertilized egg drifts along the Fallopian tube to the uterus, it divides every 15 to 20 hours. At four days it is known as a late blastocyst, a ball of 64 identical cells. At one week this has implanted in the uterus. The blastocyst's cells invade the uterine tissues – richly supplied with blood by capillaries – to obtain nutrients for growth.

3 days, morula

2½ days, 8 cells

2 days, 4 cells

1 day, 2 cells

Fallopian tube

Uterus

Capillaries

Uterine glands

Three layers of cells in the embryonic disc – seen in cross-section (**1**) – are the basis for three main groups of tissues in the body. Cells of the future ectoderm will form the external linings and layers of many body parts, such as the skin, and all the tissues of the nervous system. The future ectoderm differentiates into ectoderm proper (blue) and the neural plate, which thickens and dips to form a channel, the neural groove (**2**). Neural crest tissue splits off from the plate, which gets deeper (**3**), curves around (**4**), and joins together at the top to make the neural tube (**5**). The disc's middle layer, the mesoderm, forms the notochord, a forerunner of the spinal column, and the somites to either side, which are precursors of muscles and bones. The endoderm forms many of the body's inner organs.

By five weeks the embryo's "head-first" development is evident, and the bulges that are becoming the brain are clearly visible. The chest and abdominal organs are also forming.

In the seventh week the spinal cord has become distinct. By this stage the face and neck are forming, the fingers and toes are separating, and the tail, characteristic of all vertebrate embryos, has started to shrink away.

About four weeks after fertilization, the neural tube (seen in rear view, **left**) forms in the rapidly developing embryo. This is made when the neural groove (seen in transverse section, **left**) joins up, something like a zipper being closed. Initially it is open at both ends. At the head end, the tube enlarges and develops into the brain.

As the embryo grows, its cells gradually become different in size and shape, as some genes switch on while others turn off. Sections or segments known as somites appear along the embryo, which at this stage is hardly distinguishable from the similar-stage embryo of other backboned (vertebrate) animals. At around this time it is in the process of curling over front and back to produce the beginnings of recognizable head and tail ends.

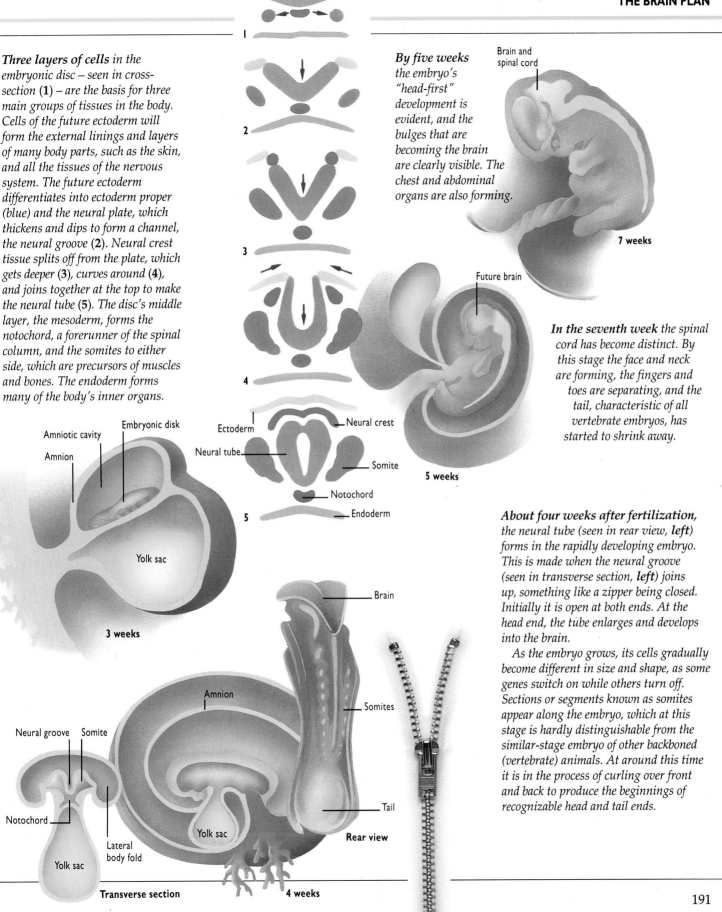

1

2

3

4

5

Ectoderm

Neural crest

Neural tube

Somite

Notochord

Endoderm

Amniotic cavity

Embryonic disk

Amnion

Yolk sac

3 weeks

Brain and spinal cord

7 weeks

Future brain

5 weeks

Brain

Amnion

Somites

Tail

Rear view

Neural groove   Somite

Notochord

Yolk sac

Lateral body fold

Yolk sac

Transverse section

Yolk sac

4 weeks

See *also*

BUILDING THE BRAIN
▶ The developing brain
192/193

▶ The cell factory
194/195

▶ Linking up
196/197

SURVEYING THE MIND
▶ Brain maps
152/159

INPUTS AND OUTPUTS
▶ Body links
202/203

▶ The long junction
204/205

▶ Keeping control
238/239

FAR HORIZONS
▶ First thoughts
264/265

STATES OF MIND
▶ The resting mind?
282/283

191

The developing brain

From its tiny embryonic beginnings, the brain grows rapidly, reaching a quarter of its adult size by birth.

About eight weeks after egg joined sperm to create a genetically unique individual, the pinpoint-sized single cell that was the fertilized egg has divided, its cells have differentiated, the early embryo has passed through various tadpolelike stages, and a miniature, recognizably human body has developed. At this time it is about as big as an adult's thumb, yet all the main body parts and organs have appeared, right down to fingers and toes. The head is grape sized and still slightly larger than the whole of the torso, since the embryo follows a head-first order of development. The brain occupies most of this head volume, with the facial features tucked below it, still small and lacking in detail.

The end of the eighth week marks a sudden change, but in name only. By scientific convention, the embryo is now referred to as a foetus. It continues to grow at an incredible rate, fuelled by oxygen and nutrients from the mother's blood obtained via the placenta and umbilical cord. While it seems to us that a newborn baby grows fast in its first few months, it is far outstripped by the foetus. At its maximum rate of size increase, the foetus is enlarging 10 times more quickly than a newborn baby. The foetal brain grows even faster. The lower portions, such as the medulla, are among the first to form. These are the more basic parts and deal with mechanical body functions and life-support systems such as heartbeat. The areas such as the cerebrum initially lag behind.

At four months the brain's full general structure is present. By the fifth month the foetus can grip, kick and hiccup, showing that reflexes and muscle control (motor) nerves are functioning. At seven months the foetus practises controlled, rather than reflex, movements such as swallowing, pushing

At seven weeks the embryo is about 1.7 cm (⅔ inch) long. The general areas of the brain – hindbrain, cerebellum, mid- and forebrain – are clearly formed. The cerebral hemispheres (in the forebrain), which will make up 90 percent of the brain's total adult volume, now constitute only about 10–15 percent of the total.

At birth a baby mammal leaves its mother's womb through the birth canal, passing through the gap in the pelvic girdle, the bowl-shaped "hipbone" at the base of the abdomen. In most mammals, the head is relatively small and slips out easily; baby dolphins are usually born tail-first. Since dolphins are supported by water, they have developed a relatively wide birth canal, so the baby dolphin's brain can be almost the full adult size at birth. In humans, since we are two-legged walkers, the mother's anatomy has evolved to put a limit on the birth canal opening. So head size, and thus brain size, is restricted.

and "breathing" as it floats in its protective pool of amniotic fluid. From this time, too, the upper brain begins to enlarge fast, and the cerebral hemispheres continue to develop their typically wrinkled appearance. At nine months the foetus is full term, ready to be born. It is an amazing change from the original single cell, the fertilized egg. This anatomical development is the result of astonishing microscopic flurries of cell multiplication and migration as a new human being – equipped with a functioning brain – is prepared for the outside world.

At three months the spinal cord of the foetus has reached its definitive structure, with an H shape of grey matter running along inside the white matter, like letters in a stick of rock. The cerebellum and cerebrum (part of the forebrain) are still fairly smooth, with few of the wrinkles characteristic of the adult brain. The foetus is about 5 cm (2 inches) long, measured from crown to rump, that is, top of head to bottom, and is lying in the typically curled "foetal position".

Midbrain

Cerebellum

Forebrain

Hindbrain

Spinal cord

Eye

7 weeks

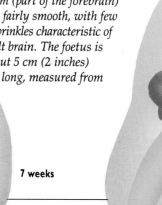

3 months

192

COLONIZING CELLS

When the neural tube is forming early in an embryo, two strips of cells are "pinched off" from the edges of the neural folds and finally flank the tube. While the neural tube goes on to form the central nervous system (CNS) – brain and spinal cord – these strips of cells, which will form part of the autonomic nervous system (ANS), multiply and migrate in waves. Known as neural crest cells, they make their way between other cell groups to set up colonies in other areas. As well as forming parts of the ganglia and nerves of the ANS, they also make up pigment cells in skin, enamel-making cells in teeth, and connective tissue bodywide.

Neural tube

Spinal ganglion

Spinal ganglion

Spinal nerve

Spinal cord

Abdominal aorta

Migrating autonomic nervous system cells

Cross section of embryo

Migrating neural crest cells leave behind colonies that develop into various body tissues, both nervous and other tissues. They include sensory neurons in the nerves connecting to the spinal cord, and neurons of the ANS that run from their ganglia to inner organs such as the heart, blood vessels and intestines.

At six months growth and development of the foetus's body has speeded up and is fast catching up with the head region. The total length is 35 cm (14 inches). In the brain, the cerebral cortex is beginning to dominate as the fastest-growing region, developing its typical convolutions on the surface.

At nine months the baby's brain looks much like the adult version. It is still more developed than other body parts, such as muscle and bone, as well as being disproportionately large. The midbrain has been obscured by the relatively huge cerebral cortex which forms most of the forebrain.

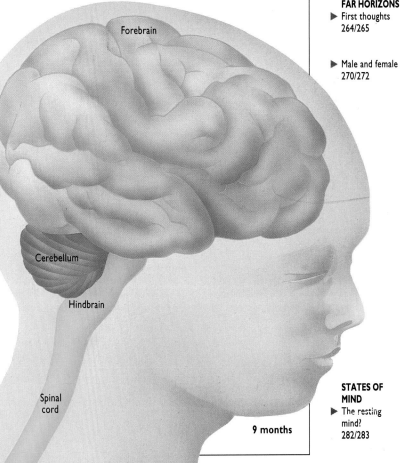

Forebrain

Cerebellum

Hindbrain

Spinal cord

6 months

9 months

The cell factory

Before birth many billions of nerve cells are created that have to find the way to their correct place in the brain.

In a newborn baby the neurons are more or less complete in number and in their basic positions within the brain. But they are not yet mature, in that their connections with other neurons are not fully established. They have all originated from cells of the layer lining the neural tube, which is present in a three-week-old embryo and is the precursor of the brain and spinal cord. They are produced by the standard cell-division process – mitosis – which gives rise to "pre-neurons", or neuroblasts. During an embryo's early weeks and months the rate of cell multiplication is enormous – 200,000 or more neuroblasts are formed every second. At any one time millions of them are migrating to their correct positions, controlled by a massively complex system of guiding factors. One of these involves "sticky" regions on cells known as cell adhesion molecules (CAMs). If two cells have similar CAMs on their surfaces, they are more likely to stay together. So one set of cells can form the route or base for another group.

There are also the so-called cell-substrate adhesion processes, in which neuroblasts attach to and travel along non-cellular lattices, scaffoldings and membranes of proteins, sugars and other molecules, formed in the extracellular environment. Migrating nerve cells are also affected by soluble chemicals such as hormones, growth factors and neurotransmitters being manufactured by their neighbours.

As each group of neuroblasts settles into position, some of their genes switch off while others switch on. The cells begin to change in shape and function and start to mature into neurons, putting out their dendrites and axons. The growth of these signifies the next phase in brain development: neurons linking up with one another.

The cerebral neocortex is the site of our most sophisticated mental processes, including thinking and awareness. In the five-week-old embryo, it is just the microthin wall of pocket-like outgrowths from the sides of the forebrain. It develops three layers. In the neuroepithelial layer the cells divide, producing neuroblasts which find their way to their brain positions by moving up guiding radial glioblasts.

A tree trunk's growth rings indicate its age in years, with two rings for each year. The light one reflects fast spring and early summer growth, the dark one late summer–autumn slowdown. Each annular ring is the result of a layer of cells, the cambium, specialized to divide and make more cells. It produces thick heartwood cells on its inside, for water transport, and softer sapwood cells on its outside, just under the bark, for nutrient and sap transport. As heartwood accumulates yearly, the trunk thickens. In a similar way, layers of cells in the brain multiply and relocate to take up set positions.

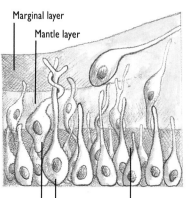
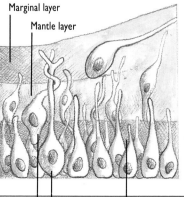

3 months

Outer limiting membrane

Marginal layer

Mantle layer

5 weeks

Radial glioblast

Neuroepithelial layer

Neuroblast

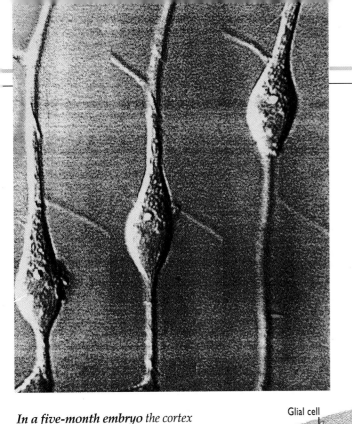

*The neuroblasts that will mature into "grey matter" neurons
of the cerebral cortex* find their way partly with the aid of glial cells.
Glia generally provide a cellular system of scaffolding, support,
protection and nourishment for the brain. Radial glioblast cells, along
the inner neuroepithelial layer lining the neural tube, grow long, thin
extensions outward, away from the centre of the tube, like the spokes
of a wheel. Each neuroblast oozes and crawls along this "glial monorail"
(**left**) and alights at its predetermined resting position.

   The process happens in waves to form the six cortical layers. The
innermost layer (VI), which is nearest to the neuroepithelial layer,
forms first. This means that successive waves of neuroblasts must
crawl between their already settled counterparts, in order to establish
their own layer on the outer side. It is like concentric rings of suburbs
growing ever outward around a city centre, using trains and roads as
their transport system.

In a five-month embryo the cortex
is developing its characteristic six
layers. Successive waves of
neuroblasts migrate from the
innermost layer to form
the outermost.

By eight months the basic physical
structure of the brain, including the
neocortex, is almost complete. To
form each of the six cortical layers, a
migratory wave of neuroblasts has
moved out along the pathfinding
extensions of the radial glioblasts and
settled in place before differentiating
into the more mature neurons
characteristic of that particular
layer: fusiform in VI, pyramidal in
V, stellate in IV and so on. The
outermost layer (I) forms last. The
axons of all the layers gather to form
the white matter below the cortex.
Some glial cells of the original
neuroepithelial layer now form the
ependymal layer, the barrier lining
the brain's fluid-filled ventricles, as
shown in the cross section (**below**)
of the eight-month-old foetal brain.

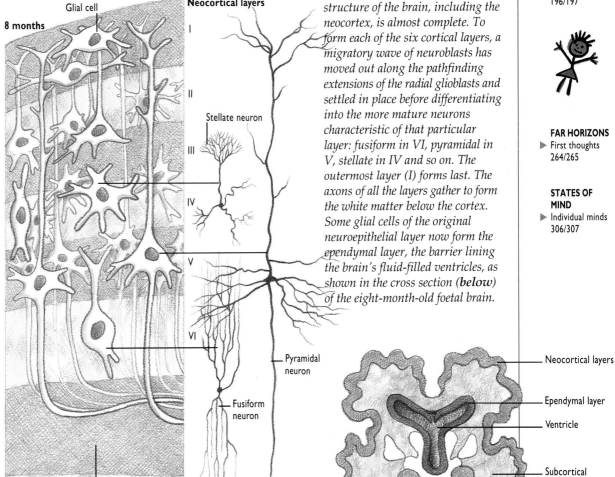

5 months

8 months

Glial cell

Neocortical layers

I

II

III

Stellate neuron

IV

V

VI

Pyramidal
neuron

Fusiform
neuron

Ependymal cell

Subcortical
white matter

Neocortical layers

Ependymal layer

Ventricle

Subcortical
white matter

Linking up

Without connections neurons could not function. How they link is one of the growing brain's most extraordinary stories.

In its first year of life, a baby's brain trebles in size, to almost three-quarters of its adult dimensions. Growth then slows dramatically, with full adult bulk attained at about 17 years. This huge and rapid initial growth in brain volume is due chiefly to the insulating myelin sheaths forming around nerve fibres. But there is another factor: the growth of neurites – dendrites and axons – from the nerve cell bodies to form links, or synapses, with one another. The dendrites elongate and snake between other cells to near neighbours. Many axons undergo incredible growth, reaching past millions of other cells and tissues to seek their target cells, perhaps in a far off organ.

Dendrites and axons find their way and link using a variety of cues and clues, from physical and positional to physiological, chemical and electrical. And during these early years the brain's connection network is "plastic" – it constantly re-wires, alters and updates, according to the environment. But by the age of 16 its physiology is mature and the molecular-cellular machinery for making new connections becomes much less efficient.

A RICHER PLACE TO BE

Researchers have discovered that rats raised in bare dark cages, with minimal sensory stimuli of any kind, develop a less sophisticated and less heavy brain cortex than normal. By contrast, those raised in a highly stimulating "enriched" environment, with plenty of extra sounds, sights, smells, tastes and touches, have a more developed brain cortex than normal. This is thought to be because the brain is at its most adaptable and plastic stage just after birth, when animals – especially mammals – begin to explore and learn about their world. With stimulation, the brain cells make more connections with one another.

Humans respond in the same way and need the senses and mind to be stimulated, too. Babies in particular need such stimulation, and are thought to thrive in an environment which is full of bright objects and in which people talk to them – even if they are unable to understand the meaning of the words.

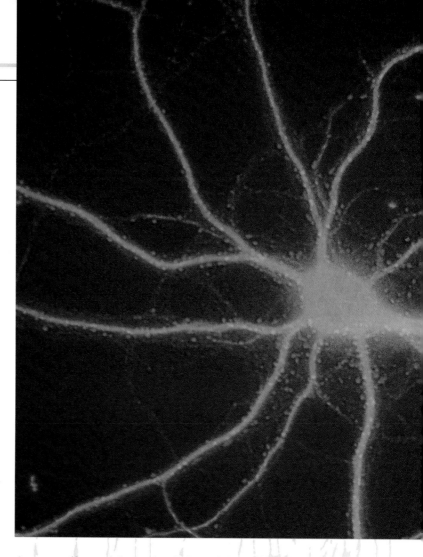

*A **nerve cell on a laboratory dish** sends lengthening neurites into its surroundings, like an octopus growing new tentacles. Their growth can be encouraged and directed by various factors, such as trails of chemicals on the glass surface, dissolved chemicals seeping from one direction through the nutrient solution, and even physical features such as scratches or cracks in the glass.*

***During the first few years of a human child's life** its brain goes through a stage of incredible activity as numerous lines of communication are set up and the bodies of the nerve cells grow slightly. But the number of cells does not increase after birth. In these early years, the action is centred on creating connections – synapses – whose networks are shaped by current needs, imitation, memory, learning and accumulating experience. Of course, this process then continues through life, although the pace is far slower in the mature brain.*

***Bees may not be bright,** but they work hard. Much of their life and behaviour is encoded in their genes. Worker bees follow strict instincts as they collect nectar from blooms and maintain the hive. In the same way, the earliest development of the human embryo follows the chemically coded instructions in the genes of its cells. These pre-programme cells to multiply, move and differentiate in certain ways, as the basic parts of the body and its nervous system take shape.*

Newborn   **3 months**

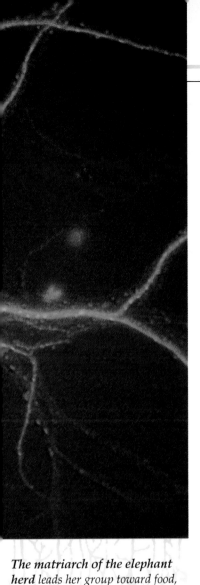

TURNING OFF THE SUICIDE SWITCH

A number of factors make a neuron's axons and dendrites, or neurites, link up with one another: genetic programming, pioneer neurons, guiding and signpost chemicals sent out by target neurons to "attract" axons and a substance known as nerve growth factor (NGF). This is a soluble protein that encourages neurons to put out neurites in its direction, like ants following a scent trail, in search of the source of NGF.

Making such connections is central to the life of each cell, since cells have suicide switches which must be switched off if the cells are to survive. A cell that has no link to any others – and thus receives no chemical message to stay alive – will "commit suicide" like a lemming (**below**) when it reaches a certain point in its life. This process effectively weeds out any neurons that are not active – and therefore not essential to the survival of the whole.

Electrical stimulation within the brain seems to have a similar role in determining which connections remain, coming into play when links between neurons have to be thinned out. Those connections that are active, and are therefore generating electrical currents typical of nerve signal transmissions, survive, while those that do not create electrical signals die.

*The matriarch of the elephant
herd* leads her group toward food,
water and safety, and away from
danger. Using clues from the
environment, such as scents and
sights, she is the pathfinder –
younger herd members follow.

In the developing brain, pioneer
neuroblasts find their way between
cells and membranes, following
directional cues from their
environment. They lay down trails
that are followed by the growing
fibres (axons) of other nerve cells,
while the cell bodies of these fibres
stay "back at base".

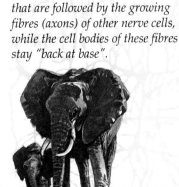

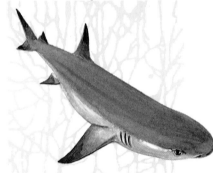

*A shark samples waterborne
substances* with incredibly
receptive chemosensory organs in its
nasal chambers. As it turns and
twists, the scents are stronger first in
one nostril, then the other. In the
developing human brain, the growing
tips of axons do the same. Receptors
on their surface detect nerve growth
factor and other chemicals given off
by target cells, and the tip heads for
their source. Repulsion chemicals
make unwanted axons turn away. As
each axon lengthens, its tip homes in
on the destination cell, to form a
synapse, or connection, there.

Play is fun with serious consequences. As the
youngster tries to put the jigsaw together, fails, tries
again and finally succeeds, millions of nerve signals flash
around the neurons of the nervous system. For the synapses
it is a case of "use it or lose it". Well-used connections
encourage further development and sophistication in that
particular part of the network. Seldom-used links soon
fade. This "wiring up" involves great competition and
natural selection at the cellular level, as some neurons
succeed while others fail and die.

The difference in the density of connections between a
newborn baby's neurons and a two year old's is incredible.
In the images left the number
of neurons at each age is
more or less the same, but
the growth in connections
comes as the infant learns.

The ageing brain

Our brain is not immune to the effects of old age, but the decline in performance is usually gradual.

Like other parts of the body, the brain and nerves succumb to the ageing process. One problem affecting all of the nervous system is that neurons are very specialized in both shape and function. They cannot multiply to replace neurons that die, unlike the cells in skin and many other tissues; indeed, some 10,000 neurons die daily from birth.

By the late teens, the brain is still constantly adapting and re-wiring itself, but the rate at which it does so begins to slow. Learning becomes more difficult and lengthy. It is estimated that our ability to learn and remember new information could decline by 50 percent between 25 and 75 years of age. The rate of cell loss in the brain begins to increase significantly after the age of 20 and is greatly hastened by consuming too much alcohol or other drugs. On average, the brain has lost 5 percent of its weight – about 70 g (2½ ounces) – by the age of 70, although we can compensate to some extent because experience helps us to anticipate, predict and find various types of short cuts.

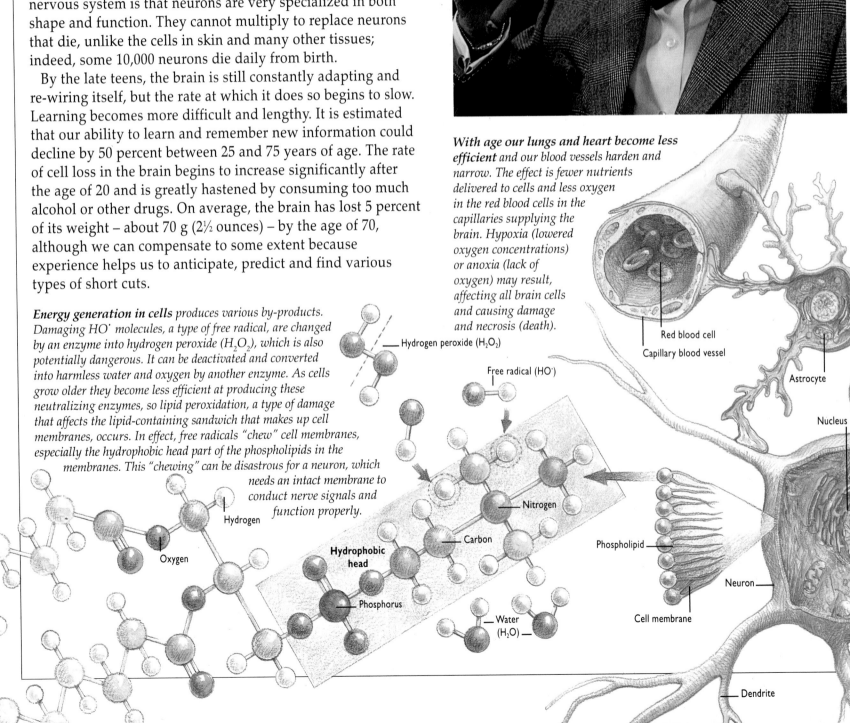

With age our lungs and heart become less efficient and our blood vessels harden and narrow. The effect is fewer nutrients delivered to cells and less oxygen in the red blood cells in the capillaries supplying the brain. Hypoxia (lowered oxygen concentrations) or anoxia (lack of oxygen) may result, affecting all brain cells and causing damage and necrosis (death).

Energy generation in cells produces various by-products. Damaging HO˙ molecules, a type of free radical, are changed by an enzyme into hydrogen peroxide (H_2O_2), which is also potentially dangerous. It can be deactivated and converted into harmless water and oxygen by another enzyme. As cells grow older they become less efficient at producing these neutralizing enzymes, so lipid peroxidation, a type of damage that affects the lipid-containing sandwich that makes up cell membranes, occurs. In effect, free radicals "chew" cell membranes, especially the hydrophobic head part of the phospholipids in the membranes. This "chewing" can be disastrous for a neuron, which needs an intact membrane to conduct nerve signals and function properly.

Hydrogen peroxide (H_2O_2)

Free radical (HO˙)

Red blood cell

Capillary blood vessel

Astrocyte

Nucleus

Nitrogen

Carbon

Hydrogen

Oxygen

Hydrophobic head

Phosphorus

Water (H_2O)

Phospholipid

Cell membrane

Neuron

Dendrite

Such is the power of the mind that it has been suggested that if people expect to lose their memory and concentration as they grow old, then they probably will. But loss of mental function is not an inevitable part of ageing. Many people in their 70s and beyond achieve wonderful feats, and make valuable contributions to their family, colleagues and society. Indeed, the comedian George Burns was still active on his 100th birthday.

HABITS AND DIETS

Some aspects of the mental diminution associated with ageing may be due to habits and activities earlier in life. These include drug use, possibly even moderate "social drinking", and levels of physical impact and injury.

Diet can play its part, too. Inhabitants of the Pacific island of Guam develop brain conditions such as Alzheimer's and Parkinson's diseases many times more frequently than average, up to 100 times the normal rate. The cause may be neurotoxic chemicals eaten in the seeds of the false sago palm (**below**). This is not a true palm tree, but a non-flowering cone-bearing evergreen tree in the cycad plant group. These trees are "living fossils" with ancient origins, appearing on Earth more than 300 million years ago. They were especially abundant at the time of the dinosaurs. Perhaps those prehistoric creatures also suffered premature ageing and senility after eating their leaves and seeds.

Ion channel

Calcium ion (Ca²⁺)

Mitochondrion

The opening of calcium ion channels in a neuron's cell membrane is a natural part of nerve transmission, but with increasing age it becomes defective. Calcium ions can build up inside the cell, and this can damage the energy-converting mitochondria.

Necrosis refers to the death of cells, tissues or parts of an organ, due to damaging external influences such as toxins, excessive heat or cold or lack of oxygen. For example, infecting bacteria may produce necrotizing poisons (toxins). Physical injury is another cause. In the brain's case, it may be a single severe blow or many small accumulating injuries, as experienced by some boxers. The dying cells release their enzymes and contents, which disrupt the local chemical environment and produce a damaging knock-on effect. The debris is cleared up by small microglia – special glial cells (a type of macrophage, literally "big eater") – that operate exclusively in the brain. They have a similar role to the macrophages found elsewhere in the body.

Degenerating axon

Damage

Axon

Degenerating neuron

Apoptosis is the death of single cells – including neurons – within an organ, and it may not be the result of an accident. It seems that there is a type of cellular death-wish pre-programmed by so-called suicide genes. The cell simply reaches the end of its natural life span and activates genes that instruct it to self destruct. Unlike necrosis, apoptosis forms part of the cell's natural life cycle.

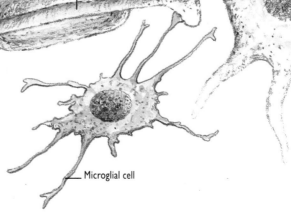

Microglial cell

DNA

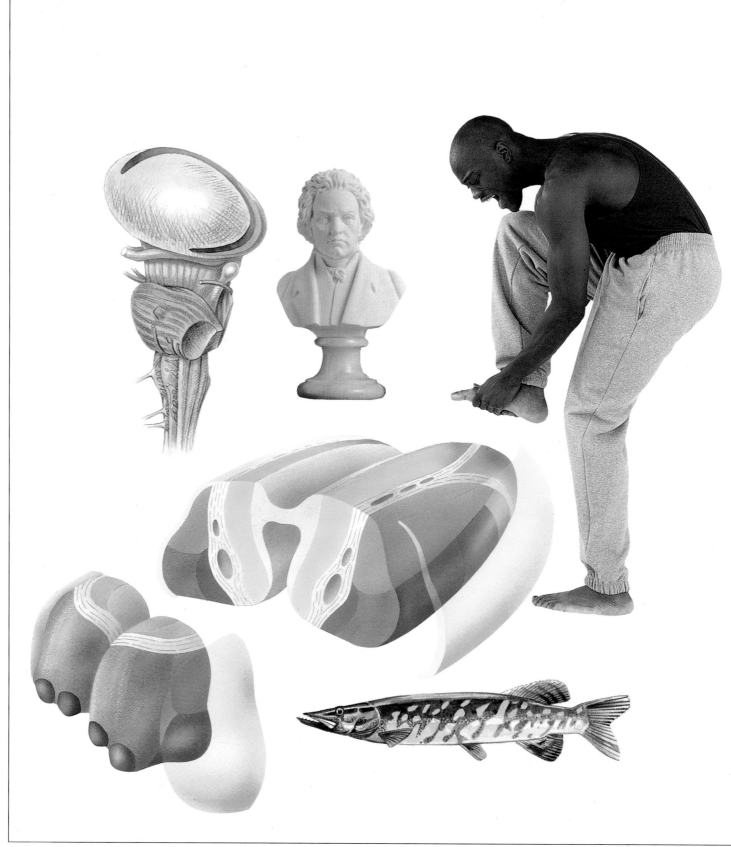

Inputs and Outputs

A s we move through the world, seeing, hearing, smelling, tasting and touching, information ceaselessly pours into and out of the brain. This information takes the form of nerve signals, the common currency of the brain and nervous system. The story of how sound, light and the other things we can detect with our senses are converted into signals is extraordinary enough. What must then happen to them if we are to become conscious of the world around us is even more fascinating. But the brain, along with its very own information superhighway, the spinal cord, does not merely help us to perceive the external world. It also monitors, controls and integrates all our movements and takes care of multiple body functions — all without our having to think about them. Never at rest, it is constantly on the lookout for potential problems and has special systems devoted to focusing awareness on either external danger or internal needs.

Left (clockwise from top): the pathways of pain from foot to brain; a fishy smell; gateway to the brain – the thalamus; sound signals and active processing; music from the mind of a deaf man.
This page (top): a fitting outcome for an odour molecule; (left) a ticklish job for the feeling sense.

Body links

The brain is just one component of the nervous system, the body's command and control network.

Any part of the body which contains neurons, or nerve cells, is part of the nervous system. Some of these parts are obvious – like the bulging brain, with its 100 billion neurons, and the spinal cord, with its long tracts of signal-carrying nerve axons or fibres. But if you look more closely at these immensely complex structures, or stray into other parts of the body, it becomes more awkward to demarcate the components of the nervous system.

In order to understand any system, it helps to divide it into separate subsystems or components. But how should the nervous system be divided up? Should structural or anatomical criteria, such as shape and size, be applied; or can functional or physiological aspects, such as which neurons link together, be used? You may as well take the whole category of road vehicles and try to define a car solely on the basis of length, or colour, or noise.

In fact, a "car" is defined by several sets of different criteria which overlap, and the nervous system can also be subdivided in different yet overlapping ways, each with its own terminology. For example, an afferent, or sensory, neuron conveys signals from a sensory part of some kind, such as the skin or eyes, toward the brain. An efferent, or motor, neuron carries nerve signals away from the brain, usually to a muscle. Yet many of the stringlike "nerves" winding through the body contain the axons of both sensory and motor neurons. Similarly, a closeknit lump or group of neuron cell bodies inside the brain or spinal cord is known as a nucleus, whereas the same type of structure in another part of the nervous system is a ganglion.

There are also large groups of nerves – for example, cranial, cervical, sacral – many of whose individual nerves have a name. Often a name is derived from a nearby bone, such as the tibial nerve which runs along the tibia (shinbone).

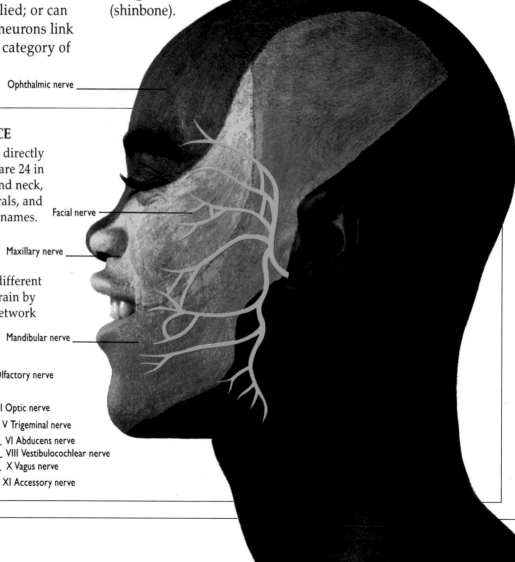

Ophthalmic nerve

Facial nerve

Maxillary nerve

Mandibular nerve

CRANIAL NERVES: BRANCHES OF HEAD OFFICE

The unique feature of cranial nerves is that they branch directly from the brain, rather than from the spinal cord. There are 24 in 12 pairs, linking the brain to parts mainly in the head and neck, but also in the trunk. They are known by Roman numerals, and their main branches also have functional or anatomical names. For example, cranial nerve VII is the facial nerve. Some nerves are purely sensory, others are mainly motor (muscle control) nerves, and still others are mixed. The coloured parts of the face (**right**) show the different areas from which sensory messages are carried to the brain by three branches of cranial nerve V, the trigeminal. The network of lines shows some of the motor branches of the facial nerve to the same areas.

Cranial nerves

III Oculomotor nerve
IV Trochlear nerve
VII Facial nerve
IX Glossopharyngeal nerve
XII Hypoglossal nerve

I Olfactory nerve
II Optic nerve
V Trigeminal nerve
VI Abducens nerve
VIII Vestibulocochlear nerve
X Vagus nerve
XI Accessory nerve

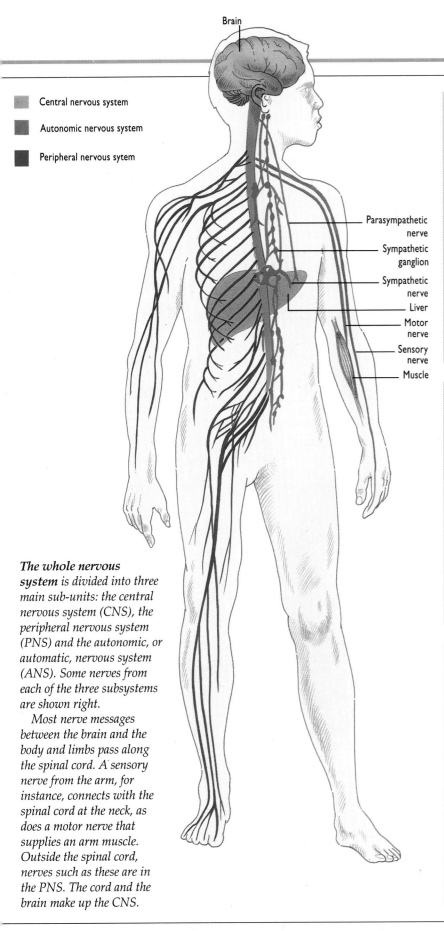

Brain

Central nervous system

Autonomic nervous system

Peripheral nervous sytem

Parasympathetic nerve

Sympathetic ganglion

Sympathetic nerve

Liver

Motor nerve

Sensory nerve

Muscle

The whole nervous system is divided into three main sub-units: the central nervous system (CNS), the peripheral nervous system (PNS) and the autonomic, or automatic, nervous system (ANS). Some nerves from each of the three subsystems are shown right.

Most nerve messages between the brain and the body and limbs pass along the spinal cord. A sensory nerve from the arm, for instance, connects with the spinal cord at the neck, as does a motor nerve that supplies an arm muscle. Outside the spinal cord, nerves such as these are in the PNS. The cord and the brain make up the CNS.

CENTRAL NERVOUS SYSTEM (CNS)

Together, the brain and spinal cord form the central nervous system. They are central in terms of their position within the head and body, and they are, of course, central to the functioning of the whole nervous system and so the entire body. They are the only parts of the nervous system that are well protected by surrounding bones, the brain inside the cranial bones of the skull, and the spinal cord within the linked vertebrae of the spinal column (backbone). The spinal cord, containing millions of nerve fibres, is the body's biggest nerve; the brain is the body's largest concentration of neurons.

PERIPHERAL NERVOUS SYSTEM (PNS)

The peripheral nerves are pale, whitish, shiny, cordlike structures snaking between the body's organs. They form the links between the CNS and other body parts, from head to toe. As well as the 12 pairs of cranial nerves, there are 31 pairs of spinal nerves that branch from along the spinal cord, at junctions known as spinal nerve roots. Some of the spinal nerves branch from the cord, join together and interweave, then branch again. Each of these networks, which look like aerial views of motorway junctions, is known as a nerve plexus.

AUTONOMIC NERVOUS SYSTEM (ANS)

The ANS controls and coordinates the body's "automatic" functions – basic life processes such as heartbeat, digestion, excretion and, to an extent, breathing. There are two major subdivisions with largely complementary roles: the sympathetic ANS generally prepares the body for action; the parasympathetic ANS has a more "peacetime" function, thus it encourages the body's digestive processes. For instance, the sympathetic system signals the liver to release glucose to give energy to the skeletal muscles. The parasympathetic changes priorities to promote the liver's digestive functions.

The long junction

Like a major highway, the spinal cord carries nerve signals to the brain from the body and vice versa.

Just as an experienced servant fetches and carries for his long-time master, so the spinal cord conveys nerve signals to and fro between the brain and the body – or, more precisely, between the brain and the chest, abdomen and limbs. (The head and face link to the brain by cranial nerves.) But the cord is no mere passive servant, simply conveying messages unaltered. It carries out its own relaying and processing of nerve signals. It also works independently of the brain when it activates various body reflexes, such as pulling your hand away from something hot. The vital nature of the cord becomes strikingly clear when it is damaged, either by disease or injury. Depending on the site and severity of the damage, the effects can range from tingling and weakness in the extremities to total paralysis, incontinence, loss of reflexes and loss of sensation.

Structurally, the spinal cord is effectively an extension of the brain: in embryonic development, both originate from the same set of cells, the neural tube. There is no obvious external join between them, only a smooth merger. So the top of the cord is usually taken to be at the level of inside the foramen magnum, the large downward-facing hole in the base of the skull. A long tube, the vertebral canal, protects and encloses

At the railway junction and marshalling yard, trains are routed through a complex maze of tracks and points, on to their correct destination. The spinal cord directs nerve signals in a similar manner, through its network of neurons and their dendrites and axons. Signals pass from the body to the brain along major ascending spinal tracts, or "up lines", and from the brain back into the body along the "down lines", or descending spinal tracts.

REFLEX ACTION

Stroke the outer part of the sole of a new baby's foot, and its toes curl. This is the Babinski reflex, one of many such reflexes – quick automatic responses to certain stimuli – in which signals from a sense organ pass along sensory nerves to the spinal cord. There the signals are processed and return ones go via motor nerves to move the muscles. Other signals go up the cord to the brain, which becomes aware of what has happened – but too late to affect the reflex. New babies are bundles of reflexes, each activating a simple survival action such as sucking, swallowing or emptying the bowel and bladder. With age children learn to control many of these responses.

the cord. It is formed by the row of holes inside the closely joined vertebrae of the spinal column, or backbone. In an adult, the spinal cord is usually about 45 cm (18 inches) long and slightly thinner than an index finger. It does not extend down the whole spine to the base of the spinal column, but tapers rapidly at the level of the first lumbar vertebra, just above the waistline, into a nerveless strip of fibrous tissue known as the *filum terminale*, which is attached to the coccyx. The vertebral canal continues below the first lumbar vertebra but contains nerves that have branched from the cord.

Membranes and fluid – more extensions from the brain above – surround and cushion the cord. There are three layers, or meninges, and cerebrospinal fluid (CSF). The cord also has a tiny tube, the central canal, along its length; this contains CSF, too, which is continuous with the CSF in the ventricles inside the brain. In its nerve layout, the cord is the "reverse" of the cerebral cortex. It has white matter – mainly myelinated nerve fibres or axons – on the outside; inside is the grey matter of connections and nerve cell bodies, such as processing interneurons, which forms a cross-sectional H or butterfly shape.

Cortex

Descending nerve

Collateral

Midbrain

Cerebrum

Cerebellum

Pons

Nerves to arm

Upper medulla

Lower medulla

8 pairs

12 pairs

5 pairs

5 pairs

Nerves to leg

Spinal tracts, or pathways, are bundles of nerve fibres, *or axons, in the white matter of the spinal cord. There are two major types of tracts, ascending and descending, named according to their positions in the cord and the brain parts that they link to.*

Ascending tracts are sensory, taking nerve signals concerned with sensation up to the brain. The posterior and anterior spinocerebellar tracts carry sensory messages about the position of joints and muscles to the brain stem, for mainly unconscious assessment of body position and posture (known as proprioception). The lateral spinothalamic tract conveys signals from the body about pain and temperature; the anterior spinothalamic tract carries information about light or coarse touch. The spinoreticulothalamic tract is grouped with these and also concerns pain. The lemniscal tracts in the back of the cord are evolutionarily newer pathways for more discriminatory messages about fine, detailed touch, which go from the skin to the somatosensory cortex, the brain's touch centre.

See also

INPUTS AND OUTPUTS
▶ Body links
202/203

▶ On the move
206/207

▶ Guided motion
208/209

▶ Sense of touch
222/223

▶ Pain pathways
224/225

▶ Keeping control
238/239

SURVEYING THE MIND
▶ Brain maps
152/159

BUILDING THE BRAIN
▶ Support and protection
164/165

▶ Sending signals
172/173

FAR HORIZONS
▶ First thoughts
264/265

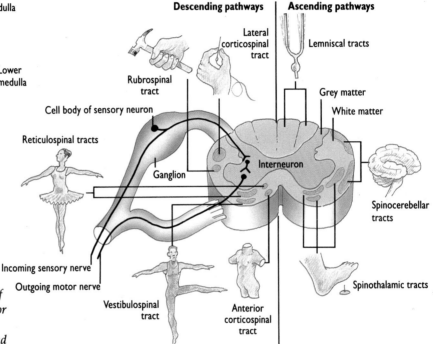

Descending pathways | **Ascending pathways**

Lateral corticospinal tract

Lemniscal tracts

Rubrospinal tract

Cell body of sensory neuron

Grey matter

White matter

Reticulospinal tracts

Interneuron

Spinocerebellar tracts

Ganglion

Incoming sensory nerve

Outgoing motor nerve

Vestibulospinal tract

Anterior corticospinal tract

Spinothalamic tracts

Spinal nerves *branch from the spinal cord in pairs between adjacent vertebrae. Their names reflect the groupings of these vertebrae: cervical (C), or neck; thoracic (T), or chest; lumbar (L), or back; and sacral (S), or low back. If you decide to move your right fingers, nerve signals pass from the left motor cortex down to the pons and medulla. As this tapers into the spinal cord, the signals cross to the right side and continue down the lateral corticospinal tract, passing out along right spinal nerves C7 to T2. Motor nerves leave the spinal cord at its front, carrying the signal down to the finger. Any returning sensory information enters the cord at its rear.*

Descending pathways in the spinal cord *carry motor nerve signals from the brain on their way to the body's muscles to make movements. The lateral (pyramidal) corticospinal tract is concerned with detailed movements of the extremities and in particular – together with the rubrospinal tract – with finger manipulation. The lateral (medullary) and medial (pontine) reticulospinal tracts convey messages to many muscles in the torso, shoulders and hips, for the seldom-noticed movements that maintain or change posture, equilibrium and balance. The signals going along the vestibulospinal tract are similar, and they also go to the limbs for fine balancing movements. The anterior (pyramidal) corticospinal tract conveys nerve signals to the muscles of the neck and torso, for bending, twisting and other voluntary movements.*

The various tracts in the spinal cord are primarily named after the areas where they start and finish. "Spino-" refers to the grey matter in the spinal cord, for instance, "thalamic" the thalamus, "cortico" the cerebral cortex, and so on. So the spinothalamic tract starts in the cord's grey matter and ends in the thalamus.

On the move

Like a puppeteer pulling strings, the brain sends signals that make the muscles contract and move the body.

To obtain the comforts of life, the brain sends out messages as nerve signals to the various systems of the body, such as the circulatory system for nourishment via the blood and the musculoskeletal system for physical motion. The body has about 640 skeletal muscles, ranging in size from the huge slab of the gluteus maximus in the buttock and upper rear thigh to the threadlike stapedius deep in the ear. Skeletal muscles work by getting shorter, or contracting. Most of them are attached by their tapering, ropelike ends (tendons) to bones. As the muscle contracts, its tendon pulls on the bone and moves it. The bone, being strong and rigid, acts as a firm inner support and moves that whole part of the body. Body movements get food, find shelter and avoid danger – helping the body and brain survive.

The skeletal muscles do not work alone. In effect, the muscular body is a robot, controlled by the brain. This sends nerve signals along motor nerves to all muscles, telling them when and how to contract and make a movement, or to relax and go floppy, so they do not oppose the work of other muscles. The more signals per second, the more the muscle contracts. Even the simplest movement such as waving goodbye is a massive cooperative effort by dozens of muscles working together in coordinated teams with split-second timing, each muscle controlled by thousands of nerve signals every second.

Several parts of the central nervous system – the brain and spinal cord – are dedicated to or partly involved in this process. A complex system of continuous monitoring and feedback makes sure movements are smooth and coordinated – and exactly what the brain requires.

Arm Trunk Leg Hand Fingers Toes Thumb Neck Brow Eye Face Lips Jaw Tongue Swallowing Primary motor cortex

The chief executives in the movement process are two strips of grey matter over the top of the brain, just under where you might wear an Alice-type hairband or a set of headphones. They are the left and right motor cortices – the left one controlling the muscles on the body's right side, and the right one those on the body's left side. The different sets of muscles in each part of the body have their own patch of motor cortex, resulting in a "strip map" of the body on the brain, from face and head on the outer (temple) side, to legs, feet and toes on the inner (midline) side. The larger the area of the cortex, the greater the precision of control. So a body part like the hand, which requires considerable precision to perform tasks such as using tools, will have a far greater area of cortex devoted to it than, say, the trunk, whose movements can be fairly imprecise.

Each body part of the motor homunculus (little man) is sized in proportion to the area of the brain's motor cortex that controls the muscles there. This indicates not the size and power of a muscle, but how precisely it can be controlled. Parts which can be moved very accurately with fine control, such as the lips, tongue and fingers, are largest.

206

FEEDBACK FOR CONTROL

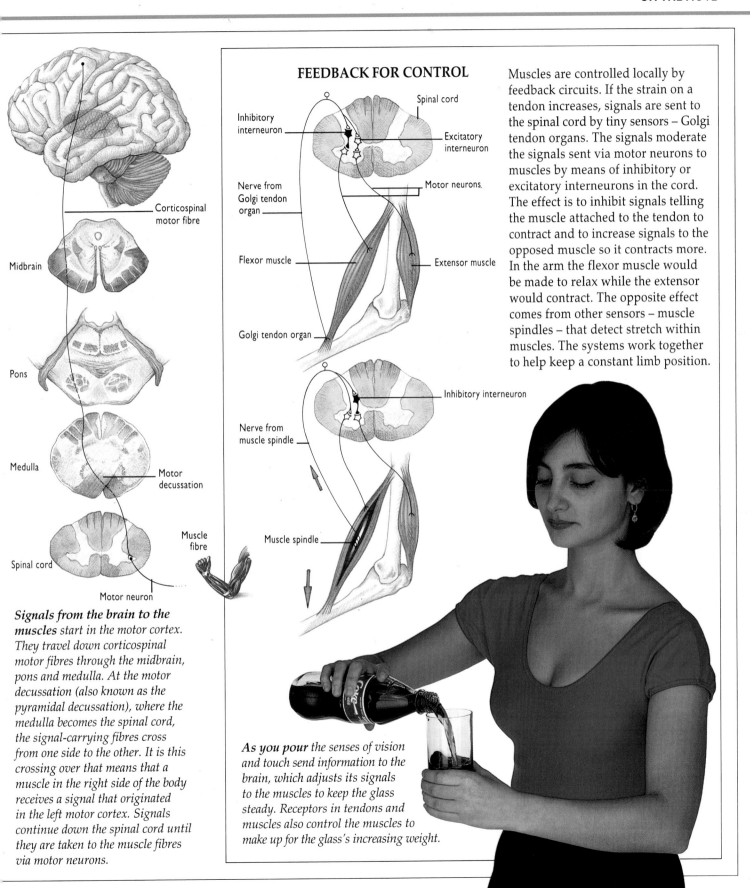

Corticospinal motor fibre

Midbrain

Pons

Medulla

Motor decussation

Spinal cord

Motor neuron

Muscle fibre

Inhibitory interneuron

Spinal cord

Excitatory interneuron

Nerve from Golgi tendon organ

Motor neurons

Flexor muscle

Extensor muscle

Golgi tendon organ

Inhibitory interneuron

Nerve from muscle spindle

Muscle spindle

Muscles are controlled locally by feedback circuits. If the strain on a tendon increases, signals are sent to the spinal cord by tiny sensors – Golgi tendon organs. The signals moderate the signals sent via motor neurons to muscles by means of inhibitory or excitatory interneurons in the cord. The effect is to inhibit signals telling the muscle attached to the tendon to contract and to increase signals to the opposed muscle so it contracts more. In the arm the flexor muscle would be made to relax while the extensor would contract. The opposite effect comes from other sensors – muscle spindles – that detect stretch within muscles. The systems work together to help keep a constant limb position.

Signals from the brain to the muscles start in the motor cortex. They travel down corticospinal motor fibres through the midbrain, pons and medulla. At the motor decussation (also known as the pyramidal decussation), where the medulla becomes the spinal cord, the signal-carrying fibres cross from one side to the other. It is this crossing over that means that a muscle in the right side of the body receives a signal that originated in the left motor cortex. Signals continue down the spinal cord until they are taken to the muscle fibres via motor neurons.

As you pour the senses of vision and touch send information to the brain, which adjusts its signals to the muscles to keep the glass steady. Receptors in tendons and muscles also control the muscles to make up for the glass's increasing weight.

See also

INPUTS AND OUTPUTS
▶ Body links 202/203

▶ The long junction 204/205

▶ Guided motion 208/209

▶ Staying upright 234/235

▶ The big picture 236/237

▶ Keeping control 238/239

▶ Survival sense 244/245

SURVEYING THE MIND
▶ Inside the mind 142/143

▶ Brain maps 152/159

BUILDING THE BRAIN
▶ Sending signals 172/173

FAR HORIZONS
▶ Parallel minds 260/261

Guided motion

Decide to make a move, and parts of the brain and spinal cord frantically send signals back and forth.

Imagine (or recall) practising a new and complex activity such as serving a tennis ball. It is painfully slow and awkward at first. Each muscle seems to need individual attention as you try to move the limbs, hands and fingers in the correct way, while retaining posture and balance. The first few times you might miss the ball or even fall over. But gradually the motor skills improve. You guide your movements more accurately, using your senses – watching the ball and racquet, feeling with your hand and fingertips, and listening for the ball's ping on the racquet strings. This sensory-guided motion is steered by feedback from the senses.

After a few more hours' practice, the serve seems to happen almost automatically, without your really thinking. It is now a subconscious motor skill, a series of pathways, connections and sequences between neurons in the brain and spinal cord. The serving movements are now well learned, faster and more powerful – a ballistic motion that, once initiated and in progress, leaves too little time to adjust and fine-tune it. It is literally hit or miss.

*A **tennis player's first serve** is usually fast and hard. The brain operates the muscles in a rapid sequence that has been programmed in during practice. This type of action, where there is no time for correction, is termed ballistic. The second serve is often slower and more controlled. The player adjusts the speed, force and angle of the racquet using proprioceptive feedback from sensors in muscles, tendons and joints.*

*A **deliberate sensory-guided movement** involves complex, ongoing messages being sent between several brain and spinal cord regions. The decision to move is usually prompted by sensory information that reaches the primary planning region, the association cortex. This sends signals to basal ganglia and to the cerebellum where movement patterns, or motor commands, are evoked and sent to the motor cortex via the thalamus. The motor cortex plays the pivotal role between receiving a motor command and executing it. It sends signals to the motor centres in the spinal cord both directly and via the brain stem. The motor centres consist of spinal interneurons and motor neurons, which send signals to make the muscles move. The motor cortex also sends data back to the cerebellum and the basal ganglia, and the various components receive feedback as sensory inputs cause ongoing corrections to the movement being made.*

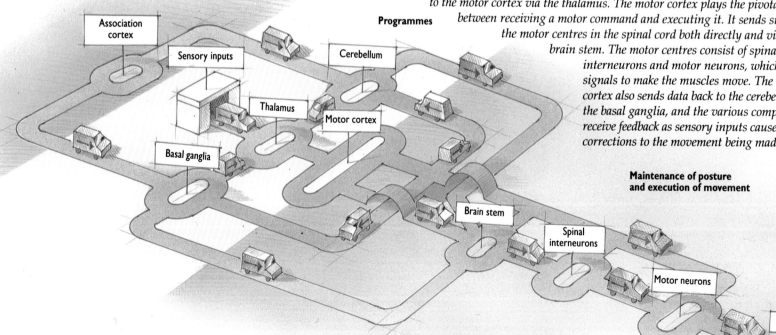

Planning

Association cortex

Sensory inputs

Programmes

Cerebellum

Thalamus

Motor cortex

Basal ganglia

Maintenance of posture and execution of movement

Brain stem

Spinal interneurons

Motor neurons

Muscles

COMPARING LITTLE BRAINS

The cerebellum, or "little brain", makes up about one-tenth of the volume of a human brain. In some fish, it is nine-tenths. In animals such as fish and reptiles it is the prime controller of body movements. In birds, and to a greater extent mammals, above all humans, the "higher" brain areas of the motor cortex take over control of voluntary movements. But the cerebellum still plays a role in precise, balanced coordination of the muscles, once a motion has begun. It receives nerve signals about the central motor programme from the cortex, and signals from microsensors in muscles, tendons and joints, about the results of a movement as it happens. The cerebellum compares the instructions and results, assesses how they match, and outputs signals to the motor cortex to modify and fine-tune the programme.

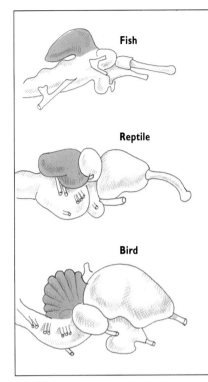
Fish
Reptile
Bird

Cat

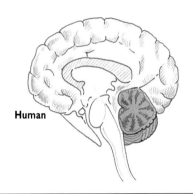
Human

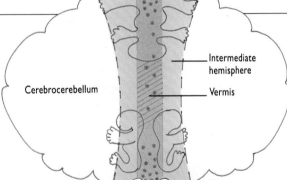
Spinocerebellum
Intermediate hemisphere
Cerebrocerebellum
Vermis
Vestibulocerebellum

Regions of the body are mapped in two distinct regions of the spinocerebellum. The maps correspond to where sensory information from the body regions arrives in the cerebellum.

Cerebrocerebellar regions (yellow) send signals to motor cortex areas and have a role in motor planning.

Ongoing movements, such as walking, are controlled by the spinocerebellum (which includes the vermis).

Signals from the inner ear concerning head movements and gravity go to the vestibulocerebellum. It controls and coordinates head–eye movements, so you can watch a speeding object pass by, moving your eyes and twisting your neck in a coordinated manner to keep it in view.

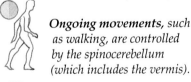
The various cerebellar regions receive and send signals to different parts of the brain and nervous system. The colours and markings (the dots, and the diagonal lines in the centre of the vermis) on the diagram of the cerebellum above indicate which signals the cerebellar regions receive and the functions that they control. Thus the cerebrocerebellum (yellow) sends signals to and receives them from the cerebral cortex and other regions including the pons (left).

The central region of the vermis receives inputs from both the visual and the auditory systems. These incoming signals assist it in controlling muscles in the trunk and other regions and in controlling and coordinating the continuing execution of movements.

The vestibulocerebellum and vermis use signals from the vestibular system to control body balance, and the muscle tensions and movements that maintain it. This means you can sit, stand and move without having to think about your posture and balance.

The spinocerebellum receives inputs from the spinal cord and other regions. It is responsible, among other things, for maintenance of muscle tone and the elimination of tremors.

Seeing the light

The story of how we see the world about us starts in the eye, where light is turned into coded nerve signals.

Humans, like their primate relations the monkeys and apes, are intensely visual animals. The eyes send millions of nerve signals every second along the optic nerves to the visual pathways in the brain, for analysis, interpretation and recording. The nerve signals represent energy transformed, or transduced, from the energy in light rays. This happens in the 2.5-cm (1-inch) diameter "biological camera", specifically in its light-sensitive layer, the retina. This is about the size and thickness of a postage stamp and lines the inner rear two-thirds of the eyeball. Around it is the blood-rich, eye-nourishing layer known as the choroid, surrounded in turn by the tough white outer sheath of the eyeball, the sclera. Within the retina is the vitreous humour, a clear jelly that gives the eyeball shape and firmness without obstructing light rays.

Rays of light that fall on the retina have already been altered to produce a clear, sharp, unblurred image there that is of suitable brightness or intensity. This is achieved by optical structures at the front of the eye. Light passes from the object being observed into the eye through its clear front, the cornea, whose domed shape does most of the focusing of the rays. It then passes through the pupil, an adjustable hole in the middle of the iris. This is a ring-shaped system of muscles which give the eye its colour. Like the aperture on a camera, the iris makes the pupil smaller in bright light conditions – to restrict the amount of light entering, which might damage the retina if too intense – and larger if it is dim, allowing the optimum amount of light in to give the best possible image.

Next, the light rays pass through the lens, which can be pulled thin or left fat by another ring of muscles around it, the ciliary muscles. This "fine tunes" the focusing, according to whether the rays come from a near or distant object, to throw a sharp image on to the retina.

Inside the eye, light rays pass through the cornea and then the pupil in the centre of the iris. The fixed cornea and adjustable lens bend light rays to focus a clear image on to the retina. As with an equivalent man-made lens, the image is inverted. But since this is the case from birth, we never know any different, and so it is not a problem.

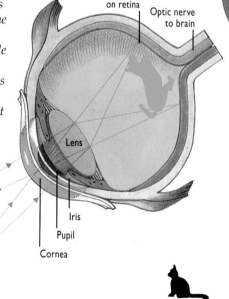

Inverted image on retina

Optic nerve to brain

Lens

Iris

Pupil

Cornea

Receptors in retina

Cones

Rods

Dendrites of bipolar and horizontal cells

Synaptic terminal

Synaptic vesicle

Mitochondrion

Nucleus

The retina has two types of light-sensitive cells – rods and cones (named after their shapes). The 125 million rods detect shades of black and white. The 5 to 7 million cones detect colour and fall into three types, each of which is most sensitive to one of the primary colours of light: red, blue and green. Most cones are in the centre of the retina, especially in the fovea – a rod-free area where vision is sharpest. Rods, and some cones, are found in the rest of the retina.

Each rod cell (above) is about 150–200 micrometres ($\frac{3}{500}$–$\frac{1}{125}$ inch) long. At one end, next to a layer of pigment cells and facing the outside of the eyeball, it has a stack of discs studded with the chemicals that play a part in transducing light energy. Toward its other end it has a nucleus and other standard cell components such as mitochondria. At its base it synapses (connects) with dendrites of intermediary cells which link it to retinal ganglion cells. These send nerve signals to the brain, and their axons (message carrying fibres) form the optic nerve. Each retina has a blind spot, a receptor-free area where all the axons leave the eye.

To find the blind spot of your right eye close your left eye and look at the black dog. Adjust the distance of the book until the cat vanishes. Repeat for the left eye but this time close your right eye and look at the cat. The dog should disappear but the lines seem continuous. The brain actively fills in with what it "thinks" should be there, in this case linking the vertical lines.

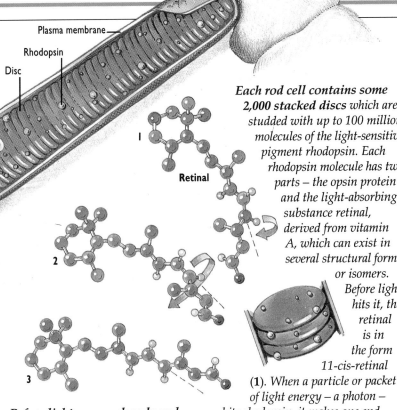

Pigment cell

Plasma membrane

Rhodopsin

Disc

Retinal

1

2

3

Before light can reach rods and cones at the rear layer of the retina it travels through several other layers. These are made up of tiny blood vessels and the so-called neural cells of the retina – bipolar, horizontal and ganglion cells – and are effectively transparent. Behind rods and cones is a layer of pigment cells which absorb any stray light and prevent it reflecting back to the retina.

Each rod cell contains some 2,000 stacked discs which are studded with up to 100 million molecules of the light-sensitive pigment rhodopsin. Each rhodopsin molecule has two parts – the opsin protein and the light-absorbing substance retinal, derived from vitamin A, which can exist in several structural forms, or isomers. Before light hits it, the retinal is in the form 11-cis-retinal (**1**). When a particle or packet of light energy – a photon – hits rhodopsin, it makes one end of 11-cis-retinal twist around (**2**) to form another isomer, all-trans-retinal (**3**). This changes the configuration of the opsin protein, too, converting the whole molecule from rhodopsin into metarhodopsin II – in the space of only one-thousandth of a second. Giving the retinal the energy to change shape is the only part light plays in this process.

The transformation of rhodopsin to metarhodopsin II triggers a series of chemical reactions within the rod. First each metarhodopsin II molecule activates hundreds of molecules of the protein transducin. Each of these in turn activates a type of enzyme known as a phosphodiesterase, which alters the structure of thousands of molecules of the neurotransmitter that stimulates cells in the retina – cyclic guanosine monophosphate (cGMP). This reduces levels of cGMP in the rod, which in darkness are high.

As the concentration of cGMP in the rod cell falls, channels which allow sodium ions to flow through its membrane close. This is because cGMP's function is to keep these channels – found in the rod cell's membrane next to the region containing the discs – open. Thus when no light falls on the retina, the channels allow a flow of positively charged sodium ions into the cell – known as the dark current – to counterbalance the diffusion of positive potassium ions out of the cell, making the inside slightly negative. When light hits the cell, sodium entry reduces but potassium exit continues, so the cell's interior becomes more negative, or hyperpolarizes.

Hyperpolarization of the rod cell reduces the release of neurotransmitters from synaptic vesicles in its 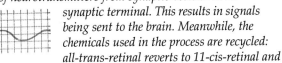 synaptic terminal. This results in signals being sent to the brain. Meanwhile, the chemicals used in the process are recycled: all-trans-retinal reverts to 11-cis-retinal and the sodium channels reopen. It all happens within one-fifth of a second of the original photon first reaching the rod cell. The process in cones is similar to that in rods but cones – which work best in bright light – require about 50 times more light to activate them to the same extent.

MORE THAN MEETS THE EYE

The human eye has the typical structure of any mammal's eye, which in turn is very similar to the eye of any vertebrate – bird, reptile, amphibian or fish. However, there are many other designs of eye, or image-forming photosensory organ, in the animal kingdom.

Insect eyes – like that of this horsefly, *Tabanis* sp. – are compound, made of hundreds, or even thousands, of closely packed light-sensitive elements known as ommatidia. Each of these – in effect a separate eye – detects light rays from only a tiny part of the scene, but the many units may combine to produce an overall image in much the same way as a mosaic is built up from many small elements. The "brain" of the insect integrates the multiple images so that although a fly cannot detect much detail with such an eye, it can pick up objects moving across its visual field fairly well.

Contrasting views

The processing of signals in the visual system starts with complex layers of nerve cells in the retina.

An orbiting space telescope takes a photograph deep in space. On the TV monitor screen back on Earth, it appears as a chaotic swirl of dark and light blobs. But the image enhancement computer sharpens differences, or contrasts, and defines clear shapes from the gloom. The retina of the eye works in a similar way. Arrays of light-sensitive photoreceptor cells – rods and cones – form its outer layer. Within this layer are further hugely complex layers of interconnected neurons.

Signals from possibly hundreds of rods and cones feed into a dozen or so bipolar cells, which then send signals to one ganglion cell. The system constitutes the receptive field of that ganglion cell and carries out what computer scientists refer to as data compression. The ganglion cell's firing rate is governed by the summation and integration of the signals from all of its photoreceptors, and is thus an indicator of the amount and distribution of light falling on its receptive field.

These data compression–convergence routes are the direct pathways for visual information, but there are also lateral pathways involving horizontal and amacrine cells. As a result of these interacting pathways, signals generated by about 130 million rods and cones are pre-processed, image-enhanced and data-compressed in the opto-neural network of the retina, producing signals that are sent from the 1 million ganglion cells in the retina to the brain. These pass as nerve impulses along the ganglion cell fibres (axons), which form the optic nerve.

An eagle could spot a rabbit at 5 km (3 miles) but we would struggle to identify it at just 1 km (3/5 mile) away. An eagle's light-sensitive rods and cones are packed five times more densely in the retina than ours, averaging more than 1 million per mm². Our retina's fovea, where cones are most concentrated to see in greatest detail, is a flattish disc. In a hunting bird it is pit shaped, which has a magnifying effect.

COLOUR-CHALLENGED

A young man applied to join the air force but after tests was turned down because his colour vision was defective. He was not colour blind, a rare state in which a person sees only in monochrome – like a black-and-white movie – but he had problems telling reds from greens. Thus he would not have been able to distinguish the umbrella in the picture on the right. This common condition is usually inherited, and it almost always affects males. Overall, colour vision defects affect about 1 in 12 men and 1 in 200 women; red–green defects are commonest. Some affected people never know, unless they are tested. They assume other people see colours in the way they do; they learn to distinguish delicate differences between similar hues, especially in bright light.

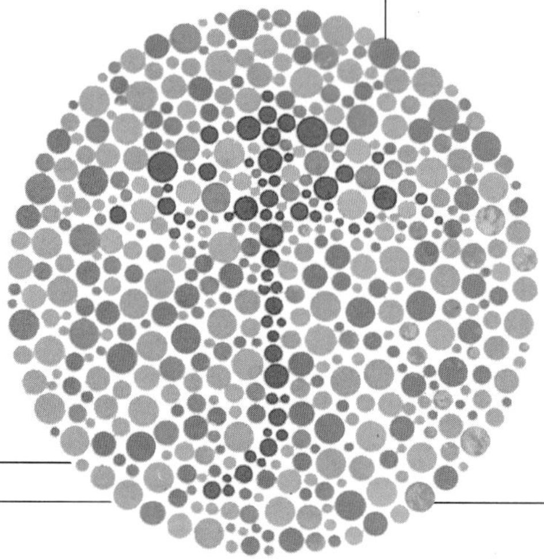

Just three colours are used to make the image above, yet the different combinations make it seem as if there are more. This is because our perception of a colour is affected by its context, that is, by the colours that are adjacent to it.

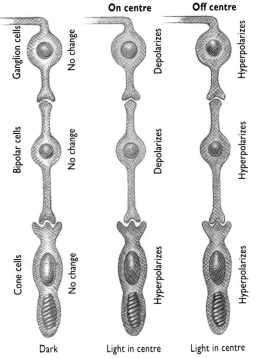

	On centre	Off centre
Ganglion cells — No change	Depolarizes	Hyperpolarizes
Bipolar cells — No change	Depolarizes	Hyperpolarizes
Cone cells — No change	Hyperpolarizes	Hyperpolarizes
Dark	Light in centre	Light in centre

Light-sensitive photoreceptor cells – rods and cones – packed into the retina do not send signals direct to the brain. Instead information is sent via bipolar cells to ganglion cells, which send signals to the brain along the optic nerve.

When illuminated, a rod or (as in this diagram) a cone hyperpolarizes. What then happens at the bipolar cell stage depends largely on the type of receptive field of the relevant ganglion cell and on the cone's position in the field. Each retinal ganglion cell has a receptive field made up of an outer ring, or surround, and an inner circle, or centre. There are two main types of receptive fields: on and off centre. In the on centre field, illuminating the cones in the middle makes them hyperpolarize, which causes depolarization in both the bipolar and ganglion cells above. This makes the ganglion cell fire faster than its normal "dark" background rate; illuminating cones in the surround makes the ganglion cell fire more slowly than normal.

When a cone in the middle of an off centre field hyperpolarizes, the bipolar cell above it also hyperpolarizes, causing the ganglion cell above to hyperpolarize, too, which reduces its rate of firing. Illuminating the cones in the surround of an off centre field makes the ganglion cell fire faster than normal. The brain interprets the patterns of changes in firing rates of the ganglion cells across the retina in the process of visual perception.

An additional feature of the system is the lateral inhibition of ganglion cells. This is carried out by horizontal cells, which attach to adjacent rod or cone cells, and amacrine cells (not shown) which link to neighbouring ganglion cells. Horizontal cells pass inhibitory signals from hyperpolarized cones to adjacent cones. Here, in this highly simplified diagram, a row of horizontal cells connects a row of illuminated, hyperpolarized cones with a row in the dark. The horizontal cells make the non-illuminated cones depolarize and this makes the bipolar cells above them hyperpolarize, lowering the rate of firing in the ganglion cells. The effect is to increase differences and sharpen contrasts, one part of retinal image enhancement.

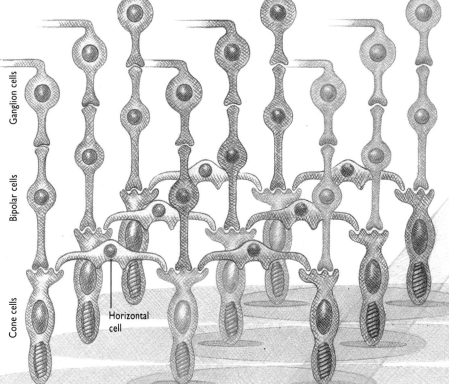

Cone cells • Bipolar cells • Ganglion cells • Horizontal cell

On centre receptive fields

▨	Cell depolarizes
▨	Cell hyperpolarizes
▨	No change in polarization

Light

Levels of seeing

More is known about how the brain processes nerve signals from the eyes than those from any other sense.

Nerve signals from the 1 million ganglion cells in the retina of each eye pass along the optic nerve to a half-crossover junction – the optic chiasma. The signals continue along the optic tracts to paired parts of the thalamus known as lateral geniculate nuclei, or LGNs. They then continue along fan-shaped optic radiations to their main destination, the visual cortex of each occipital lobe. These are sited at the lower central back of the cerebrum, just inside the part-protruding lump of the lower rear skull.

The visual cortices are sight centres concerned with decoding and analysing the nerve signals from the retinal ganglion cells. Each region of visual cortex has a number, so the primary visual cortex, the main reception area for visual signals, is V1. It is effectively a "copy map" of the retina. The activities of V1's vast patchwork of neurons represent a mosaic

A ballet dancer pirouettes and leaps gracefully, yet a few people would see a series of staccato images. This is because of damage to parts of the visual cortex, which can disrupt some aspects of vision while leaving others undisturbed. Thus shapes, outlines, colours and contours may be unaffected, but motion is perceived as disjointed.

SEEING WITHOUT KNOWING

A man who had partial blindness after a head injury underwent tests on his visual field – the area that he could still see. The doctor flashed lights across various parts of the normal visual field. The man saw and pointed to them, until the lights were in the now-blind area, when he said he could no longer see them. But when coaxed to guess where the lights were, he pointed to them in a repeated and reliable way, with a surprising degree of accuracy – yet he still denied seeing anything at all.

This condition is blindsight. The eyes and nerve pathways to the visual cortex function normally, yet the person firmly states that, in his conscious awareness, he sees nothing. But the images must register at some lower level, since the brain reacts by instructing muscles to make the arm point to them. Blindsight is associated with damage – usually severe – to the main primary visual cortex (region V1) at the lower rear of the brain. This is the chief reception site for nerve signals coming from the eyes via the major relay stations of the LGNs (lateral geniculate nuclei) in the thalamus. Possibly V1 is involved in passing signals on to other visual regions from where signals spread through the brain and enter consciousness; this does not happen in blindsight.

However, nerve pathways may be operating that send signals to other parts of the visual cortex, bypassing V1. These are thought to be from the superior colliculi and from the LGNs, which connect with region V4 from where further signals are sent to the brain's motor system. Thus the body can point to an image but no signals reach conscious perception, so the person denies the image's existence.

reflecting the pattern of signals sent in by the retinal ganglion cells. Around it in the secondary visual cortex are regions V2, V3 and so on. They sort and to an extent separately process the various aspects of vision, such as shape and form, colour, contrast, distance and depth, and movement or motion. This parallel processing seems to happen independently in different patches of visual cortex. The results are recombined as these cortical areas communicate with other parts of the cerebral cortex – notably parts of the temporal lobe – plus the language centres and other areas. By such interactions we become aware of the colour, shape, motion, distance, identity, name and meaning of what we see.

At the optic chiasma, fibres from the left of each retina (green) join, as do those from the right (red). The fibres pass to the lateral geniculate nuclei (LGNs). Each LGN sends signals along optic radiations to its primary visual cortex. Side branches of the optic tracts (orange) feed data about vision to the pretecta and the Edinger Westphal nuclei, and back via ciliary ganglia to the constrictor pupillae muscles, which control pupil size. Other side branches (blue) go to the superior colliculi which, with the LGNs, direct the gaze to anything unusual (the visual startle reflex). These regions are also involved in the visual tracking reflex which allows moving objects to be followed.

The cat has no colour and no apparent depth or movement. Yet it is instantly recognizable as a cat. In the visual cortex, nerve signals from the eyes are sorted into different aspects of vision: line, shape, colour, movement, and distance or depth. Yet from this isolated feature of an image, simply a black shape, signals may stimulate neurons "higher" in the visual hierarchy, which code for familiar shapes such as a face, cat, dog or car.

Stereoscopic, or binocular, vision allows us to judge distance and see objects, such as a cube, in three dimensions. Because of the half crossover at the optic chiasma, the left visual cortex receives signals from the left side of both retinas. In each visual cortex signals can be directly compared to detect differences in angle, shading and perspective that result from the two eyes looking at a three-dimensional object from slightly different viewpoints.

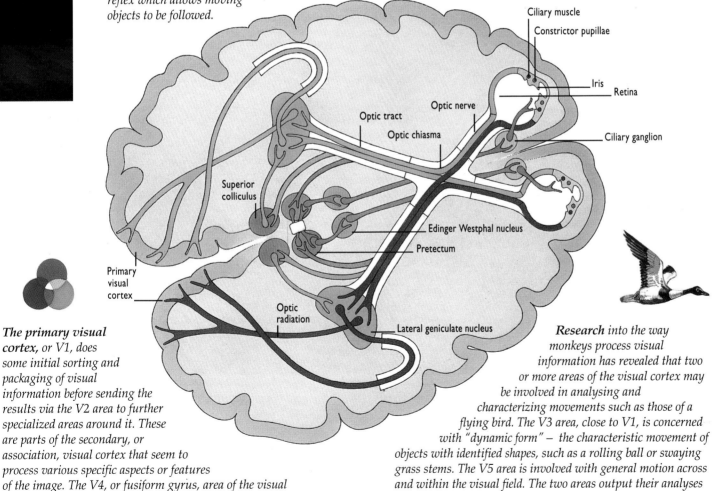

Ciliary muscle
Constrictor pupillae
Iris
Retina
Optic nerve
Optic tract
Optic chiasma
Ciliary ganglion
Superior colliculus
Edinger Westphal nucleus
Pretectum
Primary visual cortex
Optic radiation
Lateral geniculate nucleus

The primary visual cortex, or V1, does some initial sorting and packaging of visual information before sending the results via the V2 area to further specialized areas around it. These are parts of the secondary, or association, visual cortex that seem to process various specific aspects or features of the image. The V4, or fusiform gyrus, area of the visual cortex, for example, is apparently concerned mainly with the analysis and comparison of colours and contrasts.

Research into the way monkeys process visual information has revealed that two or more areas of the visual cortex may be involved in analysing and characterizing movements such as those of a flying bird. The V3 area, close to V1, is concerned with "dynamic form" – the characteristic movement of objects with identified shapes, such as a rolling ball or swaying grass stems. The V5 area is involved with general motion across and within the visual field. The two areas output their analyses to other areas, where the features of the scene are reintegrated into a complete view of the world.

Active vision

Our visual perception is based only partly on external reality – the brain makes up the rest as it goes along.

From the moment we emerge into light at birth, vision dominates our conscious perception. We learn with our eyes, and we learn to see. The brain is not merely a passive recipient of nerve signal patterns sent from the eyes. It learns to make endless assumptions, short cuts and extrapolations, so the apparently seamless scenes we see are partly guesswork. For example, the lens of the eye focuses an image on to the retina which is upside-down and back to front. But we never know any different. A baby gradually realizes that an object's image on a certain patch of the retina corresponds to a certain position in front of the body, from which the object can be picked up. By multitudes of such correlations we learn to link retinal images with the position of an object in the physical world.

There are no rods and cones where the axons of millions of ganglion cells converge in the retina to form the optic nerve. This is the blind spot, insensitive to light – a "black hole" in the visual field. But the brain learns to extend lines, shapes and colours into the blind spot. It also borrows input from the other eye, which usually looks from a slightly different angle, so the two blind spots rarely coincide. Because blood vessels fan out on the inside surface of the retina, light rays cast spidery shadows on it, throwing millions of rods and cones into darkness wherever we look. Again, the brain's visual perception fills in from experience. But the brain's leaps of assumption can be hijacked by the artificial situations of visual illusions – not fooling the eye, but tricking the brain.

There is only one triangle in this Kanizsa illusion, but gaps in the lines and black circles imply that there is another – upside-down. When it detects unexpected holes and gaps, the brain searches for an explanation. Specific neurons carry out these tasks, using experience of common line patterns and shapes.

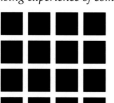

Dark patches lurk between the corners of these black squares – unless you stare at one, and then it disappears. With so many high-contrast shapes in such close proximity, the brain adds "common sense" connecting dark areas in peripheral vision. But if the image of a corner gap falls directly on the retina's cone-rich fovea (yellow spot), we see there is no such dark area.

Flicker fusion as in a movie results from the recovery of rods and cones after receiving light energy and firing nerve signals. The eyes are presented with a series of instant stationary snapshots, but the brain fills the gaps and perceives movement. In bright light, images fuse into a continuous scene when 60 per second are shown (a fly sees them as still and separate up to 300). In the dim light of a cinema, this flicker fusion frequency drops to 10 or below. So 24 images or movie frames per second produce an illusion of smooth movement.

Is it an elegant young lady in a hat looking over her shoulder, or an old crone resting her pointed chin on her chest? Once you perceive these two images, you can flip between them – but you cannot combine them. This may be due to two sets of neurons high in the visual processing system, each with a so-called projective field. One set corresponds to perception of each image, and they will be active alternately.

A BAD MEMORY FOR FACES

☤ A woman went to hospital to visit her husband who was recovering from a stroke, but when she entered the ward he showed no recognition. Only when she spoke did he realize that it was his wife. Prosopagnosia is the inability consciously to recognize or name familiar faces, even though the affected person knows that it is "a face".

Nerve signals produced in retinal ganglion cells, using information from light-sensitive rods and cones, go to various neurons at increasingly higher functional levels in the visual cortex. These neurons activate singly or in small groups only when a known whole pattern, such as a person's face, is received from their thousands of lower level inputs. This activation correlates with recognition and conscious awareness of a face. It may happen because each high-order neuron has its unique "projective field". This field consists of thousands of synaptic connections to neurons in other brain parts that code for related concepts such as the identity of the face, the person's name, associated memories such as the sound of the voice and recent conversations, plus motor actions such as saying the name.

A stroke or brain injury may destroy some of the neurons or sever their synaptic links. If certain neurons in higher-level parts of the projective field are damaged, the face's identity, associations and "meaning" are lost, even though lower-level neurons still register the image as a human face.

*Is this a scene from **Gulliver's Travels**? No, it is an Ames Room, which has distorted dimensions to fool our perception of perspective. Normally when we look at parallel lines they converge with distance. This apparently happens here with the wall edges and floor tiles, so we perceive distance. And from the context of the room, we assume comparative sizes. The brain is fooled by tricks of perspective and its own expectations into thinking (wrongly) that the person on the left is the same distance away as the people on the right, and that the room is rectangular.*

Architects sometimes play similar tricks with perspective to make it seem that buildings are taller, shorter, wider or narrower than they really are.

One of the brain's most astonishing capacities is its ability to create its own images – dreams – without any visual input from the outside world. Dreams are usually visually coherent – seamless and with places and people as they would appear in normal life, which gives them their reality. It is thought that several visual areas in the brain are active during dreaming and that data from them are integrated before being fed back into the cortex as if they were coming from outside.

All of the coloured images in this book, including the lips, are made from tiny dots in the three main printing-ink colours of yellow, cyan and magenta, plus black. Under high magnification, the eye can distinguish these separate dots and their individual colours. At normal reading distance, however, the images that the dots throw on to the retina are so small and fine that the eye's light-sensitive cone cells, which give us colour vision, cannot discern them, so the dots merge into smooth areas of graduated colour. If the printing quality is poor and the printing plates carrying the ink of the separate colours do not print on top of one another, dots in one of the individual colours can be seen as a "halo" of pure colour around the image.

On a television screen the colours are produced by the stimulation of tiny fluorescent dots in the colours red, blue and green. When the image is viewed from close up, the individual dots can be distinguished.

Children play for hours in a fantasy world based on props that give cues by sight. Such is the power of visual perception that a hat can transform reality and change behaviour. So the child might think he is a cowboy, act like one and see the world from a cowboy's viewpoint. Adults do the same – in theatre. The associations generated by a visual image, as with other sensory inputs, are almost limitless since they come from the brain which has an almost infinite memory capacity.

Sensing sound

A sound that hits the ear takes a split second to register in the mind but the journey is long and complex.

Ripples of alternating high and low pressure spreading through the air – sound waves – are produced by vibrating objects, like a bell or loudspeaker. The pitch of a sound is due to the number of vibrations per second and is measured in Hertz (Hz), with high frequency sounds being shrill and low ones being deep. You notice them because you have two tiny thin, flexible, skinlike membranes, each about the size of your little fingernail – your eardrums (tympanic membranes) – which vibrate in sympathy with sound waves. The vibrations are transferred to three tiny bones, the auditory ossicles – the malleus, incus and stapes – and from them to the oval window, another thin membrane which is part of the wall of the fluid-filled cochlea. They continue as ripples of high and low pressure spreading through this fluid and shake a strip of membranes known as the organ of Corti.

The organ of Corti is a transducer, a device that can change energy from one form to another, in this case pressure waves in the cochlear fluid into patterns of nerve signals, which go to the cochlear nerve. So sound is transformed several times: from pressure waves in the air into vibrations in the solids of the eardrums and bones, to pressure ripples in the cochlear fluid, to motion in the organ of Corti, to electrical nerve signals, which finally reach the hearing centre in the brain. Here they are decoded, analysed, compared with patterns in the memory, identified and brought into your awareness.

When glass shatters, even if you are concentrating on something else, you instantly turn your head to look at the source of the sound. In this auditory reflex, signals are sent from part of the midbrain down to a part of the brain stem that has links to motor nerves which control muscles in the neck and your head turns.

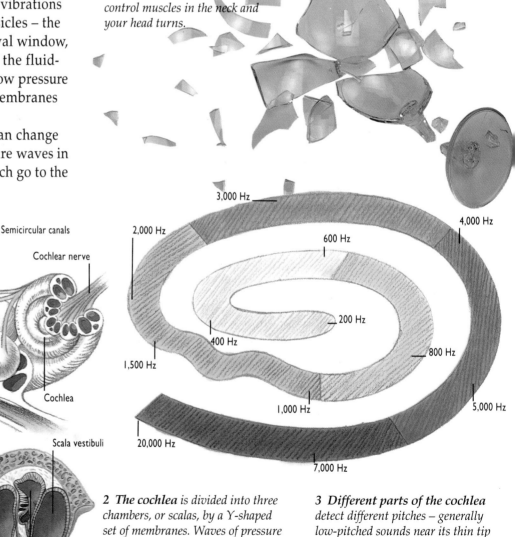

1 Sound waves funneled into the ear canal bounce off the eardrum, making it vibrate. The vibrations pass via the incus, malleus and stapes to the oval window and into the cochlea.

Semicircular canals
Cochlear nerve
Incus
Malleus
Eardrum
Ear canal
Stapes
Cochlea
Scala vestibuli
Scala tympani
Scala media

3,000 Hz
4,000 Hz
2,000 Hz
600 Hz
200 Hz
400 Hz
800 Hz
1,500 Hz
1,000 Hz
5,000 Hz
20,000 Hz
7,000 Hz

2 The cochlea is divided into three chambers, or scalas, by a Y-shaped set of membranes. Waves of pressure change make the membranes vibrate.

3 Different parts of the cochlea detect different pitches – generally low-pitched sounds near its thin tip and shrill sounds at its wider base.

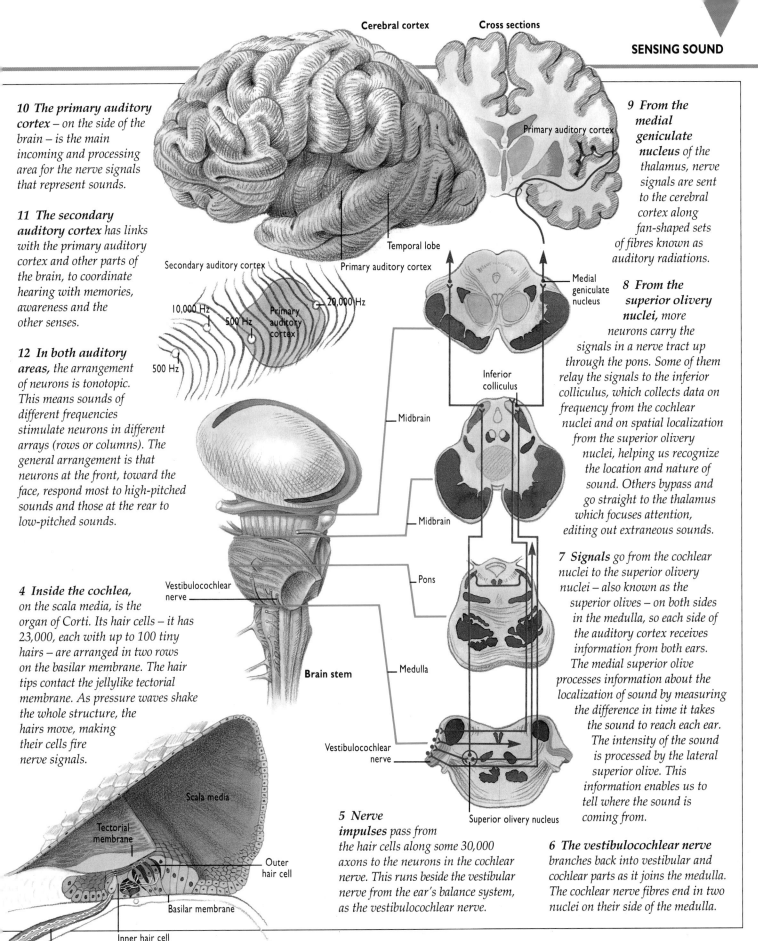

10 The primary auditory cortex – on the side of the brain – is the main incoming and processing area for the nerve signals that represent sounds.

11 The secondary auditory cortex has links with the primary auditory cortex and other parts of the brain, to coordinate hearing with memories, awareness and the other senses.

12 In both auditory areas, the arrangement of neurons is tonotopic. This means sounds of different frequencies stimulate neurons in different arrays (rows or columns). The general arrangement is that neurons at the front, toward the face, respond most to high-pitched sounds and those at the rear to low-pitched sounds.

4 Inside the cochlea, on the scala media, is the organ of Corti. Its hair cells – it has 23,000, each with up to 100 tiny hairs – are arranged in two rows on the basilar membrane. The hair tips contact the jellylike tectorial membrane. As pressure waves shake the whole structure, the hairs move, making their cells fire nerve signals.

Primary auditory cortex

Temporal lobe

Secondary auditory cortex

Primary auditory cortex

10,000 Hz

20,000 Hz

500 Hz

Primary auditory cortex

500 Hz

Midbrain

Midbrain

Pons

Medulla

Brain stem

Vestibulocochlear nerve

Vestibulocochlear nerve

Inferior colliculus

Medial geniculate nucleus

Superior olivery nucleus

Scala media

Tectorial membrane

Outer hair cell

Basilar membrane

Inner hair cell

Cochlear nerve

9 From the medial geniculate nucleus of the thalamus, nerve signals are sent to the cerebral cortex along fan-shaped sets of fibres known as auditory radiations.

8 From the superior olivery nuclei, more neurons carry the signals in a nerve tract up through the pons. Some of them relay the signals to the inferior colliculus, which collects data on frequency from the cochlear nuclei and on spatial localization from the superior olivery nuclei, helping us recognize the location and nature of sound. Others bypass and go straight to the thalamus which focuses attention, editing out extraneous sounds.

7 Signals go from the cochlear nuclei to the superior olivery nuclei – also known as the superior olives – on both sides in the medulla, so each side of the auditory cortex receives information from both ears. The medial superior olive processes information about the localization of sound by measuring the difference in time it takes the sound to reach each ear. The intensity of the sound is processed by the lateral superior olive. This information enables us to tell where the sound is coming from.

5 Nerve impulses pass from the hair cells along some 30,000 axons to the neurons in the cochlear nerve. This runs beside the vestibular nerve from the ear's balance system, as the vestibulocochlear nerve.

6 The vestibulocochlear nerve branches back into vestibular and cochlear parts as it joins the medulla. The cochlear nerve fibres end in two nuclei on their side of the medulla.

219

The mind's ear

Hearing is a long way from being a passive sense – the mind can do much to manipulate what the ears detect.

First the violins lead the orchestral swell, then come the heavy-rock guitar power chords. As you listen intently to a favourite piece of music, you might concentrate on and pick out the bass line or the noise of the cymbals. This is similar to the way that you direct your eyes and stare intently at an object that interests you visually. But this auditory "tuning in" to listen to a particular instrument is different to visual tuning in. Your ears do not move and thus they transduce all the sound waves they detect and send all the resulting nerve signals along the auditory nerves, so you must tune in within your brain, by active auditory perception. You concentrate your conscious awareness on a certain instrument by picking out and following its characteristic range of fundamental frequencies and harmonic overtones.

"Music" consists of sounds whose frequencies or pitches have mathematical relationships, and which are pleasing and harmonious to our auditory perception. "Noise" is a mixture of unconnected, discordant sounds. As you listen to your chosen musical piece, you may be distracted by a sharp noise from the side, and you try to localize it, or gauge its direction.

This is carried out partly by the two pairs of superior olivary nuclei in the brain's medulla. Because the speed of sound is relatively slow, about 340 m/sec (1,115 feet/sec), sound waves from the side arrive at the nearer ear slightly earlier than the farther ear. This time difference is less than one-thousandth of a second, yet it is detected by neurons in the medial superior olivary nuclei. To enhance it, you may tilt your head and cock an ear in the supposed direction of the sound.

The sounds are also slightly louder or more intense in the nearer ear compared to the farther one. This volume difference is detected by neurons in the lateral superior olivary nuclei. The two pairs of nuclei send summary signals to the midbrain's inferior colliculus, for relaying to the superior colliculus. This coordinates body reflexes and reactions, such as head-turning and eye-swivelling, in response to sound and sight inputs. As you turn your head, the time and intensity differences lessen, until the brain can no longer discern them – and you are facing the source of the noise.

Although this mechanism seems extraordinarily responsive, human ears have their limits, responding only to frequencies of 20–20,000 Hertz (Hz) and to volumes above 10 decibels (dB) – we simply cannot hear higher, lower and quieter sounds. So, for example, if a dog pricks up its ears and looks in a certain direction when its owner has noticed nothing out of the ordinary, it is because it can hear ultrasonic sounds above the range of human hearing and as high as 60,000 Hz.

WHALE SONG

The seas are oceans of sounds. Sound waves travel faster through water, at 1,500 m/sec (4,920 feet/sec), than through air, and they fade less quickly too. Many water animals, from sea snails to squid, fish, dolphins and whales, use a huge array of sounds for numerous reasons.

Dolphins and other toothed whales navigate and find their prey in murky waters by echolocation or sonar (sound radar), like bats in air. They send out pulses of sound, some incredibly high pitched

A capella ("in the chapel") is group singing without accompaniment. It relies heavily on vocal harmonies. A harmony is a series of notes sung or played together which are combined according to certain musical rules and which sound suited and pleasing to listen to. In fact, due to the physics of sounds and vibration rates, musical harmonies are based on simple mathematical relationships. For example, the note of middle C (c') has a pitch or frequency of 256 Hz. The "same note but higher" is upper C (c''), an octave up the musical scale. Its frequency is 512 Hz, twice that of middle C. The two notes blend virtually as one.

(up to 250,000 Hz), and detect and analyse the echoes that reflect from objects. Sperm whales can produce such powerful bursts of sound that the energy vibrations in the water stun their prey.

Many great or baleen whales produce complex songs which seem to us like clicks, squeals, howls, grunts and moans. Some of their frequencies extend into infrasound, 20 Hz and below, which is too low pitched for us to hear. So whale songs are often speeded up by tape recording or electronically pitch-raised for our listening. In a 20-hour session a mature but young humpback whale (**far left**) may repeatedly sing more than 10 songs, each up to 20 minutes long and consisting of up to 10 repeated themes. Each group of whales has its own "dialect", although the songs are unique to each individual and evolve over weeks and also from year to year. They are sung mainly in the breeding season and they may serve to attract females for mating or to warn off invaders of their territory.

THE MAESTRO'S SILENT SUFFERING

 One of music's greatest masters, Ludwig van Beethoven (1770–1827), noticed his hearing was failing when he reached the age of 30. Some 19 years later his world fell completely silent and he was forced to use conversation books in which his friends wrote questions to which he was able to speak a reply. Once a virtuoso pianist, he was also forced to give up performing, because he could no longer hear what he was playing. Yet he continued to compose, and wrote such masterpieces as the world-famous Ninth (Choral) Symphony, completed in 1823, when profoundly deaf.

From about 1800, when his ears began to buzz and whistle and high notes became inaudible, the great composer was thrown into personal turmoil. Yet from the anguish and suffering, as he lost what he termed his "noblest faculty", came some of his most emotionally charged works. It seems that the neural circuits which represent memory traces in the brain were unaffected, since Beethoven was able to compose and arrange entirely in his mind, even when he could not hear anything at all. However, it greatly affected his social world and his conversations and relationships with others. To hide the problem, he pretended to be absent-minded. To attempt a cure he flew into violent tantrums, poured strange ointments into his ears and tried many other remedies.

Historians and doctors since have discussed the possible cause of Beethoven's deafness, which may have been typhus or a similar infection. Another suggestion is Paget's disease, when the body's bone maintenance is disturbed and some bones, such as the skull, grow abnormally. This produces a characteristically large head and brow, seen in later portraits of the composer. It may also crush the auditory nerves leading from ear to brain – hence loss of hearing, but retention of musical memories.

Sense of touch

An object may feel warm or cold, wet or dry, rough or smooth, soft or hard – and all are perceived by touch.

The detection of physical contact with the body – touch – might seem straightforward. But the fact that we can not only perceive but also tell the difference between a gentle stroke of the skin and a rough pinch suggests there is more to it. In fact, the word "touch" describes only some of the sensations such as pressure, temperature, movement, vibration and pain – all based in the skin. Touch, together with proprioceptive sensations from within the body about the position and posture of various muscles, tendons and joints, makes up the somatosensory system.

Skin sensors, or cutaneous exteroceptors, are microscopic structures embedded mainly in the dermis, the lower and living layer of skin just beneath the tough, dead outer epidermis. There are about six main kinds and their distribution varies over the body, from thousands per square millimetre in highly sensitive areas such as the lips and fingertips to fewer than a hundred per square millimetre in less sensitive areas such as the small of the back. When stimulated by mechanical distortion or thermal change, these sensors produce nerve signals that

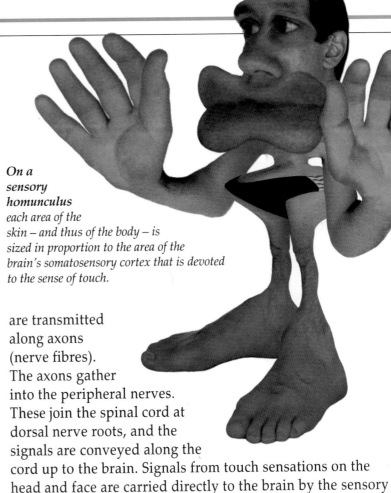

On a sensory homunculus each area of the skin – and thus of the body – is sized in proportion to the area of the brain's somatosensory cortex that is devoted to the sense of touch.

are transmitted along axons (nerve fibres). The axons gather into the peripheral nerves. These join the spinal cord at dorsal nerve roots, and the signals are conveyed along the cord up to the brain. Signals from touch sensations on the head and face are carried directly to the brain by the sensory branches of the trigeminal nerves (cranial nerves V).

In the brain, information about touch arrives at the somatosensory cortex, a strip across the top of each hemisphere, just behind the motor cortex. Here it is analysed and, after further processing in the brain's association areas, details about the type of touch enter our conscious awareness.

The brain has a "touch-map" of the body on its somatosensory cortex, or touch centre, a strip around and down the side of each parietal lobe. Different-sized patches of the centre are devoted to certain areas of skin, according to their degree of sensitivity. For example, the thumb has as much cortex devoted to it as the whole of the leg.

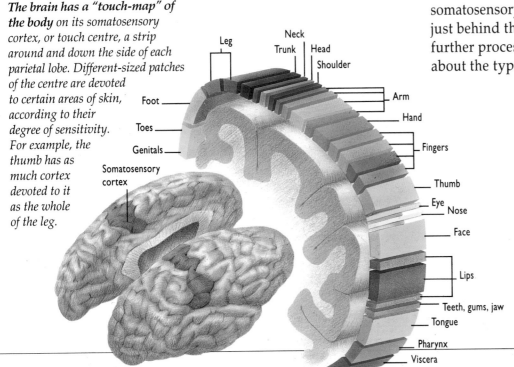

Leg
Neck
Trunk
Head
Shoulder
Foot
Arm
Toes
Hand
Genitals
Fingers
Somatosensory cortex
Thumb
Eye
Nose
Face
Lips
Teeth, gums, jaw
Tongue
Pharynx
Viscera

TOUCH TYPES

Walk on a feather and you notice little. Step in a puddle and it feels wet and cold. Stand on a pin and you feel a painful stab. These sensations show the many different aspects of touch. But how do we discern them?

Various types of sensors in the skin, cutaneous exteroceptors, detect touch. The largest and deepest are onion-shaped Pacinian endings, some over 1 mm (½₅ inch) long. They pick up heavy

659
E

READING BY TOUCH

Blind from the age of three, the teenager Louis Braille (1809–52) attended a demonstration at the National Institute for Blind Youth in Paris of a code of dots and shapes embossed on card, used by the French military for secret, silent communications. He immediately realized its potential and began to adapt the complex code for normal reading purposes. By the age of 15 he had introduced his dot-based printing-reading system for visually handicapped people, which he continued to improve over the years.

The Braille system, which was standardized in 1932, uses cells, each being a pattern of up to six raised dots in three rows of two. Each cell (there are up to 63 combinations) represents a letter of the alphabet, a number, a punctuation mark, a common word such as "and" or "with", or a speech sound such as "ch". Usually one hand feels the dots with the sensitive fingertip skin, while the other hand feels for further lines.

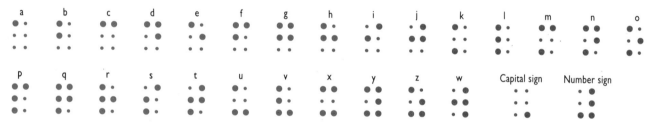

a b c d e f g h i j k l m n o

p q r s t u v x y z w Capital sign Number sign

pressure and fast vibrations, like those from a tuning fork. Smaller, egg-shaped Meissner's endings also detect vibrations, plus light touch. Both are fast-change mechanoreceptors, responding to brief mechanical stimuli by firing nerve impulses at an increased rate – but only while the stimulus is altering. Slow-change mechanoreceptors respond to more gradual alterations and

continue to fire even under unchanging pressure. They include bulb-shaped Krause and sausage-shaped Ruffini endings. Merkel endings, which may project into the lower epidermis, pick up fast and slow mechanical changes and light touch. Free nerve endings are the most numerous microsensors. They detect most types of stimuli and are thermoreceptive and nociceptive – they feel heat, cold and pain. Many different sensors may be stimulated at once, so it seems that our ability to distinguish various sensations lies – in part – in the brain's recognition of the pattern of sensory signals.

Pain pathways

Detection and perception of pain are essential if we are to protect ourselves from harmful injury.

The process of pain sensation begins with specialized, bush-shaped microsensors. They are known as free nerve endings, since the receptive parts of their membranes lack the characteristic structures of other microsensors associated with general touch. Free nerve endings are embedded in the skin at the junction between its outer epidermis and deeper dermis and they also occur in many internal body parts. Different sub-populations of free nerve endings can detect several kinds of stimuli, including those that are mechanical (touch, pressure and movement) and thermal (heat or lack of it). They are also the body's nociceptors, or "injury receivers", responding to potentially harmful events affecting body tissues.

Physical, chemical, microbial or thermal injury causes tissue cells to rupture and spill out their contents, which include potassium and other ions. To limit and mend such damage, mast cells release histamine as part of the body's inflammatory response, which causes redness, soreness, fluid accumulation and swelling. It seems that the chemicals released by these types of damage set off pulses of depolarization in the pain-specialized free nerve endings, suggesting that these receptors are mainly chemosensory (like smell and taste), detecting certain chemicals in their vicinity.

Nociceptive free nerve endings are distributed unevenly through the skin and body organs, which explains why injury to the facial skin is more painful than that to the skin at the back of the thigh, and why a damaged artery hurts more than an equivalently damaged vein. The only parts of the body lacking nociceptors are the intestines and the brain itself. This means that once the scalp, skull and meninges (protective layers over the brain) are anaesthetized, a surgeon can operate on a brain while the conscious patient feels little.

The nerve fibres carrying pain signals from the main body and limbs group into peripheral nerves that lead to the spinal cord. In the cord pain signals are carried up to the brain along two pathways – the lateral spinothalamic tract and the spinoreticulothalamic tract. Signals concerning pain in the region of the face and head are conveyed directly to the brain by the cranial nerves.

Both touch and pain sensations are dealt with by the somatosensory system. But while touch signals are sent largely unmodified to the somatosensory cortex, for conscious perception, signals representing pain can be modified and even blocked by the activity of neurons in many parts of the spinal cord and in the brain itself.

YOU CAN RUB IT BETTER

An understanding of neural circuits in the spinal cord explains why rubbing the site of a sharp pain eases the hurt. Inputs from pain and touch neurons taking signals along their fibres to the spinal cord modulate the firing rate of interneurons in the spinal cord and in projection fibres, which carry signals toward the brain. The rate at which these signals are sent to the brain determines what is perceived.

Activity rate
- Low
- Medium
- High

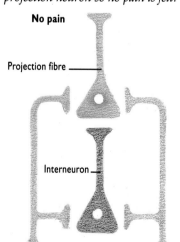

With low input from both pain and touch fibres, the interneuron continues its normally high firing rate and inhibits the activity of the projection neuron so no pain is felt.

No pain

Projection fibre

Interneuron

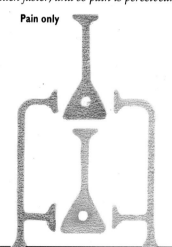

When the pain fibre fires faster this both inhibits the interneuron and excites the projection neuron. This causes the projection fibres to fire much faster, and so pain is perceived.

Pain only

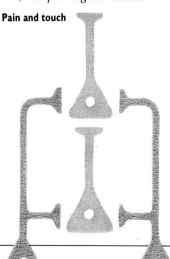

Rubbing activates the touch fibre, exciting the projection neuron and the interneuron, which resumes some inhibition of the projection fibre, and pain signals reduce.

Pain and touch

Pain fibre

Touch fibre

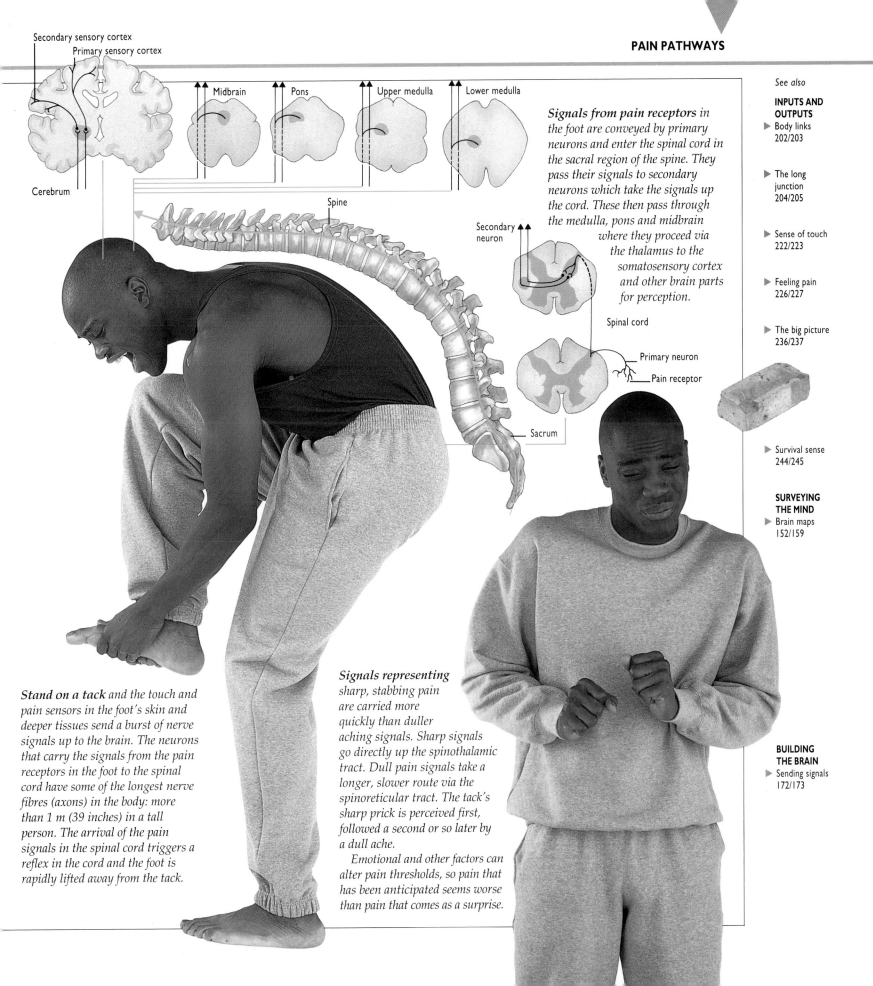

Secondary sensory cortex

Primary sensory cortex

Midbrain

Pons

Upper medulla

Lower medulla

Cerebrum

Spine

Secondary neuron

Spinal cord

Primary neuron

Pain receptor

Sacrum

Signals from pain receptors in the foot are conveyed by primary neurons and enter the spinal cord in the sacral region of the spine. They pass their signals to secondary neurons which take the signals up the cord. These then pass through the medulla, pons and midbrain where they proceed via the thalamus to the somatosensory cortex and other brain parts for perception.

See also

INPUTS AND OUTPUTS
► Body links 202/203

► The long junction 204/205

► Sense of touch 222/223

► Feeling pain 226/227

► The big picture 236/237

► Survival sense 244/245

SURVEYING THE MIND
► Brain maps 152/159

BUILDING THE BRAIN
► Sending signals 172/173

Stand on a tack and the touch and pain sensors in the foot's skin and deeper tissues send a burst of nerve signals up to the brain. The neurons that carry the signals from the pain receptors in the foot to the spinal cord have some of the longest nerve fibres (axons) in the body: more than 1 m (39 inches) in a tall person. The arrival of the pain signals in the spinal cord triggers a reflex in the cord and the foot is rapidly lifted away from the tack.

Signals representing sharp, stabbing pain are carried more quickly than duller aching signals. Sharp signals go directly up the spinothalamic tract. Dull pain signals take a longer, slower route via the spinoreticular tract. The tack's sharp prick is perceived first, followed a second or so later by a dull ache.

Emotional and other factors can alter pain thresholds, so pain that has been anticipated seems worse than pain that comes as a surprise.

Feeling pain

How you perceive pain depends on a number of factors, from state of mind to time of day.

Most people agree on the type or nature of a certain pain – sharp, shooting, stabbing, dull, aching, sore, intermittent, episodic and so on. But overlaid on this is each individual's state of body and mind. Perception of pain – its threshold, intensity, duration and other factors – is heavily influenced by feelings, emotions and knowledge. One reason for this is descending pain control. Nerve signals from the brain go along descending tracts in the spinal cord to modify the pain-related sensory inputs and their neural circuits within the cord.

An important part of the system involves the periaqueductal grey area (PAG) around the fluid-filled cerebral aqueduct between the third and fourth ventricles. Its neurons normally inhibit the activity of groups of neurons in the raphé nuclei, deep in the medulla. Researchers worked out how it operates indirectly. They found that when opiate-type substances such as the pain-relieving (analgesic) drug morphine are taken, they fit into inhibitory receptors on the PAG neurons. The activated inhibitory receptors damp down the activity of their PAG neurons, releasing the raphé neurons

Endorphins are the body's own analgesics and are made mainly in the pituitary and hypothalamus. In molecular shape they resemble opiate drugs such as morphine. Both fit into opiate-receptor sites on neurons to activate internal pain-relief systems. Enkephalins, such as methionine, are related substances made in the brain, adrenal glands and other organs.

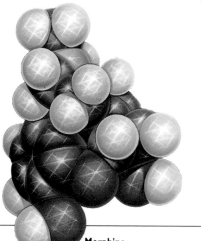

Methionine

Morphine

A runner experiences a natural high induced by the release of endorphins into the body as the race progresses. This helps the athlete to continue through the pain barrier. When the course is completed, the high – a raised physical and mental state – subsides, and the inner pain-suppressing systems die down. Now the realization of the pain breaks through, and agony follows the ecstasy.

from their inhibition. The latter then send signals down the descending tracts to stimulate interneurons in the cord, which block the input of pain signals from peripheral nerves.

At certain times the body makes and releases its own analgesic substances, known as endorphins (endogenous morphinelike substances). For example, when the body is under stress, through physical exertion, say, endorphins activate the pain control systems and act as natural painkillers.

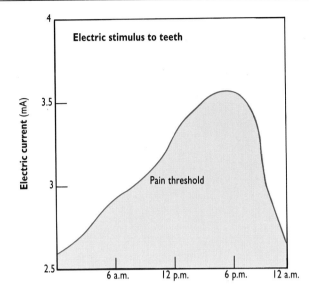

Electric stimulus to teeth

Pain threshold

Electric current (mA) — 4, 3.5, 3, 2.5

6 a.m.   12 p.m.   6 p.m.   12 a.m.

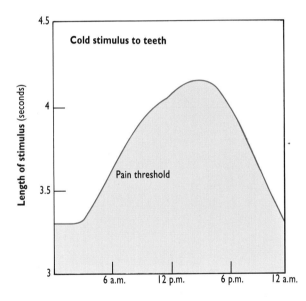

Cold stimulus to teeth

Pain threshold

Length of stimulus (seconds) — 4.5, 4, 3.5, 3

6 a.m.   12 p.m.   6 p.m.   12 a.m.

How much pain you feel varies with time of day, so make an appointment with your dentist in the afternoon if you think you are especially sensitive to pain. Experiments have shown that in the average day, experience of pain waxes and wanes, with the lowest thresholds early and late. When irritation or discomfort turns to actual pain, you have reached your pain threshold. But it is a very individual and subjective experience, related to a host of general body variables. These include hormonal and other chemical levels (and even, in women, the phase of the menstrual cycle), the wake–sleep cycle and biorhythms, your level of hunger, and your emotional state, such as happy or depressed.

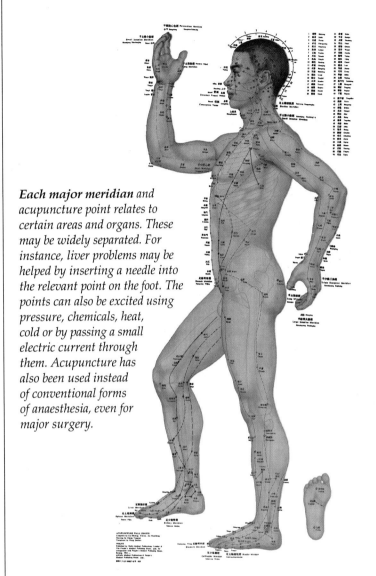

Each major meridian and acupuncture point relates to certain areas and organs. These may be widely separated. For instance, liver problems may be helped by inserting a needle into the relevant point on the foot. The points can also be excited using pressure, chemicals, heat, cold or by passing a small electric current through them. Acupuncture has also been used instead of conventional forms of anaesthesia, even for major surgery.

TO THE POINT: PREVENTING PAIN

The ancient eastern tradition of acupuncture involves inserting fine needles into the body at specific points, to relieve pain, to reduce feeling and sensation, and to help treat illness and disease. Acupuncture points lie on channels known as meridians, along which chi, or "life force", energy circulates around and through the body. Imbalance in energy distribution along the meridians may lead to ill health, but acupuncture can restore the balanced flow and with it health. One possible explanation for acupuncture's effectiveness – in terms of conventional science – is that needle insertion stimulates peripheral nerves to relay signals to the central nervous system, triggering the release of endorphins for natural pain relief.

A matter of taste

*Food without flavour would be like the seaside
without sunshine, so how do we taste what we eat?*

Complaining that it tastes horrible, an ill child refuses to take some medicine. An adult sips it and says it just tastes bland. This scenario has its roots in sensory and neural fact. Taste (gustation), like smell (olfaction), is a chemosense – it detects the presence of certain chemicals. The individual "tasters" are chemosensory receptor cells, or chemosensors. They are shaped like the segments of an orange and are grouped with supporting cells into an orange-shaped cluster of 25 to 50 cells known as a taste bud.

The specialized chemosensors are short-lived, lasting only 10 days, but they are replaced within 12 hours. The average human adult mouth has up to 10,000 taste buds, mostly on the tongue, but also on the back of the upper mouth (palate) and down toward the throat. On the tongue, taste buds are grouped mainly on the sides and around the bases of the papillae, the small lumps and bumps on the tongue's upper surface, visible to the naked eye. Each taste bud is embedded in the covering layer, or epithelium, with a small hole that opens to the surface. Dissolved chemicals from food and drink seep through the hole to the chemosensors, whose tips have tufts of tiny hairs, or microvilli, that detect the chemicals.

Why do lovers of hot and spicy foods put up with *that burning feeling when eating chilli peppers? This sensation is not taste at all. Pain-type nerve endings in the tongue and mouth are stimulated by the chemical capsaicin, found in many peppers. The receptors send signals along the trigeminal nerve to the brain. Here, any sweet flavours already being tasted are heightened, and the release of endorphins – the body's natural painkillers – is triggered, causing feelings of wellbeing and pleasure. The result: chillis in a meal boost other flavours and make you feel good.*

TASTY FEET

In humans, taste and smell are separate sensory systems. Smell deals with airborne chemicals, taste with waterborne chemicals in foods and drinks. But in other animals the distinction is more blurred. For example, a fish cannot detect airborne chemicals, only waterborne ones. So in the animal kingdom biologists group taste, smell and similar detecting systems together as chemosenses.

The distribution of the chemosensor cells on an organism is tailored by evolution to the lifestyle of the creature. We have them in the mouth, which is the first place we come into intimate contact with food. Some fish have them inside the mouth and nasal area, some on the outside of the snout and head, and others along the body. The catfish's body is covered with chemosensors, making it like a "living tongue". Flies, such as the housefly and blowfly (**right**), have chemosensors on their feet, which are especially sensitive to sweet, high-energy substances. So the fly knows at the moment of touchdown whether an object is suitable to eat.

See also

INPUTS AND OUTPUTS
▶ Body links
202/203

▶ On the scent
230/231

▶ The primal
sense
232/233

▶ The big picture
236/237

▶ Dealing with
drives
240/241

▶ Survival sense
244/245

SURVEYING THE MIND
▶ Comparing
brains
140/141

▶ Brain maps
152/159

FAR HORIZONS
▶ Conditioning
the mind
250/251

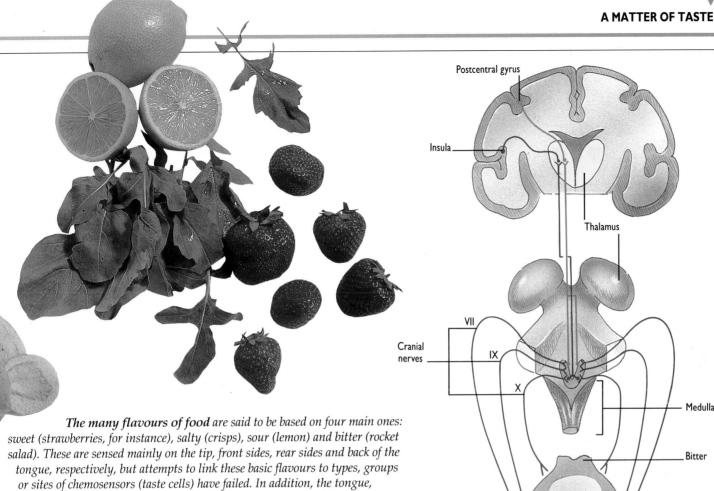

The many flavours of food are said to be based on four main ones: sweet (strawberries, for instance), salty (crisps), sour (lemon) and bitter (rocket salad). These are sensed mainly on the tip, front sides, rear sides and back of the tongue, respectively, but attempts to link these basic flavours to types, groups or sites of chemosensors (taste cells) have failed. In addition, the tongue, gums, lips and mouth lining have somatosensory receptors, which respond to touch, pressure, moisture, heat, cold and other features of food. The brain combines all this with the even more sophisticated input of the smell system. What we think of as simply "taste" is a combination of touch, smell and taste.

It seems that certain chemicals – the ones we taste – bind or lock on to receptor sites on the chemosensors' cell membranes. This probably opens sodium and other ion channels, causing depolarization in the membrane, which may in turn generate a nerve signal. The lower portions of the chemosensors have synapses with the 20 to 30 nerve fibres supplying each taste bud. Each cell probably has many different receptor sites, which respond to a variety of tastes with a complex pattern of signal-firing. When suitably stimulated by increased firing rates from the chemosensors, the fibres conduct nerve signals to the brain.

As a person ages, whole taste buds die, leaving possibly fewer than 5,000 in old age. The rate of chemosensor cell replacement also slows, so each individual taste bud has fewer chemosensors. This is why in general older people have less sensitive taste than younger people, hence the problem with the foul-tasting medicine.

Taste signals from the chemoreceptor cells on each side of the tongue and back of the mouth travel along three pairs of nerves to the brain. From the front two-thirds of the tongue they go along a branch of the facial (VII cranial) nerve; from the rear third their route is via the lingual branch of the glossopharyngeal (IX cranial) nerve; and from the palate and upper throat, it is along the superior laryngeal branch of the vagus (X cranial) nerve.

All the signals arrive in a region known as the nucleus solitarius in the medulla. They then pass along more fibres to the thalamus – the brain's relay station. This sends signals to the primary and secondary gustatory areas or "taste centres", near the somatosensory area or "touch centre" of the cerebral cortex. Nerve fibres also connect the taste system to the hypothalamus (which controls appetite) and the limbic system (which deals with emotions). This is why taste can affect feelings of hunger and mood.

On the scent

A sniff of the air sets in motion a complex train of actions that can lead to the perception of a smell.

Like taste, our sense of smell, or olfaction, is a chemosense: it detects the presence of chemicals, in this case odorants, or odour molecules. These chemicals arrive in the nose floating on a stream of indrawn breath and land on the mucus-coated interior of the nasal cavity; if they dissolve in the watery mucus, they stand a chance of detection. At the top of the nasal cavity in each side of the nose is a thumbnail-sized patch, the olfactory epithelium. This has about 10 million olfactory receptor cells. The main dendrite of each cell extends downward to the nasal cavity. It has a swollen tip bearing up to 20 microscopic hairs, or cilia, that "float" in the nasal mucus. Individual olfactory receptor neurons live for 30 to 35 days, then they are replaced by cell division.

When specific odorants lock into receptor sites on the cilia, they can generate nerve impulses in an olfactory cell. These travel from the cell's body along its axon, which projects through the thin skull bone just above, and into the olfactory bulb. The diffuse webs – one for each nostril – of axons from olfactory cells passing through the skull make up the paired olfactory nerves, also known as the I (first) cranial nerve. The bulbs process the signals and relay the results to the rest of the brain, including some so-called primitive parts involved in functions such as emotion and memory. This "hard-wiring" into these regions, parts of what is known as the paleocortex, is a major difference between smell and the other senses.

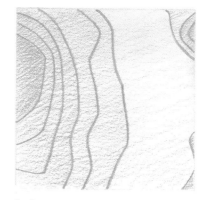

Sawdust

Banana

"Smell maps" can be derived from EEG readings of the wavelike electrical signals recorded across the olfactory bulb of a rabbit. The computer image shows the distribution of the amplitude, or strength, of the waves which represent nerve signal activity. The result is like a contour map, with the most active areas resembling hills.

From first sniff to recognition an odour passes along many pathways: through the olfactory system – from nose to olfactory cortex – to limbic system, thalamus and frontal cortex.

In the olfactory bulb nerve impulses from olfactory cells enter one of hundreds of olfactory glomeruli – small ball-like tangles of axons, synapses, dendrites and cell bodies. Next the signal goes along the olfactory tract to the secondary olfactory cortex. The anterior

A rabbit trained to recognize the odour of sawdust produces a specific pattern in its bulb (*above left*), derived from the bursts of waves produced as it inhales. When it is then familiarized with the smell of banana, a different pattern results (*above*). But the map can change with learning and experience.

olfactory nucleus links the bulbs from the two nostrils via the anterior commissure. The olfactory tubercle and the pyriform cortex project to other olfactory cortical regions and to the medial dorsal nucleus of the thalamus; they are involved in conscious perception of smell. The last two, with the amygdaloid complex and the entorhinal area, which in turn projects to the hippocampus, are pathways to the limbic system, which is why smells evoke memories and emotions.

THE WORLD IN SMELLS

A dog probably lives in a world where smells are as important to it as vision is to us. A sniffer dog, for instance, has an area sensitive to smell 30 times larger than ours, containing 10 times as many olfactory receptor cells. Dogs also have a proportionally larger area of cortex devoted to analysing smells. An average human can discern some smells at concentrations of less than 1 part in 20 billion, but sniffer dogs can detect odours at least 10,000 times weaker.

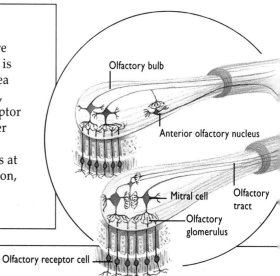

Olfactory bulb

Anterior olfactory nucleus

Mitral cell

Olfactory tract

Olfactory glomerulus

Olfactory receptor cell

Acting on the signals from a region of about 25,000 olfactory receptor cells in the nose, each glomerulus in the olfactory bulb reacts to certain odorants. The number of receptors activated indicates the strength of the smell stimulus, and their position in the nose supplies information as to the nature of the scent.

Messages are relayed from one glomerulus to the next, probably by periglomerular cells, and a pattern of activity, as shown in the sawdust and banana "maps", is generated which carries information about the odour. For this information, which is in the form of a burst of nerve signals, to get through to the rest of the brain it has to be strong enough to survive the inhibitory effects of the granule cells in the bulb. Successful messages are carried along the axons of mitral and tufted cells, which form the olfactory tract, into the olfactory cortex.

Here the signals have to pass through an intermediate layer of cells, the superficial pyramidal cells. They synapse with and excite stellate cells, as well as deep pyramidal cells. But when excited, the stellate cells inhibit the deep pyramidal cells, creating a loop of excitation (red) and inhibition (blue) that has the effect of generating bursts of nerve signals which are then transmitted to other brain regions.

Sawdust

When the rabbit inhaled sawdust again after it had learned the banana smell, a different pattern emerged. This shows how such maps are not specific to the smell itself, but appear to change with time and according to experience. Furthermore, another rabbit will almost certainly have a different map for sawdust.

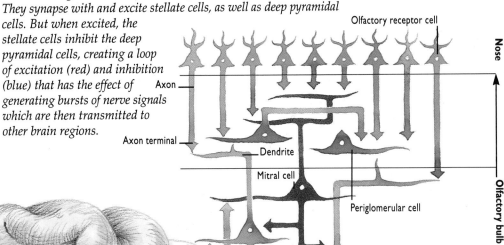

Olfactory receptor cell

Nose

Axon

Axon terminal

Dendrite

Mitral cell

Periglomerular cell

Olfactory bulb

Tufted cell

Granule cell

Medial dorsal nucleus of thalamus

Anterior commissure

Corpus callosum

Thalamus

Anterior olfactory nucleus

Olfactory bulb   Olfactory tubercle

To orbitofrontal cortex

Olfactory cortex

Superficial pyramidal cell

To Hippocampus

Stellate cell

Olfactory tract

Lateral olfactory tract

Deep pyramidal cell

Pyriform cortex

Amygdaloid complex   Entorhinal cortex

To other brain regions

231

The primal sense

Almost without our being aware of its presence, a scent can subtly affect the way we act and feel.

Unlike the other human senses, our sense of smell is linked directly by nerve pathways into the less sophisticated, more primitive, animal-like parts of the brain such as the limbic system and the sites involved in processing and storing memories. Nerve signals from the olfactory bulb, which is situated above the nasal cavity, can go directly to these parts without first passing to the cortex, where they would stimulate our conscious awareness and allow us to think about them and modify our behaviour accordingly. These direct pathways to primitive areas mean that certain smells have powerful effects on memories and emotions. We experience smells in a subconscious way, almost as the opposite of a hallucination. Whereas a smell is there, influencing our mind and behaviour although we are not obviously aware of it, a hallucination is a conscious experience, but with no external cause or stimulus.

Since we experience smells in this manner, the way in which we respond to them may have something in common with the ways that animals react to them (and perhaps to other sensed stimuli). Our own awareness is dominated by "higher" human thought processes and by the senses of vision and sound. But many creatures experience the world primarily in terms of odours, and the use of smells is widespread in animal survival, communication, mating and other types of behaviour.

For instance, biologists have found that salmon migrate, sometimes over great distances, from the sea back to the stream where they were spawned, mainly by using their chemosenses to detect and follow the "scent-taste profile" of their home water. Pike leave their home area, where they lurk to ambush potential prey, in order to get rid of body wastes. This prevents the pike's excretory smell from building up in the home area and warning other fish of the hunter's presence. There are thousands of such examples in nature, right across the animal kingdom, ranging from worms and insects to various types of mammals. The chances are that we humans are more influenced by smells than we think.

A perfumier checks a blend in the never-ending search for new scents. Years of experience have given him a "trained nose". In fact his nose is probably no more sensitive than most other people's, but he has trained his brain to focus on and isolate what it detects. Extracts of scents, smells and essences are big business for many industries, from perfume and cosmetics to food and drink, soap and hygiene products, and air fresheners and detergents.

Peppermint

Floral

Ethereal

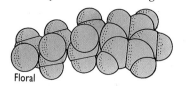

One theory of how odour molecules activate smell receptors in the nose is that they are shaped to fit into equivalently structured protein receptor sites. There may be several basic shapes, shown here. But smell seems to be based on pattern-recognition rather than being stimulus specific: most smells activate most of the olfactory cells, so the identity of the smell lies in the overall pattern of activation.

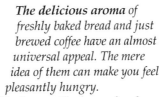

The delicious aroma of freshly baked bread and just brewed coffee have an almost universal appeal. The mere idea of them can make you feel pleasantly hungry.

"Background" odours of such evocative foods are used in many ways by supermarkets and other organizations. The bakery or coffee shop may be loss leaders – as departments, they will not make any profit; indeed, they make a loss. But their wafting odours attract people, alter their mood, increase their sense of wellbeing and perhaps – the store certainly hopes – make them spend more money. If there is no bakery or coffee shop, extracts of the relevant odours may be circulated in the air-conditioning system for the same purpose.

This is just one of many varied ways in which smells can affect our psyche subliminally. But the initial impetus is shortlived: we can usually only perceive a smell for about 30 seconds after it was first detected. This is due to a process known as habituation in which a sense stops perceiving what it detects once it has become accustomed to it. This happens more quickly in smell than in any of the other senses.

CHEMICAL COMMUNICATION

Some animals release particular sorts of chemicals, known as pheromones, into the air or water or on to objects. These are chemosensed by fellow members of their species, whose behaviour is altered as a result.

Humans are also thought to make use of pheromones, especially in the area of reproduction. These chemicals may be responsible for the phenomenon in which women who live or work together become synchronized in their menstrual cycles.

They may also explain why women in particular are often able to identify the sex of a person by the smell of his or her breath or underarm odour, and why some men can tell the stage of a woman's menstrual cycle from her vaginal odour.

Researchers are now striving to identify a pheromone that works as a sexual attractant between humans. It could have various uses and commercial rewards! But they have had little success, so far.

Musk

Camphor

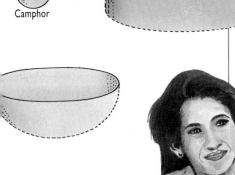

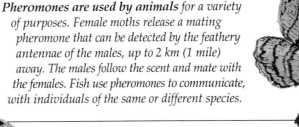

Pheromones are used by animals for a variety of purposes. Female moths release a mating pheromone that can be detected by the feathery antennae of the males, up to 2 km (1 mile) away. The males follow the scent and mate with the females. Fish use pheromones to communicate, with individuals of the same or different species.

233

Staying upright

We take balancing for granted but the nervous system's "behind the scenes" action is highly sophisticated.

Balance, often called the sixth sense, is not really a sense at all. Rather, it is a process in which the brain, using nerve signals from a range of sensory inputs, works out which muscles – in the trunk, legs, arms and so on – must move to keep an erect posture and equilibrium. One input is from the vestibular system inside the ears which detects head movements and gives information about head orientation in relation to gravity. Visual input helps work out the head's position, using verticals such as walls and trees, and horizontals such as floors.

A third input is from pressure sensors in the soles of the feet and other skin areas in contact with firm surfaces. These give data about the body's centre of gravity and leaning angle. Fourth is proprioception – the body's inner positional-posture sense. Microscopic sensors in muscles, tendons, joints and ligaments all over the body detect tension, elongation and other changes. They send signals to the cerebellum and, via the spinal cord and thalamus, to the centre for conscious positional sense in the cerebral cortex.

Coupled to these inputs are unconscious pathways that produce reflex reactions, many of which route through the cerebellum. For example, if you stand and rock back on your heels you may automatically thrust your arms forward as a counterbalance in the extensor thrust reflex.

THE RIGHTING IS ON THE FALL

A cat's marvellous agility – especially the way it almost always lands on its feet – is not a result of feline magic or lives to spare. Cats are climbing animals and over time natural selection has determined that the cats that were best able to survive falls from a height passed on their ability to future generations.

When a cat falls, its finely tuned balance mechanism swings into action: first the head rotates back to horizontal, followed by the body, next the legs stretch out and the toes spread, ready for a soft landing. This righting reflex primarily involves structures in the inner ear: the utricle and saccule. Signals from them pass to processing centres (nuclei) in the upper medulla (the lower stalklike projection of the brain) and the cerebellum, for fast analysis and reflex-type reactions. The processes are similar, but slower and more ponderous, in humans.

Eyes closed, arms by your side and standing one-legged on a cushion, you are sure to totter as so many inputs to balance are blocked. There is no visual input; the arms cannot counterbalance; and, apart from being on only one foot, data from sole sensors is blurred due to the soft cushion. A wobbly toy's low centre of gravity ensures a quick return to upright.

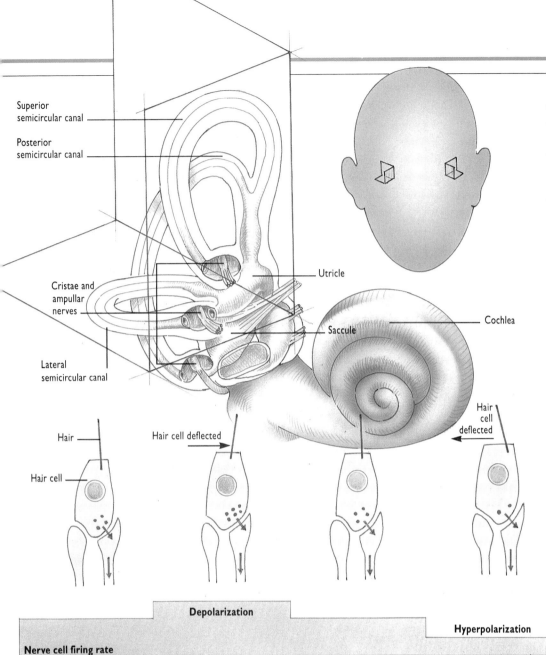

The balance, or vestibular, organs of the inner ear are the three semicircular canals, the utricle and the saccule. The semicircular canals sense chiefly acceleration, deceleration, rotation and other motions of the head. They are almost at right angles to each other, occupying three planes of space, so whichever way the head moves, at least one is affected. The utricle and saccule, also known as the otolith organs, detect mainly the position of the head in relation to gravity's downward pull and also linear acceleration and deceleration.

The vestibular system's receptor is the hair cell. When a hair cell's hairs are bent one way they convert their movement into depolarization of the cell, causing it to release more neurotransmitters which cross to the outgoing, or afferent, nerve and depolarize it. This raises its firing rate from its steady background rate.
  If the hairs are deflected the other way they cause their hair cell to hyperpolarize, reducing its neurotransmitter release and thus hyperpolarizing the afferent nerve and reducing its firing rate. The change in the firing rate in the afferent nerves is used in the balance process.

In each utricle and saccule, the hairs of hundreds of hair cells are embedded in a jellylike membrane, containing calcium carbonate crystals. As the head moves or stays still, motion and gravity drag the membrane one way, then another, bending the hairs.

Hair cells in the ampulla of a semicircular canal cover the crista. Their tips are embedded in the jellylike cupulla. Head motion sets up currents in endolymph fluid in the crista which bend the cupulla and hairs. The nerve signals pass along the ampullar nerve.

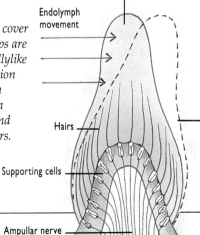

Crista movement creates nerve impulses

The big picture

Engaged in a continuous exchange of signals with the cortex, the thalamus is the brain's sensory gatekeeper.

Millions of nerve signals, representing sensory information, pour into the brain every second. They concern not only outside events as detected by light, sound, smell, taste and touch, but also internal variations such as change in posture and body temperature as well as levels of nutrients and hormones. But the brain can cope. Nerve tracts and connections route each batch of signals to appropriate sites in the brain for simultaneous analysis. A vital site is the thalamus, which consists of two egg-shaped structures about 4 cm (1½ inches) long in the core of the brain, below the corpus callosum and cerebral hemispheres.

The thalamus is a major centre for switching, routing and relaying sensory inputs to their dedicated areas of cerebral cortex for analysis and processing. It has two-way relationships and integrating functions, receiving reciprocal signals from each of the sensory cortical areas and both sending and receiving signals to and from other more general "association" areas of cortex. In addition, the ventral parts of the thalamus have a role in motor responses. They receive signals from the cerebellum and basal ganglia, coordinate these with incoming sensory information, and send further messages up to the pre-motor and motor cortex areas. Other thalamic functions include the general state of body awareness and arousal, linked to biorhythms and the wake–sleep cycle, and connections to the limbic system, associated with expressing feelings and emotions.

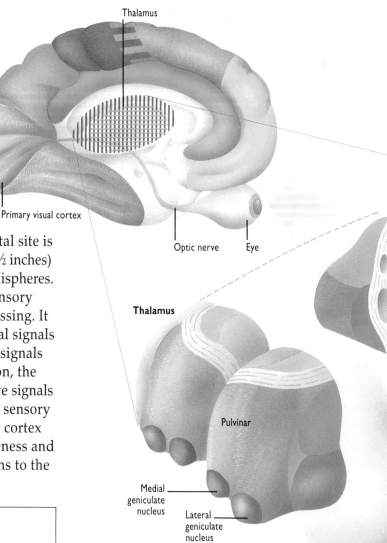

The thalamus, which nestles in the central region of the brain, has a core of grey matter, chiefly nerve cell (neuron) bodies and their connections – dendrites and synapses – covered with a thin layer of white matter, mainly nerve fibres, or message-carrying axons.

The grey matter in the thalamus is organized into "lumps", or nuclei, that are associated with certain inputs and outputs. In effect, part of the thalamus is a miniature version of the cerebral cortex. Each of its nuclear masses has two-way connections with a corresponding area of cerebral cortex, but the "map" of the thalamus has its sites shifted around slightly, compared to the map of the cortex.

*Here, the regions of the thalamus that connect with regions of the cortex have been colour matched. The medial geniculate nucleus (**above**) has connections with the primary auditory cortex (**right**) and the lateral geniculate nucleus (**above**) links to the primary visual cortex (**top** and **right**).*

THE COLOUR OF WORDS

For as long as she could remember, a woman had seen colours when she heard words or letters. The colours were consistent, so she always saw yellow with hints of green when she heard the word "king"; for instance.

The woman had synaesthesia, the mingling or even swapping of sensory information in which stimulating one sense triggers conscious experience in another. In her case words had colours, but all the senses can be confused. Thus spoken words have tastes or shapes, colours smell different, and touches on the skin have sound signatures. The condition occurs in about 1 in 25,000 people, mainly women. It seems to arise early in childhood and is consistent, involuntary and non-suppressible: it "just happens". It rarely causes great suffering, indeed some synaesthetics enjoy it.

One theory for the shared or mixed sensory experiences is that the sensory areas of the brain are "cross-wired" within the cortex or via the thalamus. We are born into this state, but – except in synaesthetics – the developing conscious separates out the senses. Another idea is that it occurs in the limbic system – and that the limbic system is the main site where sensory information normally combines to form our "big picture" of conscious experience.

Sensory inputs from the eyes and some other sense organs are relayed through nuclei of the thalamus en route to the cerebral cortex. Visual nerve signals pass along the optic nerve and through the lateral geniculate nuclei on their way to the primary visual cortex for initial processing. Smell is the only sense that does not channel its nerve signals through the thalamus before they reach the cortex.

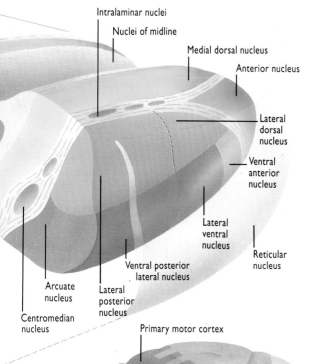

Intralaminar nuclei
Nuclei of midline
Medial dorsal nucleus
Anterior nucleus
Lateral dorsal nucleus
Ventral anterior nucleus
Lateral ventral nucleus
Reticular nucleus
Ventral posterior lateral nucleus
Arcuate nucleus
Lateral posterior nucleus
Centromedian nucleus
Primary motor cortex

A savage storm assaults the senses with sights, sounds, touch sensations and movements. The sensory receptors feed their nerve messages, mainly via the thalamus, to the "thinking" cerebral cortex. But the cortex also sends signals back to the thalamus. Perhaps by such pathways inputs from some senses can be suppressed at the thalamic level, so that we can selectively attend to just one sensory input. We can choose to pay attention to the sight of the waves crashing against the rocks, or their sound, or the needles of sea spray splattering the skin and making it prickle. Meanwhile, should any part of the big picture demand attention – possibly because it poses some threat or because it becomes "interesting" for some reason – the system quickly directs awareness to that part.

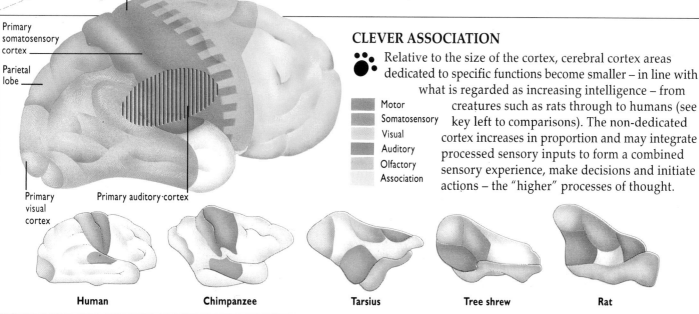

Primary somatosensory cortex
Parietal lobe
Primary visual cortex
Primary auditory cortex

CLEVER ASSOCIATION

Relative to the size of the cortex, cerebral cortex areas dedicated to specific functions become smaller – in line with what is regarded as increasing intelligence – from creatures such as rats through to humans (see key left to comparisons). The non-dedicated cortex increases in proportion and may integrate processed sensory inputs to form a combined sensory experience, make decisions and initiate actions – the "higher" processes of thought.

Motor
Somatosensory
Visual
Auditory
Olfactory
Association

Human **Chimpanzee** **Tarsius** **Tree shrew** **Rat**

Keeping control

Not only is the brain the seat of reason, perception, memory and emotions, but it also controls essential body processes.

The autonomic nervous system (ANS) controls and coordinates the body's "automatic" functions – the vital life processes such as heartbeat, blood pressure, digestion, excretion and, to an extent, breathing. We are usually unaware of ANS control because it is based in the brain stem, the "lower" part of the brain, where activities are mainly at the unconscious level. For example, in the medulla of the brain stem are two centres involved in heartbeat control: the cardio-acceleratory area (CAA) and, below it, the cardio-inhibitory area (CIA). Working together in a balanced way they make up the cardioregulatory centre, which adjusts the heartbeat rate according to sensory feedback from many parts of the body.

Other such complexes are the vasomotor centre in the lower part of the pons and medulla, which regulates blood pressure, and the respiratory centre, which is concerned with breathing. Many of these brain stem centres have links with the hypothalamus, the highest integrating area of the ANS. The hypothalamus is the main mediator between the autonomic, or unconcious, control systems in the brain stem, and the voluntary, conscious "higher" mental activities in the cerebrum and other upper parts, especially the cerebral cortex. So if a threat is perceived, signals from the hypothalamus make the brain stem generate the appropriate physical responses.

In the kitchen the chef checks the seasoning while the pressure regulator on the steam cooker keeps its internal conditions within set limits. Likewise the body uses neural receptors to test for chemicals, blood pressure and many other internal conditions. Chemosensors in the brain, blood vessels and various organs detect levels of sodium, glucose, oxygen, carbon dioxide and other substances in blood and body fluids. Barosensors in the walls of the main arteries, mainly in the neck and chest, respond to changes in blood pressure. Such sensors send their information to the brain stem's autonomic auto-control systems.

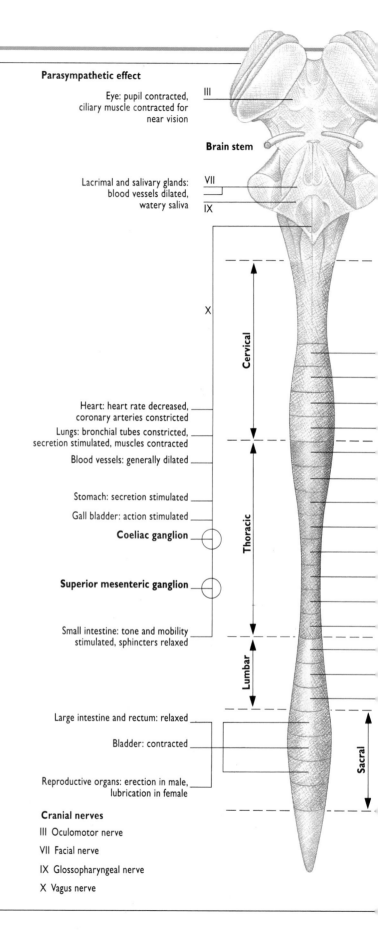

Parasympathetic effect

Eye: pupil contracted, ciliary muscle contracted for near vision — III

Brain stem

Lacrimal and salivary glands: blood vessels dilated, watery saliva — VII, IX

X

Heart: heart rate decreased, coronary arteries constricted

Lungs: bronchial tubes constricted, secretion stimulated, muscles contracted

Blood vessels: generally dilated

Stomach: secretion stimulated

Gall bladder: action stimulated

Coeliac ganglion

Superior mesenteric ganglion

Small intestine: tone and mobility stimulated, sphincters relaxed

Large intestine and rectum: relaxed

Bladder: contracted

Reproductive organs: erection in male, lubrication in female

Cervical

Thoracic

Lumbar

Sacral

Cranial nerves

III Oculomotor nerve

VII Facial nerve

IX Glossopharyngeal nerve

X Vagus nerve

Sympathetic effect

Eye: pupil dilated, ciliary muscle
relaxed for far vision

Salivary glands: blood vessels
constricted, thick saliva

Superior cervical ganglion

Stellate ganglion

Heart: heart rate increased,
coronary arteries dilated

Lungs: bronchial tubes dilated,
muscles relaxed

Liver: glycogenolysis increased

Stomach: secretion inhibited

Gall bladder: action inhibited

Small intestine: tone and mobility
inhibited, sphincters contracted

Coeliac ganglion

Adrenal gland: adrenaline and
noradrenaline secreted

Superior mesenteric ganglion

Skin: sweat glands stimulated,
peripheral blood vessels
constricted, hairs stand erect

Inferior mesenteric ganglion

Large intestine and rectum: contracted

Bladder: relaxed

Reproductive organs: orgasm

Paravertebral ganglia

The autonomic nervous system (ANS) has two major subdivisions, the sympathetic and the parasympathetic, which have balanced "push-pull" effects. Each exerts its control by sending nerve signals to many groups of muscles – those in arterial walls that control blood distribution and pressure, cardiac muscle in the heart, muscle layers in the walls of the intestines, glands and other internal organs, and skeletal muscles that move the body.

The parasympathetic subdivision's signals leave the brain stem via cranial nerves, in particular cranial nerve X (the vagus), and go to the chest and abdominal organs. They also go from the sacral portion of the spinal cord. The parasympathetic system takes the lead when the body is in its normal resting state and is relatively inactive. It promotes blood flow to the organs that deal with digestion and excretion, while keeping blood flow to the inactive skeletal muscles to a minimum; it also makes breathing easy and relaxed and the heartbeat steady.

The sympathetic subdivision sends its signals from the brain stem down the spinal cord and out along the spinal nerve roots of the cervical, thoracic and some lumbar segments. The signals travel onward to the muscles via the necklacelike chains of lumps on either side of the backbone known as paravertebral ganglia. The sympathetic system takes over when the body is in a heightened state of awareness and is ready for action. It stimulates the heart, breathing and skeletal muscles to work faster; tops up levels of high-energy glucose in the blood; and heightens conscious awareness and sensory perception, while temporarily shutting down the internal processes of digestion and excretion. In other words, it produces the classic fight-or-flight response, preparing the body for action.

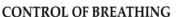

CONTROL OF BREATHING

By focusing the mind on controlled breathing, practitioners of techniques such as yoga can achieve a state of deep relaxation. One possible reason for this effect is that the brain is "fooled" by this type of breathing. Slow and even breathing resembles that of sleep, and the brain sends out signals that are appropriate to this state. These then calm the body and mind.

But most of us rarely think about our breathing at all. Instead several areas in the brain stem work together as the respiratory centre to control it. They include the inspiratory and expiratory neural circuits in the medulla's respiratory rhythmicity area. These stimulate breathing in, then out, by "see-saw" alternation of activity every few seconds. Other areas are the apneustic and pneumotaxic areas in the pons. The former encourages strong inhalations with weak exhalations, to build up air volume in the lungs; the latter inhibits this activity. These areas are in turn influenced by data coming from other parts of the brain and body such as chemosensors that detect the blood's acidity (a guide to its carbon dioxide content) and barosensors, which monitor blood pressure. Rises in both of these stimulate faster, deeper breathing.

Dealing with drives

A tiny part of the brain is vital for controlling aspects as diverse as blood pressure, body heat and thirst.

The hypothalamus, so called because it is under the thalamus, seems an unremarkable part of the brain: the size of a small, flat grape, it weighs only 0.3 percent of the brain's total. Yet it is the most important brain centre dealing with homeostatis – keeping the body's internal conditions constant – and, from its position at the heart of the limbic system, is in overall charge of many autonomic and automatic body processes, such as body temperature, blood pressure, nutrition levels and fluid balance. Nerve messages go to and from the hypothalamus and various control areas of the autonomic nervous system. It also exerts much of its control by links with the body's chief hormonal gland, the pituitary, just below.

But the hypothalamus is no "dumb autopilot". It is also the mediator between the unconscious autonomic functions in the brain stem and conscious awareness – the "higher" mental activities in the forebrain. You may be out walking, for instance, when suddenly you feel the need for a drink. This "need" is the hypothalamus, on behalf of its autonomic subsystems, breaking through into your conscious awareness and modifying your behaviour to meet your body's basic needs.

Inputs arrive in the hypothalamus as nerve signals. They may be from the senses, especially sight, taste and touch; from the limbic system or reticular formation in the brain itself (about basic needs and drives); and from internal organs such as the heart and intestines. It is also influenced by hormones circulating in the blood, and by concentrations of glucose, sodium and other substances in the blood passing through it and in the cerebrospinal fluid just above it.

Inside the hypothalamus are several pairs of relatively discrete nuclei, or areas. Some tasks of the hypothalamus are assigned to a specific pair; others seem to be spread through several areas which communicate by nerve fibres so that they can work together as a single "centre" for one main role.

The hypothalamus sends outputs as nerve signals to the motor (muscle-controlling) parts of the midbrain, the limbic system and the various autonomic centres in the brain stem that control processes such as heartbeat, blood pressure and urine production, as well as the glands producing saliva, sweat and digestive juices. It also produces hormones such as antidiuretic hormone (ADH), which makes the kidneys lose less water in urine, thus increasing blood volume and raising blood pressure. These hormones then pass to the pituitary.

Red nucleus

Basis pedunculi

Pons

Oculomotor nerve

A television studio is a hive of activity with many people working to produce a programme. They are mainly autonomous, using their training and experience to get on with the job, but occasionally they must consult the studio manager, in overall charge of operations. The studio manager passes on high-level instructions as required and is the link with the actors and directors.

The hypothalamus is the body's studio manager. In overall charge of smooth running, it leaves routine and detail to the various homeostatic subsystems. It becomes active when something unusual happens. And it mediates between the service-type homeostatic activities and the brain's higher activities of awareness and conscious thought.

THE VITAL STALK
Hanging by a stalk from the hypothalamus is the pituitary gland, the chief controller and regulator of the body's hormonal processes. The nerve fibres and portal blood vessels in the pituitary stalk are the small but vital link between the body's two communication-control systems – nervous and hormonal. The hypothalamus makes its own forerunner "pro-hormones" in neurosecretory cells. These pass along the neurosecretory cell axons in the pituitary stalk for conversion into the mature hormone and storage in the posterior

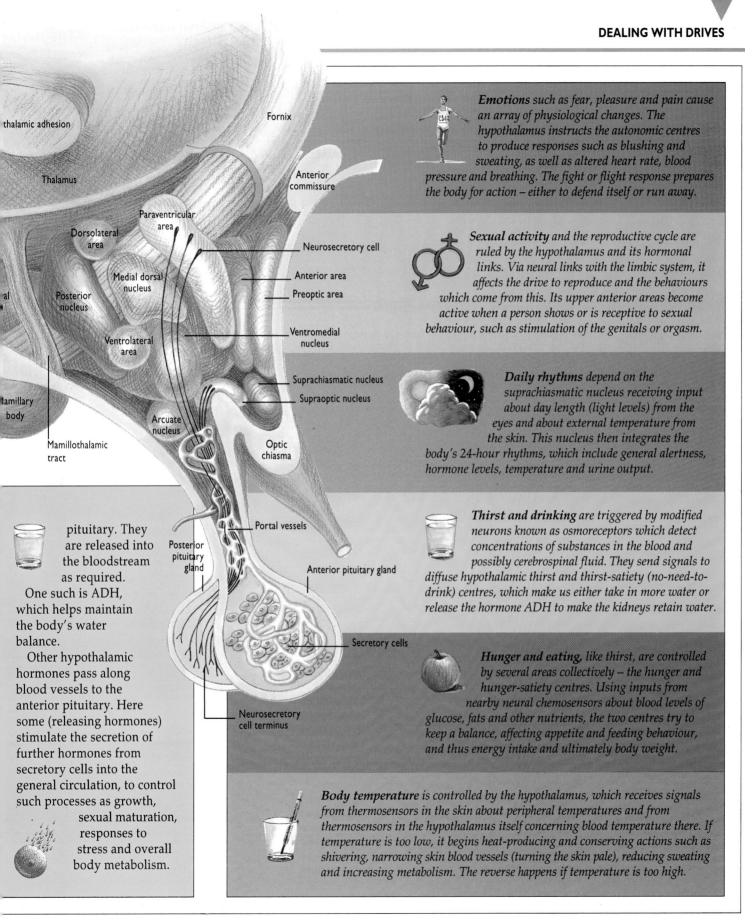

thalamic adhesion

Thalamus

Fornix

Anterior commissure

Paraventricular area

Dorsolateral area

Medial dorsal nucleus

Posterior nucleus

Ventrolateral area

Mamillary body

Mamillothalamic tract

Arcuate nucleus

Neurosecretory cell

Anterior area

Preoptic area

Ventromedial nucleus

Suprachiasmatic nucleus

Supraoptic nucleus

Optic chiasma

Portal vessels

Posterior pituitary gland

Anterior pituitary gland

Secretory cells

Neurosecretory cell terminus

pituitary. They are released into the bloodstream as required.

One such is ADH, which helps maintain the body's water balance.

Other hypothalamic hormones pass along blood vessels to the anterior pituitary. Here some (releasing hormones) stimulate the secretion of further hormones from secretory cells into the general circulation, to control such processes as growth, sexual maturation, responses to stress and overall body metabolism.

Emotions such as fear, pleasure and pain cause an array of physiological changes. The hypothalamus instructs the autonomic centres to produce responses such as blushing and sweating, as well as altered heart rate, blood pressure and breathing. The fight or flight response prepares the body for action – either to defend itself or run away.

Sexual activity and the reproductive cycle are ruled by the hypothalamus and its hormonal links. Via neural links with the limbic system, it affects the drive to reproduce and the behaviours which come from this. Its upper anterior areas become active when a person shows or is receptive to sexual behaviour, such as stimulation of the genitals or orgasm.

Daily rhythms depend on the suprachiasmatic nucleus receiving input about day length (light levels) from the eyes and about external temperature from the skin. This nucleus then integrates the body's 24-hour rhythms, which include general alertness, hormone levels, temperature and urine output.

Thirst and drinking are triggered by modified neurons known as osmoreceptors which detect concentrations of substances in the blood and possibly cerebrospinal fluid. They send signals to diffuse hypothalamic thirst and thirst-satiety (no-need-to-drink) centres, which make us either take in more water or release the hormone ADH to make the kidneys retain water.

Hunger and eating, like thirst, are controlled by several areas collectively – the hunger and hunger-satiety centres. Using inputs from nearby neural chemosensors about blood levels of glucose, fats and other nutrients, the two centres try to keep a balance, affecting appetite and feeding behaviour, and thus energy intake and ultimately body weight.

Body temperature is controlled by the hypothalamus, which receives signals from thermosensors in the skin about peripheral temperatures and from thermosensors in the hypothalamus itself concerning blood temperature there. If temperature is too low, it begins heat-producing and conserving actions such as shivering, narrowing skin blood vessels (turning the skin pale), reducing sweating and increasing metabolism. The reverse happens if temperature is too high.

See also

INPUTS AND OUTPUTS
▶ Body links 202/203

▶ The long junction 204/205

▶ Keeping control 238/239

▶ Survival sense 244/245

SURVEYING THE MIND
▶ The working mind 138/139

▶ Inside the mind 142/143

▶ Brain maps 152/159

BUILDING THE BRAIN
▶ Building blocks 162/163

▶ Food for thought 188/189

FAR HORIZONS
▶ Male and female 270/271

STATES OF MIND
▶ Motivation 302/303

Rhythms of the mind

As natural products of evolution, the human body and brain are tuned to nature's rhythms and cycles.

The dominant cycle on Earth is the 24-hour circadian cycle of light and dark, the day–night cycle. Humans are mainly visual creatures, so it makes little sense to be up and about, or active and alert, during hours of darkness. The result is sleep, a state in which conscious self-awareness disappears, the brain takes time off for other tasks, and the body rests as its systems slow down and repair processes come to the fore.

Sleep is a major phase in the body's circadian biorhythms, which involve regular changes in hundreds of substances and processes, from levels of hormones and brain chemicals to body temperature, heart and breathing rates, and urine production. These mind and body rhythms seem to be internally generated, or endogenous, and persist even when people experience constant external conditions. They are largely based in two clumps of a few thousand neurons each, the suprachiasmatic nuclei (SCNs), in the brain's hypothalamic region just above the optic chiasma (where the optic nerves cross over). SCN neurons show their own circadian variations in electrical and chemical activity, and in the production of neurologically active substances – even when individual neurons are isolated in the laboratory. They are the nearest thing to a "body clock" thus far discovered.

The SCNs' built-in rhythms are synchronized, or entrained, with the external world in several ways. One is the light–dark cycle, detected by the eye's retina and communicated by nerve fibres from retinal ganglion cells to the SCNs. There are other entrainers whose mechanisms are much less clear; one such is the level of social interaction and arousal, which may communicate to the SCNs along fibres from the thalamus.

Nerve fibres from the SCNs communicate their information to other hypothalamic nuclei involved in many basic behaviours and body drives, and also along other more tortuous neural pathways, such as down the spinal cord and out to the cervical ganglia (nerve collections adjacent to the spinal cord in the neck) and then back up to the pineal gland at the base of the brain. The pineal makes several hormones and other chemicals, among them melatonin, which is produced mainly in darkness (light inhibits melatonin production) and which causes drowsiness.

EEG recordings of "brain waves" during sleep show regular variations in both frequency and amplitude. When asleep the body passes from stage 1 (light sleep) down to stage 4 (deep sleep) and back up again, in periods of 80 to 120 minutes. These are punctuated by regular and increasingly long episodes of REM sleep (red bar), when the body becomes less active, save for rapid eye movement (REM), and dreams occur. The EEG traces from REM sleep are similar to those of wakefulness. During the day, alertness waxes and wanes in a similar cycle, thought to be related to the rise and fall in levels of neurotransmitters.

EEG changes

Levels of alertness over 24 hours

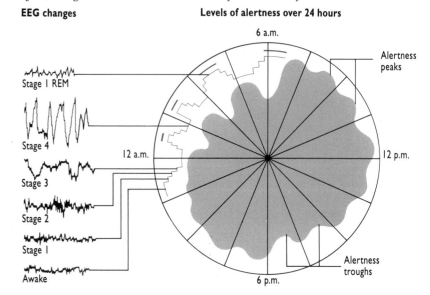

Stage I REM

Stage 4

Stage 3

Stage 2

Stage I

Awake

6 a.m.

12 a.m.

12 p.m.

6 p.m.

Alertness peaks

Alertness troughs

The sleep–wake cycle involves changing levels of neurotransmitters in the brain. There is twice as much acetylcholine present during both wakefulness and dreaming (REM sleep) as there is during non-REM, or ordinary, sleep. And while there is twice as much noradrenaline present during wakefulness as there is during non-REM sleep, there is only one-tenth the amount of it during REM sleep compared with non-REM sleep. The release of these chemicals is widespread throughout the cerebral cortex and therefore probably underpins overall changes in awareness. For instance, the variations in the alertness level over the course of a day (**left**) are thought to coincide with variations in the level of amine neurotransmitters (one of which is noradrenaline). Alertness rises with greater amine release and declines when levels are lower.

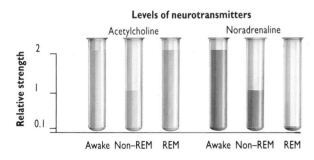

Levels of neurotransmitters

Acetylcholine   Noradrenaline

Relative strength

2

1

0.1

Awake Non–REM REM   Awake Non–REM REM

Jet lag demonstrates that the human body was not designed to chase the Sun around the globe in an aeroplane at 1,000 km/h (625 mph). The aircraft's interior and comfort make the trip more or less bearable, but problems start on arrival in a different time zone. The brain and body say sleep, while the destination's night–day cycle, temperature variation, mealtime routines and human activities upset internal biorhythms by saying stay awake. The results can be confusion, headache, memory lapses, drowsiness interspersed with sleeplessness, upset digestion and reduced resistance to infection.

It takes most long-haul travellers between two and five days to reset their body clock. One recommended way of dealing with the problem is to try to conform to local time at once. But regular international trippers on short stays may try to stay on home time if at all possible.

FREE-RUNNING IN TOTAL ISOLATION

Frenchman Michel Siffre spent six months in the constant darkness, total silence and unvarying 22° C (72° F) temperature of Midnight Cave near Del Rio, Texas. He was wired to medical equipment on the surface which monitored various functions, including body temperature; brain wave, or EEG, traces; and heart activity. There was even a device that stored his daily beard shavings to study their hormone-influenced growth.

After about three weeks Siffre's body had shifted to a 26-hour sleep–wake cycle. This became increasingly erratic, varying from 18 to 52 hours, although each seemed like a standard day length to the isolated cave-dweller. Over the six months Siffre's average cycle was 28 hours. His mental processes and his manual dexterity in particular deteriorated steadily.

Because he was deprived of all environmental cues about time, from light–dark alternation to a clock, his body rhythm was allowed to "free-run" in its own self-generated cycle of sleep, wakefulness and activity. Such studies help us to understand the body's internal clocks and rhythms, and they are of practical use to people such as submarine crews and astronauts.

See also

INPUTS AND OUTPUTS
▶ Feeling pain 226/227

▶ The primal sense 232/233

▶ Survival sense 244/245

BUILDING THE BRAIN
▶ Discovering transmitters 182/183

FAR HORIZONS
▶ Male and female 270/271

STATES OF MIND
▶ The resting mind? 282/283

▶ Feeling low 290/291

Survival sense

With our superb senses and responses we seem well equipped to cope with the modern world. But are we?

Just suppose that while walking along the road one day you came upon a lion. Surely you would be doomed? But wait; the human body in the modern form of *Homo sapiens* probably evolved on the plains of Africa, at least 100,000 years ago. Physically and physiologically, we have changed little in that time, and our distant ancestors must have encountered the occasional lion in their original home. In fact, if you pause to think about it, the human body is well suited to the situation. It is large and strong compared to most animals; its general senses are relatively sharp, especially sight. The eyes pick up the right range of electromagnetic waves, or light, to gain maximum information from the environment and discern every detail of the big cat's movements and behaviour.

The body's other senses, such as hearing and smell, are similarly tuned in to important stimuli. Our intelligent brain can turn almost anything handy into a usable weapon. And the body's nervous and hormonal systems can quickly put its interior on "red alert". Nerve signals flash through the sympathetic nervous system, and adrenaline and associated hormones pour into the bloodstream. Almost at once, heart and breathing rates rise, blood pressure goes up, pupils dilate, and blood is diverted from the skin, digestive and excretory systems to the muscles. All this happens fast and automatically, thanks largely to the brain.

At the same time your conscious mind focuses on the lion. Your brain filters out irrelevant sights and sounds. Your conscious perception is super-aware and your thought processes speed up. Your whole body

In a flight simulator a trainee pilot practises landing. All of his senses are working at their optimum as he concentrates on the task in hand. He watches the runway and the instrument displays, feels the plane's motions, and hears the engines' whine and warning buzzers. All of these mechanical and electronic systems are designed to stimulate and work with the body's senses. The brain copes with amounts of data coming along nerves from various sensory sources, such as sight, hearing, touch and motion detection, that would swamp a supercomputer.

Modern humans cannot usually deal with stress by smashing its cause to pieces. The nagging colleague is often at a distance – on the other end of the phone. But the fact that we might dearly love to take physical action could reflect our ancient instincts and the body's fighting expectations.

TOO MUCH OF A BAD THING

Unrelieved stress can eat away at both mind and body, and the list of stress-related conditions grows ever longer. A mild heightening of autonomic nervous activity stimulates many body processes, such as acid secretion by the stomach in expectation of food. But when this state is maintained over days, months and years, the excess acid erodes the stomach lining, and the result can be a gastric ulcer. Other stress-related conditions include headaches, breathlessness, asthma, heart flutters and angina, muscle twitches and aches, and many mental and emotional states such as anxiety, mood swings, depression and schizophrenia.

Comparison of stress (life events)	U.S. Rating	Europe Rating	Japan Rating
Death of spouse	1	1	1
Divorce	2	3	3
Marital separation	3	5	
Jail term	4	2	2
Death of close family member	5		4
Personal injury or illness	6		5
Marriage		4	6
Pregnancy		6	

Some of the most stressful events are perceived differently in different cultures. The top six in the United States, for example, are not the same as in Europe or in Japan.

and mind are prepared for action, in a state of heightened readiness either to battle with the foe or to flee the danger. Then you see that it is just a stuffed lion, on its way to a museum. The result is neither fight or flight. Your nervous and hormonal systems gradually subdue the body's inner processes, trying to return to normal. This may be an extreme example, but the body's state of readiness is thwarted unnaturally like this time and again in the modern world. A row at work, a traffic jam, an unreasonable neighbour, a family problem, unfair pressures from employers can all evoke the same sort of "primitive" reaction. The brain and body expect action as the response to stressful situations. But they rarely get it, and this can lead to both physical and psychological problems.

Stone Age humans coped with stress by taking action against its cause, be it a marauding leopard or rival humans from a nearby group encroaching on their territory. The human brain, nervous system and senses were geared for survival in this type of situation. And the stone axe was one of the earliest tools used to aid survival.
Another more surprising, but extremely important, aid for general survival is pain. If we did not feel pain when we stuck our hand in a fire, for instance, we would leave it there and suffer burns which could reduce our chances of survival.

See also

INPUTS AND OUTPUTS
▶ The big picture 236/237

▶ Dealing with drives 240/241

SURVEYING THE MIND
▶ What is a brain? 134/135

▶ Inside the mind 142/143

FAR HORIZONS
▶ The evolving mind 248/249

STATES OF MIND
▶ Motivation 302/303

Far Horizons

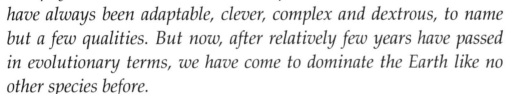

A s a species, modern humans – Homo sapiens – have been around for a comparatively short period of time. We can look back over only about 5,000 years of recorded history. And evidence from various sources suggests that we existed for perhaps a couple of hundred thousand years before that. During that time we have changed little, both in our physical and in our mental capabilities. We have always been adaptable, clever, complex and dextrous, to name but a few qualities. But now, after relatively few years have passed in evolutionary terms, we have come to dominate the Earth like no other species before.

It is the power of our mind that has enabled this. This power has given us the ability to control our environment. It has given us the means to learn and remember. And it has given us language. This, perhaps more than any ability, is the key to our success; for it allows us to communicate, passing knowledge down the generations so that it accumulates and lets us build on what has gone before.

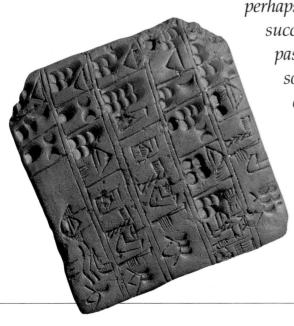

Left (clockwise from top): the developing mind in the growing child; getting a grip on interpersonal intelligence; drawing conclusions about autism; a superstitous response; memory has its high points. This page (top): rising to the intellectual challenge of chess; (left) expressing ideas in a form of writing.

The evolving mind

Due to our inbuilt intelligence our numbers have increased and our achievements in all fields have reached extraordinary heights.

Back in the mists of time, about 20 million years ago, the first of the so-called terrestrial apes evolved in Africa and inhabited the Miocene landscape. Perhaps 6 to 8 million years ago this group split into two – the modern apes and the hominids. The first hominids are called australopithecines, or southern apes; the earliest fossil remains date back about 4.5 million years. Despite the name, they had some characteristics that were distinctly unapelike. For a start they habitually walked upright and their brains were larger than would be expected in an ape with the same body size.

Scientists believe that these creatures were the ancestors of modern humans, but their brain was only about a third the volume of ours. Over millions of years brain size in succeeding species of hominids increased dramatically until the current figure was reached. So how did we get the big, efficient brains that give us our intelligence and ability to manipulate our environment?

Making and using tools was almost certainly a factor – bigger brains made for better tool makers, who were more successful still. Another suggestion is that standing upright reduced blood pressure and thus rate of flow of blood to the brain, which meant it was unable to lose enough heat. So the number of blood vessels there had to increase, which in turn led to more brain cells. Another theory links it with increasingly important social skills, especially the development of language.

The major design problem caused by increasing brain size is that the brain is an energy guzzler. Although it makes up only 2 percent of body weight, it uses 20 percent of the body's fuel in the form of glucose and oxygen. So a bigger brain demands more nutritious food – animal protein – and for our ancestors obtaining this required greater intelligence. And so came the ability to make better hunting weapons, to cooperate in hunting groups and to communicate.

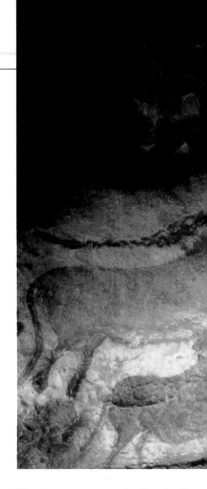

The Lascaux cave paintings *in the Dordogne in France were created by humans 25,000 years ago. The vivid use of representational and symbolic images shows that in their mental capacity these people were close to us.*

Australopithecines roamed Africa *from about 4.5 million years ago. One form was* Australopithecus robustus, *with a brain volume of about 485 cc (30 in³). By 2.5 million years ago,* Homo habilis *had emerged. They made the first stone tools and had a brain of 650 cc (40 in³). A million years later came* Homo erectus, *who made better tools, used fire, hunted big game and whose brain was around 990 cc (60 in³).* Homo sapiens neanderthalensis, *a variant of the human species, with an average brain volume of 1,640 cc (100 in³), died out 35,000 years ago. Today's* Homo sapiens sapiens, *with a brain of 1,610 cc (98 in³), originated 250,000 years ago and gradually replaced other forms.*

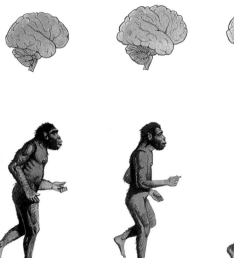

Australopithecus robustus   *Homo habilis*   *Homo erectus*   *Homo sapiens neanderthalensis*   *Homo sapiens sapiens*

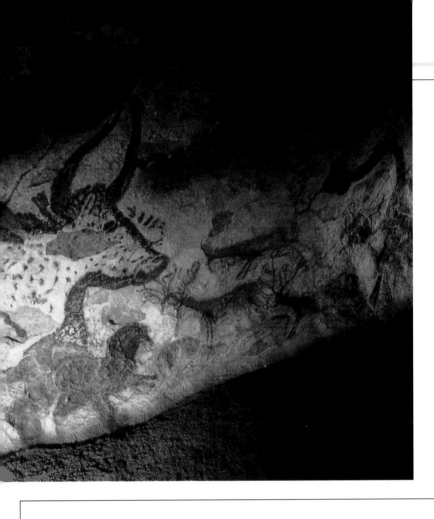

Our species survived by hunting and gathering, and the population was a constant 10 million until about 10,000 years ago. Then the agricultural revolution saw new farming techniques that generated more food. Numbers began to rise, and progress was made in other fields. Stone tools gave way to metal, settled communities allowed civilizations to grow, and the demands of trade led to written language.

Microchip

World population reached a plateau of several hundred million from the height of the Roman Empire until the Black Death, the plague that reduced the population by about one-third worldwide. The population recovered, and advances in science and culture eventually led to understanding about public health measures and food production. These, with modern medicine and mass immunization against infectious diseases, have caused numbers to rocket in recent decades.

Mass immunization

COMMUNICATING INTELLIGENCE

Some researchers believe gossip was a major factor in boosting brain size. It has been found that the bigger the cortex in the brain of a primate species, the bigger the size of a group. And being part of a sizeable group is an advantage – there is more protection, and larger hunting groups get more food.

Apes hold a group together by grooming, among other things. Language may have enabled humans to "mentally groom" many people at once by chatting with them. So those of our ancestors with the best language skills – and thus with larger cortices – enjoyed the benefits of a bigger group and were more likely to survive to pass on their large brain to further generations.

Stephenson's Rocket

Roman Empire

Discovery of New World

Galileo

Agricultural Revolution

First civilizations

Flint tool

Iron Age

Black Death

Modern Medicine

Computer Age

Clean water

Stone Age

Bronze Age

Renaissance

Scientific Revolution

Industrial Revolution

Middle Ages

| | | | | | | | | | | | | | | | | | | | |
|00|5,000|1,000|550|500|450|400|350|300|250|200|150|100|50|0|

Years ago

Population (billions)

6
5
4
3
2
1

Conditioning the mind

Learning plays a vital role in survival, but there is more to memory than recalling responses to obvious dangers.

The first time you put your hand on a hot stove will probably also be the last. The pain from the heat is such a strong stimulus that it triggers a reflex response – you snatch your hand away – and you now associate a hot stove with pain and have learned never to touch one again. In the everyday world such learned associations, or conditioned responses, exist in countless forms: a car driver brakes at a red traffic light; if a type of food makes someone ill, he or she will avoid it in future. But associations and responses can be learned that are not useful, including phobias and superstitions. A car crash can leave behind a lifelong fear of cars; wearing a certain pair of socks when an important game of soccer is won can make someone want to wear those socks whenever a game is played.

Humans are not the only creatures that learn responses to stimuli. All animals, including even flatworms, are able to learn conditioned responses because without them they would die. The first person to study learning of this type systematically was the Russian scientist Ivan Pavlov, who used dogs as his subjects. The work of Pavlov and others convinced some psychologists that all human behaviour could – if broken down into small enough sections – be explained in terms

Superstitions can be explained as conditioned responses to certain situations. For example, things occasionally fall on people when they walk under ladders, so the link has been created that walking under ladders equals bad luck. Sportspeople and actors are especially prey to these false connections, which is why they often have a lucky item of clothing, or feel they have to go through some elaborate ritual before performing to bring them luck. But most people do not get hit by objects when they walk under ladders so they have not learned to associate ladders with danger directly. Thus it seems that there is much to human behaviour that we cannot explain in terms of simple conditioned responses.

of conditioning. Much of the evidence for this idea came from work done with animals. American psychologist B.F. Skinner, for instance, showed that it was possible to teach rats and pigeons quite complicated behaviour, such as running through mazes correctly or even playing a version of table tennis.

The core idea behind Skinner's thinking was that all living creatures make small actions which have an effect on their surroundings. If one of these small actions, called an operant, has some sort of pleasant effect, the creature is likely to learn to repeat the action. The behaviour is reinforced by the pleasant effect, in Skinner's experiments usually some reward such as food. Eventually a series of small actions that lead to pleasant effects can be shaped by reinforcement into more complicated strings of behaviour. Thus a pigeon will put together a sequence of operants and play ping pong.

In fact, conditioning techniques, in the form of rewards and punishments, are used extensively in the human world, for example to teach children how to behave properly. Skinner made the distinction between two types of reinforcers. For humans primary reinforcers are things that are actually wanted, such as food, drink, sex or rest; secondary reinforcers (the most obvious of which is money) are things that enable people to obtain the primaries.

HUNGER FOR LEARNING

Ivan Pavlov (1849–1936) was a Russian physiologist who, in 1904, won the Nobel prize for his work on digestion. While researching the amount of saliva produced by dogs, he noticed something intriguing. To begin with, his dogs would salivate only when they saw food, but they soon began salivating when they heard the sound of rattling dinner bowls, without any food being present. They had learned to associate the rattling of the bowls with food.

Over many years Pavlov explored a large number of variations on this simple type of learning. It is known as classical conditioning and it occurs as a result of association of a stimulus (in this case rattling bowls) with an involuntary response (salivation) to a different stimulus (food). Pavlov linked food with lights and bells and tested how close together in time the two stimuli had to be for the dogs to make an association. He also investigated what happened when he set up connections between unpleasant stimuli – electric shocks – and neutral objects such as lights and bells. He also discovered how to extinguish connections. Applied to humans, classical conditioning could explain why there might be a rush on the ice-cream stall in a cinema when a film depicting desert scenes was shown even though the temperature in the cinema remained cool.

The lure, to some, of a one-armed bandit can be explained in terms of a particular pattern of rewards for behaviour. Psychologist B.F. Skinner found that rats and other creatures learned and then behaved in different ways depending on how he rewarded them for performing certain acts. In one experiment Skinner varied the number of times an action, such as pressing a lever, had to be performed before a rat was rewarded. He found that rats worked hardest and longest when they were rewarded at a rate of once for every five to seven actions. In another experiment, the time between the rats' actions and their receiving the reward varied unpredictably and this often led to superstitious behaviour. Humans find themselves in a similar situation when trying to dial a busy phone number; if, for example, they finally get through on several occasions after counting to 50, then they might repeat the pattern whenever they get an engaged line.

Humans are operating on a similar type of reward schedule when they gamble on a machine such as a slot machine. From time to time the machine pays out a small amount of money, encouraging the gambler to go on playing. Whether or not this explains all the reasons why some people gamble is a matter of debate. For instance, how can the fact that people still gamble when they know that in the long run they will lose be accounted for? Clearly there is more to human life than the simple stimulus and response or conditioned response behaviours that a behaviourist such as Skinner would use to explain actions.

The infinite store?

Some memories are laid down in fairly precise regions of the brain, while others are spread right across it.

What were you doing yesterday evening? Such a question probably prompts a visual image, perhaps of yourself watching television, at the gym or at a shopping mall. So is memory like a film library where all your experiences are stored waiting to be called up? The American researcher Karl Lashley believed it was and during the 1950s tried to locate the site of this library in rats' brains. He trained the animals to solve a maze and then removed different parts of the cortex to see if the loss of any area made them forget the solution. It did not.

Memory is more complicated than that. Many memories – how to ride a bicycle or the French word for cake – are not stored as images, so we have other sorts of memory. These are controlled by different parts of the brain. Studies on brain-damaged patients have shown just how specific these can be. One woman with damage to her left temporal lobe could remember the names for tools but not for animals, for instance.

Our memory capacity is huge. Some people have a vocabulary of about 100,000 words, and ancient Celtic story tellers frequently knew 350 long epic poems by heart. Such feats, as well as ordinary everyday memory, rely on certain principles. The most important of these is association: the more links there are to other similar facts the more easily a memory is recalled. So a number can be better remembered if it has a visual association, such as "legs eleven".

A model of the Eiffel tower will trigger many different memories in different people, even if they have never seen it, because it has reached the status of an icon. It will make most people think of Paris, but some may associate that with romance and moonlit walks by the Seine, while others might visualize other great structures and still others might remember a scene from a favourite film set in that city.

Memories are physically formed by strengthening the links between brain cells – the more links, the stronger the memory. There are around 100,000 billion of these connections, or synapses, which explains our virtually limitless capacity, more than the largest supercomputer. Complex chemical changes at these links make certain connections more likely and these are responsible for laying down memories.

A phone call may seem a simple act, but it can involve all the types of memory. The number may be held in the phonological loop for dialling, which requires non-declarative memory for motor skills. And without semantic and episodic memory you would not be able to discuss the previous night's events.

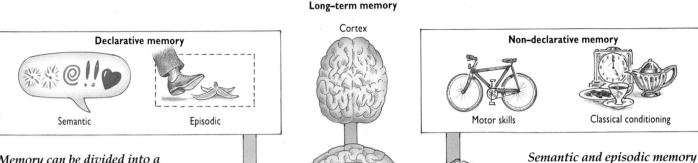

Long-term memory

Cortex

Declarative memory

Semantic   Episodic

Non-declarative memory

Motor skills   Classical conditioning

Hippocampus   Thalamus   Cerebellum

Working memory

ABC 123 — Phonological loop

45 + 7 = — Central executive

Visual–spatial scratch pad

Memory can be divided into a number of different types, thought to reside in various regions of the brain. Both declarative and non-declarative memory are part of long-term memory. Declarative memory involves the use of the hippocampus for forming memories and the cortex for storage. It covers your memory of facts such as events and names which do not need to be repeated for them to sink in. For example, if you fell over on the way to work you would remember it.

Non-declarative memory covers motor skills, such as playing football or riding a bicycle. These memories are thought to reside in the cerebellum and do not seem to involve the hippocampus. They require rehearsal and patience for you to learn the skill.

Semantic and episodic memory are subsections of declarative memory. Semantic memory is the knowledge of facts – language and concepts – which the brain files in categories and which seems to involve the left temporal lobe. Episodic memory is of an event in one's life and everything about it, including emotional reactions to it.

Classical conditioning, along with motor skills, is part of non-declarative memory. Our desire for food at a particular time of day – regardless of whether we are hungry or not – is one example of such conditioning.

Short-term, or working, memory is also divided into categories – of which there are three main ones. They all work together to keep material in the mind for a short time, and allow us to manage such tasks as putting together a sentence. The first of these is the phonological loop, which enables us to remember sequences of approximately seven digits, letters or words.

The second is the visual–spatial scratch pad. It is like a sort of inner eye, which receives and codes data into visual or spatial images. It comes into play when we need to remember where on a page we had got to when we start reading a book again. The central executive is the last of these elements. Its function is to help with such tasks as reasoning or doing mental arithmetic and as such it is rather like the RAM of a computer.

CUT OFF FROM THE PRESENT

A man had suffered from severe epileptic fits since he was 16 years old, but all drug treatments had failed. In an attempt to control the condition, his doctors decided to operate on the area of his brain that was affected, the area below the temporal lobes. This was in the 1950s, when brain surgery for all sorts of brain disorders was far more common than it is now.

In one sense the operation was a success – the man was cured of his convulsions. In another its effects were devastating: as a result of the surgery he was unable to form any new memories. Any conversation he had was forgotten after a few minutes, as was the person he spoke to. He could not remember where he lived and could read a book several times without any sense that he had read it before. Yet he did not lose skills such as language, and his memory of events some two years before the operation was normal. What is more, he taught himself to draw, showing that he could still memorize motor skills, but he had no memory of learning to do so.

The importance of this case is that it showed for the first time that the hippocampus – which was damaged on both sides of his brain by the operation – is involved in laying down memories, but it does not appear to be the place where they are stored.

Active memory

Just as vision is an active creative process, so memories seem to be remade every time we call them to mind.

Generally our memory serves us well. We remember people's faces and names, we know what we did yesterday or last week; but it does not work like a computer disc. It seems that rather than storing memories, we re-create them each time we recall them, and that means that they can change. This is why eyewitnesses are notoriously unreliable. We do not record the events like a camera, instead what we remember can be affected both by what we expect to see and by the questions we are asked about it. Many people expect bank robbers to carry guns so if shown a film of an unarmed robbery they often say that guns were used. Likewise, asking witnesses about a "car crash" as opposed to an "accident" makes it more likely they will come up with false memories of broken glass.

So-called false memories have also featured in cases of alleged sexual abuse in childhood. Numerous people in therapy claim to have uncovered long-buried memories of abuse. Some claim that certain of those memories, which may seem totally real, have been influenced by the therapist's suggestions.

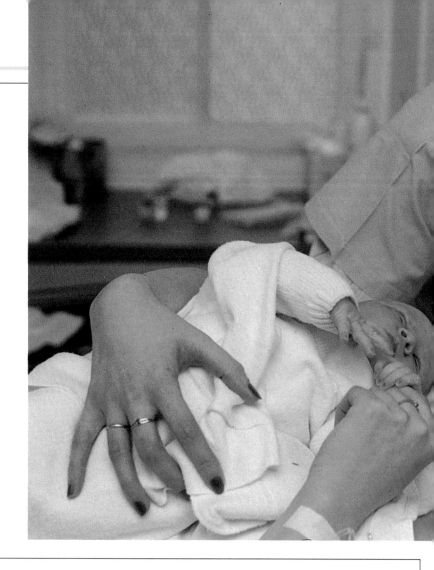

LOOKING FOR THE SEAT OF MEMORY

One of the apparently strongest pieces of evidence that memories are stored in snapshot form came from the work in the 1940s and '50s of the Canadian neurosurgeon Wilder Penfield, who developed techniques for treating epilepsy. Since epileptic fits are caused by a diseased patch on the brain, he worked to find that patch so it could be removed. To do this, he removed the top of the patient's skull, using only a local anaesthetic (to numb the scalp, the brain itself feels no pain), and stimulated the exposed brain with electrodes. The idea was that when he found the right patch, the patient would experience the feelings that normally preceded a fit.

Not only did Penfield locate the site of the disease in his patients, he also believed that he had found the seat of memory – in the temporal lobe. When this was stimulated, 40 out of about 1,000 patients reported vivid flashbacks – a fragment of a tune, a child calling, being in a room. All were marked by a dreamlike quality with no sense of time or location. He believed that this was evidence that our memories are stored in one place in a complete and recoverable form. Later researchers pointed out, however, that few of the patients recalled actual memories; so perhaps the position in the brain of the seat of memory is a mystery still to be solved.

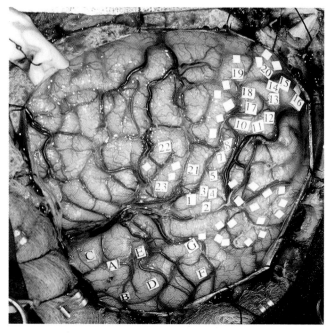

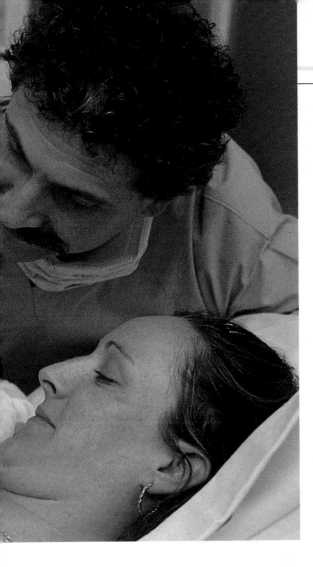

The birth of a baby is an event that no mother – or father, if he is present – will ever forget. Every moment seems etched on the mind (although women seem to be sufficiently selective about memories of the pain they experience to be prepared to do it again). But all of us, whether we are parents or not, have similar personal moments that stand out especially vividly, and which we seem to remember accurately rather than distorting with each recall. They are known as flashbulb memories and are apparently "burned" into our brains because the original experience was so powerful.

Something similar seems to happen to the victims of post-traumatic stress disorder, who often have vivid flashbacks to a terrible event – usually one that threatens their own life or that of a family member or close friend – for years after the original incident. Unlike normal memories, these remain exceptionally strong unless treated with therapy soon after the event. The symptoms of this disorder include recurring nightmares, in which sufferers relive the event, feelings of guilt at having survived, sleeplessness and a profound sense of detachment.

YOU MUST REMEMBER THIS

Imagine being able to remember huge strings of random numbers with the ease that you remember your mother's name. In 1920s Moscow, a newspaper reporter could do just that, not because he had a particularly good general memory, but because he was able to think up mnemonic tricks incredibly quickly. His technique was to visualize a familiar street or place and then associate the list of numbers or even objects that he wished to recall with particular aspects of that scene. To remember the numbers he simply had to imagine himself in the scene he had created (often many years before) and find the places he had hidden them.

A slightly different technique has been used by a British mnemonist, who associates numbers with letters, making words, and from the words creates a – sometimes bizarre – picture. For instance, faced with 36 random numbers to remember, he breaks them down into groups of 6. Using a special conversion table that he has memorized, he first gives the group a number, so that he knows

where it comes in the sequence. If he were trying to remember the fourth group, this would give the letter R, which he makes into a word by adding vowels – "ray", which he remembers as a ray of light. If that group were, say, 351639, he would get the letters MLTChMP. By breaking this down he gets MLT and ChMP, which with the addition of vowels might give the words "mallet" and "chimp". The whole gives the unlikely image of a chimp smashing a light with a mallet, one he is unlikely to forget.

In everyday life we rarely have to perform such feats of memory. But we can use similar tricks – ideally using unusual visual images, since memory works best with them – to recall more useful things. For instance, to make the name Cindy Carson memorable you might conjure up an image of a Sindy doll. Then for Carson try a picture of a car driving toward the setting sun. You will not forget a doll at the wheel of a bright pink Cadillac at sunset.

A knotted handkerchief is often used to jog memory. When you find a knotted handkerchief in your pocket, it reminds you that you have to remember something – which will usually then come back to you. Failing that, leave yourself a note – if necessary written on your hand.

Meeting of minds

*Across the animal kingdom one of the prime abilities
of the mind is communication with other minds.*

Walk into a wood, field or jungle and listen. What you
hear is communication – a cacophony of chirps, calls,
whistles and grunts as animals advertise for mates and warn
about the approach of predators. Birds stake out territory with
song, monkeys grunt and cough to make arrangements with
other members of the troop. And enter a place where humans
congregate and you will hear a hubbub of talk, see a flurry of
gestures and observe myriad postures and expressions.

You have only to look at your own dog or cat to understand
how much can be conveyed without speech. Your dog greets
you with a welcoming bark and enthusiastic wagging of the tail
when you return home; but a stranger who is perceived as a
threat is met with a snarl and a curled lip. A cat carries its tail
high over its back in greeting and purrs with pleasure when it
is stroked. All of these are unmistakable signals, conveyed by
body language and sound. But by far the most sophisticated
form of communication is human language. While nearly all
animals have only a limited and fixed number of calls and
signs, language is almost infinite in its possible combinations.

Speech was impossible until about a million years ago
because production of the complex sounds of language requires
more space in the throat than our primate ancestors had. We
acquired sufficient room by developing a longer neck and a
lower larynx; we also produced a more rounded tongue –
modifications that permitted the development of speech. But
language is much more than making sounds, it requires the
ability to use symbols and handle abstract ideas.

Primates are now considered to be more sophisticated
communicators than was previously thought and it appears
that they can learn to use symbols and signs. So it seems that
building on this ability, early humans at about the time of *Homo
erectus* 1.6 million years ago developed sign language as a
halfway house to speech. Not only had their brains become
larger, as is evident from skulls of the time, but they were also
bigger on the left – the side that controls language. In addition,
they had developed an opposable thumb, which made holding
tools and making hand signs easier. Language proper eventually
emerged about 100,000 years ago or possibly even earlier.

*A **girl sitting** with one leg
propped on her knee and hands
clasped behind her head is giving
out strong non-verbal signals. Ask
a group of people what message she
is conveying and they will agree that
she exudes arrogant self-confidence.*

*Indeed, her attitude is one that
most people will recognize as that
of a rather smug, over-confident
individual, who will expound upon
her own abilities and achievements
to the boredom of all around her.
Conversely, although it may be
easy to read the body language of
another person, we are often not
conscious of it in ourselves. But
some people learn to control their
body language. Poker players, for
instance, who do not want to give
any indication of how good or bad
their cards are, rigidly govern any
giveaway non-verbal clues – hence
the expression "pokerfaced".*

CHIMP SIGNING

In the 1960s it was announced that after five years of intensive training a chimpanzee called Washoe had learned 132 signs and could indicate general classes of objects such as "dog" or "bird". Recent research seems to indicate that young pygmy chimps, or bonobos – the type found in the rainforests of Zaire – can learn a similar number of signs fairly quickly. One bonobo, Kanzi, was able to understand 150 English words after only 17 months. Like a child, he learned language by experience, rather than by special training, and by the age of nine was able to comprehend and carry out quite detailed verbal instructions. Although incapable of speech, he was also able to express his feelings and wishes using a keyboard with 256 signs (**left**). But despite the abilities of some specially trained chimps, they lack a skill that is unique to humans. While chimps can manage to express their needs, for instance by signing that they want a banana, they cannot express ideas.

Researchers studying vervet monkeys in the wild have found that they have an extensive and complex range of calls and signals, more than was previously thought. There are several specific types of calls and signals that youngsters need to learn. One set warns of nearby predators and even distinguishes between leopards, snakes and eagles, while the other involves a number of complex social situations. From such beginnings language may have developed.

Non-verbal communication has always played an important part in transmitting messages. Researchers studying primates can tell simply from posture which of the animals is dominant or submissive, since junior monkeys appease their seniors by making a gesture which says, "Look, I'm not a threat". And the first serious research on human body language found that we, too, often use it to express rapport or to signal our state of mind. Films of conversations revealed that those who were listening often unconsciously moved their hands or head in time to the rhythm of the speaker's speech. Similarly, when people were getting on well they often sat or stood in the same way, and when they were angry or bored it was evident from their posture, even if their words appeared to be placatory or polite.

__With arms and legs crossed__, this girl conveys that she is on the defensive and probably nervous as well – an impression reinforced by her hidden hands. Perhaps she is shy, feels threatened or is having to listen to an arrogant bore.

__Nose rubbing or touching__, usually with a forefinger, which may be transmuted into rubbing an ear or an eye, generally signifies that the person is doubtful what his response should be to an awkward question or situation. It may also be accompanied by other negative gestures such as wriggling on the chair or turning sideways.

Word power

The fact that you can read and understand the words on this page means that you must be a human being.

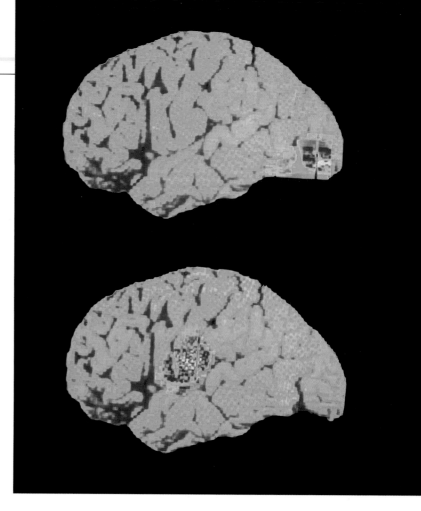

All human societies, however primitive their technology, have highly developed language, which they use to share ideas, plan complex activities and teach their children. But because we learn to speak automatically it is sometimes not appreciated what an amazing achievement language is. We not only have tens of thousands of words to describe things and ideas but we also have grammar, which is one of the features that distinguishes human from animal communication.

Grammar is the complicated and elaborate set of rules for putting words together so that they convey meaning. Even the experts find it difficult to describe grammar fully, yet by the age of two English-speaking children have, for instance, worked out the rule for making a word plural and can soon talk in reasonably grammatical sentences. For this reason, most researchers now believe that humans are born with an innate ability to learn language, just as we arrive with the

Written language first emerged in Mesopotamia about 5,200 years ago. Marks made on clay tablets with a reed pen recorded such things as grain accounts and land sales. Crude drawings of familiar objects such as human heads or animals were also used to convey ideas. Gradually the pictograms became more stylized until words were represented by symbols. The pictograms at the top are from about 4,400 years ago while the symbols, called cuneiform, were made 2,650 years ago. How the signs sounded is shown at the bottom of each column.

Language regions in the brain are shown by PET scans which detect active areas. The images of the left-hand side of the brain show the area activated by vision, including reading (**top left**); by hearing (**top right**); by speech (**bottom left**); and by the high activity generated by thinking about words and speaking them (**bottom right**).

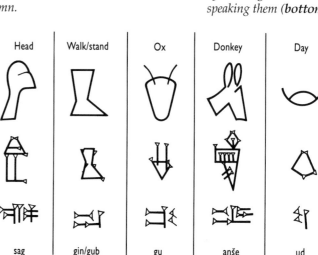

Head	Walk/stand	Ox	Donkey	Day	Water
sag	gin/gub	gu	anše	ud	a

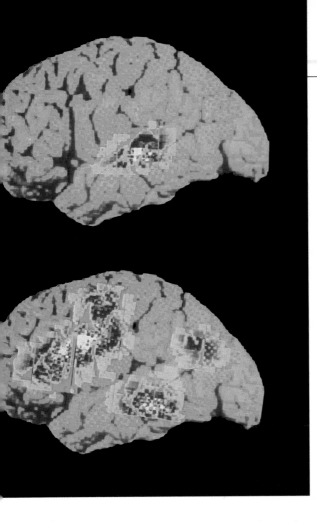

A TIME TO TALK

☤ A boy of about 10 was found wandering in the wild. He appeared healthy and had been cared for by wild animals. He was taken in but despite persistent efforts, he could not be taught to speak, even though there was nothing wrong with his vocal apparatus. It seems that unless children are exposed to speech before the age of about eight, they are unable to learn a true language.

Normally the process of learning language is marked by the same type of regular stages of development found in other pre-programmed abilities such as learning to walk. By the age of six months, on average, babies are constantly babbling, making all the sounds that are used in human languages, including some of the clicks that are a feature of a number of African languages. At a year they can manage a few words and by two years they are using two-word combinations such as "mummy ball" that show a grasp of the distinction between subject and object. Once children learn a word like "ball", they often apply it to other objects with the same function – such as bouncing – or the same form – round. What is more impressive is that they then make corrections without having to be specifically told. By the time they are four to five years old, most children have a vocabulary of several thousand words and have mastered the basic rules of grammar and syntax.

---

ability to see. Both can, however, be shaped by the world in which we find ourselves.

In places where adults – usually immigrant labourers – who do not share a common language are living together, their children will spontaneously develop a pidgin language made up of bits from all their parents' languages. What is remarkable about these pidgin languages is that among second-generation speakers clear and specific rules emerge completely spontaneously.

Language is generally processed by the left side of the brain, and damage in certain areas can lead to the loss of specific aspects of ability. For example, patients in whom part of the left frontal lobe, known as Broca's region, has been destroyed can understand language but cannot speak fluently, while damage to Wernicke's area, nearby in the temporal lobe, produces speech that is fluent but virtually meaningless.

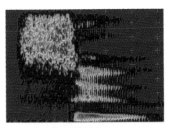

Sound: Gay

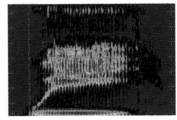

Sound: Sue

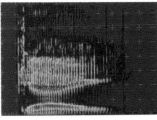

Sound: Ma

Sound: We

Voices make a combination of noises as shown in these images where sounds have been plotted according to their frequency (pitch) and volume (the lighter the colour, the louder the sound). The brain

analyses the complex sounds of speech, recognizing not only the content, in terms of grammar and the like, but also who is doing the talking by the distinct set of noises generated by each individual.

Parallel minds

Reading these words probably makes the left side of your brain work a little harder than the right.

We each have a brain in two halves. Almost without exception, every part of the brain on the left is matched by a more or less mirror image part on the right. This applies to animals, too, and in many creatures – ourselves included – each side of the brain controls the opposite side of the body.

Humans are thought to be unique, however, in that opposite structures in the cerebral cortex, the thin layer of grey matter on the outside of the brain, have become specialized, with some functions not mirrored left to right. In most people the left side, which is slightly larger, controls language and logical activities and the right controls spatial activities and tasks with a more emotional element. The essential difference between the two halves seems to be not so much the type of information that has to be processed – words versus pictures – but how it is dealt with. For instance, only the left side is involved in reading a technical manual but reading folk tales, with their strong mythic and symbolic content, requires both sides to work together.

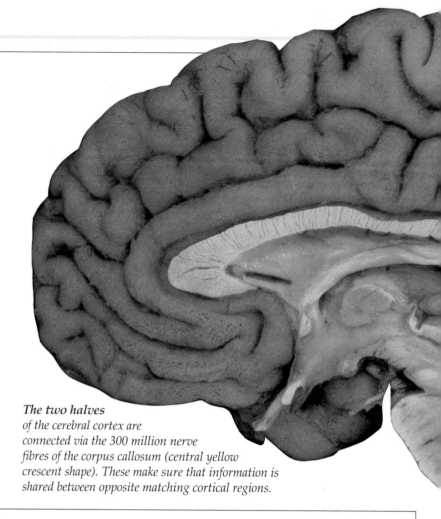

The two halves
of the cerebral cortex are connected via the 300 million nerve fibres of the corpus callosum (central yellow crescent shape). These make sure that information is shared between opposite matching cortical regions.

MUSIC IN MIND

Studies of musicians reveal that brain dominance can change as a result of learning and experience. For instance, non-musicians focus on the overall contours of the melody when listening to music and tend to use the right side of the cerebral cortex. But professionals have learned to be more analytical about it and so use the left side to break the music into its component parts.

The effect of brain damage on musical ability is also a good example of the way the two halves specialize. Damage on the right causes singing to be grossly disturbed and all sense of melody to go; but rhythm, which involves a repetitive sequence, remains. Left-side damage, however, which the French composer Ravel (1875–1937) suffered, causes problems with naming songs or recognizing written music. Similarly, recent studies with PET scans have shown that reading music involves left brain areas that are near, but separate from, those involved in reading.

WHEN THE LEFT HAND DOESN'T KNOW WHAT THE RIGHT HAND IS DOING

 Given a pencil to hold in his right hand, which is hidden from him, a man can describe it perfectly well. But ask him to do the same thing when the pencil is in his left hand, and he cannot describe it at all. Using his left hand the man can make a rough copy of a square but is unable to write the word "Sunday" – "SA" is all he can manage. With his right hand, by contrast, he can write the word perfectly well but the square is represented as five parallel lines above one another in a column.

The man suffers from severe epilepsy and has had the connection between the two halves of his cerebral cortex, the corpus callosum, cut as an extreme treatment to control his seizures. Each side is thus forced to function on its own. So the right cortex, which controls the left hand and receives sensory information from it, can neither give the pencil a name nor write a word, as it is specialized in spatial tasks. But it can instruct the left hand to draw a square. The left side, which deals with the right hand, can give the pencil a name and can write the word "Sunday" as it is specialized in language. But it cannot tell the right hand to draw a decent square.

*The left side of the brain controls the right of the body and receives sensory information from it. Similarly, the right controls and receives data from the left. Thus the left motor cortex (**below**) controls* the motions of the muscles in the right side of the body, and the left somatosensory cortex receives touch signals from the right of the body. In addition, the left primary visual cortex deals with what is in the right of the visual field and the left auditory cortex deals with sounds from the right ear.

Three areas on the left of the cerebral cortex are known to have specific language functions: Broca's area (which deals with grammar and articulation); Wernicke's area (which covers sense and understanding); and the angular gyrus (which turns images into words).

For the overwhelming majority of right-handed people the left cerebral cortex does indeed handle language and logic, and the right spatial tasks. But in left-handed or ambidextrous people, the functional specialization can be different. Sometimes there is a straight swap between the hemispheres and their specialized functions, so a left-hander's right brain might deal with language and logic. But sometimes functions are shared equally between left and right.

The ability to use and understand language and to perform fine motor skills is usually located in the left side of the cerebral cortex, as are the musical abilities of timing, sequencing and rhythm. So, too, are logic, mathematical abilities and the analysis and shaping of ideas.

The right side is, in most people, better at dealing with complex visual patterns, perspective and spatial matters generally. It is also thought to be more involved in emotions and in divergent and insightful thinking. The musical elements of tonal memory, quality of sound, melody recognition and intensity are also handled here. The right side

Motor cortex
Somatosensory cortex
Angular gyrus
Broca's area
Left primary visual cortex
Wernicke's area
Left auditory cortex

is responsible for recognizing faces and interpreting their expressions. Although each half of the cortex has its functional specializations, there is a constant flow of data between them via the corpus callosum. There is some evidence that the callosum is thicker in women, leading to speculation that the female brain may be better integrated.

Having ideas

From daydreaming to solving problems to having an original thought, the brain can do it all.

The phenomenal complexity and flexibility of our brain allows us to perform extraordinary feats. Our 100 billion neurons give us the processing power of a vast computer. This allows us to deal both with mundane everyday problems and with mentally demanding tasks such as understanding and using complicated mathematical concepts. The brain's higher functions give rise to language, technology and the arts; yet, although we all know what it means to be creative or intelligent, understanding how we do it has proved to be difficult.

Stephen Hawking theorizing about black holes, Picasso transforming a bicycle seat and handlebars into a bull's head, and a chess grand master are all operating at a high level of intelligence. But they are also doing things that require very different mental skills. And measuring mental skills is one of the most controversial areas of psychology. One way is the IQ (intelligence quotient) test, which uses multiple-choice questions to test how good people are at verbal skills – reading, writing, vocabulary – and spatial ones – arranging blocks, detecting patterns. It appears to reflect a basic division, into two types, in the way we think. The first is known as convergent and refers to organizing, analytical skills. The other is divergent and includes the brain's ability to make unexpected connections. Artists like Picasso tend to be divergent while scientists and chess players are more convergent.

Much of our high-level thinking seems to be done in the frontal lobes of the brain, but recent PET (positron emission tomography) scans, which show how much energy the brain uses, have come up with some surprising results. Not only do clever people seem to use less energy when solving problems than those of average intelligence, but male and female brains seem to tackle problems in a different way and using different areas. Such scans may eventually resolve the debate over whether there is one central quality to intelligence or several independent ones.

It takes a leap of imagination to create a work of art from unlikely materials. The bull (**left**) was made from recycled junk found on cattle ranches in New Mexico by artist Holly Hughes.

Just how or why some people are able to come up with genuinely original ideas is still not fully understood, but it seems to be linked to personality. Some researchers associate it with psychoticism while others connect it with manic-depression, or bipolar disorder.

Creativity does not feature in IQ tests because it is not easy to measure – a person's ability to create something new is hard to assess objectively in the same way as other forms of intelligence.

As far as the location of creativity in the brain is concerned, the right side seems to be most concerned with producing new images or connections, while the left is essential for evaluating and shaping them.

IDEAS ABOUT INTELLIGENCE

Linguistic intelligence is the use of language in fundamental aspects such as writing, reading and understanding speech. This is best exemplified by the creative use of language required, for instance, in writing poetry.

Personal intelligence has two forms: interpersonal intelligence – used in interactions with others; and intrapersonal intelligence – concerned with understanding and knowing yourself.

Logical-mathematical intelligence is of the type used in numerical calculation, arithmetic and logic. It involves the ability to manipulate quantities and is separate from the abilities needed for language and music. Work such as Einstein's requires this type of intelligence.

Bodily kinaesthetic intelligence is the ability to use the body expressively and skilfully, especially in fine motor-control of the hands. It is used in sport, dancing and simple everyday movements involving dexterity. Someone with a high score in this type of intelligence might perform delicate surgery well.

Musical intelligence is used in appreciating, performing and composing music. Composing has a logic of its own quite distinct from that of language. It can be one of the most striking early talents – the composer Mozart was a child prodigy.

Spatial intelligence involves being able to perceive the shape and relative position of objects. It is evident in the ability to design and build things, from tables to planes. It also involves being able to find your way around and is important in art.

The IQ (intelligence quotient) test is the best-known attempt to rate intelligence on a single scale, although it does not deal with some forms of intelligence. Psychologist Howard Gardner broadened out the idea of IQ with his multiple component theory, in which there are a number of types of intelligence (**right**). Some argue, however, that including specialized abilities like music and mathematics means his model does not apply to everyone.

Solving chess problems involves the use of spatial intelligence, logical mathematical intelligence and phenomenal feats of memory.

First thoughts

Babies' brains are very flexible and they develop rapidly after birth in response to the world around them.

A new baby is virtually helpless but it has a number of reflexes to help it feed and bond with its mother. For instance, the cries it makes when distressed – which usually bring a rapid response – are just one method it can use to ensure that it survives. And recent research has shown that even prior to birth the foetus has a number of capabilities. It does regular physical exercise in the womb, at first jerkily, but later with more coordination; it also shows disgust if the amniotic fluid that surrounds it is made bitter. Later, the foetus will be startled in response to a sudden noise and will blink when a bright light is shone on its mother's stomach. If it regularly hears a piece of music while in the womb, it recognizes and responds to it for several weeks after birth.

Some things can interfere with normal, healthy development. If a mother contracts certain diseases or takes drugs, the baby can be brain damaged, and there is evidence that intense and unhappy emotional states in the mother can also have an effect.

BORN DAMAGED

The paediatrician looking after a newborn boy noticed that the infant was small for his age, with an unusually flattened face. As the boy grew up, he became hyperactive and also showed signs of being mentally retarded.

His symptoms were due to foetal alcohol syndrome, the third most common form of birth abnormality after Down's syndrome and neural tube defects such as spina bifida. The boy's mother was an alcoholic and since mother and baby share a blood supply, drugs or deficiencies in the mother's blood can harm the baby.

The foetal brain is particularly vulnerable between 8 and 16 weeks after conception, when the brain is growing at a remarkable rate. One estimate is that 250,000 neurons are being generated every minute.

Other threats to a foetus are rubella (German measles) in the first two months of pregnancy, which can cause the baby to be retarded or deformed, and spina bifida, linked to low levels of folic acid in the diet. And there is some evidence of a link between flu during pregnancy and a slightly increased risk of schizophrenia.

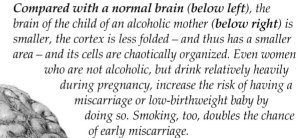

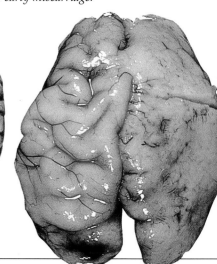

Compared with a normal brain (below left), the brain of the child of an alcoholic mother (below right) is smaller, the cortex is less folded – and thus has a smaller area – and its cells are chaotically organized. Even women who are not alcoholic, but drink relatively heavily during pregnancy, increase the risk of having a miscarriage or low-birthweight baby by doing so. Smoking, too, doubles the chance of early miscarriage.

Two inborn reflexes help a newborn to feed. The rooting reflex makes the baby turn its head toward a touch on one side of the mouth to find something to suck. It immediately begins to suck vigorously – the sucking reflex.

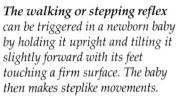

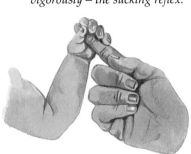

The grasp reflex is instigated by pressure in a baby's palm. For a few days after birth the grasp is so strong that a baby can support its weight by holding its mother's finger. The reflex fades by four months, but may once have ensured survival.

The walking or stepping reflex can be triggered in a newborn baby by holding it upright and tilting it slightly forward with its feet touching a firm surface. The baby then makes steplike movements.

This reflex tends to disappear by the age of two months. It is thought to become impossible as the baby gains weight because its legs become too heavy for the muscles to make them move.

True walking, usually preceded by a set order of actions including crawling and supported standing, does not happen until about 12 months, although the age does vary considerably.

For reasons of survival, a newborn baby is a totally egocentric creature. The infant's world is small and revolves around satisfying its immediate needs for food, warmth and care through its mother, since it is unable to look after itself. Thus the baby can focus on objects 25 cm (10 inches) away, about the distance to its mother's eyes when it is feeding. And it seems programmed to respond to faces. Given a number of coloured discs to look at, a baby will spend the longest time staring at the one with a crude representation of a human face on it. Within a few hours of birth a baby can follow a moving light and can recognize sounds that it heard while in the womb.

It is not known for certain what a baby experiences of the world around it. Some say the world must seem a confusing place after the peaceful darkness of the womb. Others believe that perception is probably quite coherent, but still simple and less selective. And as a baby does not have many memories about the objects it experiences, there is a theory that consciousness expands slowly as the child gains more memories and thus can make more associations about the objects it perceives. On a physical level, although the brain is rich in connections between the cells, these have not yet been organized by experience.

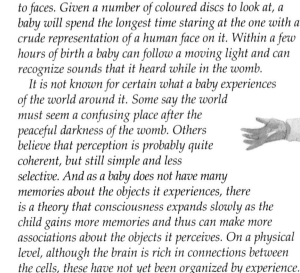

The Moro reflex can be seen when a baby is held flat on its back. If its head is allowed to drop slightly but suddenly, the baby will fling both of its arms out with the hands open and then gradually bend the arms back toward the body. This reflex usually fades by about four months. The Moro, stepping, rooting, sucking and grasp reflexes are only a few of the so-called primitive reflexes that are present at or shortly after birth and that have faded by six months or so.

Learning to be human

The process of development is not confined to physical and intellectual growth, we develop emotionally too.

A baby's relationship with its primary carer (usually the mother) has to provide the child with what it wants – food, warmth and devoted care – so that it can develop properly physically and mentally. To achieve this it is vital for the infant to establish a relationship with an adult that is close and rewarding. This usually happens right after birth, and some believe that close skin contact during these hours is vital for mother and baby to bond. Such a relationship seems so important that babies who receive no one-to-one bonding and love – such as those in some orphanages – have been known to die, although their physical needs were taken care of. From an evolutionary perspective the apparent instinct for closeness has developed because it is vital to a baby's survival.

Babies are thus emotional creatures. Many mothers believe they can detect in their expressions a wide range of emotions, including interest, surprise, joy, anger and fear, within a month or so of birth. By three months other observers can reliably see them, too, and at that age babies can recognize emotions in other people, preferring a familiar or happy face to one showing another expression, for instance. By 18 months infants can even fake emotions – acting peeved or hurt – to get what they want.

The development of interpersonal relationships starts from the earliest time and by childhood is fairly far advanced. The chances are that many of a person's character traits will also be established by this time. Play with other children seems to be important in helping children learn something of the social skills and emotional insights that are such an essential part of being human.

CUT OFF FROM THE WORLD

Children suffering from autism – a disorder that affects 4 in 10,000 – develop their motor skills very slowly but, more distressingly for their carers, they seem unable to show any affection or to form emotional connections. Instead they focus all their attention on objects and sometimes develop skills such as drawing to a high level. This image was created by an extraordinarily gifted child, Stephen Wiltshire, who has been diagnosed as autistic. Most autistic children hardly recognize parents or playmates and do not respond to them. They never look people in the eye and either ignore questions or reply by repeating them. However, they dislike change and may throw temper tantrums if the smallest detail of a daily routine alters. Until 20 years ago mothers were blamed for creating autistic children by a cold and detached style of upbringing. But now it is accepted that the disorder is almost entirely genetic.

IMPRINTED ATTACHMENT

The fact that baby chicks will follow almost any moving object – another chicken, a duck or a human – was first noted over 120 years ago, but it was animal behaviourist Konrad Lorenz who termed this instinct imprinting. Experimenting with baby geese he showed that imprinting is instinctive, that it happens during a critical period after hatching and that it cannot be reversed. In the wild it is useful because the object the chick is most likely to follow is its mother. The strong bond developed between a human baby and parent is also thought to be instinctive and is obviously useful for the baby's wellbeing.

After establishing a strong early connection, babies often go through a phase, at around eight or nine months, of being frightened by strangers and fearful of separation – they object much more when left by their mother. This also seems like a useful adaptation for our hunter-gatherer ancestors to have developed in a world where sudden change or the unknown often meant danger – especially for a helpless infant. By 14 months, however, infants are eagerly exploring their world, occasionally coming back to a secure base for reassurance. The early years, when an infant is learning so rapidly, are just as important to its emotional wellbeing as they are in other areas of mental life, because patterns of emotional attachment formed in childhood can be repeated in adult relations.

Babies who enjoy a relationship involving high levels of love and care, especially physical contact and responsiveness to their needs, are more likely to develop a close attachment to their parents. A secure early attachment also tends to result in warm and loving adult relationships. Behaviour benefits, too, so while such children enjoy being close to their parents, they are also happy to explore.

Children whose parents are withdrawn or distant, however, tend to stay detached from their parents and later keep partners at arm's length, too. Most complex are those whose parents alternated intense closeness with hostility or rejection. They become both desperate for a close relationship – thus they often make a great initial show of romance – and terrified the moment it seems likely.

Milestones of the mind

Slowly but surely the human mind develops until it is capable of phenomenal feats of logic and reasoning.

Because humans are such social creatures, we need a childhood that is about twice the length of that of any other animal if we are to absorb all the complex physical, social and language skills we need to get on as adults. This long-drawn-out learning process can be affected by many different factors, from genetic make-up to the amount of love and stimulation we receive. But whatever happens, we are all pre-programmed to go through several definite stages.

For instance, we have milk teeth before adult ones, we crawl before we can walk, we understand stories before we can follow abstract ideas. The first big mental, as opposed to physical, leap comes at around 10 months, when babies first recognize themselves in a mirror. This is something that only a few species can do and it marks the beginning of a sense of self-awareness, which later gives rise to a host of peculiarly human questions such as "Who am I?" and "Where have I come from?"

By the age of 18 months we are beginning to use symbols and by two we have laid the ground for a number of crucial adult skills. We have arrived at half our adult height – if we continued to grow at the same rate we would be about 3.5 m (11½ feet) tall by the time we reached adolescence. We have a vocabulary of about 200 words, which we use in two-word combinations. We no longer think of ourselves as the centre of the world, we ask questions, we understand stories, we set goals and achieve them, we pretend and we have formed attachments to people.

The next major milestone of change comes at puberty when we have another growth spurt. This one can be accompanied by emotional problems since it is combined with maximum self-consciousness, and growth is often uneven, leading to feelings of being gangly and awkward just at a time when attractiveness seems so important. Hormones set off the development of secondary sexual characteristics and we become better at abstract thought and more responsive to ideals. And, as if the physical upheavals were not enough, we start to question everything.

Our mental abilities are thought to develop in definite stages, a theory most famously put forward this century by the Swiss psychologist Jean Piaget. He termed the first of these – from birth to about two – the sensorimotor period, when the child's senses (sensori) and muscles (motor) develop. Between two and seven is the preoperational stage, when a child uses symbols but cannot yet manage abstract ideas. A key development of this stage is the realization that objects continue to exist, even if they are out of sight. From 7 to 11 a child is deemed to be concrete operational, capable of logical thought, but only when it is tied to concrete reality. The formal operational stage, from 11 up, is when a child learns to make up classifications and build hypotheses.

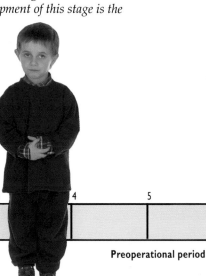

| 1 | 2 | 3 | 4 | 5 | 6 | 7 |

Sensorimotor period

Preoperational period

A famous experiment was used by Piaget to show that preoperational children could not see that the amount of liquid in a tall thin container was the same as in a short fat one. Since then some have questioned his findings, but certainly by seven children can realize that superficial changes to an object do not change its basic qualities.

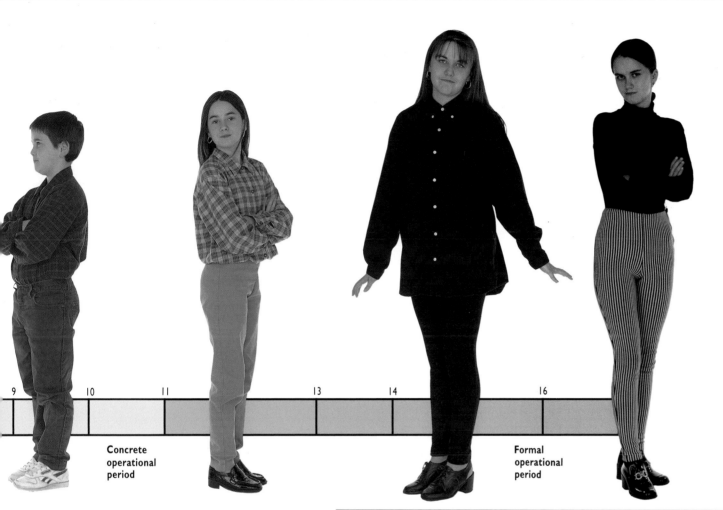

9 | 10 | 11 | 13 | 14 | 16

Concrete operational period

Formal operational period

Between birth and two we develop from being able to recognize a face and remember tunes that we have heard in the womb to being able to walk, talk and use a limited number of symbols.

By seven we are less dominated by the senses and are developing the ability to classify things, for example into groups such as animals, red objects, things made of wood and the like. At this age we start to reason abstractly, have a grip on numbers, weights and hierarchies, and are more ordered and focused.

Between about 7 and 11 we learn the basis of adult thought and reasoning, although we are limited to the concrete – reality as we have experienced it personally.

From 11 up we make the jump from concrete thought to formal operational, or abstract, thought and deduction. We are now improving our skills in logic, making up theories about the world and trying out alternatives – a process that continues throughout adulthood.

CHILDHOOD GENIUS

Infant prodigy is an enduring subject of fascination, with some parents hoping to be able to push their children forward and give them a better start in life. There are many examples, from children who go to university at the age of only 11 or 12 to icons of the past like Wolfgang Amadeus Mozart (1756–1791), who could play the harpsichord when he was just three. A year later he was playing short pieces and at five he was composing – an age at which any other parent would be proud if a child could pick out the tune of a nursery song. By the time he was 10 he had played at court in Munich and had been on a tour, performing at numerous cities in Europe. But can such genius be created? Probably not, nor can it be properly measured. The best a parent can do is to foster such gifts as their children display in whichever way seems appropriate to the child.

Male and female

Is there more to the difference between men and women than obvious physical characteristics and capabilities?

On average, men are about 7 percent taller, 30 percent stronger and 20 percent heavier than women; they also have more body and facial hair. Females have more developed breasts and tend to lay down fat on their thighs and buttocks, while weight in men gravitates to the stomach. Men are, generally, bigger and stronger, but women are designed for childbearing.

Psychological differences are less clearly defined and more controversial. Men are perceived as more aggressive and competitive and less nurturing and emotionally responsive. And some researchers suggest that moral reasoning develops differently in the two sexes, with men tending to focus on abstract, rational principles such as justice and rights, while women see morality more as a matter of caring and compassion.

In terms of abilities, women on average talk more fluently, while men are better at tasks involving spatial ability, such as reading maps. And there is some evidence that male and female brains work differently. One recent study found that when asked to judge whether strings of nonsense words rhymed, men used only the left side of the brain, while more than half the women used both sides together. In another study, when people were asked to think of nothing, men's brains were active in the more primitive part that controls physical activity, while women's were active in the regions that deal with symbols and emotions.

DEFAULTING TO THE BASIC BLUEPRINT

A girl who reached the usual age of puberty, but still had "infantile" external genitalia and was short for her age, complained to her doctor that she was not developing properly. The doctor ordered tests, which revealed that she had only one sex chromosome – an X – a condition known as Turner's Syndrome.

At fertilization each parent supplies one half of each of the 23 pairs of chromosomes. One of these pairs decides sex: two Xs give a girl; an X and a Y make a boy. A Y chromosome, which can come only from the father, imposes maleness on the basic human blueprint, which is female. The girl was given hormone treatment and developed secondary sexual characteristics and monthly vaginal bleeding, but was infertile since two Xs are needed for normal ovary development.

There are great differences between male and female in many species. The male golden toad Bufo periglenes, *found in Costa Rica, is brightly coloured and, at 2.5 cm (1 inch) long, much smaller than the mottled female. He clings to the female's back to fertilize her eggs as she lays them. There can also be differences in the roles of male and female. For instance, the male lion guards his pride against other males while the females hunt, and the male emperor penguin incubates the egg, but the female returns to feed the chick.*

The testosterone surge a male foetus receives in the womb prepares it for later male development. There is also a rise in levels of the hormone in the first year after birth and a huge one at puberty (between 10 and 16), which produces the secondary sexual characteristics of mature genitalia, deeper voice and a beard, as well as a growth spurt. After a peak in the early 20s, levels of testosterone fall slowly throughout a man's life.

Female foetuses develop ovaries, which secrete the hormone oestrogen, by eight to nine weeks. An increase in oestrogen levels at puberty (around age 12) produces a growth spurt, breasts and mature genitals. This overall rise is subject to fluctuation during a woman's menstrual cycle. And after the menopause in middle age oestrogen production diminishes rapidly until almost none is secreted.

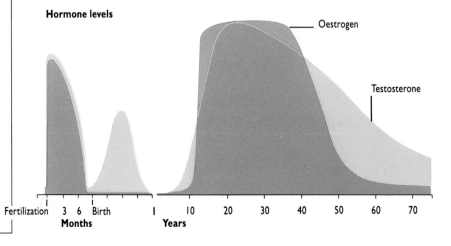

Hormone levels

Oestrogen

Testosterone

Fertilization | 3 | 6 | Birth | 10 | 20 | 30 | 40 | 50 | 60 | 70
Months — **Years**

The sex of a child *is genetically determined, but where, if at all, do children learn to be different and to conform to the behaviour that is deemed to be typical of their sex? Some theories state that this learning comes from the culture and from the expectations that exist within it. Others argue that the learning of roles and differences in behaviour come from identifying with an adult of the same sex. Still others suggest that the way children and then adults behave is genetically predetermined: the various genes and all that they are responsible for in terms of hormones and other basic differences cause not only the physical differences but also any psychological ones. It seems that children have some predetermined differences but that they also probably learn from the society around them and attempt to live up to its expectations, being rewarded when they do and discouraged when they do not.*

Whatever the case, traditionally, the ways girls and boys are treated start to differ almost immediately. In some cultures this means a boy is dressed in blue, a girl in pink. And although parents may try to avoid sexual stereotyping, boys often choose to play with a toy car rather than a doll, and girls may prefer pretty feminine dresses to jeans. As they grow older, boys will often, though not invariably, choose competitive games while girls cooperate more in their play.

Thinking together

Our ability to think and share our thoughts and ideas has played a vital part in the human success story.

Much of psychology is involved with the study of individuals – how they develop, what their personality is like, how their brain works. But it is essential not to lose sight of the fact that we are intensely social animals who can exist only in a complex web of relationships. Society strongly shapes our behaviour and gives meaning to our lives. Indeed, compared to other animals, human children need a firm social structure over a long period before they become adult.

Among early humans the value of improved social skills was probably a powerful factor driving the development of both self-consciousness and language. Groups in which people could communicate often complex ideas – only truly possible with speech – would have been at a great advantage. The success of *Homo erectus*'s migration out of Africa about a million years ago, for instance, can be attributed to improved group organization, and the Neanderthals' failure to compete with modern humans some 950,000 years later is thought to be linked to their failure to form large groups.

Modern humans are born with a powerful urge to communicate with others: a newborn baby not only responds very soon to faces but also tries to gain a response. People will do almost anything to win approval and acceptance by the group, and many psychological experiments have shown that they can be made to alter their behaviour drastically because

The pyramids of ancient Egypt are seen by many to epitomize the success of group effort. In the days before mechanization, these vast monuments to a culture could have been achieved only by the intense and dedicated labour of thousands of people working together.

Something of the same group effort is shown today in industry where, for instance, teams of workers, each one contributing his or her own particular skill, produce the thousands of motor cars that roll off the production line every year.

An earthquake such as the one that hit Mexico City in 1985 is just one of the numerous situations in which it is essential for us to work together if we are to make any major impact. People facing such a disaster will rapidly identify with those who have experienced the greatest suffering and will become selfless members of a group toiling to rescue victims at considerable risk to their own lives.

In such a situation, it will soon become necessary for a leader of some sort to emerge, and experiments have shown that the army model of an autocratic leader and obedient followers may prove the most effective, since it results in the highest level of productivity by the group. Under other conditions a more democratic approach may prove valuable, encouraging people to cooperate and share responsibility rather than blindly obeying orders or rules.

they believe that a certain type of behaviour is expected by the group. Indeed, experiments have shown that students are prepared to administer quite severe electric shocks to their fellows if sufficient pressure is exerted upon them to obey the mores of the social group and so to "belong".

One of the strongest sanctions that can be applied to anyone is expulsion from the group. Once it meant almost certain death; today complete loners are more likely to have severe mental problems, while those who do have lasting and close connections with others tend to be healthier and happier. An extreme example of the human need for togetherness can be seen in a common attitude to times of war, which are often fondly remembered – despite the hardship and suffering they entail – because of the sense of connection they create. And part of the enduring appeal of soap operas on radio and television is that they provide the illusion of being involved with a constant and familiar community.

In contrast with this is the powerful image of the lone genius in the arts or sciences, but even the most gifted base their work on what has gone before – there could, for instance, have been no Einstein without Newton. This forms the basis for our culture, for we are connected not only to the minds of those around us but to the minds of the past as well.

ANIMAL SOCIETIES

Like humans, animals gain enormous benefits from living in societies. They can gang up on predators such as eagles or lions or they can hunt in packs like wolves and bring down prey they could never manage to kill working alone. Some of the most complex societies are found among insects such as termites, ants and bees. These societies, with their single leader or queen and rigid castes, including soldiers, drones and workers, are sometimes held up as a mirror of certain human societies. The crucial difference, however, is in their lack of flexibility.

While humans do create rigid, centralized totalitarian societies, we can also form liberal, democratic and open ones. Individual ants or bees are not at all like the individuals in a human society: the ants have no choice but to follow the dictates of their genes as to how they should behave. We, however, can change, and if enough people want a different type of society they can sometimes create it by concerted action – as with the fall of the Berlin Wall in 1989 – for the power and influence of the group will is immense.

The success of social insects such as ants is clearly evident in the Amazon basin where, although they make up only 3 percent of the insect species, they form 80 percent of the total number of insects found.

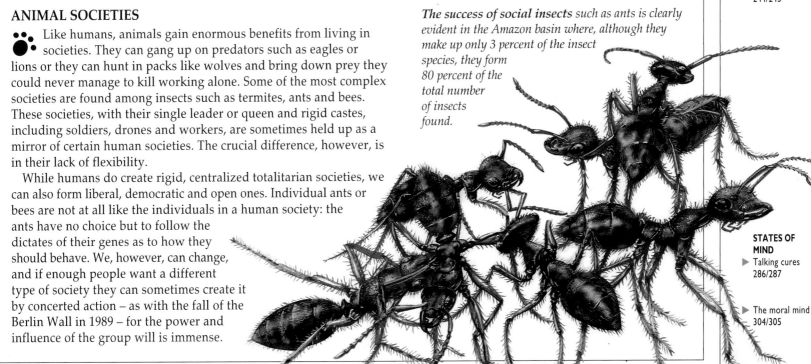

States of Mind

Consciousness is the most amazing of the brain's qualities. Without it we would be little more than automatons, merely going through the motions of life. We would, for example, have no appreciation of such aspects of existence as the subtle interplay of our own emotions and the richness of relationships with other people, each with a unique personality. Without it we would not be able to question what we do and why we do it, or to ponder moral questions and debate issues such as the existence of free will.

But the price for possessing such a remarkable mind can be high. We all experience sadness and anxiety at times but some people become overwhelmed by abnormal states of mind and fall ill. Help is at hand, though, and most recover to savour again the experiences self-awareness brings.

Left (clockwise from top): a tiny mind; object of fear; blot on the personality; a lemon squeezer made into a desirable object; a slice of sleep.
***This page (top):** if birds were neurotransmitters; (**left**) food, drink and depression.*

Emotional states

Whether you are aware of it or not, emotions suffuse everything you do, colouring every thought and action.

Happiness, rage, love and hate are just some of the feelings that make us human and not machines. They seem illogical, but may be vital to our survival as a species. Love, for instance, may have evolved to ensure we not only find a partner but stay with him or her and make sure our offspring survive. Anger and fear may help us fight off or run away from danger.

People from different cultures label emotions in different ways, but happiness, fear, anger, sadness and disgust are universal and are linked with facial or vocal expressions that are understood worldwide. Other emotions such as surprise or guilt – and the expressions associated with them – vary between cultures.

For each emotion, there are three elements. The first is how we feel subjectively – happy or sad, for example. The second is change in the body over which we have no conscious control, such as butterflies in the stomach or goose pimples. The third is the behaviour we associate with a particular emotion – running away, laughing and so on.

Different theories about emotion emphasize a different one of these elements. One view is that the feeling causes the change in the body. Another is that changes in the body create the feeling: when you tremble, the trembling makes you feel

A lovers' kiss is the perfect expression of that most discussed of all emotions – love. Some psychologists say loving is just a more intense version of liking. Others say loving and liking are very different. Freud saw love as the socially acceptable face of the libido, or sex drive. It has also been suggested that there are two kinds of love: one which stems from our need for security and inevitably leads to disappointment because it depends on the other person to satisfy it; the other which is more settled, with both partners secure and balanced. Other theories of love centre on the difference between brief all-absorbing passions and long-term affection, or on the varying balance between intimacy, passion and commitment.

CURBING HIS PASSION

A few years ago a man in California was arrested lying on a pavement trying to make love to it. When asked why, he said he found pavements irresistible. Cases like this are rare, but animal experiments in the 1930s showed how brain damage may alter emotional responses. Damage to the cortex, for instance, produced "sham rage" in cats, in which the cats showed all the signs of rage, yet purred and allowed themselves to be stroked. Damage to the amygdala of monkeys made them calm, but their sex drive became so active that they mounted anything they could and put all kinds of objects in their mouth, a change known as Klüver-Bucy syndrome after the scientist who carried out the experiment.

Attempts to connect particular emotions, such as aggression, completely to particular parts of the brain have failed, but the amygdala does seem to play an important role in emotions, linking the physical signs of emotion triggered by the hypothalamus with the mental experience of emotion in the cortex.

scared; when you smile, the smile makes you happy. Others think the feeling and the bodily changes are independent, since people who are paralysed feel emotions just as intensely as anyone else. They believe an emotion starts when the stimulus that triggers it is processed in the brain by the thalamus. The thalamus then sends signals simultaneously to the cortex, where we become aware of the emotion, and to the hypothalamus, which sets off changes in the body via the nervous system and hormones. Another theory, that of cognitive labelling, suggests that the body becomes aroused before we are aware of a particular emotion – but the emotion we feel depends on what we think aroused us. In one experiment, people injected with adrenaline laughed more at a comedy than those without the injection. In another, men on a dangerous rope bridge found a woman interviewer far more sexy than did men on a solid wooden bridge.

THE SPECTRUM OF EMOTIONS

Many psychologists believe emotion is bound up in a continuous loop of feedback between bodily changes and the feeling we are aware of. One way of looking at it may be as an interplay between arousal, drive and association. Our bodies and brains become aroused by certain stimuli – a dangerous situation or the sight of an attractive person, for instance. This arousal may also be influenced by the second of these elements – basic physiological drives, such as the need for food, sex or self-preservation. The third element is the whole range of mental associations that flood into the mind.

In the image below a white rose is illuminated with red, blue and green light. Like the subtle interplay of the lights on the rose, the shifting balance between the three elements of association, drive and arousal determines the nature of the emotion we feel and the way our bodies respond.

Associations – essentially memories or ideas that spring to mind – can move through the mind at an extraordinary rate adding texture and context to emotion. They can also alter arousal levels. Associations linked with seeing the rose may involve memories of the last time a rose played a part in a person's life. This could be a pleasant association, such as giving or receiving roses as a love token, or an unpleasant one, such as being pricked by a thorn on the stem. For some the association may be sinister since in some cultures white flowers are unlucky and can be reminders of funerals or death.

Arousal level affects emotional response. In a sense, it acts like a volume control of emotion. If arousal level is high to begin with, the response, to the rose in this case, is strong; if arousal is low the response is weak. Seeing the rose is unlikely to change your arousal level on its own unless someone attacks you with it, but it may alter it by evoking an association.

Drives have a constant input into emotional state. If you are hungry or thirsty, for example, the way you feel about anything is affected by whether it is likely to satisfy the drive or not. By itself, a rose in a vase will probably not have much impact on drives since it cannot ordinarily be eaten, drunk or made love to. However, if an association of love comes to mind, the appropriate drive may well swing into action.

The unique self

Each of us has a different personality – our individual pattern of emotion, behaviour and perception.

If you say "I am not myself today", everyone knows what you mean. But it is an odd statement. Who are you then? A string of everyday words – such as kind, happy, open – might seem to describe your "personality", but even psychologists have difficulty in getting to grips with the concept. Although you might think that you know what type of personality you are and that your behaviour is consistent with those traits, in some situations you may do something "out of character".

There are many theories as to what constitutes personality, how and whether it can be measured and how it develops. Some see it as a result of learning throughout life; others relate it to the environment, society or family; still others believe it is genetic or developed in early childhood. And personality is not set in stone – people can change, either as a result of altered circumstances or because they have made a conscious effort to change, perhaps with the help of psychotherapy.

There are also recognized personality disorders. One survey has concluded that nearly one in ten of the adult population in the United States may suffer from a disorder in which that person has traits that affect functioning – socially or at work – or cause mental anguish. A few people are even diagnosed as having multiple personality disorder, in which they have two or more distinct personalities between which they switch.

Extroverts and introverts – sociable partygoers and withdrawn stay-at-homes – are two of the broad categories of personality. Extroverts need excitement and stimulation, so they tend to be outgoing, enjoy driving fast and like working with people. Introverts already have a busy inner life so they need little additional excitement.

FOOLING ALL OF THE PEOPLE ALL OF THE TIME?

Astrology is one ancient system for describing personality which many people find to be accurate. However, this so-called accuracy may in fact be because we are not particularly adept at identifying our own personality, not because it is governed by our date of birth and the relative positions of the planets in the heavens at the time.

A classic psychology experiment involves giving a personality assessment to each member of a class and asking them to say how accurate it is. About 90 percent report that it is either a good or excellent reflection of their qualities. At the end of the test the experimenter reveals that everyone received exactly the same profile.

The key to the assessment is that it is made up of carefully constructed sentences, known as Barnum statements, which almost everyone agrees with, but – and this is the clever part – most do not believe also apply to everyone else. An example is: "Normally you are quite outgoing but underneath you are more shy". So the reason that so many people accept astrological descriptions of personality as correct is that most consist almost entirely of Barnum statements.

DESCRIBING PERSONALITY

There are 18,000 adjectives in the English language to describe people and many of them fall into clusters. So someone who is kind is often also thought of as helpful, friendly and thoughtful. Since the time of the Greeks we have assumed that these clusters point to some underlying aspect of personality. But how many clusters are necessary to describe the basic personality types?

In the second century the Graeco-Roman physician Galen outlined three clusters: the cognitive, covering the intellect; the conative, referring to intuition; and the affective, for the emotions.

A medieval system, based on one put forward in the fifth century B.C. by the Greek physician Hippocrates, had the four humours. They were fluids in the body, the proportions of which gave rise to different personalities. Blood produced a happy and lively – or sanguine – character; phlegm was linked with calm, careful, "phlegmatic" people; black bile caused melancholy and pessimism; yellow bile led to a "choleric" nature involving hastiness and excitability.

Since then, despite many statistics and extensive personality testing, we have not progressed very far. Psychologists today talk about personality dimensions or traits. One model, now rarely used, says that 100 distinct traits need to be considered to describe personality adequately; Raymond Cattell, a leading personality theorist, developed a system using 16. At the other extreme is Hans Eysenck who believes that only three basic dimensions are necessary – extroversion–introversion, psychoticism and neuroticism–stability.

Today the most generally accepted trait theory is that of the "big five", or the "five robust factors", which works with the five personality traits that recur most often in studies and theories. The most commonly occurring five characteristics can be summed up in the acronym OCEAN: Openness, covering such aspects as intelligence, the imagination and aesthetic sensitivity; Conscientiousness; Extroversion; Agreeableness, meaning someone who is good natured, friendly and easy to get on with; and Neuroticism.

The Rorschach inkblot test is one of the better known methods used for assessing personality but it is not often applied outside of psychoanalytic circles. It was devised in 1921 by Hermann Rorschach and consists of 10 symmetrical inkblot designs, each one printed on a separate card. Five of the designs are in black, white and shades of grey, five are in colour and all are non-representational.

When subjects describe what they see, aspects of their psychological make-up can be revealed. Most people will project themselves into the designs, each person interpreting an image in a different way – and thus helping the psychologist to establish elements of that person's personality or a particular mental condition.

For instance, with the coloured blots, such as this one – the only one to be fully coloured – the subject's response to the colours is believed to reflect his or her emotional life. And it is not merely detailed descriptions of colour that are important, failure to mention the colours at all can be equally significant.

Being aware

The fact that you know you are reading this illustrates the brain's most amazing quality, self-awareness.

We all know what consciousness is like from the inside. It is where we think and feel and remember. But scientists must analyse it from the outside, and so come up against the problem that there is no way to measure it, since it exists in a private world. Researchers studying such subjects as the workings of muscles can all look at the same thing, but consciousness belongs to individuals and the only person who can know what your consciousness is like is you.

Nonetheless, consciousness is obviously dependent on the brain. Drugs affect it, some even sending it crazy or knocking it out altogether. The key question is whether it can be explained entirely by the firing of brain cells. Some researchers believe that it can and that once enough information is gathered it will be possible to say that activity in a particular combination of neurons means that the subject is having a particular sensation or thought. Others claim that the very nature of consciousness means that it cannot be explained in such terms. They focus on the idea that a process of natural selection takes place among brain cells from the moment of conception, driven by the different experiences that each individual has. The result is that the precise structure of each person's brain is unique. Another argument is that some brain processes take place at a quantum level, which means they cannot be described only in terms of chemical and electrical processes.

At the heart of the debate is the puzzle of how matter – molecules – and electricity can produce something that is aware of itself. We do not just hear and respond, as a machine does, we hear and know what it is like to hear. Some claim this awareness is just a by-product of the brain's complexity – brains produce minds like clouds produce rain – others say there is a gap there that science as we know it now cannot bridge.

Dressing up is one of the ways children have of playing with newly emerging ideas of self-consciousness. To pretend you are someone else, you must first of all be aware of yourself as a separate individual. Only a few monkey species show signs of being able to do this, but by the age of four children seem able to grasp that other people have a conscious internal world as well.

Consciousness is remarkably difficult to define. Some describe it as self-awareness – that quality that differentiates humans from animals. Others use the term "soul"; still others refer to it as the mind. Are these terms all interchangeable, depending on a person's point of view, or do they refer to different aspects of the mind? A simple distinction is that a soul is something enduring, believed by many to last beyond the life span of the body or physical brain. The mind is limited by the duration of a particular life. Consciousness is what we have during waking hours, while awareness is our grasp of the here and now.

 **Soul** is for ever   **Mind** is for life   **Consciousness** is for today   **Awareness** is for now

DEAD OR ALIVE?

A young man who suffered severe head injuries in a car crash was in a coma – a state where the brain does not work at all – for some weeks. He then regained some functions: his sleep–wake cycle was restored and he was able to regulate his temperature, breathe and maintain his heartbeat and to swallow and digest food. He also withdrew from pain, could blink and his pupils contracted if a light was shone on them. He could also make some noises, such as grunts and moans, and occasionally seemed to smile. But none of his behaviour – apart from the reflexes – bore any relation to what was going on in the outside world.

He was eventually diagnosed as being in a persistent vegetative state (PVS), a condition in which, despite signs to the contrary, patients are not aware, not conscious and are said to have suffered cognitive death (cessation of thinking). His brain damage was in the higher regions, the cortex, while his signs of life were generated by the lower parts of the brain where most autoregulatory and reflex responses are dealt with. After a few years with no signs of improvement his family took medical advice and requested that feeding be withdrawn and the man died.

Just as the flavour of a stew is more than the sum of its ingredients, our mental image of an object is a composite structure that emerges when various different elements come together. The vision centres in our brain break down what we see into these elements – straight or curved lines, edges and so on – and then combine them to produce faces, trees, chairs. But we cannot understand an object by learning more and more about curves and lines.

Some neuroscientists believe that consciousness emerges as different groups of neurons – dealing with vision, memory or touch – combine and recombine. A sudden sensory input – a car braking hard, for instance – can trigger a completely different combination of neuron groups from the conscious state produced by reading or listening to music.

In this view, just as there is no single centre for vision or language, there is no seat of consciousness, no internal theatre where consciousness is a permanent spectator. Instead, what we experience as consciousness is this constant procession of waxing and waning neuronal groupings.

The resting mind?

During sleep, a time when body and mind are restored, the brain regularly switches on and dreams.

When we fall asleep we go through four stages of deepening sleep measured by changes to EEG (electroencephalogram) recordings which measure the brain's electrical activity. Moving through the stages, the brain waves get progressively slower. This lasts about 80 minutes and we then return to a state in which the brain waves look like those produced when we are awake. This state is known as REM (rapid eye movement) sleep and this is the time when we dream. These eye movements – in which the eyes flick back and forth – are the only visible sign of a number of dramatic changes. Brain cells at the top of the spine send out signals that prevent any movement so we are virtually paralysed, except for our eyeballs. Also activated is our balance system in the ear and the visual part of the cortex. After about 5 to 15 minutes of REM sleep we sink back down into deep sleep once more. We go through this cycle four or five times a night.

Throughout history, people have asked why we dream and what dreams mean. Until about 100 years ago their source was thought to be partly supernatural, perhaps involving messages from the gods. Then pioneer psychoanalyst Sigmund Freud replaced the supernatural with our own unconscious when he stated that dreams are the expression of unfulfilled desires, the more shocking of which pass through an internal "censor" that replaces them with symbols which psychoanalysts attempt to interpret. Another theory is that we dream in order to sort out memories, either adding them to the memory store or throwing away unwanted information.

More recently it has been suggested that dreams are attempts by the brain to make sense of stray thoughts. During the day our cortex interprets the information that floods in from the senses to create a picture of the world. At night, with nothing coming in, it tries to interpret the weak internal scraps of thought and link them with stored memories.

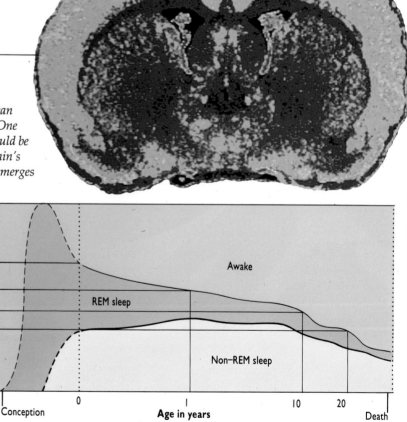

Awake

At 26 weeks a foetus is in REM (rapid eye movement) sleep 24 hours a day. In adults this is the stage at which we dream. What can a child in the womb be dreaming about? One theory is that REM sleep at this time could be nature's way of giving some of the brain's systems a trial run before the baby emerges into the real world.

The proportion of time we spend awake, asleep or dreaming (REM sleep) changes during our lives **(right)**. By the time a baby is born it still spends 16 hours a day asleep, half of those in REM sleep. As we get older we sleep less, are awake more and spend less time dreaming.

Hours

24
16
12
10
8
0

Awake

REM sleep

Non–REM sleep

−1   0   1   10   20

Conception   **Age in years**   Death

THE IMPORTANCE OF SLEEP AND DREAMS

In 1959 New York disc jockey Peter Tripp stayed awake for 200 hours to raise money for charity. He was supported by doctors and psychologists who tested his mental functioning. But his prolonged period of sleep deprivation had unexpected and unpleasant results. After about 50 hours he started having mild hallucinations, seeing cobwebs in his shoes when there were none there and thinking that specks of dirt were bugs; by 100 hours he found simple mental tests unbearable.

At 110 hours he became delirious and saw a doctor's tweed suit as a tangle of furry worms; at 120 he needed a stimulant to keep him awake. After 150 hours he was disoriented, not knowing who or where he was and he became paranoid – he backed against a wall letting no one pass behind him; by 200 hours his hallucinations had taken a sinister turn and he thought a doctor trying to examine him was an undertaker come to bury him. When it was over he slept for 13 hours, after which his paranoia and hallucinations had gone.

Oddly, when it was time for his regular broadcasts – between 5 and 8 p.m. – he was able to perform almost normally. He could carry out relatively complex tasks such as playing records and was able to talk in a fairly normal fashion to his listeners. Other, more formal, sleep-deprivation studies have had similar results. For instance, Tripp's ability to rouse himself for his broadcasts bears out the fact that subjects of experiments who have been seriously deprived of sleep can revive themselves to perform brief tasks.

REM sleep (dreaming), in particular, seems to be vital to mental health. If people are deprived only of REM sleep they will have psychological symptoms; when allowed to sleep normally again, they make up for it by spending more time proportionally in REM sleep.

REM sleep **Non–REM sleep**

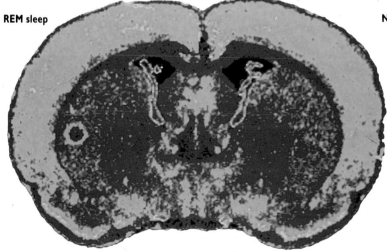

Maintenance and repair work takes place throughout the body while we sleep. Evidence for this in the human brain comes indirectly from another mammal, the rat.

*Images taken of slices of the brains of rats (**above**) reveal that protein synthesis – which is necessary for reconstructing cells – increases in the brain during non-dreaming, or non-REM, sleep compared to wakefulness or dreaming (REM sleep). In humans,* *during dreaming the amount of the brain chemical noradrenaline is also sharply reduced. Since noradrenaline seems to be involved in the process of organizing information into a coherent form, its low level during dreaming could explain why dreams appear to disregard logic and seemingly impossible things can happen.*

Elsewhere in the human body other physical changes occur during sleep. For instance, blood pressure *drops and breathing and heart rate slow down, but more growth and sex hormones are released.*

Nearly all animals, including humans, have some sort of rhythm of rest and alertness, although the reasons for this are not entirely clear. It is thought that in addition to allowing the body to repair and maintain itself, sleep could be a survival device – a time to conserve energy during periods of inactivity.

Protein synthesis

Low

High

Abnormal states

Deciding when a person's state of mind is abnormal and that they need help is not as easy as it might seem.

Every now and then all of us feel a little sad, a little anxious, a little confused. From time to time we all escape into fantasy worlds – daydreaming, reading books or watching television. But sometimes a person's responses to the world become so exaggerated that they are thought "abnormal" and perhaps in need of medical treatment. The problem is to recognize just when this is the case.

Abnormal behaviour is not simply behaviour that is not normal. Someone who dashed in front of a speeding car to save a child or even a dog would be hailed as a hero; someone who did the same to save an ant would be called insane. Yet both actions are out of the ordinary. Similarly, behaviour that seems abnormal in one situation or society might be perfectly normal in another. Flailing your arms and legs and screaming wildly is normal at a disco but distinctly odd in the office. In countries under totalitarian rule, the state controls criticism by labelling dissidents insane, as happened in the Soviet Union and in Hitler's Germany. So defining behaviour as abnormal is fraught with problems.

Today people who are unable to cope with the normal demands of everyday living, or are a menace to themselves or society, are regarded as mentally ill. In the past they might have been thought mad or possessed by demons. The idea of mental illness suggests the person suffering is sick and that an attempt should be made to diagnose the illness and effect a "cure", just as with physical illnesses. As with other branches of medicine, illnesses of the mind are broken down into categories according to a person's symptoms. But there are critics who argue that there is no such thing as mental illness. Where there is damage to the nervous system, it should be termed a neurological disease and treated as such. Where there is no obvious physical damage the sufferer is simply having problems living – and we should look for solutions, using either drug or psychological treatments, or a combination.

These revellers seem to be having a wild time, but if any of them was to behave in the same way in a different situation – in a board meeting, for instance – they might be regarded as insane. This is just one example of how behaviour that seems abnormal may be quite normal in another context. It may be that our cultural prejudices lead us to make similar mistaken judgments in less obvious ways.

Attitudes to abnormal behaviour and ways of dealing with it have changed dramatically over the years. Once sufferers were seen as being possessed by demons and were treated by the laying on of hands. Later they were regarded as dangerous and were locked up in noisy and chaotic "madhouses" and bound in chains. Such places and practices have long since vanished, but the fear and the prejudice still remain.

ENDING IT ALL

Sometimes life's problems can be so pressing that suicide seems the only way out; indeed, there are 31,000 suicides a year in the U.S. alone. For all the countries shown here, more men commit suicide than women. Hungary has the highest suicide rate in the world, while that for Greece (geographically not far distant) is one of the lowest.

Most suicides are severely depressed, but a small minority use it as a form of manipulation – perhaps to inflict revenge on someone who has rejected them, or as a cry for attention. People like this do not necessarily wish to die, but unless they receive help they may go on attempting suicide until they succeed.

	59.3											

59.3

19.8 22.3 11.7 20.4 4.8 12.1 3.4 9.7 3.1 5.9 1.6

Hungary   Japan   U.S.   U.K.   Argentina   Greece

■ Male   □ Female   Suicides per year (per 100,000 of population)

Mental illnesses are described using a number of categories and subtypes. The branches on the right represent the major divisions and broad subtypes. The most fundamental division is between those causes of abnormal behaviour that are termed organic and those that are non-organic.

Organic disorders are caused by neurological damage – such as a brain tumour, head injury, alcoholism or diseases like Parkinson's and Alzheimer's. Non-organic disorders do not have any recognizable physical cause. It is only once the illness has been properly identified that appropriate treatment can begin.

Schizophrenia

Manic–depression

Type 1

Non-organic mental illnesses are generally thought to be of two main types – psychoses and neuroses. In a neurosis the person may become unduly anxious but does not lose touch with reality. Neurotic disorders include phobias, extreme anxiety, obsessive-compulsive disorders, hysteria, depression and hypochondria. In psychosis the person has delusions and lacks contact with reality. The two main subdivisions of psychosis are manic-depression, or bipolar disorder, and schizophrenia.

Psychoses

Type 2

Neuroses

Non–organic

Organic

Manic-depression involves severe mood disturbance: sufferers often feel that they are on an emotional roller coaster, swinging between extreme – and sometimes inappropriate – elation and extreme sadness.

Type I schizophrenia describes patients with "positive" symptoms like delusions and hallucinations. Type II describes those with "negative" symptoms such as loss of will, flat emotional reactions, and motor and speech problems.

Talking cures

Physical cures for mental problems mostly treat only symptoms, but some talking cures can deal with causes.

When a person is physically ill, there is often just one recognized treatment. But when the problem is mental, this is far from so; there are almost as many different therapies as there are psychiatrists. Some approaches are physical, such as using drugs; others involve talking. Yet it would be a mistake to assume they are mutually exclusive. Many psychiatrists will treat a depressed patient, for instance, both by talking about the problem and with antidepressant drugs.

The talking cures come under the umbrella heading of psychotherapy and fall into four main areas: psychoanalytic, humanistic, behavioural and cognitive. By far the best known is psychoanalysis, developed by the legendary Sigmund Freud. This involves skilled probing into the patient's past to reveal the origins of unconscious repressed feelings, thoughts and

Fear of flying, however irrational, is something that can be crippling for sufferers. One treatment that can be used to help such phobias is behaviour therapy, which essentially deals with the abnormal behaviour itself and not necessarily any deeper cause. There are various approaches. Systematic desensitization teaches the patient to relax as he or she is exposed to anxious-making situations in a series of graduated steps, starting with something relatively minor and, when relaxation can be achieved with that, moving up to something stronger. This aims to replace one response to a particular stimulus with another. Implosion therapy, a similar but more extreme approach, involves surrounding the patient with the source of fear – not building up to it gently – on the basis that the phobia will soon subside. Operant conditioning works by giving rewards for changed behaviour.

Group therapy is one alternative to the more common pattern of one-to-one psychotherapy and has been popular since World War II, particularly with the increasing use of psychotherapists and restricted resources. For many problems it is not only less expensive, but some therapists also believe that it can be as useful as individual treatment.

In a typical group therapy session, the patients and therapist discuss the problems of one or more of the members. There are a number of reasons why this can be helpful. Perhaps the most obvious is if the group is set up for people who share a common problem, alcoholism or bereavement for instance. They can then share their experiences about that problem and come to a deeper understanding of it – and their reactions to it.

It has also been argued that other aspects specific to group therapy are valuable. The strength gained from being a member of the group is one of them – patients feel supported and so are more able to take risks and cope with criticism. Another is the sense of self-worth gained by helping other people. Members often also begin to understand themselves better – partly through seeing similar concerns and reactions in others – and learn to express themselves better.

motives. Humanistic therapists, by contrast, see the problem as a problem with how they perceive themselves, and they refer to the people they see as clients, not patients. They will not delve for unconscious motives but simply provide the support clients need to help them find their own solution.

Psychoanalysis, including the schools of psychotherapy derived from it, and humanistic therapy both tend to be long-term treatments – psychoanalysis can take years. Behaviour therapy, however, tends to be quick and direct, treating only the immediate symptoms. If a person is anxious, a behaviourist will not look for an underlying cause but will simply reduce the anxiety with appropriate stimuli. Cognitive therapy seeks to condition (teach), but here the aim is to provide the patient with a better way of thinking about a problem, since the theory is that our perception of something – distorted in the case of someone with mental illness – governs how we respond to it.

Besides these four mainstream approaches there are myriad alternatives. Gestalt therapists, for instance, focus on developing awareness, arguing that problems arise when we are unaware of our needs and leave them unfulfilled. Advocates of transactional analysis (TA) believe it is useful for everyone, not just those with "problems". TA aims to make us aware of the way we and those around us behave, and of the games we all play, so that we can direct our behaviour accordingly.

DIGGING INTO THE PAST

Sigmund Freud was the first to suggest that the causes of psychological problems could be uncovered by delving into a patient's past. He did this by encouraging his patients to lie down on a couch and relax, and then used such tools as free association and the interpretation of dreams. With free association, the fully relaxed patient says whatever comes to mind, without censoring or editing it; the analyst simply acts as a guide. The repressed memories causing the conflict and undermining the patient's ego only emerge slowly because people subconsciously offer resistances – blocks that save them from confronting painful memories. Whenever the painful topic looms, the patient may fall silent or make jokes. After a while, the analyst will try to help the patient interpret these memories. The patient may strongly resist the analyst's view at first, but this only confirms the interpretation, because strong resistance must conceal painful conflicts.

Psychoanalysts aim to remain emotionally detached from their patients, since by doing so they become a blank screen, encouraging patients to shift feelings and thoughts they have toward others – both positive and negative – on to the analyst. This process, known as transference, helps bring out the suppressed conflicts.

Physical cures

There are some powerful remedies available for relief of mental symptoms.

Much mainstream psychiatric treatment relies upon physical rather than psychological methods. Physical treatments fall into three groups: psychosurgery, electroconvulsive therapy (ECT) and drug therapy. The first two are controversial and not common, whereas the use of drugs is relatively uncontroversial and widespread. Drugs have, in fact, revolutionized treatment of mental illness since they were first widely used in the 1950s. Now millions of patients worldwide benefit from drug therapy.

But psychiatrists who rely too heavily on drugs have been criticized because of the side effects of some and because of the dependency others encourage. Other doubts arise since many of the major drugs were discovered by accident, and it is not known why their action at the cellular level is therapeutic. It is often possible to see how they operate on certain neurotransmitters in the brain – but no one knows why this has particular psychological effects. And no drug actually cures a problem, it simply relieves symptoms.

Four main groups of drugs are used to treat mental illness: antipsychotics; antidepressants; antianxiety drugs; and those for manic-depression. Antipsychotics commonly used to treat schizophrenia are phenothiazines such as chlorpromazine (Largactyl and Thorazine). They are thought to work by blocking the receptors for the neurotransmitter dopamine in the brain – particularly in the limbic system, which is deeply involved in our emotions, and the hypothalamus, which is involved in our basic drives such as sex and food. By blocking the nerve impulses transmitted by dopamine, they damp down emotional response and interrupt basic drives, reducing symptoms.

Antidepressants were discovered by accident in 1952, when tuberculosis patients receiving the drug iproniazid started

Psychotropic (mind-affecting) drugs almost all have their action at the synapse, the gap between nerve cells (neurons). They modify how one neuron communicates across the gap with another neuron. Some drugs, for instance, alter the amount of neurotransmitters (chemicals that carry messages across the synapse) made in the sending neuron. With more available for release, say, the chances are that communication will be stronger. In the same way, if carrier pigeons breed there will be more birds to carry messages.

About 50,000 people – the number of M's in the Manhattan telephone directory – had prefrontal lobotomy operations in the '40s, '50s and '60s, in which the frontal lobes of the brain are cut away. Usually performed on schizophrenics, the operation often left patients much calmer – but only because they were virtual vegetables. Psychosurgery is performed very infrequently today.

A SHOCKING BUSINESS

All attempts at alleviating the severe depression of a patient in a psychiatric hospital failed. After some months, doctors resorted to electroconvulsive therapy (ECT), which consisted of six treatments over two weeks. At the end of that time the patient's spirits lifted and eventually he recovered.

The idea behind ECT evolved when it was noticed that epileptics who suffer convulsions are rarely schizophrenic. This led people to attempt to cure mentally disturbed patients by inducing convulsions. Eventually, a jolt of electricity to the brain, delivered via electrodes attached to the head, was chosen as the means of setting off the convulsions. The current causes a brain seizure lasting a few minutes in which neurons all over the brain fire out of control. In the early days people were often hurt as they thrashed about after the shock. In modern treatments a muscle relaxant and anaesthetic are given to prevent damage and to reduce anxiety.

ECT is used only for severe depression when all else fails; it often seems to work. No one is quite sure why it works, although one theory is that it increases neurotransmitter activity and corrects a deficit in noradrenaline levels and perhaps also in serotonin. Some people experience memory loss and confusion after ECT but this is usually temporary.

But its use is controversial, and clinicians have widely differing opinions about it. It is viewed by some as an extreme and frightening measure and this, together with associated memory problems and uncertainty about how it works, has led to a marked decline in its use since its 1950s heyday.

STUMBLING ON A TREATMENT

In 1949 Australian psychiatrist John Cade (**right**) was carrying out experiments on guinea pigs to test a theory that high levels of uric acid in the body caused mania. To facilitate absorption of the uric acid by the guinea pigs he mixed it with lithium. But when he injected the mix he noticed that the animals grew calmer, not more lively as he had predicted. He began to suspect that the calming might be due to the lithium and when he gave it to a group of manic patients, he found that it calmed them down and regularized their mood. At the time, lithium had just been banned in the U.S. because it had caused several deaths when used as a substitute for common salt. It was not until 1970 that it was approved for use in treating bipolar disorders (manic-depression) there.

Lithium was a breakthrough and is effective in reducing both the up and the down mood swings of bipolar disorder. Its use has to be carefully monitored, however, since too high a dose can cause kidney problems.

Some drugs alter the release rate of neurotransmitters. The more released by the sending neuron, the greater the chance that the message will get across strongly. Similarly, the more carrier pigeons released, the more are likely to deliver their message.

In the synaptic gap neurotransmitter levels are reduced by the action of enzymes that break them into non-active components, like the hunter killing carrier pigeons. With *fewer neurotransmitters carrying the message the communication becomes weaker.* Some drugs have the opposite effect and inhibit the action of enzymes, thus raising neurotransmitter levels and boosting communication.

The availability of special sites, known as receptors, on the neuron receiving a message affects how well neurotransmitters deliver a message. Some drugs have the effect of blockading the receptor sites thus stopping or reducing the strength of the signals. Others, conversely, increase the availability of receptor sites, enhancing the communication. It is like the carrier pigeons being unable to get into their "home" (**below**) or having plenty of spaces to enter (**right**).

getting "high". This, too, works by altering levels of neurotransmitters in the brain, usually by boosting noradrenaline and/or serotonin.

In the 1950s, the only effective sedatives, or antianxiety drugs, were barbiturates which are rarely used today because they are so addictive and potentially dangerous. Since 1960, the benzodiazepines such as Librium (chlordiazepoxide) and Valium (diazepam) have been available. These seem to have a more specific and subtle chemical action than barbiturates. But they are addictive and at one time were overprescribed. Their use now is limited to short periods only. Anxiety is also sometimes treated with antidepressants.

Feeling low

If sadness persists and deepens, people can feel trapped in the downward spiral that leads to depression.

Nearly all of us feel miserable and depressed sometimes – perhaps when a love affair ends, when a job is lost or even just when the weather is wet. But for some depression is not merely a passing mood; it develops into a way of life. They become overwhelmed by sadness, pessimism and a sense of failure. They have difficulty concentrating and feel that any effort is futile. And they find it hard to get to sleep, still harder to wake up and often lose their appetite. It affects people from all walks of life, but manual workers and those from lower income groups are more likely to suffer than the middle classes, and more women suffer than men. About 15 percent of adults will have a severe episode of clinical depression at some time.

There are many theories as to the cause of depression, including genetic predisposition, the effects of childhood trauma, a chemical imbalance, and the idea that people become victims of "learned helplessness". They develop feelings of helplessness, perhaps because they have little control over their lives or because in the past they have been in situations where they could do little to relieve their distress.

A few people swing between deep depression and wild excited euphoria when they believe, perhaps, they can conquer the world. This condition is known as manic-depression, or bipolar disorder (in contrast to continuous unipolar, or clinical, depression), and seems to respond well to treatment with the drug lithium. Unipolar depression is much harder to treat, and psychiatrists deal with it using a combination of antidepressant drugs and psychotherapy.

Certain foods, including red wine and cheese, contain the chemical tyramine, which is normally broken down by the enzyme monoamine oxidase in the liver. If they are eaten when MOAIs are being taken for depression, tyramine accumulates, raising blood pressure beyond safe levels.

THE CHEMISTRY OF DEPRESSION

Varying levels of brain chemicals and patterns of brain activity seem to play a major part in depression. According to one theory, high levels of the brain chemical serotonin (one of the monoamine group) keep the brain in a state where it is at a low level of arousal – in effect, in a depressed state. Paradoxically, treatment involves raising serotonin levels even higher. This is thought to work by bombarding brain cells with so much of the chemical that they lose their sensitivity to it; cells thus become more active, arousal levels rise and the depression lifts in about 10 days as the cells' sensitivity levels gradually decrease.

Two general classes of drugs raise serotonin levels: the first stops it being reabsorbed and includes the tricyclics, a subgroup of the monoamine re-uptake inhibitors (MARIs), and the selective serotonin re-uptake inhibitors (SSRIs) such as fluoxetine (Prozac). The second class, the monoamine oxidase inhibitors (MOAIs), stops serotonin being broken down, thus maintaining levels of the chemical.

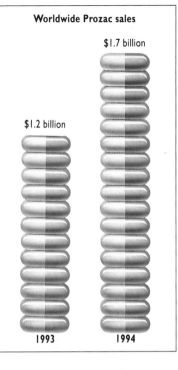

Worldwide Prozac sales

HAPPY PILLS

No antidepressant drug has attracted more attention than fluoxetine, better known by its trade name Prozac. Since it was introduced in the late 1980s, use of the drug has soared in the United States. It seems to work with a variety of depressed patients, who typically show an improvement three weeks after being prescribed Prozac. The drug inhibits the re-uptake of serotonin, so boosting levels of this chemical in the brain and having the net effect of moving it into a higher state of arousal.

Many depressives swear that Prozac has been their salvation, and even those who are not clinically depressed use it to help their social life go with a swing. For some it has become a way of life. But the drug has unpleasant side effects – such as nausea and agitation – and it is also addictive. Critics argue that Prozac pushes people into a state of perpetual mindless sensuality, with no thought for others.

$1.7 billion

$1.2 billion

1993   1994

Depression is a natural reaction at times, for example after the death of a loved one. In such instances the cause of the depression is obvious – but it is not so clear why some people recover rapidly and others do not. Whatever the case, the grieving process takes time and should not be hurried, neither should the fact of a loved one's death be hidden away or ignored. Bereavement is a common experience: every year more than 8 million people in the U.S. experience the death of a member of their immediate family.

Where there is an identifiable cause, such as bereavement or physical illness, psychiatrists talk of exogenous depression. Where there is no such obvious cause and the depression appears to be coming from within, it is known as endogenous. Even so, this type of depression may have an external cause – perhaps buried in the person's past – that is simply hard to identify.

Energetic sports such as aerobics may be a simple way of helping to fight clinical depression. Most people experience a feeling of wellbeing as a result of strenuous physical activity because it causes the brain to release endorphins, natural painkillers that help to alleviate discomfort and stress. And some psychiatrists think that if patients follow an increasingly demanding daily schedule of activities – especially social activities – they are likely to become more confident, which will assist in lifting their depression.

The mind adrift

A number of factors – genetic, physical and environmental – may contribute to schizophrenia.

Sometimes, the inner world of the schizophrenic can be confusing and even terrifying. A cacophony of sensations bombards the mind; angry inner voices shout orders; gibberish trips off the tongue. Yet the symptoms are not always so extreme. Indeed, they vary so much, and the line between schizophrenia and normality can be so blurred, that it is often impossible to diagnose with complete certainty.

Schizophrenia is one of the most serious psychiatric disorders. Usually symptoms are divided into two types: positive (Type I) and negative (Type II). Positive symptoms include hearing voices, suffering from delusions and hallucinations, and behaving strangely; they are more dramatic, but tend to be short-lived. Negative symptoms include apathy, depression and confused speech; they last longer and occur more often, some think, as the illness tightens its hold. Schizophrenia typically strikes in early adulthood and total recovery after a major attack is rare. Positive symptoms can be eased by tranquillizers and psychotherapy, but the victim's ability to carry on normally between tends to decline.

Dopamine pathways in the brain

Labels: Striatum, Frontal cortex, Amygdala, Ventral tegmental area, Substantia nigra

Brain cross section

Normal ventricles   Enlarged ventricles

The brain chemical dopamine is implicated in schizophrenia. Major dopamine pathways go from the substantia nigra to parts involved in movement and from the ventral tegmental area to areas that link sensory perceptions with memories and emotions.

Schizophrenics are often acutely aware of the bewildering array of information pouring into their brains all the time from their senses. Most people manage to filter out some of these sensations – just as you mentally block out background sounds in a noisy café and focus on your friends' voices. But schizophrenics are unable to do this. So they find their minds constantly bombarded by intense sights and sounds.

*Physical abnormalities in the brain can be linked to schizophrenia, but it is not certain whether these signs of damage cause the disorder or are caused by it. MRI scans reveal larger ventricles in the brain of a schizophrenic twin than in his or her healthy identical sibling (**left**). PET scans show that the prefrontal cortex – crucial to forming memories – is much less active in sufferers. So, too, is the hippocampus, which is also important in memory. Post mortems have shown that the prefrontal cortex of schizophrenics is often atrophied, and this shrinking of brain tissue seems also to enlarge some of the cavities or ventricles.*

WORD SALAD

☤ A woman was delighted to receive a letter from her son abroad, but distraught when she read it: "Dear mother... I am writing on paper. The pen I am using is from a factory called Perry and Co. The factory is in England. The city of London is in England. I know this from my school days. Then I always liked geography. My last teacher in that subject was Professor August A. He was a man with black eyes. There are also blue and grey eyes and other sorts too. I have heard it said that snakes have green eyes. All people have eyes. There are some, too, who are blind."

He was later diagnosed as being schizophrenic. Sufferers often have difficulty using language to communicate. They cannot make small talk and tend to answer questions with a single word. Although they do not lose their linguistic ability – their word play can appear to border on genius – they lose the power of abstract thought and seem to flit from one phrase to the next by random association without any shaping strand. One word may follow another simply because it rhymes or conjures up particular images. This may also be because working memory, used to help us speak sentences, is affected. A schizophrenic will not retain the memory of the beginning of a sentence and so finishes it with nonsense.

Genetic factors may play a role in causing schizophrenia. Studies have shown that the disorder is more likely to develop in the relatives of schizophrenics than in those of non-schizophrenics, and the closer the relationship, the greater the chance of having it. For example, if one identical twin suffers from schizophrenia, the other twin (whose genes are identical) has a 40–60 percent chance of developing the illness. With non-identical twins, the likelihood drops to 17 percent.

The hunt is on for the guilty gene. By analysing the DNA of at least 200 pairs of afflicted siblings, scientists hope to pinpoint the position of genes that could be linked to the disorder. Some researchers also think that a genetic defect could disrupt the migration of neurons in the developing brain, leading to abnormal connections between the cortex and the limbic system, thought to play a role in emotion and motivation. The illness occurs to the same degree worldwide and it still exists, suggesting that the gene that carries it must have other evolutionarily important factors.

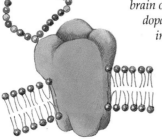

Environment can be the trigger for schizophrenia. Emotional strife in the family is one such factor. In "double-bind" situations, a parent gives contradictory messages. A child may be told "don't be so obedient", for instance. Where there is marital discord, a child may be encouraged by mother or father to take a side, thus fostering guilt feelings about split loyalties.

Usually children are taught how to respond to social cues – to a frown or smile – and to moderate behaviour accordingly. If this does not happen, they may concentrate on irrelevant cues such as the hum of a computer.

Scientists believe schizophrenia is linked either to raised levels of the neurotransmitter dopamine in the brain or to increased sensitivity of dopamine receptors, both of which induce a high state of arousal. Symptoms can be treated by drugs like phenothiazine which block dopamine receptors in brain cells and so reduce the chemical's effect. Conversely, drugs which boost dopamine levels, such as L-dopa (given to Parkinson's sufferers), create schizophrenia-like symptoms in healthy people. There are five different dopamine receptors, D1 to D5. Schizophrenics have more D2 receptors in the basal ganglia part of the midbrain, but disruption is not limited to this area. The problem may be caused by changes in certain fats in neuron membranes, which alter the way dopamine works.

Anxious states

It is natural to feel worried sometimes, but for a number of people anxiety can be both disabling and distressing.

From time to time all of us get worried or anxious – before a major exam, or when a loved one is late coming home, for instance. But for some people, anxiety can become so extreme, or can be provoked by so little, that they are said to be suffering from anxiety disorder. They become tense, nervous and distressed, and sometimes panic. They may spend a lot time worrying about why they are so anxious, and then become frustrated because they cannot see why. And they may be beset by a whole range of somatic, or physical, symptoms. Some break out in a sweat, others tense their muscles, possibly causing headaches, still others hyperventilate, which makes them dizzy, or develop high pulse rate or blood pressure – all signs of a body aroused by fear for "fight or flight". Indeed, each individual's anxiety is expressed with a different range of physical symptoms, from stomach cramps to susceptibility to colds – or simply pacing around the room or tapping fingers.

There are as many kinds of anxiety disorder as there are anxious people, but five main categories can be identified: phobias, obsessive-compulsive disorders, panic attacks, generalized anxiety and stress disorders. The last of these includes post-traumatic stress syndrome, which occurs when, after a terrible event such as a fire or car accident, victims suffer from recurring painful memories, nightmares and flashbacks, often so vivid that they feel they are reliving the event.

For some people a particular situation seems to induce greater anxiety levels. The reason for this is not known, but a genetic predisposition and how they were treated in childhood are possible theories. Panic attacks can come from out of the blue, with no apparent cause. According to one theory they are caused because a person is highly sensitive to a few physical sensations and thinks they foretell the failure of some vital bodily function. Another theory attributes them to the emergence of long-repressed painful memories or difficult emotions.

Anxiety disorders affect 15 percent of people at some time. Since they are more common in technologically advanced societies, they are thought to be caused by the stress of modern living – noisy cities, fast pace, the breakdown of communities and relationships, urban isolation and competitive lifestyles.

Singer Joan Baez suffered from severe stage fright in the past. The symptoms can include breaking out in a cold sweat or getting "butterflies" in the stomach before going out in front of an audience. These stage fright symptoms are part of the body's automatic responses to anxiety. Joan Baez dealt with this problem, and others, using psychotherapy, yoga and visualization techniques, among other things.

Stress affects us physically because we react to it with the "fight or flight" response. In preparation for either staying and fighting or fleeing from danger, heart and breathing rates speed up, to get more oxygen to the brain; the digestive system "shuts down" temporarily to avoid wasting energy; and skin temperature drops, because of sweating and the constriction of small blood vessels in the skin, turning it paler and redirecting blood to the muscles.

It is thought that these physical responses may be in part responsible for stress-related heart disease. One theory is that since stress narrows blood vessels and boosts heart rate, it puts the coronary arteries under strain. Another is that hormones activated by stress make blood pressure waver, weakening blood vessels. A third is that stress adds lipids (fats) to the bloodstream, clogging the arteries. To reduce the risk of heart disease, people are advised to modify their reaction to stress.

Anxiety disorder can be triggered by stress, which may make us more likely to suffer from all kinds of physical illness. Stress is essentially caused by a situation in which we feel challenged or threatened in some way – one in which we must either adapt or cope. Things that cause stress – called stressors by psychiatrists – can range from missing a train to buying a house.

Various studies have rated the stress level of different life events. Such ratings are inevitably rather arbitrary – events which are stressful for some are not for others – but they give an idea of how things might affect us. Since the late 1960s, psychiatrists in the U.S. have used the SRRS (social

readjustment rating scale), which gives scores to 43 stressors that affect our lives. At the top of the list, with a tally of 100, comes the death of a husband or wife. Next comes divorce (73), a broken relationship (65), a prison sentence (63), the death of a close family member (63) and personal injury or illness (53). Marriage comes next on the list with a score of 50. Down near the bottom of the scale are holidays (13) and Christmas (12), which are both in theory pleasant but can also cause some stress.

Learning to relax can be an effective way of combating stress. Even if you cannot avoid stressful situations, you may be able to modify your reaction to them. Some people suggest relaxing by exercise – sport, aerobics, dancing and so on – or transcendental meditation, which has been shown to reduce stress and improve physical health. Something as simple as walking the dog can also help. And letting your emotions out or even just laughing can have a restorative effect. Others suggest a cognitive approach – that is, modifying your way of thinking. If you get stressed when someone cuts in front of you in the car, for instance, remind yourself that it really makes very little difference.

Buspirone

$5HT_{1A}$ autoreceptor

Cell body

5HT–producing cell

Axon

5HT

THE CHEMISTRY OF ANXIETY TREATMENTS

Clearly, stress and individual personality play a major part in anxiety disorder, but some physical explanations have also been suggested. The overall levels of certain brain chemicals – such as GABA (gamma-aminobutyric acid) and serotonin (5HT) – are thought to be important. GABA, for instance, has an inhibitory effect; it reduces the sensitivity of neurons, so it takes more to excite them. It may be deficient in anxious people, allowing the brain to become overaroused and causing anxiety. So raising GABA levels or enhancing its effect might reduce anxiety. The

benzodiazepine (BDZ) tranquillizers, such as Librium (chlordiazepoxide) and Valium (diazepam), work partly by increasing GABA activity. At the cell-membrane level, BDZ binds to a receptor site on a GABA receptor and enhances the effect of GABA, causing the GABA chloride channel to open more often. The influx of chloride ions hyperpolarizes the cell making it less likely to fire.

Another antianxiety drug is buspirone which has the net effect of reducing the output of 5HT in the brain. Lowering 5HT levels is thought to reduce anxiety. Buspirone binds as an agonist to an autoreceptor, known as the $5HT_{1A}$ autoreceptor, on a 5HT-producing cell. An autoreceptor regulates the output of a neuron, acting a bit like the thermostat on a electric iron. If the cell produces too much neurotransmitter, in this case serotonin, the amount binding to its autoreceptors rises, telling the cell to cut its output.

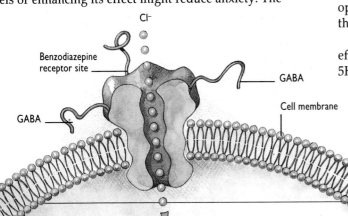

Cl^-

Benzodiazepine receptor site

GABA

GABA

Cell membrane

Fears and fixations

There are many unfortunate twists and turns in the paths of human thought – some are truly terrifying.

Imagine stepping out on to the balcony of your holiday hotel. Suddenly, it shakes violently, the hand rail disintegrates, the floor dissolves, a bottomless chasm gapes open beneath your feet and you start to fall. Naturally you are terrified. This is what going out on a balcony is like all the time for someone who suffers from acrophobia, an abnormal fear of heights. Acrophobia is just one of many phobias – abnormal fears – that may afflict some people. Phobias are not unusual – according to some research about 8 percent of women and 3.5 percent of men suffer from a phobia at some time.

Phobias are essentially excessive, unreasonable fears, in which someone is terrified of something – a situation, activity or object – that holds little or no danger. A phobia becomes a problem when it affects a person's ability to live a normal life or when it makes someone extremely unhappy or anxious. When this is the case the person is said to suffer from a phobic disorder. Phobias break down into three broad categories. There are simple phobias, fear of such things as spiders, water, darkness, birds and so on. There are social phobias, fear of being criticized by others, which makes people petrified of

Unwanted thoughts and irresistible urges, which can be neither understood nor controlled, are thought to beset about 1 person in 40. Obsession is when a person's mind becomes dominated by an image or impulse which the sufferer cannot get rid of. The thought takes over the person's life and guides his or her actions – and seems impossible to fight against.

Compulsion is when someone is overcome by an irresistible urge to perform a meaningless act repeatedly. Some people become so obsessed by cleanliness, for instance, that they compulsively wash their hands hundreds of times a day. If these thoughts or actions – either on their own or together – inhibit their everyday life or make them unduly anxious then they are said to have obsessive-compulsive disorder.

Obsessive-compulsive disorder may have something in common with "stereotyped" behaviour in animals. This occurs when cagebound animals repeat the same movement again and again in a highly agitated manner with no apparent purpose.

A different use of the word obsession describes the sexual obsession of fetishism. The key feature is that sexual urges and arousing fantasies are fixated on an inanimate object or unexpected body part. A fetishist might think of or handle the object while masturbating or, if the object is an item of clothing, would not be able to have intercourse unless a sexual partner were wearing it. The range of fetishistic objects is vast; in fact, almost anything can be a fetish – from wrists to rubber.

EATEN UP BY FEAR OF FAT

Thousands of people – usually teenage girls – suffer from one of two major eating disorders: anorexia nervosa and bulimia nervosa, both of which are serious. (Between 5 and 20 percent of anorexics die from the damage done to their bodies.) In recent years the number of males with anorexia has increased; some put the ratio of males to females with this problem at 1 to 10. Anorexics refuse to eat enough – often to the point of starvation. No one knows what causes the disease, and it is difficult to treat. Most sufferers see themselves as fat – even when emacíated – and stubbornly refuse to eat. Bulimics are similarly concerned about their weight, but they alternate binges, when they stuff themselves with food, and purges, when they get rid of it with laxatives or by making themselves sick. It is also hard to treat, since bulimics often isolate themselves to hide their behaviour.

A common phobia is arachnophobia, an irrational fear of spiders. People can develop irrational fears of all kinds of things, and there are conflicting theories as to how phobias come about. The behaviourist John B. Watson carried out a famous, if by today's standards unethical, experiment early in the 20th century to show how phobias might be learned by association of genuinely frightening stimuli with "harmless" ones. He gave a year-old baby named Albert a white rat to play with and then frightened the infant by banging on a metal bar. After repeating this several times Albert became frightened of the rat. He also became afraid of white dogs and rabbits. But there is some debate as to whether his reactions were as strong as a phobia, and the case for phobias being caused by this type of association, or conditioning, is not proven. Other theories state that phobias arise more often when society is unstable; that they are manifestations of defence mechanisms to control underlying anxiety; or that a predisposition to certain phobias is built into the human mind by evolution. But none of the theories seems able to explain phobias fully.

talking to the opposite sex, eating in public, meeting new people and so on; these are rarer than simple phobias. And there is agoraphobia, the most common of all, especially for young women. Agoraphobia, literally, fear of the market place, is usually defined as fear of open spaces, and some agoraphobics are indeed terrified of being alone in wide open spaces. But for most it is a fear of being in public places, especially if they do not have a friend or family member with them. Many are afraid that they might not be able to escape from such a place if they lost control of some bodily function or fainted. When severe it can confine people to their homes.

Usually, phobics are completely aware of how irrational their fear is and are often upset by their inability to overcome it. Some are successfully treated by hypnosis, but the medical profession usually tries behaviour therapy. In systematic desensitization, a phobic's ability to cope with the fear is built up by gradual exposure to more and more of what frightens him or her. Someone who was terrified of spiders might initially be asked to think about a spider, then to look at a picture of one and so on, building up to being able to handle a spider. The opposite approach is taken in "flooding" – exposing the phobic to their fears. Thus taking an acrophobic to the top of a high building or a nyctophobic into a darkened room forces them to realize that nothing bad happens to them. "Implosion therapy" is midway between the two, encouraging phobics to live through their worst fears – but only in their imagination.

NAME THAT PHOBIA

Animals	Zoophobia
Being afraid	Phobophobia
Being alone	Autophobia
Being buried alive	Taphophobia
Being dirty	Automysophobia
Being stared at	Scopophobia
Birds	Ornithophobia
Blood	Haematophobia
Body odours	Osphresiophobia
Books	Bibliophobia
Cancer	Carcinomatophobia
Cats	Ailurophobia
Choking	Pnigophobia
Crowds	Ochlophobia
Darkness	Nyctophobia
Death	Thanatophobia
Dirt	Mysophobia
Disease	Nosophobia
Dogs	Cynophobia
Enclosed spaces	Claustrophobia
Faeces	Coprophobia
Failure	Kakorraphiaphobia
Fire	Pyrophobia
Flying	Aerophobia
Food	Sitophobia
Foreigners	Xenophobia
Germs	Spermophobia
Heights	Acrophobia
Human beings	Anthropophobia
Insanity	Lyssophobia
Insects	Entomophobia
Light	Photophobia
Machinery	Mechanophobia
Men	Androphobia
Motion	Kinesophobia
Nakedness	Gymnophobia
New	Neophobia
Noise or loud talking	Phonophobia
Open spaces	Agoraphobia
Pain	Algophobia
Physical love	Erotophobia
Pleasure	Hedonophobia
Poverty	Peniaphobia
Punishment	Poinephobia
Reptiles	Batrachophobia
Robbers	Harpaxophobia
School	Scholionophobia
Sea	Thallassophobia
Sharp objects	Belonophobia
Sleep	Hypnophobia
Spiders	Arachnophobia
String	Linonophobia
Thunder	Keraunophobia
Travel	Hodophobia
Vomiting	Emetophobia
Water	Hydrophobia
Women	Gynophobia
Words	Logophobia
Work	Ergasiophobia
Writing	Graphophobia

The failing mind

Most people have a fully functioning mind all their life; a few, however, slowly lose their higher faculties.

Nowhere is the connection between brain cells and all the processes that we think of as making us uniquely human made more clear than in cases of dementia. In such cases, over years, sometimes decades, the brain cells which play a part in understanding, memory and language slowly die off until there is little of the mind left that is recognizably human. When the degeneration begins sufferers become detached from friends and relatives. Later, over half of them become paranoid and believe they are being persecuted. Day-to-day activities, such as using the telephone, writing cheques and driving, become increasingly difficult. Later still, patients need help in feeding, dressing, washing and going to the lavatory.

Dementia is largely a disease of old age, affecting only one percent of 60 to 64-year-olds but 30–40 percent of those over 85. It can be caused by blood clots in the brain as well as by Parkinson's disease. The hallmark of Parkinson's is shaking hands and a shuffling walk, but 40 percent of sufferers can also experience severe intellectual decline. It is caused when cells in the substantia nigra of the midbrain, which are involved in controlling movement, start to die off.

But the leading cause of dementia is Alzheimer's disease, accounting for 50–60 percent of cases. In the brains of sufferers, whole areas are filled with deposits, or plaques, and tangled whorls of protein that damage the surrounding neurons. There is no known cure but in some countries the drug tacrine, which blocks the enzyme that destroys the neurotransmitter acetylcholine, has boosted intellectual performance in the short term. The cause is still unknown but people are more likely to succumb if members of their family have had it, if they have suffered a head injury or if they have Down's syndrome.

Genes that seem to be associated with Alzheimer's have been discovered. One such is FAD3 – familial Alzheimer's disease gene no. 3 – linked to the uncommon early-onset form. Carriers of an abnormal FAD3 gene start sliding into dementia in their 40s. An increased chance of developing the more common late-onset form of Alzheimer's is linked with a mutated gene for the protein ApoE, normally involved in transporting fats in the blood. Just how these genes have their effect is still unclear.

Alzheimer's disease is no respecter of rank or privilege. It is now official that former president of the United States Ronald Reagan suffers from this debilitating illness. The man called "the great communicator" made one of his last public appearances, with his wife Nancy, at a gala in Washington to celebrate his 83rd birthday in February 1994.

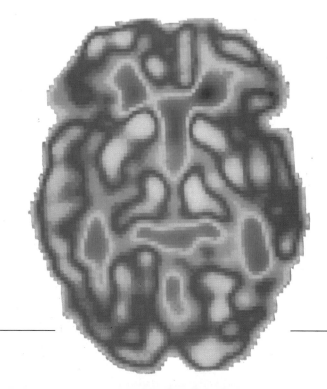

*PET scans show brain activity levels from low (blue) to high (yellow). The normal brain (**below left**) shows symmetrical high activity in the left and right cerebral hemispheres. The scan of an Alzheimer's sufferer (**below right**) shows patchiness and reduction in general activity.*

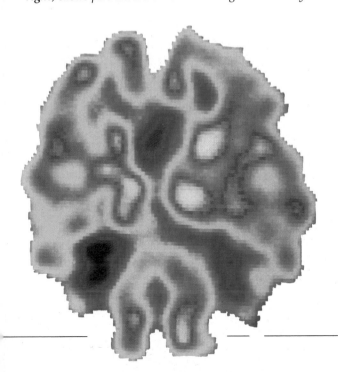

THE LOSS OF A MIND

The relatives of an elderly woman living alone became worried when her neighbours complained, on several occasions, about the smell of burning from the woman's apartment. She often grilled her food but became prone to forget that she had put it under the heat, where it caught fire. The problem grew steadily worse until she was no longer able to look after herself and had to move into a nursing home. There she stopped talking, did not recognize her relatives and eventually died after some years. When the woman began to burn her food she was in the early stages of Alzheimer's disease.

As people age, plaques and tangles begin to build up in the brain, especially in the hippocampus, an area that is involved in laying down new memories. These lumps or plaques of protein in the brain and tangles of nerve filaments gradually damage the surrounding neurons, leading to forgetfulness, but they do not, to any real extent, affect the power of the mind.

In Alzheimer's disease, the plaques and tangles are far more numerous than usual and are found all over the brain, including in the cerebral cortex – the realm of higher functions. At the heart of the plaques is a short chain of protein, known as beta amyloid, which has been chemically severed off a much larger protein – beta amyloid precursor protein. Normally the beta amyloid is cut in two but the trouble starts when, for some reason not yet understood, the enzymes isolate intact beta amyloid, which is then liberated and starts to cause damage.

The progress of dementia is marked by a thinning of the cortex. While the medial temporal lobe (MTL) of a normal healthy ageing person thins gradually over time, the MTL of someone with Alzheimer's or dementia of an Alzheimer's type shrinks rapidly on average from the time of diagnosis. Death usually comes when the brain in this region is 3 mm (⅛ inch) thick.

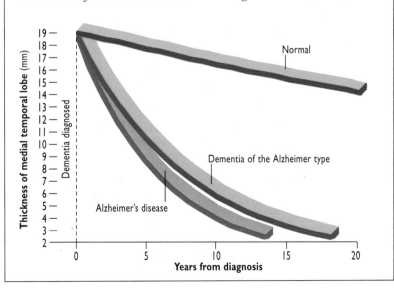

Thickness of medial temporal lobe (mm) — y-axis: 19, 18, 17, 16, 15, 14, 13, 12, 11, 10, 9, 8, 7, 6, 5, 4, 3, 2

Dementia diagnosed

Normal

Dementia of the Alzheimer type

Alzheimer's disease

Years from diagnosis — 0, 5, 10, 15, 20

Drugs of abuse

Most people use drugs daily – to wake them up, to relax, to get a buzz – even if they don't classify them as such.

It seems such a modern problem, yet people have been taking drugs to alter their mood since the dawn of civilization. Today drug taking is the norm: many people drink tea, coffee and alcohol; many smoke cigarettes; many young people have tried illegal drugs such as Ecstasy or cannabis at least once in their lives; and a huge number take tranquillizers or antidepressants.

Yet however commonplace they may seem, a lot of drugs can be harmful. Some, such as tobacco, cause huge physical damage if used heavily over long periods. Others can do psychological damage. Frequent use of amphetamines can bring on paranoia and psychosis similar to schizophrenia. Heavy drinkers suffer both physical (cyrrhosis of the liver) and psychological (Korsakoff's syndrome, the inability to store memories) damage. But many drugs – including alcohol – are only really harmful if taken in excess. However, most people could not argue with the idea that if either an individual or society is harmed by a person's taking of a drug then the drug is being abused. When abuse has been perceived as a threat at various times and in different cultures, certain drugs have been declared illegal.

A house of cards is an exceptionally delicate structure and must be perfectly balanced if it is to remain standing. The slightest puff of wind will have the cards cascading to the ground. The brain is an infinitely more complex structure whose equilibrium is easily disturbed, and drugs that interfere with the chemicals that send signals within it can have catastrophic effects on that balance.

People become addicted to drugs such as cocaine (snorted as "coke" and smoked as "crack"), heroin and alcohol when the body becomes dependent – the drug takers cannot function normally either physically or psychologically without the drug. If they stop taking the drug, they suffer withdrawal symptoms – often so hard to bear that they feel compelled to seek immediate relief in the drug again. This is why addicts find it so hard to wean themselves off the drugs.

Slightly less serious than dependence is tolerance, when the body adapts to the continual presence of the drug. As a result the drug taker has to take ever larger quantities to achieve the same effect. This happens quite frequently with drugs such as alcohol and Ecstasy and may lead to addiction.

When a person becomes addicted, or even just tolerant, the problems of obtaining and paying for the drug are added to the physical and psychological dangers of excess. This results not only in potential harm to the individual but also in danger to society.

See also

STATES OF MIND
▶ Abnormal states 284/295

▶ Physical cures 288/289

▶ Feeling low 290/291

▶ The mind adrift 292/293

▶ Fears and fixations 296/297

▶ The moral mind 304/305

BUILDING THE BRAIN
▶ Discovering transmitters 182/183

INPUTS AND OUTPUTS
▶ Feeling pain 226/227

▶ Keeping control 238/239

PSYCHOACTIVE DRUGS

Drugs which alter mood, behaviour and consciousness – known as psychoactive drugs – come in many forms, but all contain substances such as the caffeine in tea or the alcohol in beer which alter the brain's chemistry in some way. Some boost levels of a particular chemical, for instance; others make a certain brain chemical act more or less effectively or even mimick it. By altering the brain's chemistry, these substances change our state of mind. Such drugs can be grouped into four categories – narcotics, depressants (downers), stimulants (uppers) and hallucinogens (psychedelic drugs) – and although numerous types already exist, chemists are searching for new ones all the time.

Narcotics include the original narcotic opium, made from the poppy, as well as other opiates – natural narcotics such as heroin, morphine and codeine – and opioids, or synthetic narcotics, such as meperidine and methadone. The word narcotic comes from the Greek for "numbness" and these drugs are the most powerful of all painkillers.

Drug abusers take them for the feeling of relaxed euphoria, the "high", they give. They work by mimicking endogenous morphines or endorphins, the body's natural painkilling neurotransmitters, heightening the pain relief and euphoria of a natural release of endorphins. The more narcotics a person takes, the fewer endorphins the body makes, increasing tolerance and dependence. Eventually, natural endorphin production falls so low that any reduction in drug dosage brings horrible withdrawal symptoms – chills, sweating, stomach cramps, headaches and vomiting. Worse still, the body's greater tolerance for the drug spurs the abuser to take ever higher doses to achieve a high, so increasing the risk of a fatal overdose.

Depressants, including alcohol, sedative-hypnotics like barbiturates and tranquillizers, do not make you depressed; they depress or slow down the activity of the central nervous system, which is why some of them are known as downers. Small doses raise your mood, relax you and free you of inhibitions. High doses can make you moody, anxious and irritable. They also slow your reflexes, slur your speech and upset your balance and judgment. Alcohol, for instance, seems to work by reducing the effectiveness of dopamine and other neurotransmitters. In small doses it excites you because it slows down only the inhibitory nerve pathways – those that keep you in check. But high doses make you drunk because they also slow down the nerve pathways that excite and arouse you.

Stimulants include substances such as caffeine, nicotine (in tobacco), amphetamine (speed), cocaine and MDMA (3,4-methylenedioxymethamphetamine, or Ecstasy). In small doses, they wake you up and give you a high by exciting the central nervous system. In high doses, they can make you anxious and irritable and even psychotic. All of them can be addictive.

Caffeine is the drug in many national drinks – coffee in the U.S., tea in Britain, guarana in Brazil – and in chocolate and cola drinks. It perks you up by stimulating the heart and suppressing the effects of adenosine, one of the brain's inhibitory chemicals. Speed arouses you even more, inducing a high by boosting levels of the brain chemicals noradrenaline and dopamine and keeping them in action longer by preventing their re-uptake from the synapse by nerve cells. High doses also affect levels of serotonin. Cocaine works in much the same way, but affects noradrenaline and serotonin more, and gives a brief high, rather than long arousal. Ecstasy gives a feeling of euphoria and sociability and seems to work directly on the brain's serotonin pathways, slowing the re-uptake of the chemical from synapses.

Nicotine seems to stimulate respiration and heart rate and depress appetite by activating nicotine-sensitive nerve receptors and mimicking transmission of the brain chemical acetylcholine. It is highly addictive and the dangers it poses to health are well documented.

Hallucinogens alter the way a person perceives things, either mildly like marijuana or dramatically like "acid" (LSD; lysergic acid diethylamide), mescaline, psilocybin (magic mushrooms) and PCP (phencyclidine), which all induce hallucinations. Most (but not marijuana, PCP or mescaline) affect the serotonin system that reaches up from the brain stem to the rest of the brain, which is why they have such a profound effect on consciousness. One theory is that serotonin usually stops us dreaming when we are awake, and inhibiting the serotonin fountain allows us to do just that. But these drugs affect people differently, giving some a wonderful dream and others a nightmarish bad trip.

Marijuana seems to affect the brain chemical GABA (gamma-aminobutyric acid). It may induce mild relaxation, but it can also make time seem to pass slowly or even cause hallucinations.

Motivation

Why do you get up in the morning? What makes you go to work or school? What makes you do anything?

Questions of motivation – why people do what they do – are among the most difficult to answer. Early this century, psychologists such as William James tried to explain them in terms of "instinct" – automatic responses inherited from our parents, including "physical" instincts such as sucking and "mental" ones such as jealousy. Everything we do would be motivated by a different instinct. But as the list of instincts rose over 10,000, theorists realized this approach was not quite right.

Then psychologists came up with the idea of "drives" – compelling desires to satisfy the physical need for such basics as food, water, sleep, warmth and sex. Ultimately, some argued, everything we do could be understood in terms of an attempt to satisfy, or reduce the clamour of, these drives. One problem with this theory is that humans and other primates are naturally curious, exploring for the joy of it, and this is hard to explain in terms of physiological needs. Now psychologists simply try to explore the links between brain physiology and motivation, and to develop theories of our needs and ways of thinking.

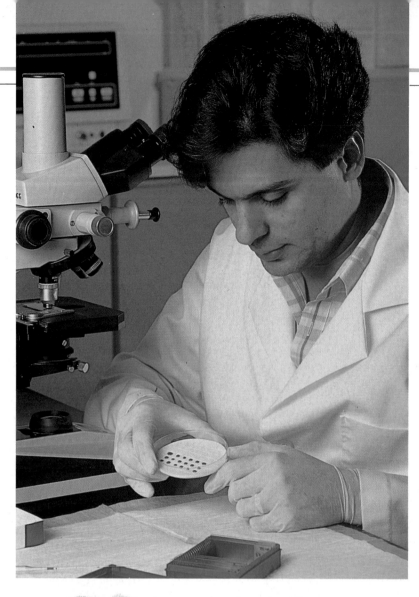

People talk about the sex drive *as if it were a basic physiological need like the need for food. But while people have to eat to avoid starvation, a lack of sex will not kill anyone. Yet people still seek out sexual pleasure even though it is not essential to their immediate survival. Sexual desire is linked with many motivations, including the needs for love, power and physical closeness, to name but a few. Although they are different types of drive, both hunger and sexual desire are influenced by the hypothalamus in the brain. It stimulates the pituitary gland to release the sex hormones. When levels of these hormones fall, so does sexual desire.*

The stylish lemon squeezer (left) *represents a common human trait, the desire to create surroundings full of aesthetically pleasing things, from everyday implements to works of art.*

Many people are highly motivated *to acquire wealth and the possessions that it can buy. And there are few who could honestly say that they do not gain pleasure from material objects. What these are depends largely on the values of the culture in which a person lives. In some parts of the world a powerful car is the object of desire, while in others it might be expensive jewellery. Objects can be perceived to bestow status on their owners and thus raise their self-esteem.*

The scientist's constant quest *for knowledge is one of the many examples of human curiosity – a human activity which cannot be explained in terms of physiological needs. Some psychologists argue that we are curious because we are trying to control our environment. But other factors may motivate people to achieve in this field. Peer-group admiration and the knowledge that your work might benefit society can both be immensely gratifying.*

PRIMARY NEEDS

A mother's love for her offspring is so common among all species of animals that it is easy to understand in terms of instinct. Our needs for food and drink, too, are easily understood in terms of basic drives. But what about everything else we do? Many psychologists think we are motivated as much by social needs as by physiological drives and instinct. They argue that we are prompted by, for instance, a need for affiliation, which makes us seek out friends and join groups, or a need to achieve, which makes us look for challenges. The need to achieve is common to all of us, some believe, but its form varies from culture to culture – and from person to person.

Psychologist Abraham Maslow (1908–70) suggested that we are motivated by a need hierarchy: only when we have satisfied the lower levels of needs do we try to satisfy the higher ones. At the bottom are physiological needs such as those for food and drink. Above that is the need for safety and security. Then comes the need to belong and be loved. Next is the need for self-esteem. Above that are so-called cognitive needs, which include exploration, curiosity and the search for meaning and knowledge, followed by aesthetic needs for beauty, order and symmetry. And at the top comes the need for "self-actualization" – the need to fulfil our true potential.

The sow with her piglets is highly protective of her offspring. She behaves in a way that promotes their wellbeing and enhances their chances of growing up and eventually reproducing. Although what she does might seem selfless – she looks after her offspring often to her own detriment – it might be seen as the satisfaction of a longer-term biological need. Evolution is driven by the survival of the fittest, especially those who are most successful at reproduction. Thus successful nurturing behaviour becomes part of the genetic inheritance as instinctive behaviour.

Scientists used to think that we felt hungry when our stomach contracted. Now they know the brain, and in particular the hypothalamus, plays a major role too. The lateral hypothalamus (LH) seems to be a switch that makes us want to eat; the ventromedial hypothalamus (VMH) tells us to stop eating. The LH and VMH may respond to changing levels of nutrients in the blood – the LH going into action when levels drop, and the VMH coming into play when they rise again. One theory suggests that the hypothalamus tries to keep each of us at a particular set weight, established by the number of fat cells in the body when we are born. Extreme obesity may be caused by damage to the hypothalamus.

The regulation of body temperature is a physiological essential: if we get too hot or too cold we die. Automatic temperature regulation is controlled by the hypothalamus: we sweat to cool down and shiver to warm up. We also control body temperature voluntarily, finding shade when the sun is hot and dressing warmly when the air is cold. But some people deliberately choose hot sunny holiday destinations. This is not because they are cold – they have other associations with the sun, such as the pleasure of freedom from everyday cares.

The moral mind

You know when you are doing wrong, or at least you should if you have developed a set of morals.

News headlines trumpeting "Crime wave brings terror to city streets!" make us feel crime is too much the norm. Yet most of us behave well nearly all the time and few would even think of stealing an ice cream from the hands of a child. Even though our appetites may tell us to grab the goodies, our minds stop us. Most of us have a strong moral sense and are essentially altruistic. Why?

The problem for scientists is that our altruism is apparently at odds with Darwin's theory of evolution, which shows how species evolve as the fittest (best-adapted) individuals survive to pass on their genes. Some have tried to apply this notion to human nature and society, with terrifying results: the idea that some people and races are fitter lay behind the "science" of eugenics, which culminated in the holocaust and the Nazis' horrific experiments with genetics. Some people still believe that humans are innately aggressive, competitive and selfish, yet the evidence is overwhelmingly against them. Most of the world's population follow religions that specifically frown on aggression and selfishness. Even non-religious people usually condemn them, and altruistic acts – a fire fighter plunging into a burning building to rescue someone – are common.

How do we acquire a set of morals? We only develop the power to make moral judgments as we mature. Moral sense comes, it seems, with increasing ability to reason; from social learning from parents and teachers; with the development of emotion, especially empathy; and from biological needs and drives. American psychologist Lawrence Kohlberg sees us as going through three moral stages. He used as an example the dilemma of a man whose dying wife can be saved only by a drug sold by a profiteering chemist. He cannot raise the money, so decides to steal the drug. In the first stage (7–10 years old), when we simply try to avoid punishment, we would worry only about his getting caught or his wife dying. In the second, when moral conventions guide our judgments (10–16 years), we might reason that it is bad to steal or good to take care of a dying wife. In the third stage, adults judge for themselves and might worry about the social consequences of stealing or the balance between preserving life and upholding the law.

EVERY ACT AN ANIMAL ACT?

A creature that helps others – especially at risk to itself – will, in strictly Darwinian terms, reduce its chances of surviving and producing offspring. So we would expect evolution to rule out altruism. And yet the animal world shows plenty of examples of altruistic behaviour that would be considered "moral" in humans.

A rabbit endangers itself by stopping to thump its feet to warn other rabbits of the approach of a predator. Songbirds sing to warn other birds of danger – even though by singing they draw attention to themselves. And despite the fact that they will produce no offspring, sterile worker bees spend all their lives sustaining the queen.

One answer to this apparent paradox is the idea of the selfish gene – a theory which has also been applied to human actions – that altruism is really selfishness at the genetic level. A mother fox will risk her life to save her cubs because her genes will survive in them.

Another theory is that of "delayed reciprocal altruism", the idea that one good turn deserves another. Young female baboons, for instance, groom dominant adult females who may later become powerful allies; young males groom less dominant females who, in turn, let them mate.

WHAT IS A SIN?

Every society and every culture has its own system of morals, from the Ten Commandments handed down from God to Moses in Judaeo-Christianity to the pronouncements of the Islamic prophet Muhammad. Sometimes these are given extra weight by religious dogma or are enforced by the power of the law – yet even societies which have no organized religion or legal system almost always have an underlying guiding morality, as is evident from the table on the right.

What is remarkable about moral systems is not only how diverse they are, but also how much they have in common.

	Anglican	Catholic	Judaism	Islam	Hinduism	Buddhism	Secular
Blasphemy	Sin	Sin	Wrong	Sin	Not a sin	Not applicable	Acceptable
Non-observance of religious events	Sin	Sin	Wrong	Sin	Not a sin	Not harmful	Normal
Murder	Sin	Sin	Wrong	Sin	Sin	Harmful	Wrong
Adultery	Sin	Sin	Wrong	Sin	Sin	Harmful	Wrong
Theft	Sin	Sin	Wrong	Sin	Sin	Harmful	Wrong
Lying	Sin	Sin	Wrong	Sin	Sin	Harmful	Wrong
Premarital sex	Sin	Sin	Wrong	Sin	Sin	Not harmful	Normal
Homosexual practices	Sin	Sin	Wrong	Sin	Sin	Not harmful	Normal
Divorce	Not a sin	Sin	Permitted	Not a sin	Sin	Not harmful	Acceptable
Masturbation	Sin	Sin	Wrong	Not mentioned	Sin	Not harmful	Normal
Suicide	Not a sin	Sin	Wrong	Sin	Sin	Harmful	Acceptable
Cruelty to animals	Not a sin	Not a sin	Permitted	Not a sin	Sin	Harmful	Wrong

Feeling guilt is one of the most notable instances of the moral mind at work. Most of us feel uneasy if we do something we perceive – or know – to be wrong. In Japan, such feelings have been exploited at notorious accident blackspots by installing plastic policemen; these artificial enforcers of the law have proved effective in slowing down the traffic and preventing accidents.

Indeed, a feeling of guilt can be so powerful that it lasts a lifetime, and a misdeed committed in early childhood can haunt us for many years. We are not always aware of our guilt, yet it rises to the surface in unconscious ways, affecting our behaviour, like Shakespeare's sleepwalking Lady Macbeth rubbing her hands and crying, "Out damned spot!" as she tries to rid herself of the guilt of killing Duncan.

Individual minds

Each person's unique mind leads to unique thoughts and actions, but do individuals choose what they do?

Should a gangster's son turn to lawlessness, people say, "like father, like son", as if crime was an inevitable consequence of his parentage. We accept that our physical make-up comes from our parents. Could it be that behaviour does too? One branch of psychology – sociobiology – says so. It argues that everything we do, everything we are, is a product of evolution and our genetic inheritance.

Many behaviourist psychologists, on the other hand, argue that what we do is determined by our past experiences; our lives, they say, are completely "programmed" by the pattern of rewards and punishments we encounter. What both the behaviourists and the sociobiologists have in common, though, is that they suggest that our every action is predetermined and inevitable. This is not as outrageous as it sounds. All classical science works on the premise that there is a cause for every event and that one thing inevitably leads to another.

In fact, most psychologists must work on this assumption too – that there is a reason for everything we do or feel. But if everything we do or feel is caused inevitably by something else, do we have any real freedom of choice? Is there such a thing as free will? The problem with this idea is that it runs counter to our own personal experience and to the way society is run. We all feel as if we are making free choices (within certain constraints) all the time, and our legal system is based on the assumption that we are each responsible for our actions.

To deal with this apparent paradox, many psychologists adopt something similar to the idea of "soft determinism". They believe that for psychology as a science, determinism works best, but since there is more to life than science, free will works best in relation to subjective, everyday experience. Essentially, soft determinists say everything has a cause, but they recognize free will as a cause, just like any "external" one. They argue that we act freely when we are neither constrained nor coerced. Clearly, a prisoner is constrained from doing what he or she wants to do; or a gun held to the head may coerce someone into doing something he or she does not want to. But the idea allows constraints and coercion

Leonardo da Vinci's self-portrait is just one of his many remarkable works of art. Were these and his brilliant scientific studies due to his own genetic allocation or were they a result of his inevitable experiences and memories of his environment? Many would say it was Leonardo's unique genius; deterministic psychologists would counter that he could not help but do what he did.

to work much more subtly and deeply than this. We might be constrained by a childhood fear, for instance.

Still other psychologists maintain that to contrast free will with determinism is misleading. They argue that as we are material beings in a world where everything has a cause, our actions must also be based in causality. But since the causes are so numerous, they are effectively indeterminate, and so we have freedom of choice. It is, they say, our biology that makes us free because our biology has made us into creatures who are always creating our own mental and material environments.

OUT OF THE SILENT DARKNESS

Born a normal baby, Helen Keller (1880–1968) suffered a fever at 19 months which left her deaf and blind and soon afterward she became unable to speak. With only her senses of smell, taste and touch remaining, the child was, in effect, cut off from the world. When Helen was about 6 years old, her parents sought help with her education and a remarkable 20-year-old woman – Anne Sullivan – came to teach her. Anne, who had herself been blind at one time but had had her sight partially restored, was a graduate of a school for the blind. Anne "spoke" to Helen by spelling words on her palm, teaching her the names of objects which Helen could feel. Later Anne helped Helen to learn to speak by allowing Helen to feel the vibrations in her throat as she spoke.

Helen proved such an adept pupil that by the age of 10 she could read braille and at 24 she graduated from university, with the constant help of Anne who accompanied her to lectures where she spelled out the lectures on Helen's hand. Soon after graduating Helen wrote her biography, later becoming a famous author. She dedicated her life to helping the blind and deaf and went on worldwide lecture tours to promote their education. Everyone who met her, including writer Mark Twain, was enthralled by her vivacity, warmth and intelligence. Stories like this, of human beings who live remarkable lives despite severe handicaps, persuade many people to believe that there is more to being human than genetic programming. There is little more striking evidence of the willpower of the individual human mind than Helen Keller's story.

Helen Keller's unique circumstances generated a unique individual. Unable to hear or see, she was nevertheless able to communicate and make an extraordinary contribution to the world around her.

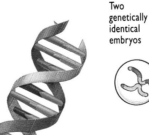

Identical twins are as alike as two humans can be – their genes are identical. Yet despite physical similarities they have unique minds. The genes they share can be expressed in divergent ways and subtle differences in experiences will give each one unique capabilities and memories and thus a unique way of responding to events.

The coming together of an egg and a sperm creates a genetically unique fertilized egg, which develops into a genetically unique person. No other human egg has had the same genes – nor will it have in the future – unless it splits in two, which happens occasionally. In that case, two genetically identical eggs form, giving rise to two genetically identical twins. But almost from the moment the two identical eggs appear, environmental influences act upon them, and the embryos, later babies, and then adults develop along slightly different, individual lines.

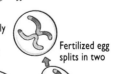

Two genetically identical embryos

Fertilized egg splits in two

Fertilized egg

Eggs

Mother

Father

Sperm

Bibliography

Agur, Anne and Ming Lee *Grant's Atlas of Anatomy* Williams and Wilkins, Baltimore, Maryland and London, 9th ed., 1991

Alexander, R. McNeill *The Human Machine* Natural History Museum Publications, London, 1992
——*American Medical Association Home Medical Library* Reader's Digest, Pleasantville, New York, 1992
——*Atlas of the Body and Mind* Mitchell Beazley, London, 1976

Bevan, James *A Pictorial Handbook of Anatomy and Physiology* Mitchell Beazley/Reed International Books, London, 1994

Birren, James E. and Warner K. Schraie *Handbook of the Psychology of Aging* Van Nostrand, New York, 1977

Blakemore, Colin et al. *The Mind Machine* BBC Books, London, 1988

Bodanis, David *Being Human* Century Publishing, London, 1984

Carlson, Neil R. *Physiology of Behavior* Allyn and Bacon, Inc., Boston and London, 3rd ed., 1986

Carola, Robert et al. *Human Anatomy and Physiology* McGraw-Hill, Inc., New York, 1992

Charness, N. (ed.) *Aging and Human Performance* John Wiley and Sons, Chichester, 1985

Comer, Ronald J. *Abnormal Psychology* W.H. Freeman and Company, New York, 1992

Cooper, Jack R. et al. *The Biochemical Basis of Neuropharmacology* Oxford University Press, Oxford and New York, 6th ed., 1991

Crick, Francis *The Astonishing Hypothesis: The Scientific Search for the Soul* Touchstone Books, London and New York, 1994

Cunningham, John D. *Human Biology* Harper & Row, New York, 1989

Dawkins, Richard *The Selfish Gene* Penguin, London, 1986

Dennet, Daniel C. *Consciousness Explained* Penguin, New York, 1993

Diamond, Marian C. et al. *The Human Brain Coloring Book* Barnes & Noble Books, New York and London, 1985

Dixon, Bernard *Health and the Human Body* Perseus Press, London, 1986

Dorit, Robert L., Warren F. Walker Jr. and Robert D. Barnes *Zoology* Saunders College Publishing, Philadelphia, Pennsylvania, 1991

Dox, Ida, Biagio John Melloni and Gilbert M. Eisner *Melloni's Illustrated Medical Dictionary* Wilkins and Wilkins, Baltimore, Maryland, 1979

Downer, John *Supersense* BBC Books, London, 1988

England, Marjorie A. and Jennifer Wakely *A Colour Atlas of the Brain & Spinal Cord* Wolfe Publishing Ltd., London, 1991

Farndon, John *The All Color Book of the Body* Arco Publishing, Inc., New York, 1985

FitzGerald, M.J.T. *Neuroanatomy Basic and Applied* Baillière Tindall, London, 1985

Gallahue, David L. and John C. Ozmun *Understanding Motor Development* Brown & Benchmark, Madison, Wisconsin, 1995

Giese, Arthur C. *Cell Physiology* W.B. Saunders Company, Philadelphia, Pennsylvania, 1979

Glees, Paul *The Human Brain* Cambridge University Press, Cambridge and New York, 1988

Gold, Jay J. and John B. Josinovich (eds.) *Gynaecologic Endocrinology* Harper, Hagerstown, Maryland, 1980

Gould, Stephen Jay *Wonderful Life* Hutchinson Radius, London, 1989
——*Ever Since Darwin* Penguin, London, 1991

Graham, Robert B. *Physiological Psychology* Wadsworth Publishing Company, Belmont, California, 1990
——*The Guinness Book of Records* Guinness Publishing Limited, London, 1994

Greenfield, Susan G. *Journey to the Centers of the Mind: Toward a Science of Consciousness* W.H. Freeman and Company, New York, 1995

Gregory, R.L. *Eye and Brain: The Psychology of Seeing* Oxford University Press, Oxford, 1990
——*Oxford Companion to the Mind* Oxford University Press, Oxford, 1987

Guyton, Arthur C. *Textbook of Medical Physiology* W.B. Saunders Company, Philadelphia, Pennsylvania, 6th ed., 1981

Hobson, J.Allan *Sleep* Scientific American, Inc., New York, 1989
——*The Human Body* Arch Cape Press, New York, 1989

Huxley, Aldous *The Doors of Perception* Perennial Library, New York, 1954

Jennett, Sheila *Human Physiology* Churchill Livingstone, Edinburgh, 1989

Jones, Steve *The Language of the Genes* Flamingo, London, 1994

Kandel, Eric R. et al. *Principles of Neural Science* Prentice-Hall International Inc., London and New Jersey, 1991

Kirkpatrick, C.T. *Illustrated Handbook of Medical Physiology* John Wiley and Sons, Chichester, 1992

UNDER PRESSURE

The force with which blood is pushed against the walls of blood vessels is the blood pressure. While pressure is usually measured in pounds per square inch or Newtons per square metre (Pascals), blood pressure is measured in millimetres of mercury, or mmHg. This refers to the height to which a column of mercury can be raised by the pressure. The typical pressure in the main arteries caused by the contraction of the heart's left ventricle is enough to raise a column of mercury by 120 mm.

ACID TEST

The acidity or alkalinity of a solution is measured using the pH scale. A pH of 1 is very acid and a pH of 14 is very alkaline; a pH of 7 is neutral. The pH of pure water is 7. The pH of the blood is between 7.35 and 7.45, making it slightly alkaline. The term pH stands for "power of hydrogen" and the scale reflects the number of free hydrogen ions and the number of free hydroxyl ions in a solution. Each whole number change on the scale represents a tenfold change in the number of ions.

MEASURE FOR MEASURE

In the metric system a millimetre (mm) is a thousandth of a metre ($\frac{1}{25}$ inch); a micrometre, or micron (μm), is a millionth of a metre ($\frac{1}{25,000}$ inch); and a nanometre (nm) is a billionth of a metre ($\frac{1}{25,000,000}$ inch). A millivolt (mv) is a thousandth of a volt (V); a microvolt is a millionth of a volt.

In this book, a billion is 1,000 million, or 10^9; a trillion is a million million, or 10^{12}.

Koestler, Arthur *The Ghost in the Machine* Macmillan, New York, 1967

Kuby, Janis *Immunology* Freeman, New York, 1994

Kuffler, Stephen W. et al. *From Neuron to Brain* Sinauer Associates Inc. Publishers, Sunderland, Massachusetts, 2nd ed., 1984

Levitan, Irwin B. and Leonard K. Kaczmarek *The Neuron: Cell and Molecular Biology* Oxford University Press, Oxford and New York, 1991

Lyons, A. and R.J. Petrucelli, II *Medicine – An Illustrated History* Abradale Press/Harry N. Abrams Inc. Publishers, New York, 1987

McArdle, William D., Frank I. Katch and Victor L. Katch *Exercise Physiology* Lea & Febiger, Malvern, Pennsylvania, 1991
——*Man's Body an Owner's Manual* Paddington Press Ltd., New York, 1976

Nieuwenhuys, Rudolf *Chemoarchitecture of the Brain* Springer-Verlag, New York, 1985

Ornstein, Robert *Psychology* Harcourt Brace Jovanovich, New York, 1988
——*The Evolution of Consciousness: The Origins of the Way We Think* Touchstone, New York, 1992

Parker, Steve *The Body Atlas* Dorling Kindersley, London, 1993
——*Eyewitness Science: Human Body* Dorling Kindersley, London, 1993
——*Eyewitness Science: Medicine* Dorling Kindersley, London 1995
——*How the Body Works* Dorling Kindersley, London, 1994

Penrose, Roger *The Emperor's New Mind* Oxford University Press, Oxford, 1989

Pinchot, Roy B. (ed.) *The Brain* Torstar Books, New York, 1984

Roberts, Jean *Mastering Human Biology* Macmillan, London, 1991

Roitt, Ivan M., Jonathan Brostoff and David K. Male *Immunology* Churchill Livingstone, Edinburgh, 1985

Ronan, Colin A. *Science Explained* Doubleday, London, 1993; Henry Holt, New York, 1993

Rose-Neil, Wendy *The Complete Handbook of Pregnancy* Warner Books, London, 1993

Russell, Peter *The Brain Book* Routledge, London, 1989

Silverstone, Trevor and Paul Turner *Drug Treatment in Psychiatry* Routledge, London and New York, 5th ed., 1995

Smith, Anthony *The Mind* Hodder & Stoughton, London, 1984

Smith, Jillyn *Sense and Sensibilities* Wiley Science Editions, New York and Chichester, 1989

Snyder, Solomon *Drugs on the Brain* Scientific American Inc., New York, 1986

Steinberg, Robert *In Search of the Human Mind* Harcourt Brice, Orlando, Florida, 1995

Steur, Faye B. *The Psychological Development of Children* Brooks/Cole Publishing Company, Pacific Grove, California, 1994

Stockley, Corinne, Chris Oxlade and Jane Wertheim *The Usborne Illustrated Dictionary of Science* Usborne, London, 1988

Strickberger, Monroe W. *Evolution* Jones and Bartlett Publishers, Boston, Massachusetts, 1990

Tortora, Gerard J. and Nicholas P. Anagnostakos *Principles of Anatomy and Physiology* Canfield Press, San Fransisco, California, 1978

Whitfield, Philip *The Natural History of Evolution* Doubleday, London, 1993

Whitfield, Philip and Ruth Whitfield *Why Does My Heart Beat?* British Museum (Natural History), London, 1988

Williams, Peter L. et al. (eds.) *Gray's Anatomy* Churchill Livingstone, Edinburgh, 38th ed., 1995

Wills, Christopher *The Runaway Brain* Flamingo, London, 1993

Winfree, Arthur T. *The Timing of Biological Clocks* Scientific American Inc., New York, 1987

Zeki, Semir *A Vision of the Brain* Blackwell Scientific Publications, London and Boston, 1993

Suggested journals and periodicals

Nature Macmillan Magazines, London
New Scientist IPC Magazines Ltd., London
Scientific American Scientific American, Inc., New York

IN SHORT – WHAT THE LETTERS MEAN

ADH	antidiuretic hormone	DNA	deoxyribonucleic acid	LH	luteinizing hormone
ADP	adenosine diphosphate	ECG	electrocardiogram	MEG	magnetoencephalography
ANS	autonomic nervous system	ECT	electroconvulsive therapy	MHC	major histocompatibility protein
ATP	adenosine triphosphate	EEG	electroencephalogram	MRI	magnetic resonance imaging
BMR	basal metabolic rate	5-HT	5-hydroxytriptamine (serotonin)	PET	positron emission tomography
CAM	cell adhesion molecule	FSH	follicle-stimulating hormone	PNS	peripheral nervous system
CAT	computerized axial tomography	fMRI	functional magnetic resonance imaging	PSP	postsynaptic potential
CNS	central nervous system	GABA	gamma-aminobutyric acid	PVS	persistent vegetative state
CSF	cerebrospinal fluid	LGN	lateral geniculate nucleus	RNA	ribonucleic acid

Index

Acknowledgments

l = left; *r* = right; *c* = centre; *t* = top; *b* = bottom.

Picture credits
2*t* Mehau Kulyk/Science Photo Library; 2*b* John Barlow; 10*t* Mark Conlin/Telegraph Colour Library; 10*b* Peter Aprahamtan/Sharples Stress Engineers Ltd/Science Photo Library; 12/13 Mark Conlin/Telegraph Colour Library; 13 The Ronald Grant Archive; 16 John Barlow; 18/19 John Barlow; 19*l* Wellcome Institute Library, London; 19*r* Peter Aprahamtan/Sharples Stress Engineers Ltd/ Science Photo Library; 20/21 John Barlow; 23 Corey Ross/Professional Sport; 24 Wellcome Institute Library, London; 24/25 Dr. Philip J. Benson; 26 Philip Quirk/Wildlight Photo Agency; 28 Adam Hart-Davis/Science Photo Library; 28/29 Alan Brooke/Telegraph Colour Library; 30 John Barlow; 30/31 Michael Fogden/Oxford Scientific Films; 31 Avon Rubber P.L.C.; 32*l* Dr. Ray Clark/Science Photo Library; 32*r* John Barlow; 34/35 Paul Lowe/Network; 36/37 Alan Becker/ The Image Bank; 37 Gray Mortimore/Allsport; 38 Dr. Ray Clark/Science Photo Library; 40 John Barlow; 50/51 D.C. Lowe/Tony Stone Images; 52–56 John Barlow; 60*t* E.T. Archive; 60*c&b* John Barlow; 63*l* John Barlow; 63*r* François Gohier/ Ardea; 64 John Barlow; 68 Bill Dobbins/Allsport; 69 Wellcome Institute Library, London; 70/71 A.B. Dowsett/Science Photo Library; 72/73 Tom van Sant/Geosphere Project, Santa Monica/Science Photo Library; 74 Arnulf Husmo/Tony Stone Images; 74 John Barlow; 76 Chicago Historical Society; 80/81 Scott Frances/Esto/Arcaird; 82/83 Randy Wells/Tony Stone Images; 84 John Massey Stewart; 88 J.C. Revy/Science Photo Library; 89 John Barlow; 91 E.T. Archive; 92/93 Dr. Arnold Brody/Science Photo Library; 94/95*t* John Barlow; 94/95*b* Jerry Mason/Science Photo Library; 96*t&c* John Barlow; 96*b*–99 J. Feingersh/Zefa Picture Library; 100 Martel/Rapho/Network; 100/101 CNRI/ Science Photo Library; 103 Richardson/Custom Medical Stock Photo/Science Photo Library; 106/107 John Barlow; 107 G.A. Maclean/Oxford Scientific Films; 110/111 John Shaw/NHPA; 115 John Barlow; 118/119 F. Guenet/Imapress/ Camera Press; 120/121 Zefa Picture Library; 126/127 Zigy Kaluzny/Gamma/Frank Spooner Pictures; 128 Larry Lefever/Zefa Picture Library; 129 Sinclair Stammers/Science Photo Library; 130*t* Alan Brooke/Telegraph Colour Library; 130*b* John Barlow; 132*l* Michael W. Davidson/ Science Photo Library; 132*tr* Science & Society Picture Library; 132*br* John Barlow; 11 Warren Anatomical Museum, Harvard Medical School, Boston; 134/135 Animals Unlimited; 136 Science & Society Picture Library; 138 John Barlow; 140/141 Alain Compost/Bruce Coleman; 141, 142 John Barlow; 142/143 Dan Bosler/Tony Stone Images; 143*t&br* John Barlow; 143*bl* Warren Faioley/Oxford Scientific Films; 144*t* Manfred Kage/Science Photo Library; 144*b* Michael W. Davidson/Science Photo Library; 145*tl&b* John Barlow; 145*tr* US Department of Energy/Science Photo Library; 146 Warren Anatomical Museum, Harvard Medical School, Boston; 148*t* Guy's Hospital anatomy department; 148*b* Mike Powell/ Allsport; 150 Tim Beddow/Science Photo Library; 150/151*t* Mehau Kulyk/Science Photo Library; 150/151*b* The National Hospital for Neurology and Neurosurgery; 160*t* John Barlow; 160*b* Dr. Pietro De Camilli, Yale University School of Medicine, and Dr. Michela Matteoli, University of Milan; 162/163 Steve Hopkin/Planet Earth Pictures; 165 Guy's Hospital Anatomy Department; 168/169 John Barlow; 170 Bruce Forster/Tony Stone Images; 171 Max-Planck-Institut für Medizinische Forschung; 172/173 Lori Adamski Peek/Tony Stone Images; 174 Don Fawcett/Science Photo Library; 176/177 John David Begg; 178 Science Photo Library; 178/179 Leo Mason/ The Image Bank; 180, 182 John Barlow; 184 G.I. Bernard/Oxford Scientific Films; 184/185 Duncan Wherrett/Tony Stone Images; 186/187 Litsios/ Frank Spooner Pictures; 187 Mehau Kulyk/Science Photo Library; 188/189 John Barlow; 190 John Lawlor/Tony Stone Images; 191, 194 John Barlow; 195 Mary E. Hatten; 196/197*t* Dr. Pietro De Camilli, Yale University School of Medicine, and Dr. Michela Matteoli, University of Milan; 196/197*b* Harvard University Press, graphic from the postnatal development of the human cerebral cortex by Jesse Leroy Conel vol. 1, 1939, 1959; 198 The Kobal Collection; 200, 201, 202 John Barlow; 204*t* Mel Lindstrom; Tony Stone Images; 204*b*, 206, 207 John Barlow; 208 Bolcina/Frank Spooner Pictures; 211 Claude Nuridsany and Marie Perennou/Science Photo Library; 212 Institute of Opthalmology; 212/213 Stephen Dalton/NHPA; 214/215 Images Colour Library; 216/217*t* Emile Luider/Rapho/Network; 216/217*b* Maxim Ford; 218 John Barlow; 220 James D. Watt/Planet Earth Pictures; 221*t* Eve Arnold/Magnum Photos; 221*b*, 222 John Barlow; 223*t* Terry Vine/Tony Stone Images; 223*b*, 225 John Barlow; 226 Allsport; 228*b* Anthony Bannister/NHPA; 228/229*t* John Barlow; 230 Frank Spooner Pictures; 232/233 Roger Hutchings/Network; 233, 234/235 John Barlow; 237 Kim Westerskov/Tony Stone Images; 238 John Barlow; 239 Alon Reininger/Colorific!; 240 F. Henry/Rea/Katz; 242/243 Paul Lowe/ Network; 243 Michel Siffre; 244 John Barlow; 244/245*t* James King-Holmes/Science Photo Library; 244/245*b* Museum of London; 246*l&tr* John Barlow; 247*l* Michael Holford; 247*r* John Barlow; 248/249 L.D. Gordon/The Image Bank; 250 John Barlow; 250/251 Range/Bettmann; 251 Nostalgia Amusements; 252 John Barlow; 254 William Feindel, Wilder Penfield Archive, Montreal Neurological Institute; 254/255 Petit Format/Bubbles; 255 John Barlow; 256/257*t* Anna Clopet/Colorific!; 256/257*b* John Barlow; 258 Michael Holford; 258/259 Wellcome Dept. of Cognitive Neurology/Science Photo Library; 260 Lou Jones/The Image Bank; 260/261 Dr. Colin Chumbley/Science Photo Library; 262 E. Ferrorelli/ Colorific!; 263 John Barlow; 264 Sterling K. Claren, Prof. of Pediatric Dept., University of Washington School of Medicine; 264/265 John Barlow; 266/267 Kunsthistorisches Museum, Vienna/ The Bridgeman Art Library; 267*t* Range/ Bettmann/UPI; 267*b*, 268/269 John Barlow; 270 Michael Fogden/Oxford Scientific Films; 271 Penny Gentieu/Tony Stone Images; 272 Alex Webb/Magnum Photos; 272/273 Robert Harding Picture Library; 274*tl* Image courtesy of Peter Ramm, Imaging Research Inc.; 274*tr* James Stevenson/Science Photo Library; 274*bl* John Barlow; 274*bc* Rorschach H., Rorschach-Test © Verlag Hans Huber AG, Bern, Switzerland, 1921, 1948, 1994; 274*br* Neil Fletcher; 275 John Barlow; 276/277 Werner Bokelberg/The Image Bank; 277 John Barlow; 278/279 C. Poulet/Frank Spooner Pictures; 279 Rorschach H., Rorschach-Test © Verlag Hans Huber AG, Bern, Switzerland, 1921, 1948, 1994; 280/281 John Barlow; 282 James Stevenson/Science Photo Library; 282/283 Image courtesy of Peter Ramm, Imaging Research Inc.; 284 Antonio Ribeiro/Frank Spooner Pictures; 284/285 Eric Bouvet/Frank Spooner Pictures; 286 John Barlow; 286/287 Paul Grendon/Select; 287 Freud Museum, London/© Sigmund Freud; 288/289, 290 John Barlow; 290/291 Don McCullin/ Magnum Photos; 291 Bruce Ayres/Tony Stone Images; 292/293 John Barlow; 294/295 David Redfern/Redferns; 296 Ariel van Straten; 297 Neil

Fletcher; 298 Tim Beddow/Science Photo Library; 298/299 Range/Reuter/Bettman; 299 Tim Beddow/Science Photo Library; 300 Eugene Richards/Magnum Photos; 300/301 John Barlow; 302t Matt Meadows/Science Photo Library; 302b John Barlow; 303t Nigel Cattlin/Holt Studios International; 303b John Barlow; 304 The Kobal Collection; 305 Douglas Dickins; 306 Biblioteca Reale, Torino/Scala; 307t Range/Bettmann; 307b Michael Nichols/Magnum Photos

If the publishers have unwittingly infringed copyright in any illustration reproduced, they would pay an appropriate fee on being satisfied to the owner's title.

Illustration credits
David Ashby 88/89, 100/101, 102/103, 162/163; John Barlow 206/207, 222/223; John Bavosi 114/115; Richard Bonson 56/57, 162/163, 164/165, 166/167, 194/195, 198/199; Sarah Bowers 122/123; Richard Coombes 84/85; Michael Courtney 42/43, 66/67, 118/119; Bill Donahoe 56/57, 108/109, 120/121, 146/147, 174/175, 180/181, 182/183, 214/215, 288/289; Andrew Farmer 12/13, 14/15, 38/39, 58/59, 80/81, 82/83, 88/89, 126/127, 136/137, 138/139, 140/141, 148/149, 196/197, 210/211, 214/215, 216/217, 232/233, 240/241, 248/249, 262/263, 264/265, 268/269, 280/281, 294/295, 300/301; Chris Forsey 22/23, 26/27, 36/37, 52/53, 62/63, 72/73, 110/111, 116/117, 134/135, 202/203, 204/205, 208/209, 228/229, 234/235, 252/253, 284/285, 292/293; David Gifford 68/69; Ed Gillah 18/19; Mick Gillah 58/59; Greensmith Associates 82/83; Gary Hinks 70/71, 90/91, 92/93, 190/191, 192/193, 236/237; Frank Kennard 14/15, 26/27, 28/29, 42/43, 64/65; Sally Launder 218/219, 230/231, 240/241; Mainline Design 16/17, 28/29, 34/35, 40/41, 46/47, 54/55, 68/69, 74/75, 76/77, 78/79, 102/103, 104/105, 114/115, 122/123, 124/125, 142/143, 146/147, 168/169, 170/171, 172/173, 176/177, 178/179, 184/185, 188/189, 206/207, 212/213, 226/227, 238/239, 242/243, 270/271, 278/279, 282/283, 290/291, 294/295, 298/299, 304/305, 306/307; Tom McArthur 128/129; Annabel Milne 22/23; Ed Musy 18/19; Lillith Pollock 122/123; Paul Richardson 118/119; Peter Sarson 20/21, 24/25, 38/39, 66/67, 84/85; Mike Saunders 30/31, 76/77, 78/79, 86/87, 186/187, 206/207, 222/223, 224/225, 272/273; Sue Sharples 106/107; Les Smith 44/45, 48/49, 66/67, 116/117; Technical Art Services

258/259; Richard Tibbets 152/153, 154/155, 156/157, 158/159, 260/261, 292/293; Zhang Tongyun 226/227; Mark Watkinson 168/169; Stephen Wiltshire 266/267

Marshall Editions would like to thank the following:

Authors: Jerome Burne 146–51, 248–73, 278–79
              John Farndon 134–45, 276–77, 284–95, 300–7
              Steve Parker 12–31, 162–99, 202–45
              Dr. Philip Whitfield 34–59, 62–95, 98–129

Copy editor: Isabella Raeburn
Managing editor: Lindsay McTeague
Editorial director: Sophie Collins
DTP editors: Mary Pickles, Pennie Jelliff, Kate Waghorn
Research: Jolika Feszt, Michaela Moher
Index: Caroline S. Sheard
Art assistant: Eileen Batterberry
Production: Sarah Hinks

David Mellor for the loan of frying pan, stainless steel knife, sieve, plate, glass and cutlery; Kristin Baybars for the loan of toy giraffe; The Algerian Coffee Shop for the loan of cafetière; Pravins Jewellers Ltd for the loan of watch; Racing Green for the loan of man's top; Olympus Sport for the loan of man's sports clothes and trainers; Jubilee Sports for the loan of rugby ball; James Bodenham & Co. for the loan of pot-pourri and toiletries.

George Bridgeman and Jo Tomlin at Guy's Hospital anatomy department. David Weeks "Magician" (0171–582 9186) for card tricks. Dr. Deirdre O'Gallagher for prescription drugs.

The Independent (8 June, 1995); Olympus Sport for man's track suit bottom; Quicks Archery for bow and arrow; Chappell of Bond Street, London, for Beethoven's bust; Freed of London for woman's leotard; David Mellor for pressure cooker, cruet, casserole and cooking utensils; Chess & Bridge for chess board and pieces; BMW for car keys; Body Active for dumbells; Reject Shop for cushions. The Family Flynn. John Barlow for retouching and imaging. Jo Neild for cooking the casserole. Dawn Lane for make-up.

Dr. P.W. Atkins, University Lecturer in Physical Chemistry and Fellow in Chemistry, Lincoln College, Oxford. George Bridgeman at Guy's Hospital Anatomy Department. Dr. John Coleman and Mr.

Andrew Slater, Oxford University Phonetics Department. Dr. Huw Dorkins, Senior Research Fellow and Tutor in Medicine, St. Peter's College, Oxford. Dr. Andrew King, Senior Research Fellow, University Laboratory of Physiology, Oxford University. Dr. John Morris, University Lecturer in Human Anatomy and Wellcome-Franks Tutor, St. Hugh's College, Oxford. Dr. J. Stein, Lecturer in Physiology, Oxford University Medical School, and Fellow of Magdalen College, Oxford.